PENGUIN CLASSICS

PENGUIN ENGLISH POETS
GENERAL EDITOR: CHRISTOPHER RICKS

JOHN DRYDEN: VIRGIL'S AENEID

PUBLIUS VERGILIUS MARO (70–19 BC), usually called Virgil or Vergil, was from an agricultural family living near Mantua. He studied in several Italian cities, including Rome, and in time attracted the patronage of the emperor Augustus' associate Maecenas and of Augustus himself. He became, most have thought, the pre-eminent poet of the Augustan Age, elevated above Horace and Ovid, among others. The main poems attributed to Virgil are the ten pastoral *Eclogues*, the *Georgics*, a four-part meditative, philosophical poem on farming, and the *Aeneid*, an epic for Rome comparable to Homer's epics for Greece. Not only his poems, but the sequence of them in his career, became exemplary for later poets. The progress from pastorals, to poetry such as the *Georgics*, to an epic established a pattern prominent in the careers of Spenser and Pope and discernible in the careers of others, including Milton and Wordsworth.

JOHN DRYDEN was born in 1631, into a rural family, and was educated at Westminster School, London, and Trinity College, Cambridge. He became the major English poet and man of letters of the late seventeenth century, and was also the most influential poet of his time on poetry of the eighteenth century, sometimes called the 'neo-classical' or 'Augustan' period. Dryden distinguished himself as the author of occasional poems such as *Annus Mirabilis* (1667); various works for the theatre, including the tragedy *All for Love* (1677); satires, most notably *Absalom and Achitophel* (1681); polemical, didactic poems such as *The Hind and the Panther* (1687); criticism, in the early *Of Dramatick Poesy, an Essay* (1668); and, especially towards the end of his life, translations. His translation of the *Aeneid* was an act of homage to a classical poet whom he had long revered and, to a certain extent, it stood for the epic which Dryden himself wished to write. He became Poet Laureate in 1668 and, soon after, became Historiographer Royal. However, he lost these positions in the 'Glorious' Revolution of 1688. John Dryden died in 1700.

FREDERICK M. KEENER is Professor Emeritus of English at Hofstra University. His publications include *English Dialogues of the Dead, An Essay on Pope* and *The Chain of Becoming*. He has also written essays directed towards a history of the comprehension of literature and co-edited, with Susan E. Lorsch, *Eighteenth-Century Women and the Arts*.

VIRGIL'S AENEID
TRANSLATED BY JOHN DRYDEN

Edited by FREDERICK M. KEENER

PENGUIN BOOKS

PENGUIN BOOKS

Published by the Penguin Group
Penguin Books Ltd, 80 Strand, London WC2R 0RL, England
Penguin Group (USA) Inc., 375 Hudson Street, New York, New York 10014, USA
Penguin Group (Canada), 90 Eglinton Avenue East, Suite 700, Toronto, Ontario, Canada M4P 2Y3
(a division of Pearson Penguin Canada Inc.)
Penguin Ireland, 25 St Stephen's Green, Dublin 2, Ireland
(a division of Penguin Books Ltd)
Penguin Group (Australia), 707 Collins Street, Melbourne, Victoria 3008, Australia
(a division of Pearson Australia Group Pty Ltd)
Penguin Books India Pvt Ltd, 11 Community Centre, Panchsheel Park,
New Delhi – 110 017, India
Penguin Group (NZ), 67 Apollo Drive, Rosedale, Auckland 0632, New Zealand
(a division of Pearson New Zealand Ltd)
Penguin Books (South Africa) (Pty) Ltd, Block D, Rosebank Office Park,
181 Jan Smuts Avenue, Parktown North, Gauteng 2193, South Africa

Penguin Books Ltd, Registered Offices: 80 Strand, London WC2R 0RL, England

www.penguin.com

This edition first published 1997

018

Copyright © Frederick M. Keener, 1997
All rights reserved

Filmset in 10/11.5 pt Postscript Monotype Ehrhardt
Set by Rowland Phototypesetting Ltd, Bury St Edmunds, Suffolk
Printed in England by Clays Ltd, St Ives plc

ISBN: 978-0-140-44627-2

www.greenpenguin.co.uk

MIX
Paper from
responsible sources
FSC
www.fsc.org   FSC® C018179

Penguin Books is committed to a sustainable
future for our business, our readers and our planet.
This book is made from Forest Stewardship
Council™ certified paper.

CONTENTS

PREFACE

John Dryden kept the Latin title *Æneis* for his English translation of what we call Virgil's *Aeneid*, a translation first published in 1697 and enduringly valuable. Besides offering attractive access to one of the three outstanding classical epics, the translation is an important, magisterial and moving English poem. Historically very influential as well, Dryden's poem is particularly useful in preparing readers to understand and enjoy eighteenth-century English poetry.

A taste for this poetry must be acquired. It is distinctly stylized, in ways which Dryden did much to create or establish. Less obviously, acquiring the requisite taste presupposes other acquisitions. The eighteenth century, unlike some literary periods, pointedly expected readers to have a certain amount of learning, including some familiarity with the Roman classics.

This poem of Dryden's, more fully and concentratedly than any other single text, combines much of the eighteenth century's distinctive poetic style with the requisite substance; with indeed, in Virgil's poem, the historic centrepiece of that substance. At first these two aspects, of substance and style, may seem obstacles. As they become familiar, they reveal themselves to be aspects of the translation's merit and interest.

This edition seeks to help readers make that transition, and this preface, while providing some explanation and support for the claims already made in it, concentrates on the translation's distinctive substance and style. Without seeking to be interpretatively definitive about the enormous topics involved – Virgil and Dryden have both been subjects of commentary for a long time – the preface addresses first Virgil's contribution to Dryden's poem, then Dryden's own contribution, and finally, though only suggestively, the relation of the two.

The edition comes as close as is desirable – very close – to presenting Dryden's *Æneis* in a form in which it made itself known to its original readers. A glance at the text will reveal some notable peculiarities of presentation. The spelling and punctuation, the capitalization, the italics, the occasional long bracket in the margin: these provide only the most conspicuous signs that the text in some ways suits conventions of Dryden's era, not our own. But the reader unfamiliar with those conventions will quickly become accustomed to them, and will gain something from the experience: not just the satisfaction of being able to negotiate a text of a distant time in, by and large, its own terms; also – a further point which this preface seeks to illuminate – some appreciation of how those textual conventions contribute to the poem's special meaning and worth.

Ways In

At first the poem may seem unwelcoming. It begins as if the reader already knows the legendary, historical, and geographical subject-matter which the story involves, even the story itself. But the translation, as originally published and as reproduced here, comes equipped with a summary, the prose 'arguments' (by young Joseph Addison, to become famous as an author of the *Spectator*) introducing the poem's twelve parts or 'books'. And the poem soon tells most if not all of what a reader needs in order to make sense of the narrative: about Aeneas, Juno, Rome, and the rest of what is temporarily assumed at the start.

This edition supplements the text with maps and a Glossary. These aids, though selective, will answer a good many questions which the poem raises beyond those it soon answers. Dryden provided a number of useful answers himself in the prose apparatus published with his poem, including both a long preface in the form of a Dedication (to John Sheffield, Marquess of Normanby and Earl of Mulgrave, whose writings Pope was to edit), and a short Postscript to the Reader. Dryden's *Æneis* was published together with his translations of Virgil's *Eclogues* and *Georgics*, the whole presented as an edition of Virgil's *Works*. That edition also included a set of 'Notes and Observations' by Dryden on all these poems.

Dryden's commentary might have been printed here but has been largely omitted as distracting, particularly for readers making their initial approach to the poem, and not least because the apparatus itself requires a good deal of explanation; Dryden certainly did not give to the apparatus the quality of attention he gave to the poem. The apparatus is, however, readily available: complete in the grand California Edition of *The Works of John Dryden* as well as in some older editions of Dryden including *The Poetical Works* edited by George R. Noyes. James Kinsley's edition of Dryden's *Poems* and George Watson's of Dryden's critical writings have the Dedication and Postscript, though Watson abridges the former where it is largely a transcription of an earlier commentary. The present edition's list of Further Reading includes these editions, together with some studies bearing on the *Æneis*. (My quotations from the Dedication are from the 1698 second edition of the translation, my copy-text as will be explained here. Citations for these quotations and other references are to that edition, but because it is not readily accessible to most readers the citations also include, in italics, the pertinent page numbers in the California Edition.)

To begin to understand the poem and make substantial headway is much easier than finishing the process. Absorbingly, the poem has dimension on dimension, notably but not exclusively corresponding to the multiple temporal perspectives involved. Virgil narrates a story set in what was antiquity for him, a thousand years before his time. The story, its events and other circumstances – as well as the narration of them – have precedents in other authors, including those ancient for Virgil himself. The *Aeneid* is clearly a sequel to Homer's epics, especially to the *Iliad*, which, against the backdrop of the Greeks' ten-year siege of Troy, concentrates on the hero Achilles and particularly on the effects of his quarrel with the general of the Greek forces, Agamemnon, king of Mycenae. The Greek campaign was initiated in retribution for the elopement to Troy of Helen, wife of Agamemnon's brother, King Menelaus of Sparta, with Paris, son of the Trojan king Priam. The *Aeneid* also weaves in some of the other Homeric epic. The *Odyssey* concentrates on the Greek hero Odysseus – Ulysses, in Latin – as he makes his way home from the war to his island of Ithaca. Ulysses' route and adventures prefigure those of Aeneas, notably Ulysses' visit to Hades and his protracted amorous delay with the nymph Calypso. It has frequently been remarked that the first half of the *Aeneid* resembles the *Odyssey*, as Aeneas struggles to reach Italy, and the second half resembles the *Iliad*, narrating a war, though not directly a war of conquest. Aeneas battles to provide his displaced Trojan people with a secure Italian home.

Virgil also writes his story as it prophetically or otherwise adumbrates history up to and even beyond his own time. Dryden adds comparable perspectives, on such history and on Virgil but also proceeding from his own particular historical standpoint. Politics provides the sharpest examples. Dryden had comparatively close experience of two major revolutions against Stuart monarchs. First there were the Civil Wars of his youth which had reached their conclusion with the execution of Charles I in 1649 and, in the 1650s, Charles's replacement by the Protector, Oliver Cromwell. Then, though in 1660 the Restoration reinstituted the monarchy in the person of Charles's son, Charles II, the next king, James II, was driven from the throne into exile in 1688. James's Roman Catholicism had been a cause of protest for years, and he was supplanted by the Dutch, Protestant prince William of Orange, who reigned as William III together with his wife Mary, James's daughter. Dryden remained loyal to the departed king. Recent scholarship (including books by William Frost and Steven N. Zwicker listed in Further Reading) has emphasized the topical overtones of the translation, for example in its preference for words such as 'exil'd' and 'restor'd'.

There are historical, Virgilian parallels as well. Virgil's poetry reflects his experience of Rome's similar transition, from a republic dominated by the Senate to what in our terms was a dictatorship, a transition in two major stages involving one ruling family, that of Julius Caesar. The autocratic control seized by Julius Caesar, which was cut short by his assassination, his adopted son Caesar Augustus secured for himself.

Such historical parallels contribute to the significance of Virgil's and Dryden's poems. So does the fact that in Dryden's time the prevalent theory of epic, mainly based on Virgil's precedent and enunciated by René Le Bossu's *Traité du poëme épique* (1675), viewed the hero as personifying the actual, historical monarch of the poet's nation. For Virgil, then, Aeneas is Augustus, though Le Bossu had complicated the matter, as Dryden's Dedication acknowledges at least in passing (206, *271*), by observing that the hero, so long as he is virtuous in some respects, need not be above criticism in others. For Dryden the matter is still more complicated, because Aeneas, particularly the wandering Aeneas of the first six books, would seem to be James, not William.

But Virgil's story has also to do with the native prince Turnus whose expectations, certainly legitimate in some respects, must contend with those of the hero and his army whom Turnus suddenly finds on his shores. Single-minded reading or translation is not something which the *Aeneid* invites or very readily permits. The tradition that Virgil had not completed the poem when he died offers some explanation for those parts of the text which are difficult or impossible to reconcile with others. Perhaps the most unavoidable example has to do with Aeneas' behaviour at the end. Just what Virgil thought his poem meant, however, is a topic too difficult and large for consideration here, as is what Dryden thought it meant, though some of his opinions will be mentioned.

Poetical Vigour

The translation comes highly recommended, most memorably by the period's splendid translator of Homer, Alexander Pope. In the Preface to his version of the *Iliad* Pope proclaims Dryden's *Aeneid* 'the most noble and spirited translation that I know in any language'. The leading critic of the period, Samuel Johnson, in what has come to be called his *Lives of the English Poets* (ed. George Birkbeck Hill, 3 vols., 1905; reprinted New York: Octagon, 1967), evidently reaffirms Pope's delight by repeating that compliment (I, 449) and saying much to justify it when extolling Dryden's general poetic achievements. For Johnson, Dryden's is 'a vigorous genius operating upon large materials' (I, 457). That genius is palpable in Dryden's historic transfiguration of English verse, especially his establishment of a new, august standard so influential as to be epochal.

Johnson declares that Dryden 'refined the language, improved the sentiments, and tuned the numbers of English Poetry. . . . The new versification, as it was called, may be considered as owing its establishment to Dryden; from whose time it is apparent that English poetry has had no tendency to relapse to its former savageness' (I, 421). That concluding generality may still take a reader's breath away, yet Johnson was not alone in believing it. Pope would have agreed, as the major beneficiary of Dryden's accomplishments. Pope could not have been the great poet he was, in the way he was, without Dryden and particularly Dryden's *Aeneid*, which reverberates throughout not only Pope's *Iliad* and *Odyssey* but also his other writing, even apart from the mock-heroic *Rape of the Lock* and *Dunciad*.

By 'sentiments' Johnson especially means the expression of thoughts suiting the subject-matter. By 'numbers', he means the versification, including a relatively sustained metre but not that alone. In view of Johnson's claims of refinement, however, readers may wonder how Dryden's genius could be so 'vigorous', especially given the fact that much of Dryden's verse, including most of the *Æneis*, is in rhymed iambic pentameter couplets, like much eighteenth-century verse. The form permits some conspicuous liberties: mainly, there may be an occasional line in hexameter, and sometimes a line may be added to and rhymed with a couplet to form a triplet. A triplet is conventionally signalled by that single, flamboyant three-line bracket in the right-hand margin. Abstractly, nevertheless, the form would seem to constrain vigour – yet Pope commends Dryden for his 'Energy divine' (*The First Epistle of the Second Book of Horace*, line 269).

The words 'vigour' and 'energy' have overlapping senses. For Johnson, 'vigour' encompasses physical but also mental force, acuity as well as the broader 'energy'. 'Vigour' may be more appropriate to a translation of the *Aeneid* because it is a Latin word, used there by Virgil, notably to describe the fiery power of the seminal principles of all life: what Dryden translates as 'Etherial Vigour' (6.988).

Pope's *Essay on Man* has a simile variously useful here, from the grafting of plants:

> As Fruits, ungrateful to the planter's care,
> On savage stocks inserted, learn to bear;
> The surest Virtues thus from Passions shoot,
> Wild Nature's vigour working at the root.   (2.181–4)

The literal point identifies vigour with the emotions. Figurative reference to grafting is frequent in Virgil; though a matter of literal, practical concern in the *Georgics*, it is also, there and elsewhere, a topic figuratively expressing an intimate, healthful relation between Roman culture and its agricultural origins. The slip or scion of a plant being cultivated gains strength from the stock into which it is inserted. Dryden speaks of his translation in terms of grafting – in one passage comparing his own phrasing to a scion on Virgil's

'Stock, which I may call almost inexhaustible, of figurative, elegant, and sounding Words' (244, *333*). Regarding what he has himself contributed to the translation, supplementing Virgil, Dryden hopes it 'will seem (at least I have the Vanity to think so,) not stuck into him, but growing out of him', and Dryden also compares Virgil's diction to a scion grafted on the stock of the English language (242, *329–30*). Some of the vigour of the translation, then, is Virgilian, some not only from Dryden but also from English, the language in which he had long thrived.

Johnson comments on Dryden's refinement of poetic language:

Every language of a learned nation necessarily divides itself into diction scholastick and popular, grave and familiar, elegant and gross; and from a nice distinction of these different parts arises a great part of the beauty of style. But if we except a few minds, the favourites of nature, . . . [t]here was . . . before the time of Dryden no poetical diction; no system of words at once refined from the grossness of domestick use and free from the harshness of terms appropriated to particular arts. Words too familiar or too remote defeat the purpose of a poet. From those sounds which we hear on small or on coarse occasions, we do not easily receive strong impressions or delightful images; and words to which we are nearly strangers, whenever they occur, draw that attention on themselves which they should transmit to things.   (I, 420)

Some thirty years later, Wordsworth would resoundingly condemn what he called 'poetic diction', elevating in its place diction selected from the more natural 'language really used by men' (Preface to *Lyrical Ballads*, 2nd ed., 1800). He supported his opinion by quoting a renowned eighteenth-century poem, Thomas Gray's 'Sonnet' (1742) on the death of Richard West, distinguishing the lines in it which were acceptable from those which were not. Wordsworth elsewhere criticized Dryden's poetry for inadequate observation of natural objects and singled out the translation of Virgil in this respect (*The Letters of William and Dorothy Wordsworth*, I, ed. Ernest de Selincourt, 2nd ed., rev. Chester L. Shaver (Oxford: 1967), 641). It may be that Wordsworth had in mind Dryden's translation of the *Georgics* and *Eclogues* with their distinctively rural subject-matter.

Poetical Diction

If the reader seeks some common ground in opinions on the face of them so radically different as those of Johnson and Wordsworth, yet apparently both of some value, it is sensible to respond that a style in the manner of Dryden's, which at its inception and for most of a century had seemed freshly perceptive about Johnson's 'things' if not Wordsworth's natural objects, had at last become routine and, at least for some subject-matter, definitely imperceptive. What is poetic diction? We may immediately think of phrases such as 'finny race', for fish. Though neither Wordsworth's comments nor the lines he quotes from Gray contain exactly that kind of phrase, examples readily arise in Dryden's translation as well as in Pope and elsewhere. Dryden at 3.868 refers to a shepherd's 'woolly Care', his sheep. But an objection such as Wordsworth's concerning an object described in a poem presupposes the larger question of what the object being addressed really is, in view of the poet's objectives.

Johnson's description of what he meant suggests a vocabulary of a middling sort: neither too much this nor too much that. Yet this vocabulary has certainly been 'refined' (Johnson's word); that is, this vocabulary is in the direction of a style high more than otherwise: a style more rather than less suitable for an exalted, heroic genre such as epic, with all objects subordinated to that objective. Dryden's Dedication begins:

A Heroick Poem, truly such, is undoubtedly the greatest Work which the Soul of Man is capable to perform. The Design of it, is to form the Mind to Heroick Virtue by Example; 'tis convey'd in Verse, that it may delight, while it instructs. . . . Even the least portions . . . must be of the Epick kind; all things must be Grave, Majestical, and Sublime. . . .   (203, 267)

Those adjectives, particularly 'Sublime', refer to the style as well as other things.

But Dryden's prose discussion of his objectives in the *Æneis* was open to more attention than he gave it. For example (though this particular point would not have troubled Le Bossu), as Dryden's Dedication proceeds it raises more doubts about the moral example set by Aeneas than it lays to rest, particularly regarding Aeneas' departure from the Carthaginian queen, Dido. Though the translation certainly has the qualities Dryden mentions in that passage from the Dedication, they are not the translation's constant, only qualities. In general, for example, if a character's behaviour is on occasion not majestic, the poem cannot be so in 'all things'. But the moral objectives of epic, as Dryden conceived them to be, are not undermined by any moral lapses the poem represents so long as the text as a whole retains majesty and the other qualities which Dryden stipulated.

'Moral', in usage such as Dryden's, is not directly equivalent to 'morally didactic'. Rather, it means that the focus of the poem, suited to the poet's most comprehensive object and objectives, is on human behaviour as related to good or evil (or on 'manners', as Dryden would say, meaning what the Romans called *mores*). Even the single small phrase may express moral responsibility and concern, as those of the shepherd's life are represented in 'woolly Care'. Less obviously, the phrase 'finny Coursers' (1.211) maintains Dryden's moral focus, among the other functions it may perform. The literal range of 'Coursers' includes 'chargers', war-horses. The word expresses a relation to human behaviour – whether virtuous, indifferent, or vicious – in the management of horses. That behaviour includes effects on other, including human, beings. The metaphorical extension to sea-creatures preserves this sense, and does so even though the coursers are Neptune's, given the like-nesses between human and divine behaviour. Because Dryden's primary object is emphatically the moral dimension of things, he does not become directly descriptive of natural objects.

But the whole question of Dryden's and the eighteenth century's diction has become complicated more fundamentally because the vocabulary to which Johnson especially refers is now not widely understood, a state of affairs tending towards fulfilment of Pope's prophecy in *An Essay on Criticism*: 'such as Chaucer is, shall Dryden be' (line 483). Some of Dryden's diction – Pope's too, and even Wordsworth's – has been obscured by time. And the words 'poetic' and 'poetical' themselves, when applied to diction or anything else, may obscure consideration of it; these words may be taken to mean that the presence or absence of the diction so described is a sign of poetic merit, or deficiency. It is best to use just one of those words so as not to suggest any distinction between them. This preface relies on 'poetical' from here on, and does so with the stipulation that the word means only 'typical of one or more verse styles', implying no evaluation.

Dryden's poetical diction does involve a special linguistic world, with its own semantic values even apart from questions about what is literal and what figurative. In that special world, for example, a 'race', oddly to our ears, may refer to an individual person. It is also a world in which darkness may regularly 'involve' the sky, including its 'racks' and 'vault', though not 'involving' it as we use that word. When serpents are involved, and in one sense they always are, they have 'curls' and even 'spires', and come in 'volumes'. In a manner related to the special matter of the *Aeneid* already touched on here, this special world is one in which neither 'Africa' nor 'Asia' is a 'continent' as we use these words. This world is also such that a 'desert' may abound with growing things; that something never broken may be 'fixed' or 'mended'; and that something already at hand may nevertheless be 'supplied'.

More subtly when the words are more abstract, this world is one in which it may well be the giver rather than the receiver who is 'grateful', and a person may be 'generous' without ever giving anyone anything; where something other than an outcome or a person may be 'doubtful', and an article of furniture may be 'conscious'; where to 'conspire' may entail no dishonesty, but it may be 'dishonest' for a person to die in a certain way, even if through no fault of that person; where to be 'amazed' may involve no surprise, and where one may regularly be 'unhappy' without knowing it; where something may be 'preferred' with no comparison stated or implied; where the 'unexpected' may certainly be anticipated; where to be 'prevented' implies not the slightest hindrance; where to 'deplore' and even to 'denounce' may express no condemnation; where what is 'obscene' need not be 'vulgar', and what is 'promiscuous' may very well have no vulgarity about it; where everyone 'expires' repeatedly with no adverse effects, but anyone may very well die from being 'bored' or 'baffled', especially in a 'debate', and 'devoting' oneself to something is regularly fatal.

Though most of the special vocabulary represented by these examples entails Latin roots and senses, not all of it does, nor is some of the vocabulary untypical of poetry preceding Dryden's. Perhaps the oddest thing to our ears and eyes is that all of these words are familiar; only some of the senses in which they are used are not, and would not have been even for some of Dryden's original readers. As Dryden employs such words, they have exceptional range and force, even have 'Wild Nature's vigour working at the root', whether the root is Latin or English, and the vigour includes Dryden's own, 'wild' at least in often being historically unconventional. The Glossary in the present edition seeks to explain any special meanings which the poem assigns to its vocabulary.

Yet like Wordsworth's sense of verbal propriety, Johnson's or even Pope's sense of the refinement appropriate to the diction of sublime verse does not extend back to Dryden in all respects, as the reader will certainly notice. One glaring example is Dryden's repeated use of the word 'fries', especially as he turns it to describe the sea's seething. The word is sufficiently – redolently – popular, familiar, even gross. Pope's verse scrupulously avoids this usage. Not only the usage, however, but also its implicit voice, is undoubtedly Dryden's. And as Johnson ultimately confessed himself fonder of Dryden than of Pope (op. cit., III, 222–3), we may find it in our minds to enjoy the unregenerate vigour of the word and others like it in the text.

Poetical Syntax

There is another distinctive, apparently very influential, stylistic trait of Dryden's poem which deserves or even requires attention here, more perhaps for readers' encouragement than for their enlightenment. Calling attention to it points to the fact that, for both Johnson and Wordsworth as well as everyone else, poetical style is not simply a matter of diction. The additional element has to do with the arrangement of words, phrases, and clauses within a sentence, and I call it 'poetical syntax' for want of a better, established term. The word 'syntax' refers to the relations of words and groups of them whereby they form a sentence permissible in a given language, whether that sentence is in prose or verse. By 'poetical syntax' I mean a certain relation of poetry to English syntax, and, as earlier, by 'poetical' I mean only 'typical of one or more verse styles', with no evaluation implied. Poetical syntax, as will become evident, has an important bearing not only on comprehension of Dryden's Æneis but also on the issue of how much of its original punctuation ought to be preserved.

The poem frequently departs from the word-order that is

standard in colloquial and much other English, including the 'language really used' in daily transactions. For example, it departs from the word-order of 'Then I came home'. With equal syntactic correctness and equal intelligibility, that sentence may be 'Home then I came' or even 'Then I home came' (and these examples do not exhaust the permissible permutations). Ordinarily, however, if such a sentence is not formed as it is in the first of these examples, the reader or hearer will probably wonder why not, and may become less interested in where that 'I' went, more in why the sentence has its unusual shape (and perhaps where its author comes from, or what its author is up to). Distinctions about diction and other elements of language regarded as poetical are general distinctions; they do not mean that such elements cannot or often do not enter prose and speech. Nevertheless, English as idiomatically spoken or written in everyday exchanges does not normally, and never did, include constructions such as 'Home then I came'. Unless facetious, they are not principally for offhand reference to narrow, normal rounds, but only for declarations of momentous journeys, to somewhere extraordinary: 'To Carthage then I came' (as T. S. Eliot in *The Waste Land* quotes St Augustine). Such constructions inverting ordinary word-order have a technical name, anastrophe, and whatever else they do, they generally heighten English style.

Some inclusion of commas in the second and particularly the third of the examples just given here might ease a reader's progress through them, but the additional punctuation is not necessary. English syntax sometimes requires assistance from punctuation; in most cases it does not. But anastrophic constructions call for some circumspection and even patience on the reader's part because, slight as any sentence's departure from ordinary word-order may be, that departure delays or suspends the reader's identification of the particular syntactic relations which the sentence expresses. Anastrophe temporarily conceals a sentence's syntactic relations, holding those relations, and the reader, in a state of suspense. Such suspension of syntactic relations is what I am calling 'poetical syntax'.

Though anastrophe is frequent in Dryden's *Æneis* and in eighteenth-century poetry, that device is only the simplest form of such syntax, which may involve more than the order of words in a given clause, extending to departure from the ordinary English order of clauses in a sentence. Such a departure particularly distinguishes the kind of sentence called 'periodic'. If a sentence contains several clauses, at least one of them dependent, and if the main independent clause or at least a crucial part of it is not given until the end, the sentence is distinctly periodic. Like an anastrophe but on a larger scale, a periodic sentence is suspenseful, in syntax and in effect. Long periodic sentences characterize the kind of style which is at once most formal and very solemn or grand, as in Cicero or Milton or Johnson. Long or not so long, these sentences occur in Dryden's *Æneis* and in eighteenth-century poetry as well, heightening the style more than anastrophe does, yet for the most part the sentences in such poetry might best be described as having a periodic quality rather than being fully periodic. That is most noticeably so because a distinctly periodic sentence builds inexorably to an emphatic, even ringing conclusion when its main clause is at last supplied or completed, whereas in Dryden's poem and others like it a sentence frequently declines in, and then recovers, intensity, or builds steadily to what seems to be a conclusion – and then continues, extending the suspense that makes its syntax 'poetical'.

Poetical syntax, frequently combined with other devices of artful word- and clause-ordering and often involved with rhyme, is a central, ubiquitous trait of eighteenth-century poetry; witness Pope's anastrophic 'The surest Virtues thus from Passions shoot'. Yet Wordsworth does not cite Gray for such departures in the sonnet on West, where one of the lines which Wordsworth found unexceptionable is 'A different object do these eyes require'. Wordsworth's acceptance of this line is significant not only because his own verse regularly displays poetical syntax but also because so much verse of various times does. The poetry of a particular era is usually quite distinguishable from that of others, but some of what is poetical at one time is also so at other times.

To look into the uses of poetical syntax in Dryden's translation, it may be most equitable to instance the first paragraph – the poem's 'proposition' (to employ a term from traditional analysis of epic). At first the reader may be struck by what seems very strange punctuation:

> Arms, and the Man I sing, who forc'd by Fate,
> And haughty *Juno*'s unrelenting Hate;

> Expell'd and exil'd, left the *Trojan* Shoar:
> Long Labours, both by Sea and Land he bore;
> And in the doubtful War, before he won
> The *Latian* Realm, and built the destin'd Town:
> His banish'd Gods restor'd to Rites Divine,
> And setl'd sure Succession in his Line:
> From whence the Race of *Alban* Fathers come,
> And the long Glories of Majestick *Rome*.   (1, 1–10)

It is tempting to streamline the punctuation, perhaps sharply minimizing it in a way consistent with today's standards:

> Arms and the Man I sing who, forc'd by Fate
> And haughty *Juno*'s unrelenting Hate,
> Expell'd and exil'd left the *Trojan* Shoar.
> Long Labours both by Sea and Land he bore
> And in the doubtful War before he won
> The *Latian* Realm and built the destin'd Town,
> His banish'd Gods restor'd to Rites Divine,
> And setl'd sure Succession in his Line –
> From whence the Race of *Alban* Fathers come
> And the long Glories of Majestick *Rome*.

Instead of fifteen punctuation marks, now there are seven, and readers may think the result an improvement, despite what may seem a comparative hastiness.

Why an author of Dryden's time, his immediate audience, and many of their successors thought differently is another topic too large for full examination here. This preface emphasizes a reader's negotiation of the main obstacles to understanding Dryden's translation, as a basis for promoting the capacity to enjoy the poem and others like it. I mainly confine my comments now to the ways in which the punctuation and other things affect the sense of the passage. The sense differs subtly but substantially in the two versions. I should add that the topic is large because it involves various considerations, including the history of punctuation. Especially, colons used to be employed where we would use a semicolon or perhaps a period, except that those marks could be followed by a clause syntactically subordinate to a clause preceding them.

This broad topic also involves another matter already touched

on here: the art, and the taste for it, of writing poems, even
long narratives, in couplets. The quoted short passage has artistic
features to which I can only begin to pay adequate attention, for
example the way in which the sound of 'forc'd' in the first line,
permeating and softening the couplet division, flourishes into the
rhymes 'Shoar' and 'bore' and then subsides in the half-line, half-
rhyme 'War', a word which Dryden seems to have heard in a range
between 'care' and 'far' (as in 1.326–7, 358–9) – only, contributing
to pull the couplets together, to become pronouncedly restored in
'before' and even the very word 'restor'd'.

I concentrate on one example of poetical syntax, related to the
way in which lines 5–8 run more smoothly in the revised version
than they do in Dryden's. A comma instead of a colon in line 6
brings out the element of parallelism in all three lines, emphasizing
their common pattern, making them readily graspable as a unit –
as are these lines from Wordsworth's 'Tintern Abbey', with their
periodic quality, about a certain 'sublime' and 'serene' state of
mind,

> that blessed mood,
> In which the burthen of the mystery,
> In which the heavy and the weary weight
> Of all this unintelligible world,
> Is lightened . . .   (lines 37–41)

Dryden's colon at the end of line 6 makes his lines less easy to
grasp than these from Wordsworth, and less soothing, more rous-
ing or vigorous. The colon has this effect at least in part because
a rhymed couplet typically ends with a mark of punctuation that
is comparatively strong in the context. But here this norm does
not provide the whole explanation. Dryden seems not to have
wanted the three lines to be perfectly parallel. The proof of that
is line 7, which departs from the general word-order of the pattern.
That is, line 7 departs from the parallelism which may be schemat-
ized as:

he	won	the Latian	realm,
	built	the destined	town,
	settled	sure	succession. . . .

The subject 'he' is the same in all these clauses, though only implied in two of them. In each clause this subject is followed by a past-tense verb, then an adjective with or without the article 'the', and then the object of each verb – all in that natural-seeming order. But line 7 begins with the last two of these predicate elements, the adjective and object, and only afterwards gets to the verb. This anastrophic line appears reckless, wild. In some sense it is. It could easily have been accommodated to the parallelism of the surrounding lines because that change would have preserved the rhyme: 'Restor'd his banish'd Gods to Rites Divine'. Instead the line all by itself exhibits poetical syntax, and does so in such a way as to complicate the different, dominant pattern and poetical syntax of the passage as a whole. The asymmetrical line makes the passage in its entirety less readily graspable. Perverse, one may think; perversification.

There can be explanatory recourse, alternatively or also, to a desire for elegant variety, a desire demonstrably active in Dryden's time. But still another explanation may be best. It identifies what it was that Dryden was apparently reckless of in this poem, and perhaps why this poem was the right place to be so.

Heightening of style by means of poetical syntax, including the periodic quality with anastrophe, does not adequately explain the matter. Such syntax is recurrent in Dryden's text, even in the passage quoted, even with present-day punctuation. 'Arms and the man I sing', brief as it is, is a complete example. So is the longer 'Long Labours both by Sea and Land he bore'. (The asymmetrical line commented on above may be said to be symmetrical with these.) A more modest example is 'who[,] forc'd . . . exil'd, left the Trojan Shoar'. One fact about all these examples and many like them that follow throughout the poem is, as I have said, that poetical syntax, in elevating the style, produces suspense in the reader. The text at least temporarily suspends full disclosure of the applied particular syntactic and other sense of the word or phrase or clause in question, requiring the reader to suspend syntactic and other resolution of it. Such particular resolution of the sentence is not immediately discovered by the text or the reader.

Such poetical syntax has various uses. It can be put to witty purposes, as for example when what seems to be introduced as a grammatical object turns out surprisingly to be the subject, but this kind of wit is not very prominent in Dryden's poem. And once the reader comes to expect such syntax, peculiarities of punctuation gain point – for example the comma which may seem *very* awkwardly placed after the first word of the poem, 'Arms'. Explanation is possible. The poet sings, or sings of, two grammatical objects, the 'Man . . . who' and those 'Arms', but those arms, except in some distinctly metaphorical way quite different from what literally happened to that man, were not 'forc'd', etc. 'Man' here is literal; 'Arms' is not, referring to war and other things. The formal parallel, with both nouns combined as the objects of 'sing', leaves still unresolved the question of any parallel in sense. The comma may be explained as acknowledging and signalling these facts.

And concerning especially the 'whence' in line 9, what is its antecedent? It is 'Line', but it is also 'Succession' in the line preceding, which ends with a colon. A comma might do, but the colon may be taken to indicate an equivalence between the last two lines of the passage and the two lines before, and such an equivalence makes sense as far as it goes. (The way in which those two last lines extend a sentence already syntactically complete and conclusive-seeming as far as it has gone, extending it in a manner which the reader has little reason to expect, exemplifies the case of sentences which have the periodic quality without being exactly periodic.) The 'whence' makes sense as referring to almost the whole paragraph. This may be thought a subtle point. A reader would pause over the 'whence', wondering about its exact application, only if alert to the recurrence of temporarily unresolved constructions in the poem. On the other hand it is not objectionably fastidious – it is comprehending – to see that the lines introduced by 'whence' depend, as much as anything else in the paragraph, on (or from) 'Arms, and the Man I sing'.

Most of the poem's many examples of such recurrence are not distinctly subtle. A striking example comes only some fifty lines later when Juno expresses an angry, invidious comparison of herself with another goddess, and introduces another comparison involving an eagle:

> Cou'd angry *Pallas*, with revengeful Spleen,
> The *Grecian* Navy burn, and drown the Men?
> She for the Fault of one offending Foe,
> The Bolts of *Jove* himself presum'd to throw:

> With Whirlwinds from beneath she toss'd the Ship,
> And bare expos'd the Bosom of the deep:
> Then, as an Eagle gripes the trembling Game,
> The Wretch yet hissing with her Father's Flame,
> She strongly seiz'd, and with a burning Wound,
> Transfix'd and naked, on a Rock she bound.   (1, 60–69)

Dryden himself introduces the eagle comparison in more ways than one; it is not in Virgil.

This passage might be said to illustrate all the potential obstacles which are the main subject of this preface. For readers who do not recognize the legendary event described, the present Glossary provides enough information in the entry 'Pallas'. Dryden's spelling is peculiar – 'gripes', for example – yet it takes but an instant to recognize 'grips'. There is salient poetical diction. 'Spleen' might have been given a Glossary entry because the word is so prominent in eighteenth-century verse, but the appropriate meaning is still current enough and sufficiently defined in any dictionary. Perhaps the main example of poetical diction is the circumlocution 'trembling Game'. A rabbit? – quite possibly.

This item of poetical diction, though, rapidly turns out to involve what I have called poetical syntax, especially as represented by the 'Wretch'. Involved too is the fact that the preceding line has introduced a standard component of the classical epic, a simile, and the fact that epic similes are typically long. There is so much rapidity in these lines that I slow down reception of them, to register each stage of their vigorous mental action – both the narrator's and the reader's. The 'Wretch' of line 67 immediately seems a reference to the preceding 'Game', syntax possibly and appositively identifying the two. Then (the 'hissing' suggests) the 'Game' is a 'snake', and 'her' suggests a female snake – if the antecedent of 'her' is not the 'Eagle'. If the antecedent is 'Eagle', then the 'Game' is still possibly a rabbit. But why next a reference to the Eagle's 'Father' and particularly to that 'Father's Flame'? The eagle is the 'Bird of *Jove*', an epithet elsewhere in the poem, but the eagle is not thereby the child of Jove. Yet the 'Flame' may be that of the thunderbolts 'of *Jove*' back in line 63, where Pallas is said to have thrown them, and Jove is Pallas' father. So the 'her' may well refer to Pallas, that reference signifying possible termination of what now seems conceivably a very brief simile –

one much briefer than originally appeared. And the beginning of line 68 immediately certifies the fact that the 'Wretch' of line 67 is not the 'Game', except by way of the simile. 'She strongly seiz'd' has no grammatical object if it is not the 'Wretch', who, as distinguished from his figurative representation in the simile, is literally the 'one offending Foe' of line 62.

What is central to the poet's mental activity in this instance, and what most requires the reader to perform comparably, is, again, poetical syntax. Line 67 could have begun with an explicit reference to Pallas or even to her seizing the 'Wretch', making her parallel with the 'Eagle' or even making her action parallel with the bird's in the simile, but Dryden willed otherwise. Moreover, he willed to continue in the same vein, so that the sequence 'and with a burning Wound,/Transfix'd and naked, on a Rock' also hangs – as does the wretched object it represents, yet only poetically suspended – until the subject and verb relating these phrases to the 'Wretch' belatedly enter. And there are additional instances of temporary syntactical irresolution in the quoted passage.

My principal point here does not much concern the pleasures of ambiguity. Most generally, what I have called poetical syntax specifies the suspenseful, at least temporary irresolution of particular syntactic relations as a poem proceeds, together with the active thought thus expressed and required of the reader, especially the vigour, the energy of it. To emphasize a labyrinthine confinement in the couplet form is to underestimate the constraint-bending, gravity-defying strength and passion with which the form, in the best hands, may coexist. And to descend to questions of punctuation, that of the last four lines of the passage as originally presented happens to be everything we could wish – certainly it subserves the syntax in its process of revealing itself. Discovery of that syntax ultimately depends on grammatical comprehension, and also on logical comprehension, especially of what is equivalent to what: the continual, almost continuous, very energetic mental activity which the poetical syntax of the *Æneis* distinctively expects of readers. The poem can be so saliently vigorous in some respects because it is subtly so rigorous in others.

Johnson adds to his description of Dryden's vigour when he contrasts that poet's prose, 'a natural field . . . diversified by the varied exuberance of abundant vegetation', with Pope's, 'a velvet lawn, shaven by the scythe, and levelled by the roller' (op. cit.,

III, 222). Johnson might have applied to all Dryden's writing Pope's line 'A Wild, where weeds and flow'rs promiscuous shoot' (*An Essay on Man*, 1.7; where 'promiscuous' means, as it usually did until after the eighteenth century, 'mixed and disorderly', only possibly with any sexual overtone). Johnson did object that Dryden 'delighted to tread upon the brink of meaning' (I, 460). Dryden could write so vigorously because the capable reader would pay close grammatical and logical attention to how the branches, not to mention the roots, are involved. Such a reader, in even an exuberant, seemingly tangled wild, would be able to distinguish each of the constituent plants and the relations among all of them.

The frequent, almost always temporary instances of syntactic irresolution in the translation have conceivable bases in Virgil's text – as reputedly and evidently incomplete when Virgil died and also as a fruit of the liberty, especially of word-ordering, available to Virgil as a poet in Latin. Latin is a highly inflected language. (Inflections are internal modifications of words which signify specific syntactic relations: for example, *amor* is 'love'; *amoris*, 'of love'; *amata*, 'she who is loved'.) In Latin, within limits broader than those of English, in a given sentence a word can be placed anywhere without substantially changing the sense of the sentence as the whole finally pulls it together. In Latin verse, poetical syntax is virtually constant. Such verse is also tolerant of ellipsis, of the omission of words if they are syntactically implicit. Dryden's poetical word-order and frequent ellipsis, and also his apparent lack of punctilio about consistent punctuation (even, as we shall see in a moment, about inserting words inadvertently omitted from the text), would seem to have drawn leeway and encouragement from these precedents, as well as from the expectation that readers would have acquired the abilities needed to understand poetical syntax.

Such considerations do much to justify a remark of Dryden's about matters including the 'pointing' or punctuation of the translation, a remark which otherwise may seem not merely reckless but feckless. It occurs in his 'Errata' list, which was published with other unpaginated front-matter in the first edition and which includes corrections of errors in his *Æneis*. The remark is that besides those errors which Dryden here corrects, 'There are other Errata both in false pointing, and omissions of words [in] the Poem, which the Reader will correct without my trouble.' There is no reason to doubt that Dryden had that confidence, though there is certainly reason to discount Dryden's next remark: 'I omit [correction of such errors] because they only lame my *English*, not destroy my meaning.' In some sense this is certainly a courtly invitation to clamorous rebuttal, like Dryden's reference to his 'Vanity' quoted earlier. Dryden does not elsewhere in the volume speak as if the translation had been seriously impaired by its printing. If the instances of improper punctuation he refers to are in any proportion to the omissions of words which he mentions in the same breath, he cannot have had in mind many instances of the former because the text has so few instances of the latter. And the 'Errata' list, with this remark, was itself omitted in the corrected second edition.

The general point, moreover, might have been made much more positively. In a poem mostly about a person, Aeneas, who must summon and act on moral resolution and do so almost always in unresolved conditions – 'doubtful' conditions, the poem would say, conditions in which Aeneas' information about his circumstances and directions is almost always incomplete, open to questions and worries – it makes sense that the translation's syntactic and other features would emphasize suspense. But it makes sense too that the translation would, also emphatically, relate that suspense to the possible reliability of something implicit, whether the trustworthiness of gods and oracles or only matters of common good faith, including that of grammar. And it may make the largest sense historically that the translation would dramatize concern about the relations of such alternative perspectives in a manner which appears expressive of Dryden's mind and those of many of his contemporaries and eighteenth-century successors, intensely interested as so many of these people were in finding constructive or tolerable relations among the clashing perspectives which had unforgettably made the seventeenth century so tumultuous and harsh, not to say bloody as in the case of Charles I and many others.

In eighteenth-century poetry as influenced by Dryden, however, the nearly ubiquitous, distinctively prominent poetical syntax, while still addressing the relations of disparate perspectives, may serve less directly dramatic purposes than it does in the *Æneis*. Pope's *Essay on Criticism*, for example, moves quickly towards these lines seeking to reconcile different, difficultly various considerations involved in critical judgment:

> First follow Nature, and your judgment frame
> By her just standard, which is still the same:
> Unerring Nature, still divinely bright,
> One clear, unchang'd, and universal light,
> Life, force, and beauty, must to all impart,
> At once the source, and end, and test of Art.   (lines 68–73)

The alert, able reader cannot miss the vigorous syntactical reorientation which occurs after 'universal light'. Until well into the third couplet, the second couplet seems only backwards-applying and corroboratively subordinate to the first, as if like the first it ought to end with a colon. But the third couplet eventually reveals that the second couplet has begun a new independent clause markedly periodic in its quality. Or the passage reveals this when the reader has sorted out the anastrophic 'Life, force, and beauty, must to all impart', discovering what the subject and objects of 'must . . . impart' are; and whether the objects include 'light'; and, if they do, whether the adjectives 'One clear, . . .' apply to 'Life, force, and beauty'; and what the reference of 'all' is; and what is 'At once' fully the reference of 'the source, and end, and test'.

One odd fact about Dryden's Æneis, complementing its poetical syntax and distinguishing this translation from translations in general, is that for the most part the original readers of the English poem, and certainly those whom Dryden would have regarded as his most competent readers, were already familiar to some considerable degree with the untranslated text, having studied Virgil in school and, some of them, having returned to the Latin poem afterwards. For these readers, the relation of the translation to the original was inevitably to some extent that of variation to theme. A number of Dryden's readers would even have known some of Virgil's poem by heart, and they and others would have known and remembered other translations. The consequence was that for those readers, and for Dryden translating with them in mind, the experience of the translation was inevitably bifocal or multi-focal, entailing multiple perspectives. The relation of the translation to the original and other things was always in play and was in some sense necessarily a matter of play, and not only because no translation can be identical in sense with its original. To many of its readers, Dryden's Æneis was for all practical purposes not meant to be read as a substitute for its foreign-language original, with which it necessarily maintained a definite, continuous, complementary relation. (Occasionally Dryden's grafting is such that a reference to the original is helpful or even necessary to clarify a given expression, and the Glossary of the present edition at times puts Virgil's text to this use.)

And more than is usually the case with translations now, in Dryden's version of the *Aeneid* there is necessarily and otherwise some adjustment of the sense of the original poem, and in some cases Dryden's adjustments are quite distinctive. Sometimes his sentiments become exaggerated, sentimental, as Restoration sentiments often did. Sometimes his poetical syntax becomes baroquely, distractingly ornate. His adjustments become distinctly vigorous when he emphasizes his interest in moral issues, in one tone or another. Grandly responsive to Virgilian solemnity as the translation can be, it can also – as in the case of 'fries' but more pointedly – become co-operative with other than wholly high possibilities. A case in point is Dryden's expressing certain non-Virgilian tendencies of his own in his reference to 'Chargers, Bowls, and all the Priestly Trade' (12.430). That final word not only recalls 'priestcraft' from the beginning of his *Absalom and Achitophel* but also, craftily, and with an effect like that of poetical syntax, retrospectively revises the sense of words earlier in the line. This is to defy gravity with levity. What Dryden's eyes required was from time to time less plain, single-minded, and sober, more elaborate, playful, satirical, and even sometimes reckless, than what Wordsworth's eyes sought, or Johnson's, or even Pope's to some extent, for substantially explainable reasons in all these cases.

Such considerations could lead to the topic of how the translation differs, in the sense it makes, from Virgil's original, another topic too large except for a glance here; that topic would introduce cases including those wherein Dryden is judgmentally grave, more emphatically moralizing and even solemn than Virgil, as in their treatments of the death of Mezentius at the end of Book 10: particularly the way in which Dryden's Mezentius, who 'to the Sword his Throat apply'd', is still more suicidal than Virgil's.

The Text

The text is almost entirely the one presented by the second edition, that is, the version in *The Works of Virgil: Containing His Pastorals Georgics, and Æneis. Translated into English Verse; By Mr Dryden. . . . The Second Edition* (London: 1698). (I gratefully acknowledge permission to use as copy-text a microfilmed copy of this edition belonging to the Folger Shakespeare Library, shelf mark 'V617'.) Without going into the complexities of the relevant printing and publishing history, matters set forth extensively in the California Edition, I may provide the four main pertinent facts: (1) only the first and second editions appeared before Dryden's death; (2) they include corrections made by him; (3) the first edition exists in two main states, the second of these correcting the first to some extent; and (4) the second edition in its differing states includes new corrections but does not include some corrections that had appeared in the corrected state of the first edition. It is because the second edition in its most corrected state is evidently the most correct edition, and therefore requires the least editorial modification, that I have employed an example of it as my copy-text.

But though retaining many features of the copy-text, the present edition is not a facsimile. It does not seek to reproduce fonts and other simply physical characteristics. The design and letters are modern. For example, though the original text often has a space between a word and a punctuation mark following it, no such spaces appear here, and the *f*-like long *s* (ſ) has been replaced with our standard short *s*.

The main purpose of this edition, as this preface has now fully indicated, is generally to remove useless obstacles to comprehension and enjoyment of especially the narrative sense made by a vigorous poem – while preserving, as much as is reasonable, the authenticity of the text as it was presented in its best form with authorial sanction to its original public. Some obstacles remain, but would do so in any responsibly edited version even if it were fully modernized. For example, some of Dryden's rhymes no longer rhyme and will therefore occasionally give pause to the reader, probably not usefully with regard to following the narrative.

Editorial licence, though, does not extend to the updating of rhymes.

This topic of rhyming is so uncomplicated in certain respects that it offers a good opportunity to acknowledge the difficulty of coming to definitive conclusions about many of the subjects touched on in this preface. The sentence just above, about some of Dryden's rhymes no longer rhyming, squints, especially skirting candour about the fact already suggested here that the question of exactly what words did rhyme in Dryden's time and for Dryden is a large one – not that good answers are unavailable, or that some are not self-evident.

The project of emendation is delicate, since the object is not to shave and level the text, and especially not to deprive it of any of Dryden's distinctive vigour, even where wild. My odd phrase about useless obstacles implies that some obstacles are useful, as some are, such as barriers to walking over a cliff. But it may be generally preferable to preserve Johnson's lawn–field metaphor and specifically to preserve Pope's about weeds and flowers, and to concentrate on weeds, since the topic now is emendation, which begins with something like weeding. That is, emendation has two aspects – removing something unwanted and often replacing it with something else: weeding and then planting.

Weeds are typically worthless where they are found, yet in certain cases telling the weeds from the flowers or other not-worthless plants is a relative matter, relative to considerations which may not be obvious. Two major considerations affecting Dryden's text as originally published concern its language and art, both related to the poem's vigour.

The original text in its first two editions gives ample opportunity for editorial regularization, subtle as well as unsubtle. It is not a very subtle fact that the text typically italicizes names. That the text has its own peculiar system in this and other respects – and also that in such respects it is sometimes irregular – are subtler matters. Yet such regularity or irregularity is not likely to prove an aid or obstacle to readers' comprehension and enjoyment. To continue the example, names in the original text are sufficiently identifiable as such on other grounds, and the reader would have had to become familiar with a now-outmoded use of italics in order to be stopped by any lapses in this respect. The present edition does not regularize italicization and some other things yet to be addressed here.

Less subtle are the instances of spellings different from those which have become standard. The reader will immediately notice many instances of this peculiarity and would have encountered still more of them had the text not undergone some modest, strictly systematic editorial intervention. In view of this edition's purpose, some of the received text's spelling peculiarities are worthless. Into this category falls everything which is certainly a typographical error, or all but certainly so. The certain errors are: inverted letters and punctuation marks; doubling of words ('the the') or tripling of a letter which needed only doubling ('eee'); incorrect line-numbering; and failure to capitalize the first word of a line. All such certain errors are silently corrected in the text.

The all-but-certain typographical errors are: lack of a space between what in context can only be two words; inclusion of a space within what in context can only be a single word, and in that case any definitely and unequivocally certain missing letter; some such letters printed unclearly; and unaccountable transposition of letters within a word. It will be clear that identification of such errors generally involves editorial judgment and depends especially on historical, linguistic decisions, though in the vast majority of instances such decisions are not difficult or contestable. In the present text all such errors have been corrected, most of them silently.

The exceptions raise historical questions about spelling. In Dryden's time the standard spelling of a word was within a generous range of acceptable alternatives. Retention of words in now non-standard forms at least keeps readers aware that this is an old poem in a developing language with promiscuous shoots, its own and Dryden's, but such editorial fidelity is more useful than that. The fact that some forms of words fall either inside or outside historically permissible ranges is something for which the reader of literature may well wish to cultivate at least a sensitivity. And in the text at hand such historical ranges pertain not only to Dryden's English but also to his Latin as it enters the text, mainly in names, some of them neither in standard Latin form nor in a form familiar in English, often because the person named is not very famous. Hence forms of a word distinctly, egregiously outside the ranges in question quite probably involve identifiable typographical errors and have therefore been corrected, silently; thus 'Rhadamanthus' replaces 'Shadamanthus' (6.764). Other, less obvious corrections having to do with spelling as well as other features of the text are identified in the part of the present edition entitled 'Emendations'. Most of these – and corrections such as that of 'Shadamanthus' might have been included in that list had they been less clearly warranted – are based on alternatives provided by an example of the corrected state of the first edition. (I gratefully acknowledge use of such a copy in the Adelphi University Library, shelf mark 'Folio. PA6807. A1. D7. 1697'.) And if, as is rarely the case, peculiar spelling of a word, when it is considered in its context, permits confusingly multiple possibilities of identification, that word has an entry in the Glossary.

Considerations of art as well as those of language affect such judgments about spelling. In his Dedication, anticipating the categories in which Johnson was to praise him, Dryden says that Virgil sought 'to excel' especially in 'Propriety of Thought, Elegance of Words, and Harmony of Numbers' (235, *318*). Dryden also speaks tantalizingly in the Dedication about having 'long had by me the Materials of an English *Prosodia*, containing all the Mechanical Rules of Versification, wherein I have treated with some exactness of the Feet ... and the Pauses' (236–7, *321*). No such *prosodia* by Dryden (a treatise on prosody or a particular system of verse-writing) was ever published or is known to have otherwise survived.

Regarding the less obvious category 'Harmony of Numbers' (recall Johnson's comparably musical 'tuned the numbers'), Dryden mentions a pair of principles directly helpful here. First, he says he has been careful not to leave 'one Vowel gaping on another'. Thus 'where a Vowel ends a word, the next begins either with a Consonant, or what is its equivalent; for our W and H aspirate. . . .' Behind Dryden's comment are two conventions of Virgilian, Latin versification: that of elision, whereby a vowel ending a word goes unpronounced and metrically uncounted if the next word begins with a vowel or h; and that of hiatus, whereby in certain circumstances the principles of elision may be ignored. Dryden took these considerations very seriously, here going into further detail: 'The greatest latitude I take is in the letter Y, when it concludes a word, and the first Syllable of the next begins with a Vowel. Neither need I have call'd this a latitude, which is only an explanation of this general Rule: That no Vowel can be cut off before another, when we cannot sink the Pronunciation of it; as *He, She, Me, I*, &c.' (236, *320*). The sinking would be by way of elision, as in 'th'' for 'the'. Elision of that *e* is permissible but elision affecting the pronouns which Dryden cites is not.

The point relates to the text of the *Æneis*, for example to its variant forms of the name of Dido's would-be suitor, 'Hyarba' or 'Hyarbas'. Dryden's text usually employs the former spelling (4.283, 471, 775), but includes the terminal *s* on the one occasion when the following word begins with a vowel (4.51). The text apparently does so to avoid hiatus. It happens that those different forms of this name have Latin precedents. Yet the idea that Latin names in Dryden's text ought to be corrected simply according to standard Latin or particularly Virgilian usage, when possible, is open to question, because of this and other considerations. Some Latin names in Dryden's text are both definitely anglicized and made so in such a way that their Latin spelling would conflict with the metre (for example, 'Tyburs' in 7.931 for Virgil's 'Tiburtus'), not that the preservation of invariable metre is everything. And when Dryden calls Virgil's Doto 'Dotis' (9.119) the reason may be that Dryden's next word is 'and'; and her mother is Doris.

The way both English and Latin permit ranges of spelling is patent regarding the letter *i*. Generally in both languages, when it is not the first or last letter of a word, *i* is often interchangeable with *y*. In Latin spelling, *i* may also be replaced by *j*, as is the case here in some names. Thus the plural 'Fabij' is pronounced 'Fabii', and another name, 'Iulus', is spelled 'Julus' the first two times it appears but nevertheless has three syllables, as does 'Jasius', where the *i* functions as almost a *y* commencing the final syllable, or just about entirely so as it does in the name 'Maja'. Also, broadly speaking, the ligatures *æ* and *œ* may be replaced by *e*. Without going into the historical details, 'Chimaera' and 'Phoenician' have also become 'Chimera' and 'Phenician' in English; Dryden on occasion spells 'Aeneas' 'Eneas'. And strictly, it is often not self-evident whether a Latin word given in the poem ought to be considered as Latin or English, with regard to spelling and especially pronunciation. The ligatures *æ* and *œ*, for example, as each occupies any given syllable in the text, should probably be pronounced in the classical Latin manner. Such pronunciation of *æ* is like present-day pronunciation of the English word 'high', without the initial *h*. Classical Latin *œ* is comparable with our 'joy', ignoring the *j*. But the classical Latin pronunciation of *e* may include that of the vowel in the English word 'say'.

Here enters the second of the artistic considerations I have specified, one which Dryden describes rather generally, declaring that he has emulated both Virgil's 'placing [his words] for the sweetness of the sound' and his doing so with such success that 'he who removes them from the Station wherein their Master sets them, spoils the Harmony'. Here too Dryden elaborates, contrasting English with Latin. Latin poets are 'forced upon' frequent elision

because they have a redundancy of Vowels in their Language. Their Metal is so soft, that it will not Coyn without Alloy [i.e. consonants] to harden it. On the other side, . . .'tis all we can do to give sufficient sweetness to our Language: We must not only chuse our Words for Elegance, but for Sound. To perform which, a Mastery in the Language is requir'd; the Poet must have a Magazin[e] of Words, and have the Art to manage his few Vowels to the best advantage, that they may go the farther. He must also know the nature of the Vowels, which are more sonorous, and which more soft and sweet; and so dispose them as his present Occasions require: All which, and a thousand Secrets of Versification beside, he may learn from *Virgil*, if he will take him for his Guide. (235–6, *319–20*)

(The last comment may incidentally remind us of Virgil's part in Dante's *Divine Comedy*, besides suggesting the extent of Virgil's enormous influence on poetry.) Dryden subsequently laments that emulation of Virgil's copious diction has strained his own lexical resources, especially towards the end of the poem (244–5, *333–4*), and the reader may notice that when a word unusual in the text crops up, it tends to do so more than once, in proximity.

Whatever else the topic of poetic musicality involves, it must include some attention to the repetition of sounds in a given line and those near it. It certainly involves much else, however, enough to make the topic both difficult and historically speculative. Nevertheless, to give some attention to one example of the worth of the point: the text at 6.639 mentions Dido's deceased husband for the fifth and last time (the other instances are at 1.472, 4.26, 4.726, 4.907). As twice before, his name is spelled 'Sicheus' here, instead of 'Sichæus'. In the Underworld, rebuffing Aeneas, Dido

> whirl'd away, to shun his hateful sight,
> Hid in the Forest, and the Shades of Night.
> Then sought *Sicheus*, thro' the shady Grove,
> Who answer'd all her Cares, and equal'd all her Love.

A Latin *æ* would rhyme with 'sight' and 'Night', these made emphatic by rhyme. A Latin *e*, stressed as it is in this word, would rhyme with 'hateful', 'Shades', 'shady' (the second of these two made emphatic by repetition), and 'cares'. The case is less clear-cut than it is in other instances, but there is no reason why such cases have to be perfect, and here there is a definite preponderance of the Latin *e*-sound, justifying the spelling. Much more could be said about this particular example. The broad conclusion I draw for the purposes of this edition is simply that, where the text's given, original spelling is not distinctly egregious – egregious enough to make the reader pause over it in some definitely unuseful way – it ought to be preserved for the benefit of the reader as well as the poem, because a major aspect of the art of the poem is very likely to be somehow expressed in it.

To cite a few other examples: when the text has Virgil's Velini as 'Velinum' in a phrase with 'from' (7.982) there is good reason not to correct Dryden's Latin. Comparably the text's 'Janicula' where Virgil has 'Janiculum' makes harmonic sense with the 'Saturnia' accompanying it (8.469), and so does the text's 'Semethis', in place of Virgil's Sebethis, in a reference to the 'Nymph *Semethis*' (7.1015). The names of especially the many warriors who figure only ephemerally in the poem are often not in Virgil's or other standard Latin spelling; for example, Virgil's warrior Idas is 'Ida' in his instant of fame at 9.781. Most such variations, which have little bearing on comprehension of the narrative sense of the poem (no reader is likely to confuse this Ida with the others in Dryden's text), are not emended here or accorded comment in any way. If the words involved require explanation, as some particularly geographical names do, there are entries in the Glossary with mention of the change in spelling.

Dryden more or less drastically changes some of the names in Virgil. As Kinsley notes (IV, 2056), at Dryden's 12.790 Virgil's Cretheus has become Cisseus, though Cisseus was killed in Dryden's 10.442 and at the corresponding place in Virgil. Even so, that Cisseus should be emended to Cretheus in Dryden's Book

12 is not self-evident – and not only because Dryden, like Virgil, might be given some benefit of doubt: if someone appears to have been slain twice, the name may apply to more than one person. The Cisseus slain in Dryden's earlier passage, it should be added, is an enemy of Aeneas, and the one slain afterwards is an ally.

In a note to *Georgics* 4.477, Dryden expresses both impatience with Virgil's multiplication of names and some additional, related dismay: 'The Poet here records the Names of Fifty River Nymphs. And for once I have Translated them all. But in the *Æneis* I thought not my self oblig'd to be so exact; for in naming many Men who were kill'd by Heroes, I have omitted some, which would not sound in *English* Verse.' Did 'Cretheus' not 'sound', to Dryden's ear? The additional death of Dryden's Cisseus, or charitably the death of Dryden's additional Cisseus, occurs in the line 'Nor *Cisseus* cou'dst thou scape from *Turnus* hand', and the least that may be said about the line as it stands is that 'Cisseus' contributes to the swarm of sibilants more than 'Cretheus' would have done, and that Dryden's repetition of the name Cisseus is unlikely to confuse readers.

Particularly prominent in Dryden's text are names exhibiting anomalous use of the ligatures *æ* and *œ*. When considerations including those of sound are taken into account, some such instances become more problematical than they initially seem; others, less so. The problems may entail the possibility that Dryden in some instances was misled by the spelling of another translator (California Edition, page 1018, note to 5.213); and also the difficulty for authors, compositors, and proofreaders of distinguishing an *a* from an *o* in some instances of ligatures, especially if in italic type or in script; and even the odd historical fact that either ligature may be replaced by *e*, though the two ligatures themselves are not interchangeable. On the positive side, considerations of sound may provide circumstantial evidence for identification of a typographical error. For example, when 'Phœnix' of 2.38 recurs as 'Phænix' in 2.1036, that the immediate context of the latter lacks the 'high' sound of Latin *æ* but includes the words 'Troy' and 'Spoils' is evidence, beyond considerations of etymology, standard practice, and Virgilian precedent, that *æ* here requires correction. But when the name of the town Cære, in the second of its two appearances (8.627, 10.264), is spelled 'Cœre', directly after a line containing 'noisom[e]' and with no 'high'-sounding word nearby, it may well be wondered whether Dryden is here exercising poetic licence; in other cases too, including the text's spelling of 'Alœan' in the clause 'Here lye the Alæan twins' (6.784).

In such cases, which concern names more important than some others in the poem – Dryden's poem as well as Virgil's – more important at least in part because these names have a certain definite standing outside the poem, the text's spelling has on occasion been silently corrected. (In standard spelling, the other such words are 'Barcæan', 'Celæno', 'Chimæra', 'Chorœbus' [2.519, 549, 575], 'Eubœan', 'Rhœtean', and 'Rhœtus' [9.463].) But in most cases of historically anomalous substitution exchanging the ligatures in question, cases in which the names affected are not important apart from the poem and the reader is not likely to be confused by the peculiarity, the spelling remains as in the copy-text. The text retains not only the additional Cisseus but also some other minor characters, such as Dryden's Menætes, whose names Virgil evidently spelled differently.

Questions of what may be called weeds and worth go further. In this respect the punctuation appears to be the most critical matter. Unsubtly, for example, apostrophes are abundant. The main function of the apostrophe in the poem is to elide a verb ending so as to make it fit the metre. Sometimes an apostrophe indicates a possessive or a plural – but, contrary to our usage, never both. Hence the reader has to get used to 'Cyclop's' or 'Syren's' or the like as a plural possessive, but can certainly do so, especially because, unless apostrophes had been added in abundance, the reader will have quickly become used to singular possessives with no apostrophe. Sometimes as such the apostrophe goes against its main metrical function here, but not often enough to interfere with that any more than other departures from iambic pentameter couplets do, for example the occasional line exceeding pentameter. The question is basically whether the reader is hampered, and, for one reason or another, it is unlikely that the reader will be.

More important: the very system of punctuation is not ours in some major ways. Ordinarily in Dryden's text, the relative force of the main punctuation marks, in ascending order, is , ; : . But as with other features, the text in all original versions employs these marks inconsistently, and it is clear that regularization of the text in this and other respects is not necessarily the best scholarly response, though modern editions with some reason have adopted it more or less fully. The plainest sign of the problems involved is the fact that in every original edition and state the text frequently employs the strongest marks of punctuation – the period as well as the question mark and the exclamation point which is often, excitedly, interchangeable with it – as if they are not final. There is persistent fluidity in the text facilitated by the extreme permeability of the original punctuation. Frequently, that is, in a manner familiar to composition-teachers, and in a manner supporting poetical syntax, what is punctuated as if it were a stopped sentence nevertheless persists syntactically into what is punctuated as the next sentence. Yet does so intelligibly. (The same often holds for the text's colons, which, if they held a clause more securely, would correspond roughly to our semicolons.) The most fundamental and urgent question concerning regularization of this poem's punctuation is therefore not whether it is prudent but whether with this text such emendation is even possible, according to either past or present systems, in any manner that substantially expresses and clarifies this text's distinctly more fundamental, crucial and vigorously overriding relations of syntax, suspended and resolved.

Almost no emendations in the present edition have to do with errors of syntax. Of those the copy-text has almost none apart from instances of dramatic error, readily identifiable as deliberately and expressively poetical, in which normal syntactic relations are disrupted in order to represent emotional distress (for example, at 10.865, this device called anacoluthon). What few kinds of actual syntactic errors by our standards there are in the text will nearly all be intelligible and familiar to us – for instance, determining the number of a verb by the plural object of a prepositional phrase modifying that verb's singular subject ('A Choir of *Nereids* meet him', 10.312) – suggesting a certain naturalness about them after all, by some system not reconcilable with the language as ordinarily used by instructors of English. Whether or not historically an error, a certain looseness in the reference of pronouns is the difficulty – syntactic, logical, or both – which the text most frequently presents, a difficulty sometimes compounded by ellipsis, as in the way Pyrgo begins her speech at 5.843: 'No Beroe this', where 'this' resolves itself clearly as a reference to the person representing herself as Beroe – or so resolves itself when the reader has inferred that the construction implies an elliptical *is*, and that there is a metaphor here, supposing a class of people named Beroe to which this person does not belong, and also that the construction is anastrophic for 'This is not a Beroe'.

Addison's argument to Book 1 opens a momentary gap when the second sentence says 'the Tempest sinks one'. The word 'sinks' must describe a relation, at least between the thing that sinks and the thing it sinks in, and 'one' has to be related semantically as well as syntactically to its context, yet Addison has not said or directly implied what is sunk. The problem of comprehension his expression poses, however, is small: what may literally and typically be said to sink is a ship, and the context of the expression proves helpful enough. The little gap here might be said to furnish an introduction to the text's poetical syntax, evident promptly in the text's first line as we have seen and actually still more evident there because only logic determines that 'who' refers to the 'Man' rather than to the 'I' doing the singing.

The consequence of the various claims adjudicated in this preface is that, but for a minimum number of corrections, including some very un-useful punctuation (identified within the Emendations), this generally unidealized edition preserves the peculiarities of the 1698 copy on which it is based, in the belief that readers not only ought to, but will, quickly find nearly all these peculiarities as negotiable as editors do, not insuperable, and that the effect of dealing with the poem's useful, typically temporary obstacles largely suits its vigour. On the whole, this edition remains authentically representative of the second, corrected edition in a copy which Dryden's contemporaries read.

The Glossary

The Glossary is introduced by some practical guidelines, chiefly concerning the way in which it is organized. An account of its purpose and scope may well be given here as following from matters in this preface and completing the reader's sense of what this edition offers.

The purpose of the Glossary is to supply intermediate information apparently assumed by the text and necessary for comprehension of the story it tells. Mainly, the Glossary explains the

reference or literal sense of expressions, including names and epi-
thets, when the text itself does not sufficiently provide such infor-
mation in the vicinity of the expressions, or has not already done
so earlier, or has already done so but not very emphatically; and
when sufficient information is not directly available from the maps;
and when such information is neither common knowledge nor a
matter of speculation. There is an entry for Pallas chiefly because
Dryden's text initially assumes some now relatively uncommon
knowledge about why the goddess dealt as she did on a particular
occasion with exactly whom. But because the Glossary is not an
index, this entry does not mention that Pallas is also the name of
other characters in the *Æneis*, most conspicuously Evander's son.
The text is promptly clear enough in that respect. Nor is there an
entry regarding Evander's murder of his guest Argus. Beyond what
is in the text there is evidently nothing very significant to be
discovered about this event and this Argus.

The Glossary attends particularly to archaic, obsolete, or
historically technical expressions including those related to ancient
customs (military, political, religious, and so forth), and any now-
unusual sense of an expression, especially if, as the poem employs
any familiar word, its standard range of senses is somehow notice-
ably at odds with the sense of its immediate context. Dryden's
'grateful', for example, usually carries the now-uncommon sense
of 'pleasing'. The Glossary gives this sense but assumes the reader
will notice those instances in which the reference is to gratitude
instead. More than one sense may apply in a given instance, and,
though the sense of a negative form of a word (for example,
'ungrateful', or 'unhappy') may also depend on the uncommon
sense of the positive form, the Glossary relies on readers to recog-
nize the possibility of such extensions. Samuel Johnson's *Dictionary
of the English Language*, already employed here to explain his
understanding of certain words including 'vigour' and cited biblio-
graphically in the introduction to the Glossary, provides definitions
for some examples of poetical and other diction.

In keeping with the remarks about spelling earlier here, the
Glossary identifies any word spelled so strangely by modern stan-
dards that a standard pronunciation may not make clear which
word it is. The obstacle typically involves more than an apostrophe,
a letter or two, or both. Hence the Glossary omits 'Quire' (for
choir) as well as 'Meen' (for mien) – and 'Appollo' for Apollo,

'Troys' (for Troy's), 'Crow'd' (for crowd), and 'crudled' (for curdled) – but includes 'Yough' (for yew) as well as the possibly confusing 'humane' (for human).

The Glossary also seeks to clarify expressions which are obdurately obscure in syntax as Dryden peculiarly constructs them. (To his credit, as I have indicated, such expressions are rare.) Though this edition is meant to be *not* particularly interpretative, so as to encourage as well as help readers to be thoughtfully so themselves, the Glossary in this way approaches the brink of positive interpretation. The Glossary also approaches that brink when cross-references analytically combine into a single entry some material dispersed in the text but related to one particular topic, such as the text's direct and indirect references to its most prototypical hero, Hercules.

The Glossary makes some use of Dryden's apparatus, and of some sources of the *Aeneid* which Dryden calls attention to there: Homer's epics and Apollonius Rhodius' *Argonautica*, a four-book Greek epic of the third century B.C. about the expedition of the Argonauts, the crew of the ship *Argo*, led by Jason. In a general note within the 'Notes and Observations', to Virgil's Book 5, Dryden remarks: 'A great part of this Book is borrow'd from *Apollonius Rhodius*. And the Reader may observe the great Judgment and distinction of our Author in what he borrows from the Ancients, by comparing them.' In another such note, to Book 2, Dryden comments, with reference to the early Roman victory over a nearby town: 'The Destruction of *Veii* is here shadow'd under that of *Troy*: *Livy* in his Description of it, seems to have emulated in his Prose, and almost equal'd the Beauty of *Virgil*'s Verse.' The Roman historians, particularly Livy, with his lively stories in *Ab Urbe Condita* – the history of the city of Rome from its origin – are rich supplements to Virgil. The Glossary occasionally cites Livy for particular points and might have done so more expansively.

Like Livy's history and as explained earlier here, the poem combines various historical viewpoints, most conspicuously when it includes prophecies to Aeneas about events which were history to Virgil. Many things which the poem represents as ancient are also, in some manner, tacit prefigurations of later and even topical matters: events, people, issues, perspectives, and so forth – even to Dryden's time and beyond. There are certainly, for example, overtones of post-ancient chivalry and romance. Though the scope for contemplation opened by such considerations is far too vast to be practicable in the Glossary, several entries suggest recognition of those and other dimensions contributing to this English poem's fundamental, enduring worth. If this edition succeeds in making some of that more apparent to readers than it might have been otherwise, credit is particularly due to the substantial assistance and encouragement of Paul Keegan and Christopher Ricks, and, nearer by, of my wife, children, other family members, and friends, including my colleagues at Hofstra University and its Axinn Library, and Steven Brock.

FURTHER READING

Editions

Frost, William, *The Works of Virgil in English*, in Alan Roper, *The Works of John Dryden*, Vols. V–VI (Berkeley, Los Angeles; London: University of California Press, 1987).

Kinsley, James, *The Poems of John Dryden*, 4 vols. (Oxford: Clarendon Press, 1958).

Noyes, George R., *The Poetical Works of Dryden* (*The Cambridge Edition of the Poets*), rev. ed. (Boston: Houghton Mifflin, 1950).

Watson, George, *John Dryden: Of Dramatic Poesy and Other Critical Essays* (*Everyman's Library*), 2 vols. (London: Dent; New York: Dutton, 1962).

Criticism and Biography

Corse, Taylor, *Dryden's Aeneid: The English Virgil* (Newark: University of Delaware Press; London and Toronto: Associated University Presses, 1991).

Frost, William, *Dryden and the Art of Translation* (*Yale Studies in English*, Vol. CXXVIII) (New Haven: Yale University Press; London: Geoffrey Cumberland, Oxford University Press, 1955).

——, *John Dryden: Dramatist, Satirist, Translator* (New York: AMS, 1988).

Winn, James Anderson, *John Dryden and His World* (New Haven: Yale University Press, 1987).

Zwicker, Steven N., *Politics and Language in Dryden's Poetry: The Arts of Disguise* (Princeton: Princeton University Press, 1984).

THE FIRST BOOK OF THE ÆNEIS

The Argument

The Trojans, *after a Seven Years Voyage, set sail for* Italy, *but are overtaken by a dreadful Storm, which* Æolus *raises at* Juno's *Request. The Tempest sinks one, and scatters the rest:* Neptune *drives off the Winds and calms the Sea.* Æneas *with his own Ship, and six more, arrives safe at an* Affrican *Port.* Venus *complains to* Jupiter *of her Son's Misfortunes.* Jupiter *comforts her, and sends* Mercury *to procure him a kind Reception among the* Carthaginians. Æneas *going out to discover the Country, meets his Mother in the Shape of an Huntress, who conveys him in a Cloud to* Carthage; *where he sees his Friends whom he thought lost, and receives a kind Entertainment from the Queen.* Dido *by a Device of* Venus *begins to have a Passion for him, and after some Discourse with him, desires the History of his Adventures since the Siege of* Troy, *which is the Subject of the Two following Books.*

Arms, and the Man I sing, who forc'd by Fate,
And haughty *Juno*'s unrelenting Hate;
Expell'd and exil'd, left the *Trojan* Shoar:
Long Labours, both by Sea and Land he bore;
5 And in the doubtful War, before he won
The *Latian* Realm, and built the destin'd Town:
His banish'd Gods restor'd to Rites Divine,
And setl'd sure Succession in his Line:
From whence the Race of *Alban* Fathers come,
10 And the long Glories of Majestick *Rome*.

O Muse! the Causes and the Crimes relate,
What Goddess was provok'd, and whence her hate:
For what Offence the Queen of Heav'n began
To persecute so brave, so just a Man!
15 Involv'd his anxious Life in endless Cares,
Expos'd to Wants, and hurry'd into Wars!
Can Heav'nly Minds such high resentment show;
Or exercise their Spight in Human Woe?

Against the *Tiber*'s Mouth, but far away,
20 An ancient Town was seated on the Sea:
A *Tyrian* Colony; the People made
Stout for the War, and studious of their Trade.
Carthage the Name, belov'd by *Juno* more
Than her own *Argos*, or the *Samian* Shoar.
25 Here stood her Chariot, here, if Heav'n were kind,
The Seat of awful Empire she design'd.
Yet she had heard an ancient Rumour fly,
(Long cited by the People of the Sky;)
That times to come shou'd see the *Trojan* Race
30 Her *Carthage* ruin, and her Tow'rs deface:
Nor thus confin'd, the Yoke of Sov'raign Sway,
Should on the Necks of all the Nations lay.

She ponder'd this, and fear'd it was in Fate;
Nor cou'd forget the War she wag'd of late,
35 For conq'ring *Greece* against the *Trojan* State.
Besides long Causes working in her Mind,
And secret Seeds of Envy lay behind.
Deep graven in her Heart, the Doom remain'd
Of partial *Paris*, and her Form disdain'd:
40 The Grace bestow'd on ravish'd *Ganimed*,
Electra's Glories, and her injur'd Bed.
Each was a Cause alone, and all combin'd
To kindle Vengeance in her haughty Mind.
For this, far distant from the *Latian* Coast,
45 She drove the Remnants of the *Trojan* Hoast:
And sev'n long Years th' unhappy wand'ring Train,
Were toss'd by Storms, and scatter'd through the Main.
Such Time, such Toil requir'd the *Roman* Name,
Such length of Labour for so vast a Frame.
50   Now scarce the *Trojan* Fleet with Sails and Oars,
Had left behind the fair *Sicilian* Shoars:
Ent'ring with chearful Shouts the wat'ry Reign,
And ploughing frothy Furrows in the Main:
When lab'ring still, with endless discontent,
55 The Queen of Heav'n did thus her Fury vent.
      Then am I vanquish'd, must I yield, said she,
And must the *Trojans* reign in *Italy*?
So Fate will have it, and *Jove* adds his Force;
Nor can my Pow'r divert their happy Course.
60 Cou'd angry *Pallas*, with revengeful Spleen,
The *Grecian* Navy burn, and drown the Men?
She for the Fault of one offending Foe,
The Bolts of *Jove* himself presum'd to throw:
With Whirlwinds from beneath she toss'd the Ship,
65 And bare expos'd the Bosom of the deep:
Then, as an Eagle gripes the trembling Game,
The Wretch yet hissing with her Father's Flame,
She strongly seiz'd, and with a burning Wound,
Transfix'd and naked, on a Rock she bound.
70 But I, who walk in awful State above,
The Majesty of Heav'n, the Sister-wife of *Jove*;
For length of Years, my fruitless Force employ

Against the thin remains of ruin'd *Troy*.
What Nations now to *Juno*'s Pow'r will pray,
75   Or Off'rings on my slighted Altars lay?
    Thus rag'd the Goddess, and with Fury fraught,
The restless Regions of the Storms she sought.
Where in a spacious Cave of living Stone,
The Tyrant *Eolus* from his Airy Throne,
80   With Pow'r Imperial curbs the strugling Winds,
And sounding Tempests in dark Prisons binds.
This Way, and that, th' impatient Captives tend,
And pressing for Release, the Mountains rend;
High in his Hall, th' undaunted Monarch stands,
85   And shakes his Scepter, and their Rage Commands:
Which did he not, their unresisted Sway
Wou'd sweep the World before them, in their Way:
Earth, Air, and Seas through empty Space wou'd rowl,
And Heav'n would fly before the driving Soul.
90   In fear of this, the Father of the Gods
Confin'd their Fury to those dark Abodes,
And lock'd 'em safe within, oppress'd with Mountain
        loads:
Impos'd a King, with arbitrary Sway,
To loose their Fetters, or their Force allay.
95   To whom the suppliant Queen her Pray'rs addrest,
And thus the tenour of her Suit express'd.
    O *Eolus!* for to thee the King of Heav'n
The Pow'r of Tempests, and of Winds has giv'n:
Thy Force alone their Fury can restrain,
100   And smooth the Waves, or swell the troubl'd Main.
A race of wand'ring Slaves, abhorr'd by me,
With prosp'rous Passage cut the *Thuscan* Sea:
To fruitful *Italy* their Course they steer,
And for their vanquish'd Gods design new Temples there.
105   Raise all thy Winds, with Night involve the Skies;
Sink, or disperse my fatal Enemies.
Twice sev'n, the charming Daughters of the Main,
Around my Person wait, and bear my Train:
Succeed my Wish, and second my Design,
110   The fairest, *Deiopeia*, shall be thine;
And make thee Father of a happy Line.

To this the God – 'Tis yours, O Queen! to will
The Work, which Duty binds me to fulfil.
These airy Kingdoms, and this wide Command,
115 Are all the Presents of your bounteous Hand:
Yours is my Sov'raigns Grace, and, as your Guest,
I sit with Gods at their Cœlestial Feast.
Raise Tempests at your Pleasure, or subdue;
Dispose of Empire, which I hold from you.
120 He said, and hurld against the Mountain side,
His quiv'ring Spear, and all, the God apply'd.
The raging Winds rush through the hollow Wound,
And dance aloft in Air, and skim along the Ground:
Then settling on the Sea, the Surges sweep;
125 Raise liquid Mountains, and disclose the deep.
South, East, and West, with mix'd Confusion roar,
And rowl the foaming Billows to the Shoar.
The Cables crack, the Sailors fearful Cries ⎫
Ascend; and sable Night involves the Skies;   ⎬
130 And Heav'n it self is ravish'd from their Eyes. ⎭
Loud Peals of Thunder from the Poles ensue,
Then flashing Fires the transient Light renew:
The Face of things a frightful Image bears,
And present Death in various Forms appears.
135 Struck with unusual Fright, the *Trojan* Chief,
With lifted Hands and Eyes, invokes Relief.
And thrice, and four times happy those, he cry'd,
That under *Ilian* Walls before their Parents dy'd.
Tydides, bravest of the *Grecian* Train,   ⎫
140 Why cou'd not I by that strong Arm be slain,   ⎬
And lie by noble *Hector* on the Plain,   ⎭
Or great *Sarpedon*, in those bloody Fields,
Where *Simois* rowls the Bodies, and the Shields
Of Heroes, whose dismember'd Hands yet bear
145 The Dart aloft, and clench the pointed Spear?
Thus while the Pious Prince his Fate bewails,
Fierce *Boreas* drove against his flying Sails,
And rent the Sheets: The raging Billows rise,
And mount the tossing Vessel to the Skies:
150 Nor can the shiv'ring Oars sustain the Blow;
The Galley gives her side, and turns her Prow:

While those astern descending down the Steep,
Thro' gaping Waves behold the boiling deep.
Three Ships were hurry'd by the Southern Blast,
155 And on the secret Shelves with Fury cast.
Those hidden Rocks, th' *Ausonian* Sailors knew,
They call'd them Altars, when they rose in view,
And show'd their spacious Backs above the Flood.
Three more, fierce *Eurus* in his angry Mood,
160 Dash'd on the Shallows of the moving Sand,
And in mid Ocean left them moor'd a-land.
Orontes Barque that bore the *Lycian* Crew,
(A horrid Sight) ev'n in the Hero's view,
From Stem to Stern, by Waves was overborn:
165 The trembling Pilot, from his Rudder torn,
Was headlong hurl'd; thrice round, the Ship was tost,
Then bulg'd at once, and in the deep was lost.
And here and there above the Waves were seen
Arms, Pictures, precious Goods, and floating Men.
170 The stoutest Vessel to the Storm gave way,
And suck'd through loosen'd Planks the rushing Sea.
Ilioneus was her Chief: *Alethes* old,
Achates faithful, *Abas* young and bold
Endur'd not less: their Ships, with gaping Seams,
175 Admit the Deluge of the briny Streams.
      Mean time Imperial *Neptune* heard the Sound
Of raging Billows breaking on the Ground:
Displeas'd, and fearing for his Wat'ry Reign,
He reard his awful Head above the Main:
180 Serene in Majesty, then rowl'd his Eyes
Around the Space of Earth, and Seas, and Skies.
He saw the *Trojan* Fleet dispers'd, distress'd
By stormy Winds and wintry Heav'n oppress'd.
Full well the God his Sister's envy knew,
185 And what her Aims, and what her Arts pursue:
He summon'd *Eurus* and the Western blast,
And first an angry glance on both he cast:
Then thus rebuk'd; Audacious Winds! from whence
This bold Attempt, this Rebel Insolence?
190 Is it for you to ravage Seas and Land,
Unauthoriz'd by my supream Command?

To raise such Mountains on the troubl'd Main?
Whom I – But first 'tis fit, the Billows to restrain,
And then you shall be taught obedience to my Reign.

195   Hence, to your Lord my Royal Mandate bear,
The Realms of Ocean and the Fields of Air
Are mine, not his; by fatal Lot to me
The liquid Empire fell, and Trident of the Sea.
His Pow'r to hollow Caverns is confin'd,
200   There let him reign, the Jailor of the Wind:
With hoarse Commands his breathing Subjects call,
And boast and bluster in his empty Hall.
He spoke: And while he spoke, he smooth'd the Sea,
Dispell'd the Darkness, and restor'd the Day:
205   *Cymothoe*, *Triton*, and the Sea-green Train
Of beauteous Nymphs, the Daughters of the Main,
Clear from the Rocks the Vessels with their hands;
The God himself with ready Trident stands,
And opes the Deep, and spreads the moving Sands;
210   Then heaves them off the sholes: where e're he guides
His finny Coursers, and in Triumph rides,
The Waves unruffle and the Sea Subsides.
As when in Tumults rise th' ignoble Crow'd,
Mad are their Motions, and their Tongues are loud;
215   And Stones and Brands in ratling Vollies fly,
And all the Rustick Arms that Fury can supply:
If then some Grave and Pious Man appear,
They hush their Noise, and lend a list'ning Ear;
He sooths with sober Words their angry Mood,
220   And quenches their innate Desire of Blood:
So when the Father of the Flood appears,
And o're the Seas his Sov'raign Trident rears,
Their Fury falls: He skims the liquid Plains,
High on his Chariot, and with loosen'd Reins,
225   Majestick moves along, and awful Peace maintains.
The weary *Trojans* ply their shatter'd Oars,
To nearest Land, and make the *Lybian* Shoars.
     Within a long Recess there lies a Bay,
An Island shades it from the rowling Sea,
230   And forms a Port secure for Ships to ride,
Broke by the jutting Land on either side:
In double Streams the briny Waters glide.

Betwixt two rows of Rocks, a Sylvan Scene
Appears above, and Groves for ever green:
235   A Grott is form'd beneath, with Mossy Seats,
To rest the *Nereids*, and exclude the Heats.
Down thro' the Cranies of the living Walls
The Crystal Streams descend in murm'ring Falls.
No Haulsers need to bind the Vessels here,
240   Nor bearded Anchors, for no Storms they fear.
Sev'n Ships within this happy Harbour meet,
The thin Remainders of the scatter'd Fleet.
The *Trojans*, worn with Toils, and spent with Woes,
Leap on the welcome Land, and seek their wish'd Repose.
245   First, good *Achates*, with repeated Stroaks
Of clashing Flints, their hidden Fire provokes;
Short Flame succeeds, a Bed of wither'd Leaves
The dying Sparkles in their Fall receives:
Caught into Life, in fiery Fumes they rise,
250   And, fed with stronger Food, invade the Skies.
The *Trojans*, dropping wet, or stand around
The chearful blaze, or lye along the Ground:
Some dry their Corn infected with the Brine,
Then grind with Marbles, and prepare to dine.
255   *Æneas* climbs the Mountain's airy Brow,
And takes a Prospect of the Seas below:
If *Capys* thence, or *Antheus* he cou'd spy;
Or see the Streamers of *Caicus* fly.
No Vessels were in view: But, on the Plain,
260   Three beamy Stags command a Lordly Train
Of branching Heads; the more ignoble Throng
Attend their stately Steps, and slowly graze along.
He stood; and while secure they fed below,
He took the Quiver, and the trusty Bow
265   *Achates* us'd to bear; the Leaders first
He laid along, and then the Vulgar pierc'd:
Nor ceas'd his Arrows, 'till the shady Plain
Sev'n mighty Bodies, with their Blood distain.
For the sev'n Ships he made an equal Share,
270   And to the Port return'd, Triumphant from the War.
The Jarrs of gen'rous Wine, (*Acestes* Gift,
When his *Trinacrian* Shoars the Navy left)

He set abroach, and for the Feast prepar'd;
In equal Portions, with the Ven'son shar'd.
275 Thus while he dealt it round, the pious Chief,
With chearful Words, allay'd the common Grief.
Endure, and conquer; *Jove* will soon dispose
To future Good, our past and present Woes.
With me, the Rocks of *Scylla* you have try'd;
280 Th' inhuman *Cyclops*, and his Den defy'd.
What greater Ills hereafter can you bear?
Resume your Courage, and dismiss your Care.
An Hour will come, with Pleasure to relate,
Your Sorrows past, as Benefits of Fate.
285 Through various Hazards, and Events we move
To *Latium*, and the Realms foredoom'd by *Jove*.
Call'd to the Seat, (the Promise of the Skies,)
Where *Trojan* Kingdoms once again may rise.
Endure the Hardships of your present State,
290 Live, and reserve your selves for better Fate.
  These Words he spoke; but spoke not from his Heart;
His outward Smiles conceal'd his inward Smart.
The jolly Crew, unmindful of the past,
The Quarry share, their plenteous Dinner haste:
295 Some strip the Skin, some portion out the Spoil; ⎫
The Limbs yet trembling, in the Cauldrons boyl: ⎬
Some on the Fire the reeking Entrails broil. ⎭
Stretch'd on the grassy Turf, at ease they dine;
Restore their Strength with Meat, and chear their Souls
  with Wine.
300 Their Hunger thus appeas'd, their Care attends,
The doubtful Fortune of their absent Friends:
Alternate Hopes and Fears, their Minds possess,
Whether to deem 'em dead, or in Distress.
Above the rest, *Æneas* mourns the Fate
305 Of brave *Orontes*, and th' uncertain State
Of *Gyas*, *Lycus*, and of *Amycus*:
The Day, but not their Sorrows, ended thus.
When, from aloft, Almighty *Jove* surveys
Earth, Air, and Shoars, and navigable Seas,
310 At length on *Lybian* Realms he fix'd his Eyes:
Whom, pond'ring thus on Human Miseries,

When *Venus* saw, she with a lowly Look,
Not free from Tears, her Heav'nly Sire bespoke.
   O King of Gods and Men, whose awful Hand, ⎫
315 Disperses Thunder on the Seas and Land; ⎬
   Disposing all with absolute Command: ⎭
How cou'd my Pious Son thy Pow'r incense,
Or what, alas! is vanish'd *Troy*'s Offence?
Our hope of *Italy* not only lost,   ⎫
320 On various Seas, by various Tempests tost, ⎬
   But shut from ev'ry Shoar, and barr'd from ev'ry Coast. ⎭
You promis'd once, a Progeny Divine,
Of *Romans*, rising from the *Trojan* Line,
In after-times shou'd hold the World in awe,
325 And to the Land and Ocean give the Law.
How is your Doom revers'd, which eas'd my Care;
When *Troy* was ruin'd in that cruel War?
Then Fates to Fates I cou'd oppose; but now,
When Fortune still pursues her former Blow,
330 What can I hope? What worse can still succeed?
What end of Labours has your Will decreed?
Antenor, from the midst of *Grecian* Hosts,
Could pass secure, and pierce th' *Illyrian* Coasts:
Where rowling down the Steep, *Timavus* raves,
335 And through nine Channels disembogues his Waves.
At length he founded *Padua*'s happy Seat,
And gave his *Trojans* a secure Retreat:
There fix'd their Arms, and there renew'd their Name,
And there in Quiet rules, and crown'd with Fame.
340 But we, descended from your sacred Line,
Entitled to your Heav'n, and Rites Divine,
Are banish'd Earth, and, for the Wrath of one,
Remov'd from *Latium*, and the promis'd Throne.
Are these our Scepters? These our due Rewards?
345 And is it thus that *Jove* his plighted Faith Regards?
To whom, the Father of th' immortal Race,
Smiling with that serene indulgent Face,
With which he drives the Clouds, and clears the Skies:
First gave a holy Kiss, then thus replies.
350   Daughter, dismiss thy Fears: To thy desire
The Fates of thine are fix'd, and stand entire.

Thou shalt behold thy wish'd *Lavinian* Walls,
And, ripe for Heav'n, when Fate *Æneas* calls,
Then shalt thou bear him up, sublime, to me;
355 No Councils have revers'd my firm Decree.
And lest new Fears disturb thy happy State,
Know, I have search'd the Mystick Rolls of Fate:
Thy Son (nor is th' appointed Season far)
In *Italy* shall wage successful War:
360 Shall tame fierce Nations in the bloody Field,
And Sov'raign Laws impose, and Cities build.
'Till, after ev'ry Foe subdu'd, the Sun
Thrice through the Signs his Annual Race shall run:
This is his time prefix'd. *Ascanius* then,
365 Now called *Julus*, shall begin his Reign.
He thirty rowling Years the Crown shall wear:
Then from *Lavinium* shall the Seat transfer:
And, with hard Labour, *Alba-longa* build;
The Throne with his Succession shall be fill'd,
370 Three hundred Circuits more: then shall be seen,
Ilia the fair, a Priestess and a Queen.
Who full of *Mars*, in time, with kindly Throws,
Shall at a Birth two goodly Boys disclose.
The Royal Babes a tawny Wolf shall drain,
375 Then *Romulus* his Grandsire's Throne shall gain,
Of Martial Tow'rs the Founder shall become,
The People *Romans* call, the City *Rome*.
To them, no Bounds of Empire I assign;
Nor term of Years to their immortal Line.
380 Ev'n haughty *Juno*, who, with endless Broils,
Earth, Seas, and Heav'n, and *Jove* himself turmoils;
At length atton'd, her friendly Pow'r shall joyn,
To cherish and advance the *Trojan* Line.
The subject World shall *Rome*'s Dominion own,
385 And, prostrate, shall adore the Nation of the Gown.
An Age is ripening in revolving Fate,
When *Troy* shall overturn the *Grecian* State:
And sweet Revenge her conqu'ring Sons shall call,
To crush the People that conspir'd her Fall.
390 Then *Cæsar* from the *Julian* Stock shall rise,
Whose Empire Ocean, and whose Fame the Skies

Alone shall bound. Whom, fraught with *Eastern* Spoils,
Our Heav'n, the just Reward of Human Toyls,
Securely shall repay with Rites Divine;
395   And Incense shall ascend before his sacred Shrine.
Then dire Debate, and impious War shall cease,
And the stern Age be softned into Peace:
Then banish'd Faith shall once again return,
And Vestal Fires in hallow'd Temples burn,
400   And *Remus* with *Quirinus* shall sustain,
The righteous Laws, and Fraud and Force restrain.
Janus himself before his Fane shall wait,
And keep the dreadful issues of his Gate,
With Bolts and Iron Bars: within remains
405   Imprison'd Fury, bound in brazen Chains:
High on a Trophie rais'd, of useless Arms;
He sits, and threats the World with vain Alarms.

He said, and sent *Cyllenius* with Command
To free the Ports, and ope the *Punique* Land
410   To *Trojan* Guests; lest ignorant of Fate,
The Queen might force them from her Town and State.
Down from the Steep of Heav'n *Cyllenius* flies,
And cleaves with all his Wings the yielding Skies.
Soon on the *Lybian* Shoar descends the God;
415   Performs his Message, and displays his Rod:
The surly Murmurs of the People cease,
And, as the Fates requir'd, they give the Peace.
The Queen her self suspends the rigid Laws,
The *Trojans* pities, and protects their Cause.
420   Mean time, in Shades of Night *Æneas* lies;
Care seiz'd his Soul, and Sleep forsook his Eyes.
But when the Sun restor'd the chearful Day,
He rose, the Coast and Country to survey.
Anxious and eager to discover more:
425   It look'd a wild uncultivated Shoar:
But whether Human Kind, or Beasts alone
Possess'd the new-found Region, was unknown.
Beneath a ledge of Rocks his Fleet he hides;
Tall Trees surround the Mountains shady sides:
430   The bending Brow above, a safe Retreat provides.

Arm'd with two pointed Darts, he leaves his Friends,
And true *Achates* on his steps attends.
Loe, in the deep Recesses of the Wood,
Before his Eyes his Goddess Mother stood:

435 A Huntress in her Habit and her Meen;
Her dress a Maid, her Air confess'd a Queen.
Bare were her Knees, and knots her Garments bind; ⎫
Loose was her Hair, and wanton'd in the Wind; ⎬
Her Hand sustain'd a Bow, her Quiver hung behind. ⎭

440 She seem'd a Virgin of the *Spartan* Blood: ⎫
With such Array *Harpalice* bestrode ⎬
Her *Thracian* Courser, and outstrip'd the rapid Flood. ⎭
Ho! Strangers! have you lately seen, she said, ⎫
One of my Sisters, like my self array'd; ⎬

445 Who crost the Lawn, or in the Forest stray'd? ⎭
A Painted Quiver at her Back she bore; ⎫
Vary'd with Spots, a *Linx*'s Hide she wore: ⎬
And at full Cry pursu'd the tusky Boar? ⎭
Thus *Venus*: Thus her Son reply'd agen;

450 None of your Sisters have we heard or seen,
O Virgin! or what other Name you bear
Above that style; O more than mortal fair!
Your Voice and Meen Cœlestial Birth betray!
If, as you seem, the Sister of the Day;

455 Or one at least of Chast *Diana*'s Train,
Let not an humble Suppliant sue in vain:
But tell a Stranger, long in Tempests tost,
What Earth we tread, and who commands the Coast?
Then on your Name shall wretched Mortals call;

460 And offer'd Victims at your Altars fall.
I dare not, she reply'd, assume the Name
Of Goddess, or Cœlestial Honours claim:
For *Tyrian* Virgins Bows and Quivers bear,
And Purple Buskins o're their Ankles wear.

465 Know, gentle Youth, in *Lybian* Lands you are:
A People rude in Peace, and rough in War.
The rising City, which from far you see,
Is *Carthage*; and a *Tyrian* Colony.

Phenician Dido rules the growing State,
470   Who fled from *Tyre*, to shun her Brother's hate: ⎫
      Great were her wrongs, her Story full of Fate; ⎬
      Which I will sum in short. *Sicheus* known ⎭
      For wealth, and Brother to the *Punic* Throne,
      Possess'd fair *Dido*'s Bed: And either heart
475   At once was wounded with an equal Dart.
      Her Father gave her, yet a spotless Maid;
      Pigmalion then the *Tyrian* Scepter sway'd:
      One who contemn'd Divine and Humane Laws.
      Then Strife ensu'd, and cursed Gold the Cause.
480   The Monarch, blinded with desire of Wealth;
      With Steel invades his Brother's life by stealth;
      Before the sacred Altar made him bleed,
      And long from her conceal'd the cruel deed:
      Some Tale, some new Pretence, he daily coin'd,
485   To sooth his Sister, and delude her Mind.
      At length, in dead of Night, the Ghost appears ⎫
      Of her unhappy Lord: The Spectre stares, ⎬
      And with erected Eyes his bloody Bosom bares. ⎭
      The cruel Altars, and his Fate he tells,
490   And the dire Secret of his House reveals.
      Then warns the Widow, with her household Gods,
      To Seek a Refuge in remote abodes.
      Last, to support her, in so long a way,
      He shows her where his hidden Treasure lay.
495   Admonish'd thus, and seiz'd with mortal fright,
      The Queen provides Companions of her flight:
      They meet; and all combine to leave the State,
      Who hate the Tyrant, or who fear his hate.
      They seize a Fleet, which ready rigg'd they find:
500   Nor is *Pigmalion*'s Treasure left behind.
      The Vessels, heavy laden, put to Sea
      With prosp'rous Winds; a Woman leads the way.
      I know not, if by stress of Weather driv'n,
      Or was their fatal Course dispos'd by Heav'n;
505   At last they landed, where from far your Eyes
      May view the Turrets of new *Carthage* rise:
      There bought a space of Ground, which *Byrsa* call'd
      From the Bulls hide, they first inclos'd, and wall'd.

But whence are you, what Country claims your Birth?
510   What seek you, Strangers, on our *Lybian* Earth?
    To whom, with sorrow streaming from his Eyes,
And deeply sighing, thus her Son replies:
Cou'd you with Patience hear, or I relate,
O Nymph! the tedious Annals of our Fate!
515   Thro' such a train of Woes if I shou'd run,
The day wou'd sooner than the Tale be done!
From ancient *Troy*, by Force expell'd we came,
If you by chance have heard the *Trojan* Name:
On various Seas by various Tempests tost,
520   At length we landed on your *Lybian* Coast.
The Good *Æneas* am I call'd, a Name,
While Fortune favour'd, not unknown to Fame:
My houshold Gods, Companions of my Woes,
With pious Care I rescu'd from our Foes.
525   To fruitful *Italy* my Course was bent,
And from the King of Heav'n is my Descent.
With twice ten Sail I crost the *Phrygian* Sea;
Fate and my Mother Goddess, led my Way.
Scarce sev'n, the thin Remainders of my Fleet,
530   From Storms preserv'd, within your Harbour meet:
My self distress'd, an Exile, and unknown, ⎫
Debarr'd from *Europe*, and from *Asia* thrown, ⎬
In *Lybian* Desarts wander thus alone. ⎭
    His tender Parent could no longer bear;
535   But, interposing, sought to sooth his Care.
Who e're you are, not unbelov'd by Heav'n,
Since on our friendly Shoar your Ships are driv'n:
Have Courage: To the Gods permit the rest,
And to the Queen expose your just Request.
540   Now take this earnest of Success, for more:
Your scatter'd Fleet is join'd upon the Shoar;
The Winds are chang'd, your Friends from danger free,
Or I renounce my Skill in Augury.
Twelve Swans behold, in beauteous order move,
545   And stoop with closing Pinions from above:
Whom late the Bird of *Jove* had driv'n along,
And through the Clouds pursu'd the scatt'ring Throng:

Now all united in a goodly Team,
They skim the Ground, and seek the quiet Stream.
550 As they, with Joy returning, clap their Wings,
And ride the Circuit of the Skies in Rings:
Not otherwise your Ships, and ev'ry Friend,
Already hold the Port, or with swift Sails descend.
No more Advice is needful, but pursue
555 The Path before you, and the Town in view.
Thus having said, she turn'd, and made appear
Her Neck refulgent, and dishevel'd Hair;
Which flowing from her Shoulders, reach'd the Ground,
And widely spread Ambrosial Scents around:
560 In length of Train descends her sweeping Gown,
And by her graceful Walk, the Queen of Love is known.
The Prince pursu'd the parting Deity,
With Words like these: Ah! whither do you fly?
Unkind and cruel, to deceive your Son
565 In borrow'd Shapes, and his Embrace to shun:
Never to bless my Sight, but thus unknown;
And still to speak in Accents not your own.
Against the Goddess these Complaints he made;
But took the Path, and her Commands obey'd.
570 They march obscure, for *Venus* kindly shrouds,
With Mists, their Persons, and involves in Clouds:
That, thus unseen, their Passage none might stay,
Or force to tell the Causes of their Way.
This part perform'd, the Goddess flies sublime,
575 To visit *Paphos*; and her native Clime:
Where Garlands ever green, and ever fair,
With Vows are offer'd, and with solemn Pray'r:
A hundred Altars in her Temple Smoke,
A thousand bleeding Hearts her Pow'r invoke.
580   They climb the next Ascent, and, looking down,
Now at a nearer Distance view the Town:
The Prince, with Wonder, sees the stately Tow'rs,
Which late were Huts, and Shepherd's homely Bow'rs.
The Gates and Streets; and hears, from ev'ry part,
585 The Noise, and busy Concourse of the Mart.
The toiling *Tyrians* on each other call,
To ply their Labour: Some extend the Wall,

Some build the Citadel; the brawny throng,
Or dig, or push unweildy Stones along.
590   Some for their Dwellings chuse a Spot of Ground,
Which, first design'd, with Ditches they surround.
Some Laws ordain, and some attend the Choice
Of holy Senates, and elect by Voice.
Here some design a Mole, while others there
595   Lay deep Foundations for a Theatre:
From Marble Quarries mighty Columns hew,
For Ornaments of Scenes, and future view.
Such is their Toyl, and such their busy Pains,
As exercise the Bees in flow'ry Plains;
600   When Winter past, and Summer scarce begun,
Invites them forth to labour in the Sun:
Some lead their Youth abroad, while some condense
Their liquid Store, and some in Cells dispence.
Some at the Gate stand ready to receive
605   The Golden burthen, and their Friends relieve.
All, with united Force, combine to drive
The lazy Drones from the laborious Hive;
With envy stung, they view each others Deeds;
The fragrant Work with Diligence proceeds.
610   Thrice happy you, whose Walls already rise;
Æneas said; and viewed, with lifted Eyes,
Their lofty Tow'rs; then ent'ring at the Gate,
Conceal'd in Clouds, (prodigious to relate)
He mix'd, unmark'd, among the busy Throng,
615   Born by the Tide, and pass'd unseen along.
    Full in the Centre of the Town there stood,
Thick set with Trees, a venerable Wood:
The _Tyrians_ landing near this holy Ground,
And digging here, a prosp'rous Omen found:
620   From under Earth a Courser's Head they drew,
Their Growth and future Fortune to foreshew:
This fated Sign their Foundress _Juno_ gave,
Of a Soil fruitful, and a People brave.
Sidonian Dido here with solemn State
625   Did _Juno_'s Temple build, and consecrate:
Enrich'd with Gifts, and with a Golden Shrine;
But more the Goddess made the Place Divine.

On Brazen Steps the Marble Threshold rose,
And brazen Plates the Cedar Beams inclose:
630 The Rafters are with brazen Cov'rings crown'd,
The lofty Doors on brazen Hinges sound.
What first *Æneas* in this place beheld,
Reviv'd his Courage, and his Fear expel'd.
For while, expecting there the Queen, he rais'd
635 His wond'ring Eyes, and round the Temple gaz'd;
Admir'd the Fortune of the rising Town,
The striving Artists, and their Arts renown:
He saw in order painted on the Wall,
Whatever did unhappy *Troy* befall:
640 The Wars that Fame around the World had blown,
All to the Life, and ev'ry Leader known.
There *Agamemnon*, *Priam* here he spies,
And fierce *Achilles* who both Kings defies.
He stop'd, and weeping said, O Friend! ev'n here
645 The Monuments of *Trojan* Woes appear!
Our known Disasters fill ev'n foreign Lands:
See there, where old unhappy *Priam* stands!
Ev'n the Mute Walls relate the Warrior's Fame,
And *Trojan* Griefs the *Tyrians* Pity claim.
650 He said, his Tears a ready Passage find,
Devouring what he saw so well design'd;
And with an empty Picture fed his Mind.
For there he saw the fainting *Grecians* yield,
And here the trembling *Trojans* quit the Field,
655 Pursu'd by fierce *Achilles* through the Plain,
On his high Chariot driving o're the Slain.
The Tents of *Rhesus* next, his Grief renew,
By their white Sails betray'd to nightly view.
And wakeful *Diomede*, whose cruel Sword
660 The Centries slew; nor spar'd their slumb'ring Lord.
Then took the fiery Steeds, e're yet the Food
Of *Troy* they taste, or drink the *Xanthian* Flood.
Elsewhere he saw where *Troilus* defy'd
Achilles, and unequal Combat try'd.
665 Then, where the Boy disarm'd with loosen'd Reins,
Was by his Horses hurry'd o're the Plains:

Hung by the Neck and Hair, and drag'd around,
The hostile Spear yet sticking in his Wound;
With tracks of Blood inscrib'd the dusty Ground.

670   Mean time the *Trojan* Dames oppress'd with Woe,
To *Pallas* Fane in long Procession goe,
In hopes to reconcile their Heav'nly Foe:
They weep, they beat their Breasts, they rend their Hair,
And rich embroider'd Vests for Presents bear:
675 But the stern Goddess stands unmov'd with Pray'r.
Thrice round the *Trojan* Walls *Achilles* drew
The Corps of *Hector*, whom in Fight he slew.
Here *Priam* sues, and there, for Sums of Gold,
The lifeless Body of his Son is sold.
680 So sad an Object, and so well express'd,
Drew Sighs and Groans from the griev'd Heroes Breast:
To see the Figure of his lifeless Friend,
And his old Sire his helpless Hand extend.
Himself he saw amidst the *Grecian* Train,
685 Mix'd in the bloody Battel on the Plain.
And swarthy *Memnon* in his Arms he knew;
His pompous Ensigns, and his *Indian* Crew.
Penthisilea there, with haughty Grace,
Leads to the Wars an *Amazonian* Race:
690 In their right Hands a pointed Dart they wield;
The left, for Ward, sustains the Lunar Shield.
Athwart her Brest a Golden Belt she throws,
Amidst the Press alone provokes a thousand Foes:
And dares her Maiden Arms to Manly Force oppose.
695 Thus, while the *Trojan* Prince employs his Eyes,
Fix'd on the Walls with wonder and surprise;
The Beauteous *Dido*, with a num'rous Train,
And pomp of Guards, ascends the sacred Fane.
Such on *Eurota*'s Banks, or *Cynthus*'s hight,
700 *Diana* seems; and so she charms the sight,
When in the Dance the graceful Goddess leads
The Quire of Nymphs, and overtops their Heads.
Known by her Quiver, and her lofty Meen,
She walks Majestick, and she looks their Queen:
705 *Latona* sees her shine above the rest,
And feeds with secret Joy her silent Breast.

Such *Dido* was; with such becoming State,
Amidst the Crowd, she walks serenely great.
Their Labour to her future Sway she speeds,
710 And passing with a gracious Glance proceeds:
Then mounts the Throne, high plac'd before the Shrine;
In Crowds around the swarming People joyn.
She takes Petitions, and dispenses Laws,
Hears, and determines ev'ry private Cause.
715 Their Tasks in equal Portions she divides,
And where unequal, there by Lots decides.
Another way by chance *Æneas* bends
His Eyes, and unexpected sees his Friends:
Antheus, *Sergestus* grave, *Cloanthus* strong,
720 And at their Backs a mighty *Trojan* Throng:
Whom late the Tempest on the Billows tost,
And widely scatter'd on another Coast.
The Prince, unseen, surpriz'd with Wonder stands,
And longs, with joyful haste to join their Hands:
725 But doubtful of the wish'd Event, he stays,
And from the hollow Cloud his Friends surveys:
Impatient 'till they told their present State,
And where they left their Ships, and what their Fate;
And why they came, and what was their Request:
730 For these were sent commission'd by the rest,
To sue for leave to land their sickly Men,
And gain Admission to the Gracious Queen.
Ent'ring, with Cries they fill'd the holy Fane;
Then thus, with lowly Voice, *Ilioneus* began.
735 O Queen! indulg'd by Favour of the Gods,
To found an Empire in these new Abodes;
To build a Town, with Statutes to restrain
The wild Inhabitants beneath thy Reign:
We wretched *Trojans* tost on ev'ry Shore,
740 From Sea to Sea, thy Clemency implore:
Forbid the Fires our Shipping to deface, ⎫
Receive th' unhappy Fugitives to Grace, ⎬
And spare the remnant of a Pious Race. ⎭
We come not with design of wastful Prey,
745 To drive the Country, force the Swains away:

Nor such our Strength, nor such is our Desire,
The vanquish'd dare not to such Thoughts aspire.
A Land there is, *Hesperia* nam'd of old,
The Soil is fruitful, and the Men are bold:
750   Th' *Oenotrians* held it once, by common Fame,
Now call'd *Italia*, from the Leaders Name.
To that sweet Region was our Voyage bent,
When Winds, and ev'ry warring Element,
Disturb'd our Course, and far from sight of Land,
755   Cast our torn Vessels on the moving Sand:
The Sea came on; the South with mighty Roar,
Dispers'd and dash'd the rest upon the Rocky Shoar.
Those few you see escap'd the Storm, and fear,
Unless you interpose, a Shipwreck here;
760   What Men, what Monsters, what inhuman Race,
What Laws, what barb'rous Customs of the Place,
Shut up a desart Shoar to drowning Men,
And drive us to the cruel Seas agen!
If our hard Fortune no Compassion draws,
765   Nor hospitable Rights, nor human Laws,
The Gods are just, and will revenge our Cause.
Æneas was our Prince, a juster Lord,
Or nobler Warriour, never drew a Sword:
Observant of the Right, religious of his Word.
770   If yet he lives, and draws this vital Air:
Nor we his Friends of Safety shall despair;
Nor you, great Queen, these Offices repent,
Which he will equal, and perhaps augment.
We want not Cities, nor *Sicilian* Coasts,
775   Where King *Acestes Trojan* Lineage boasts.
Permit our Ships a Shelter on your Shoars,
Refitted from your Woods with Planks and Oars;
That if our Prince be safe, we may renew
Our destin'd Course, and *Italy* pursue.
780   But if, O best of Men! the Fates ordain
That thou art swallow'd in the *Lybian* Main:
And if our young *Julus* be no more,
Dismiss our Navy from your friendly Shoar.
That we to good *Acestes* may return,
785   And with our Friends our common Losses mourn.

Thus spoke *Ilioneus*; the *Trojan* Crew
With Cries and Clamours his Request renew.
The modest Queen a while, with down-cast Eyes,
Ponder'd the Speech; then briefly thus replies.
790   *Trojans* dismiss your Fears: my cruel Fate,
And doubts attending an unsettled State,
Force me to guard my Coast, from Foreign Foes.
Who has not heard the story of your Woes?
The Name and Fortune of your Native Place,
795   The Fame and Valour of the *Phrygian* Race?
We *Tyrians* are not so devoid of Sense,
Nor so remote from *Phœbus* influence.
Whether to *Latian* Shores your Course is bent,
Or driv'n by Tempests from your first intent,
800   You seek the good *Acestes* Government;
Your Men shall be receiv'd, your Fleet repair'd,
And sail, with Ships of Convoy for your guard;
Or, wou'd you stay, and joyn your friendly Pow'rs,
To raise and to defend the *Tyrian* Tow'rs;
805   My Wealth, my City, and my Self are yours.
And wou'd to Heav'n the Storm, you felt, wou'd bring
On *Carthaginian* Coasts your wand'ring King.
My People shall, by my Command, explore
The Ports and Creeks of ev'ry winding shore;
810   And Towns, and Wilds, and shady Woods, in quest
Of so renown'd and so desir'd a Guest.
Rais'd in his Mind the *Trojan* Heroe stood,
And long'd to break from out his Ambient Cloud;
Achates found it; and thus urg'd his way;
815   From whence, O Goddess born, this long delay?
What more can you desire, your Welcome sure,
Your Fleet in safety, and your Friends secure?
Only one wants; and him we saw in vain
Oppose the Storm, and swallow'd in the Main.
820   *Orontes* in his Fate our Forfeit paid,
The rest agrees with what your Mother said.
Scarce had he spoken, when the Cloud gave way,
The Mists flew upward, and dissolv'd in day.
The *Trojan* Chief appear'd in open sight,
825   August in Visage, and serenely bright.

His Mother Goddess, with her hands Divine,
Had form'd his Curling Locks, and made his Temples
    shine:
And giv'n his rowling Eyes a sparkling grace;
And breath'd a youthful vigour on his Face:
830 Like polish'd Iv'ry, beauteous to behold,
Or *Parian* Marble, when enchas'd in Gold:
Thus radiant from the circling Cloud he broke;
And thus with manly modesty he spoke.
    He whom you seek am I: by Tempests tost,
835 And sav'd from Shipwreck on your *Lybian* Coast:
Presenting, gracious Queen, before your Throne,
A Prince that owes his Life to you alone.
Fair Majesty, the Refuge and Redress
Of those whom Fate pursues, and Wants oppress.
840 You, who your pious Offices employ
To save the Reliques of abandon'd *Troy*;
Receive the Shipwreck'd on your friendly Shore,
With hospitable Rites relieve the Poor:
Associate in your Town a wandring Train.
845 And strangers in your Palace entertain.
What thanks can wretched Fugitives return,
Who scatter'd thro' the World in exile mourn?
The Gods, (if Gods to Goodness are inclin'd,)
If Acts of mercy touch their Heav'nly Mind;
850 And more than all the Gods, your gen'rous heart,
Conscious of worth, requite its own desert!
In you this Age is happy, and this Earth:
And Parents more than Mortal gave you birth.
While rowling Rivers into Seas shall run,
855 And round the space of Heav'n the radiant Sun;
While Trees the Mountain tops with Shades supply,
Your Honour, Name, and Praise shall never dye.
What e're abode my Fortune has assign'd,
Your Image shall be present in my Mind.
860 Thus having said; he turn'd with pious hast, ⎫
And joyful his expecting Friends embrac'd: ⎬
With his right hand *Ilioneus* was grac'd, ⎭
Serestus with his left; then to his breast ⎱
Cloanthus and the Noble *Gyas* prest; ⎰
865 And so by turns descended to the rest. ⎭

The *Tyrian* Queen stood fix'd upon his Face,
Pleas'd with his motions, ravish'd with his grace:
Admir'd his Fortunes, more admir'd the Man;
Then recollected stood; and thus began.

870   What Fate, O Goddess born, what angry Pow'rs
Have cast you shipwrack'd on our barren Shores?
Are you the great *Æneas*, known to Fame,
Who from Cœlestial Seed your Lineage claim!
The same *Æneas* whom fair *Venus* bore

875   To fam'd *Anchises* on th' *Idæan* Shore?
It calls into my mind, tho' then a Child,
When *Teucer* came from *Salamis* exil'd;
And sought my Father's aid, to be restor'd:
My Father *Belus* then with Fire and Sword

880   Invaded *Cyprus*, made the Region bare,
And, Conqu'ring, finish'd the successful War.
From him the *Trojan* Siege I understood,
The *Grecian* Chiefs, and your Illustrious Blood.
Your Foe himself the *Dardan* Valour prais'd,

885   And his own Ancestry from *Trojans* rais'd.
Enter, my Noble Guest; and you shall find,
If not a costly welcome, yet a kind.
For I my self, like you, have been distress'd;
Till Heav'n afforded me this place of rest.

890   Like you an Alien in a Land unknown;
I learn to pity Woes, so like my own.
She said, and to the Palace led her Guest,
Then offer'd Incense, and proclaim'd a Feast.
Nor yet less careful for her absent Friends,

895   Twice ten fat Oxen to the Ships she sends:
Besides a hundred Boars, a hundred Lambs,
With bleating cries, attend their Milky Dams.
And Jars of gen'rous Wine, and spacious Bowls,
She gives to chear the Sailors drooping Souls.

900   Now Purple Hangings cloath the Palace Walls,
And sumptuous Feasts are made in splendid Halls:
On *Tyrian* Carpets, richly wrought, they Dine;
With loads of Massy Plate the Side-boards shine.
And Antique Vases all of Gold Emboss'd;

905   (The Gold it self inferiour to the Cost:)

Of curious Work, where on the sides were seen ⎤
The Fights and Figures of Illustrious Men; ⎬
From their first Founder to the present Queen. ⎦

The Good *Æneas*, whose Paternal Care
910 *Iulus* absence could no longer bear,
Dispatch'd *Achates* to the Ships in hast,
To give a glad Relation of the past;
And, fraught with precious Gifts, to bring the Boy
Snatch'd from the Ruins of unhappy *Troy*:
915 A Robe of Tissue, stiff with golden Wire;
An upper Vest, once *Hellen*'s rich Attire;
From *Argos* by the fam'd Adultress brought,
With Golden flow'rs and winding foliage wrought;
Her Mother *Læda*'s Present, when she came
920 To ruin *Troy*, and set the World on flame.
The Scepter *Priam*'s eldest Daughter bore,
Her orient Necklace, and the Crown she wore;
Of double texture, glorious to behold;
One order set with Gems, and one with Gold.
925 Instructed thus, the wise *Achates* goes:
And in his diligence his duty shows.

But *Venus*, anxious for her Son's Affairs,
New Councils tryes; and new Designs prepares:
That *Cupid* should assume the Shape and Face
930 Of sweet *Ascanius*, and the sprightly grace:
Shou'd bring the Presents, in her Nephew's stead,
And in *Eliza*'s Veins the gentle Poison shed.
For much she fear'd the *Tyrians*, double tongu'd,
And knew the Town to *Juno*'s care belong'd.
935 These thoughts by Night her Golden Slumbers broke;
And thus alarm'd, to winged Love she spoke.
My Son, my strength, whose mighty Pow'r alone
Controuls the Thund'rer, on his awful Throne;
To thee thy much afflicted Mother flies,
940 And on thy Succour, and thy Faith relies.
Thou know'st, my Son, how *Jove*'s revengeful Wife,
By force and fraud, attempts thy Brother's life.
And often hast thou mourn'd with me his Pains: ⎤
Him *Dido* now with Blandishment detains; ⎬
945 But I suspect the Town where *Juno* reigns. ⎦

For this, 'tis needful to prevent her Art,
And fire with Love the proud *Phœnician*'s heart.
A Love so violent, so strong, so sure,
As neither Age can change, nor Art can cure.
950 How this may be perform'd, now take my mind:
Ascanius, by his Father is design'd
To come, with Presents, laden from the Port,
To gratifie the Queen, and gain the Court.
I mean to plunge the Boy in pleasing Sleep,
955 And, ravish'd, in *Idalian* Bow'rs to keep;
Or high *Cythœra*: That the sweet Deceipt
May pass unseen, and none prevent the Cheat,
Take thou his Form and Shape. I beg the Grace ⎤
But only for a Night's revolving Space; ⎟
960 Thy self a Boy, assume a Boy's dissembled Face. ⎦
That when amidst the fervour of the Feast,
The *Tyrian* hugs, and fonds thee on her Breast,
And with sweet Kisses in her Arms constrains,
Thou may'st infuse thy Venom in her Veins.
965 The God of Love obeys, and sets aside
His Bow, and Quiver, and his plumy Pride:
He walks *Iulus* in his Mother's Sight:
And in the sweet Resemblance takes Delight.
     The Goddess then to young *Ascanius* flies,
970 And in a pleasing Slumber seals his Eyes;
Lull'd in her Lap, amidst a Train of Loves,
She gently bears him to her blisful Groves:
Then with a Wreath of Myrtle crowns his Head,
And softly lays him on a flow'ry Bed.
975 *Cupid* mean time assum'd his Form and Face,
Foll'wing *Achates* with a shorter Pace;
And brought the Gifts. The Queen, already sate
Amidst the *Trojan* Lords, in shining State,
High on a Golden Bed: Her Princely Guest
980 Was next her side, in order sate the rest.
Then Canisters with Bread are heap'd on high; ⎤
Th' Attendants Water for their Hands supply; ⎟
And having wash'd, with silken Towels dry. ⎦
Next fifty Handmaids in long order bore
985 The Censers, and with Fumes the Gods adore.

Then Youths, and Virgins twice as many, join
To place the Dishes, and to serve the Wine.
The *Tyrian* Train, admitted to the Feast,
Approach, and on the painted Couches rest.
990 All on the *Trojan* Gifts, with Wonder gaze;
But view the beauteous Boy with more amaze.
His Rosy-colour'd Cheeks, his radiant Eyes,
His Motions, Voice, and Shape, and all the God's disguise.
Nor pass unprais'd the Vest and Veil Divine,
995 Which wand'ring Foliage and rich Flow'rs entwine.
But far above the rest, the Royal Dame,
(Already doom'd to Love's disastrous Flame;)
With Eyes insatiate, and tumultuous Joy,
Beholds the Presents, and admires the Boy.
1000 The guileful God, about the Heroe long,
With Children's play, and false Embraces hung;
Then sought the Queen: She took him to her Arms,
With greedy Pleasure, and devour'd his Charms.
Unhappy *Dido* little thought what Guest,
1005 How dire a God she drew so near her Breast.
But he, not mindless of his Mother's Pray'r, ⎫
Works in the pliant Bosom of the Fair; ⎬
And moulds her Heart anew, and blots her former Care. ⎭
The dead is to the living Love resign'd,
1010 And all *Æneas* enters in her Mind.
    Now, when the Rage of Hunger was appeas'd,
The Meat remov'd, and ev'ry Guest was pleas'd;
The Golden Bowls with sparkling Wine are crown'd,
And through the Palace chearful Cries resound.
1015 From gilded Roofs depending Lamps display
Nocturnal Beams, that emulate the Day.
A Golden Bowl, that shone with Gems Divine, ⎫
The Queen commanded to be crown'd with Wine; ⎬
The Bowl that *Belus* us'd, and all the *Tyrian* Line. ⎭
1020 Then, Silence through the Hall proclaim'd, she spoke:
O hospitable *Jove*! we thus invoke,
With solemn Rites, thy sacred Name and Pow'r!
Bless to both Nations this auspicious Hour.
So may the *Trojan* and the *Tyrian* Line,
1025 In lasting Concord, from this Day combine.

Thou, *Bacchus*, God of Joys and friendly Cheer,
And gracious *Juno*, both be present here:
And you, my Lords of *Tyre*, your Vows address
To Heav'n with mine, to ratifie the Peace.
1030 The Goblet then she took, with *Nectar* crown'd,
(Sprinkling the first Libations on the Ground,)
And rais'd it to her Mouth with sober Grace,
Then sipping, offer'd to the next in place.
'Twas *Bitias* whom she call'd, a thirsty Soul,
1035 He took the Challenge, and embrac'd the Bowl:
With Pleasure swill'd the Gold, nor ceas'd to draw,
'Till he the bottom of the Brimmer saw.
The Goblet goes around: *Jopas* brought
His Golden Lyre, and sung what ancient *Atlas* taught.
1040 The various Labours of the wand'ring Moon,
And whence proceed th' Eclipses of the Sun.
Th' Original of Men, and Beasts; and whence ⎫
The Rains arise, and Fires their Warmth dispence; ⎬
And fix'd, and erring Stars, dispose their Influence. ⎭
1045 What shakes the solid Earth, what Cause delays
The Summer Nights, and shortens Winter Days.
With Peals of Shouts the *Tyrians* praise the Song;
Those Peals are echo'd by the *Trojan* Throng.
Th' unhappy Queen with Talk prolong'd the Night,
1050 And drank large Draughts of Love with vast Delight.
Of *Priam* much enquir'd, of *Hector* more; ⎫
Then ask'd what Arms the swarthy *Memnon* wore; ⎬
What Troops he landed on the *Trojan* Shore. ⎭
The Steeds of *Diomede* vary'd the Discourse,
1055 And fierce *Achilles*, with his matchless Force.
At length, as Fate and her ill Stars requir'd,
To hear the Series of the War desir'd.
Relate at large, my God-like Guest, she said,
The *Grecian* Stratagems, the Town betray'd;
1060 The fatal Issue of so long a War,
Your Flight, your Wand'rings, and your Woes declare.
For since on ev'ry Sea, on ev'ry Coast,
Your Men have been distress'd, your Navy tost,
Sev'n times the Sun has either Tropick view'd,
1065 The Winter banish'd, and the Spring renew'd.

THE SECOND BOOK OF THE ÆNEIS

The Argument

Æneas *relates how the City of* Troy *was taken, after a Ten Years Siege, by the Treachery of* Sinon, *and the Stratagem of a Wooden Horse. He declares the fixt Resolution he had taken not to survive the Ruins of his Country, and the various Adventures he met with in the Defence of it: at last having been before advis'd by* Hector's *Ghost, and now by the Appearance of his Mother* Venus, *he is prevail'd upon to leave the Town, and settle his Houshold-Gods in another Country. In order to this, he carries off his Father on his Shoulders, and leads his little Son by the Hand, his Wife following him behind. When he comes to the Place appointed for the general Rendezvouze, he finds a great confluence of People, but misses his Wife, whose Ghost afterwards appears to him, and tells him the Land which was design'd for him.*

All were attentive to the God-like Man;
When from his lofty couch he thus began.
Great Queen, what you command me to relate,
Renews the sad Remembrance of our Fate.
5   An Empire from its old Foundations rent,
And ev'ry Woe the *Trojans* underwent:
A Peopl'd City made a Desart Place;
All that I saw, and part of which I was:
Not ev'n the hardest of our Foes cou'd hear,
10   Nor stern *Ulysses* tell without a Tear.
And now the latter Watch of wasting Night,
And setting Stars to kindly Rest invite.
But since you take such Int'rest in our Woe,
And *Troy*'s disast'rous end desire to know:
15   I will restrain my Tears, and briefly tell
What in our last and fatal Night befel.

       By Destiny compell'd, and in Despair,
The *Greeks* grew weary of the tedious War:
And by *Minerva*'s Aid a Fabrick rear'd,
20   Which like a Steed of monstrous height appear'd;
The Sides were planck'd with Pine, they feign'd it made
For their Return, and this the Vow they paid.
Thus they pretend, but in the hollow Side,
Selected Numbers of their Souldiers hide:
25   With inward Arms the dire Machine they load,
And Iron Bowels stuff the dark Abode.
In sight of *Troy* lies *Tenedos*, an Isle,
(While Fortune did on *Priam*'s Empire smile)
Renown'd for Wealth, but since a faithless Bay,
30   Where Ships expos'd to Wind and Weather lay.
There was their Fleet conceal'd: We thought for *Greece*
Their Sails were hoisted, and our Fears release.

The *Trojans* coop'd within their Walls so long,
Unbar their Gates, and issue in a Throng,
35   Like swarming Bees, and with Delight survey
The Camp deserted, where the *Grecians* lay:
The Quarters of the sev'ral Chiefs they show'd, ⎤
Here *Phœnix*, here *Achilles* made abode,   ⎬
Here join'd the Battels, there the Navy rode, ⎦
40   Part on the Pile their wond'ring Eyes employ,
(The Pile by *Pallas* rais'd to ruin *Troy*.)
Thymœtes first ('tis doubtful whether hir'd,
Or so the *Trojan* Destiny requir'd)
Mov'd that the Ramparts might be broken down,
45   To lodge the Monster Fabrique in the Town.
But *Capys*, and the rest of sounder Mind,
The fatal Present to the Flames design'd;
Or to the watry deep: At least to bore
The hollow sides, and hidden Frauds explore:
50   The giddy Vulgar, as their Fancies guide,
With Noise say nothing, and in parts divide.
Laocoon, follow'd by a num'rous Crowd,
Ran from the Fort; and cry'd, from far, aloud;
O wretched Country-men! what Fury reigns?
55   What more than Madness has possess'd your Brains?
Think you the *Grecians* from your Coasts are gone,
And are *Ulysses* Arts no better known?
This hollow Fabrick either must inclose,
Within its blind Recess, our secret Foes;
60   Or 'tis an Engine rais'd above the Town,
T' o'relook the Walls, and then to batter down.
Somewhat is sure design'd; by Fraud or Force;
Trust not their Presents, nor admit the Horse.
Thus having said, against the Steed he threw
65   His forceful Spear, which, hissing as it flew,
Pierc'd through the yielding Plancks of jointed Wood,
And trembling in the hollow Belly stood.
The sides transpierc'd, return a ratling Sound,
And Groans of *Greeks* inclos'd come issuing through the
        Wound.
70   And had not Heav'n the fall of *Troy* design'd, ⎤
Or had not Men been fated to be blind,   ⎬
Enough was said and done, t' inspire a better Mind: ⎦

Then had our Lances pierc'd the treach'rous Wood,
And *Ilian* Tow'rs, and *Priam*'s Empire stood.
75 Mean time, with Shouts, the *Trojan* Shepherds bring
A captive *Greek* in Bands, before the King:
Taken, to take; who made himself their Prey,
T' impose on their Belief, and *Troy* betray.
Fix'd on his Aim, and obstinately bent
80 To die undaunted, or to circumvent.
About the Captive, tides of *Trojans* flow;
All press to see, and some insult the Foe.
Now hear how well the *Greeks* their Wiles disguis'd,
Behold a Nation in a Man compris'd.
85 Trembling the Miscreant stood, unarm'd and bound;
He star'd, and rowl'd his hagger'd Eyes around:
Then said, Alas! what Earth remains, what Sea
Is open to receive unhappy me!
What Fate a wretched Fugitive attends,
90 Scorn'd by my Foes, abandon'd by my Friends.
He said, and sigh'd, and cast a ruful Eye:
Our Pity kindles, and our Passions dye.
We chear the Youth to make his own Defence,
And freely tell us what he was, and whence:
95 What News he cou'd impart, we long to know,
And what to credit from a captive Foe.
    His fear at length dismiss'd, he said, what e're
My Fate ordains, my Words shall be sincere:
I neither can, nor dare my Birth disclaim,
100 *Greece* is my Country, *Sinon* is my Name:
Though plung'd by Fortune's Pow'r in Misery,
'Tis not in Fortune's Pow'r to make me lye.
If any chance has hither brought the Name
Of *Palamedes*, not unknown to Fame,
105 Who suffer'd from the Malice of the times;
Accus'd and sentenc'd for pretended Crimes:
Because these fatal Wars he would prevent;
Whose Death the Wretched *Greeks* too late lament;
Me, then a Boy, my Father, poor and bare ⎤
110 Of other Means, committed to his Care: ⎬
His Kinsman and Companion in the War. ⎦

While Fortune favour'd, while his Arms support
The Cause, and rul'd the Counsels of the Court,
I made some figure there; nor was my Name
115   Obscure, nor I without my share of Fame.
But when *Ulysses*, with fallacious Arts,
Had made Impression in the Peoples Hearts;
And forg'd a Treason in my Patron's Name,
(I speak of things too far divulg'd by Fame)
120   My Kinsman fell; then I, without support,
In private mourn'd his Loss, and left the Court.
Mad as I was, I could not bear his Fate
With silent Grief, but loudly blam'd the State:
And curs'd the direful Author of my Woes.
125   'Twas told again, and hence my Ruin rose.
I threatn'd, if indulgent Heav'n once more   ⎫
Wou'd land me safely on my Native Shore,   ⎬
His Death with double Vengeance to restore.   ⎭
This mov'd the Murderer's Hate, and soon ensu'd
130   Th' Effects of Malice from a Man so proud.
Ambiguous Rumors thro the Camp he spread,
And sought, by Treason, my devoted Head:
New Crimes invented, left unturn'd no Stone,
To make my Guilt appear, and hide his own.
135   'Till *Calchas* was by Force and Threatning wrought:
But why – Why dwell I on that anxious Thought?
If on my Nation just Revenge you seek,
And 'tis t' appear a Foe, t' appear a *Greek*;
Already you my Name and Country know,
140   Asswage your thirst of Blood, and strike the Blow:
My Death will both the Kingly Brothers please,
And set insatiate *Ithacus* at ease.
This fair unfinish'd Tale, these broken starts, ⎫
Rais'd expectations in our longing Hearts;   ⎬
145   Unknowing as we were in *Grecian* Arts.   ⎭
His former trembling once again renew'd,
With acted Fear, the Villain thus pursu'd.
    Long had the *Grecians* (tir'd with fruitless Care,
And weary'd with an unsuccessful War,)
150   Resolv'd to raise the Siege, and leave the Town;
And had the Gods permitted, they had gone.

But oft the Wintry Seas, and Southern Winds,
Withstood their passage home, and chang'd their Minds.
Portents and Prodigies their Souls amaz'd;
155   But most, when this stupendous Pile was rais'd.
Then flaming Meteors, hung in Air, were seen,
And Thunders ratled through a Skie serene:
Dismay'd, and fearful of some dire Event,
Eurypylus, t' enquire their Fate, was sent;
160   He from the Gods this dreadful Answer brought; ⎫
O *Grecians*, when the *Trojan* Shores you sought, ⎬
Your Passage with a Virgin's Blood was bought: ⎭
So must Your safe Return be bought again;
And *Grecian* Blood, once more attone the Main.
165   The spreading Rumour round the People ran;
All fear'd, and each believ'd himself the Man.
Ulysses took th' advantage of their fright;
Call'd *Calchas*, and produc'd in open sight:
Than bade him name the Wretch, ordain'd by Fate,
170   The Publick Victim, to redeem the State.
Already some presag'd the dire Event,
And saw what Sacrifice *Ulysses* meant.
For twice five days the good old Seer withstood
Th' intended Treason, and was dumb to Blood.
175   Till tir'd with endless Clamours, and pursuit
Of *Ithacus*, he stood no longer Mute:
But, as it was agreed, pronounc'd, that I
Was destin'd by the wrathful Gods to die.
All prais'd the Sentence, pleas'd the storm should fall
180   On one alone, whose Fury threatn'd all.
The dismal day was come, the Priests prepare
Their leaven'd Cakes; and Fillets for my Hair.
I follow'd Natur's Laws, and must avow
I broke my Bonds, and fled the fatal blow.
185   Hid in a weedy Lake all Night I lay,
Secure of Safety when they sail'd away.
But now what further Hopes for me remain,
To see my Friends or Native Soil again?
My tender Infants, or my careful Sire;
190   Whom they returning will to Death require?

Will perpetrate on them their first Design,
And take the forfeit of their Heads for mine?
Which, O if Pity Mortal Minds can move!
If there be Faith below, or Gods above!
195 If Innocence and Truth can claim desert,
Ye *Trojans* from an injur'd Wretch avert.
False Tears true Pity move: the King Commands
To loose his Fetters, and unbind his Hands:
Then adds these friendly Words; dismiss thy Fears,
200 Forget the *Greeks*, be mine as thou wert theirs.
But truly tell, was it for Force or Guile,
Or some Religious End, you rais'd the Pile?
Thus said the King. He full of fraudful Arts,
This well invented Tale for Truth imparts.
205 Ye Lamps of Heav'n! he said, and lifted high
His hands now free, thou venerable Sky,
Inviolable Pow'rs, ador'd with dread,   ⎫
Ye fatal Fillets, that once bound this head, ⎬
Ye sacred Altars, from whose flames I fled! ⎭
210 Be all of you adjur'd; and grant I may,
Without a Crime, th' ungrateful *Greeks* betray!
Reveal the Secrets of the guilty State,
And justly punish whom I justly hate!
But you, O King, preserve the Faith you gave,
215 If I to save my self your Empire save.
The *Grecian* Hopes, and all th' Attempts they made,
Were only founded on *Minerva*'s Aid.
But from the time when impious *Diomede*,
And false *Ulysses*, that inventive Head,
220 Her fatal Image from the Temple drew,
The sleeping Guardians of the Castle slew,
Her Virgin Statue with their bloody Hands
Polluted, and prophan'd her holy Bands:
From thence the Tide of Fortune left their Shore,
225 And ebb'd much faster than it flow'd before:
Their Courage languish'd, as their Hopes decay'd,
And *Pallas*, now averse, refus'd her Aid.
Nor did the Goddess doubtfully declare
Her alter'd Mind, and alienated Care:

230   When first her fatal Image touch'd the Ground,
      She sternly cast her glaring Eyes around;
      That sparkl'd as they rowl'd, and seem'd to threat:
      Her Heav'nly Limbs distill'd a briny Sweat.
      Thrice from the Ground she leap'd, was seen to wield
235   Her brandish'd Lance, and shake her horrid Shield.
      Then *Calchas* bad our Host for flight prepare,
      And hope no Conquest from the tedious War:
      'Till first they sail'd for *Greece*; with Pray'rs besought
      Her injur'd Pow'r, and better Omens brought.
240   And now their Navy ploughs the Wat'ry Main,
      Yet, soon expect it on your Shoars again,
      With *Pallas* pleas'd; as *Calchas* did ordain.
      But first, to reconcile the blue-ey'd Maid,
      For her stoln Statue, and her Tow'r betray'd;
245   Warn'd by the Seer, to her offended Name
      We rais'd, and dedicate this wond'rous Frame:
      So lofty, lest through your forbidden Gates
      It pass, and intercept our better Fates.
      For, once admitted there, our hopes are lost;
250   And *Troy* may then a new *Palladium* boast.
      For so Religion and the Gods ordain;
      That if you violate with Hands prophane
      Minerva's Gift, your Town in Flames shall burn,
      (Which Omen, O ye Gods, on *Grecia* turn!)
255   But if it climb, with your assisting Hands,
      The *Trojan* Walls, and in the City stands;
      Then *Troy* shall *Argos* and *Mycenæ* burn,
      And the reverse of Fate on us return.
        With such Deceits he gain'd their easie Hearts,
260   Too prone to credit his perfidious Arts.
      What *Diomede*, nor *Thetis* greater Son,
      A thousand Ships, nor ten years Siege had done:
      False Tears and fawning Words the City won.
      A greater Omen, and of worse portent,
265   Did our unwary Minds with fear torment:
      Concurring to produce the dire Event.
      Laocoon, *Neptune*'s Priest by Lot that Year,
      With solemn Pomp then sacrific'd a Steer.

When, dreadful to behold, from Sea we spy'd ⎫
270   Two Serpents rank'd abreast, the Seas divide, ⎬
And smoothly sweep along the swelling Tide. ⎭
Their flaming Crests above the Waves they show,
Their Bellies seem to burn the Seas below:
Their speckled Tails advance to steer their Course,
275   And on the sounding Shoar the flying Billows force.
And now the Strand, and now the Plain they held,
Their ardent Eyes with bloody streaks were fill'd:
Their nimble Tongues they brandish'd as they came,
And lick'd their hissing Jaws, that sputter'd Flame.
280   We fled amaz'd; their destin'd way they take,
And to *Laocoon* and his Children make:
And first around the tender Boys they wind,
Then with their sharpen'd Fangs their Limbs and Bodies
        grind.
The wretched Father, running to their Aid
285   With pious Haste, but vain, they next invade:
Twice round his Waste their winding Volumes rowl'd,
And twice about his gasping Throat they fold.
The Priest, thus doubly choak'd, their Crests divide,
And tow'ring o're his Head, in Triumph ride.
290   With both his Hands he labours at the Knots,
His Holy Fillets the blue Venom blots:
His roaring fills the flitting Air around.
Thus, when an Oxe receives a glancing Wound,
He breaks his Bands, the fatal Altar flies,
295   And with loud Bellowings breaks the yielding Skies.
Their Tasks perform'd, the Serpents quit their prey,
And to the Tow'r of *Pallas* make their way:
Couch'd at her Feet, they lie protected there,
By her large Buckler, and protended Spear.
300   Amazement seizes all; the gen'ral Cry
Proclaims *Laocoon* justly doom'd to die.
Whose hand the Will of *Pallas* had withstood,
And dar'd to violate the Sacred Wood.
All Vote t' admit the Steed, that Vows be paid,
305   And Incense offer'd to th' offended Maid.
A spacious Breach is made, the Town lies bare,
Some hoisting Leavers, some the Wheels prepare,

And fasten to the Horses Feet: the rest
With Cables haul along th' unweildy Beast.
310 Each on his Fellow for Assistance calls:
At length the fatal Fabrick mounts the Walls,
Big with Destruction. Boys with Chaplets crown'd,
And Quires of Virgins sing, and dance around.
Thus rais'd aloft, and then descending down,
315 It enters o're our Heads, and threats the Town.
O sacred City! built by Hands Divine!
O valiant Heroes of the *Trojan* Line!
Four times he struck; as oft the clashing sound
Of Arms was heard, and inward Groans rebound.
320 Yet mad with Zeal, and blinded with our Fate,
We hawl along the Horse, in solemn state;
Then place the dire Portent within the Tow'r.
Cassandra cry'd, and curs'd th' unhappy Hour;
Foretold our Fate; but by the Gods decree
325 All heard, and none believ'd the Prophecy.
With Branches we the Fanes adorn, and wast
In jollity, the day ordain'd to be the last.
Mean time the rapid Heav'ns rowl'd down the Light,
And on the shaded Ocean rush'd the Night:
330 Our Men secure, nor Guards nor Centries held,
But easie Sleep their weary Limbs compell'd.
The *Grecians* had embark'd their Naval Pow'rs
From *Tenedos*, and sought our well known Shoars:
Safe under Covert of the silent Night,
335 And guided by th' Imperial Galley's light.
When *Sinon*, favour'd by the Partial Gods,
Unlock'd the Horse, and op'd his dark abodes:
Restor'd to vital Air our hidden Foes,
Who joyful from their long Confinement rose.
340 *Tysander* bold, and *Sthenelus* their Guide,
And dire *Ulysses* down the Cable slide:
Then *Thoas*, *Athamas*, and *Pyrrhus* hast;
Nor was the *Podalyrian* Heroe last:
Nor injur'd *Menelaus*, nor the fam'd
345 *Epeus*, who the fatal Engine fram'd.
A nameless Crowd succeed; their Forces join
T' invade the Town, oppress'd with Sleep and Wine.

Those few they find awake, first meet their Fate,
Then to their Fellows they unbar the Gate.
350   'Twas in the dead of Night, when Sleep repairs
Our Bodies worn with Toils, our Minds with Cares,
When *Hector*'s Ghost before my sight appears:
A bloody Shrowd he seem'd, and bath'd in Tears.
Such as he was, when, by *Pelides* slain,
355   *Thessalian* Coursers drag'd him o're the Plain.
Swoln were his Feet, as when the Thongs were thrust
Through the bor'd holes, his Body black with dust.
Unlike that *Hector*, who return'd from toils
Of War Triumphant, in *Æacian* Spoils:
360   Or him; who made the fainting *Greeks* retire,
And lanch'd against their Navy *Phrygian* Fire.
His Hair and Beard stood stiffen'd with his gore;
And all the Wounds he for his Country bore,
Now stream'd afresh, and with new Purple ran: ⎤
365   I wept to see the visionary Man: ⎬
And while my Trance continu'd, thus began.   ⎦
O Light of *Trojans*, and Support of *Troy*,
Thy Father's Champion, and thy Country's Joy!
O, long expected by thy Friends! from whence
370   Art thou so late return'd for our Defence?
Do we behold thee; weary'd as we are,
With length of Labours, and with Toils of War?
After so many Fun'rals of thy own,
Art thou restor'd to thy declining Town?
375   But say, what Wounds are these? What new Disgrace
Deforms the Manly Features of thy Face?
To this the Spectre no Reply did frame;
But answer'd to the Cause for which he came:
And, groaning from the bottom of his Breast,
380   This Warning, in these mournful Words express'd.
O Goddess-born! escape, by timely flight,
The Flames, and Horrors of this fatal Night.
The Foes already have possess'd the Wall,
Troy nods from high, and totters to her fall.
385   Enough is paid to *Priam*'s Royal Name,
More than enough to Duty and to Fame.

If by a Mortal Hand my Father's Throne
Cou'd be defended, 'twas by mine alone:
Now *Troy* to thee commends her future State,
390   And gives her Gods Companions of thy Fate:
From their assistance happier Walls expect,
Which, wand'ring long, at last thou shalt erect.
He said, and brought me, from their blest abodes,
The venerable Statues of the Gods:
395   With ancient *Vesta* from the sacred Quire,
The Wreaths and Relicks of th' Immortal Fire.

    Now peals of Shouts come thund'ring from afar,
Cries, Threats, and loud Laments, and mingl'd War:
The Noise approaches, though our Palace stood
400   Aloof from Streets, encompass'd with a Wood.
Louder, and yet more loud, I hear th' Allarms
Of Human Cries distinct, and clashing Arms:
Fear broke my Slumbers; I no longer stay,
But mount the Terrass, thence the Town survey,
405   And hearken what the frightful Sounds convey.
Thus when a flood of Fire by Wind is born,
Crackling it rowls, and mows the standing Corn:
Or Deluges, descending on the Plains,
Sweep o're the yellow Year, destroy the pains
410   Of lab'ring Oxen, and the Peasant's gains:
Unroot the Forrest Oaks, and bear away
Flocks, Folds, and Trees, an undistinguish'd Prey.
The Shepherd climbs the Cliff, and sees from far,
The wastful Ravage of the wat'ry War.
415   Then *Hector*'s Faith was manifestly clear'd;
And *Grecian* Frauds in open light appear'd.
The Palace of *Deiphobus* ascends
In smoaky Flames, and catches on his Friends.
Ucalegon burns next; the Seas are bright
420   With splendor, not their own; and shine with *Trojan* light.
New Clamours, and new Clangors now arise,
The sound of Trumpets mix'd with fighting cries.
With frenzy seiz'd, I run to meet th' Alarms,
Resolv'd on death, resolv'd to die in Arms.
425   But first to gather Friends, with them t' oppose,
If Fortune favour'd, and repell the Foes.

Spurr'd by my Courage, by my Country fir'd,
With sense of Honour, and Revenge inspir'd.
   Pantheus, Apollo's Priest, a sacred Name,
430   Had scap'd the *Grecian* Swords, and pass'd the Flame;
With Reliques loaden, to my Doors he fled,
And by the hand his tender Grand-son led.
What hope, O *Pantheus*! whither can we run?
Where make a stand? and what may yet be done?
435   Scarce had I said, when *Pantheus*, with a groan,
Troy is no more, and *Ilium* was a Town!
The fatal Day, th' appointed Hour is come,
When wrathful *Jove*'s irrevocable Doom
Transfers the *Trojan* State to *Grecian* Hands.
440   The Fire consumes the Town, the Foe commands:
And armed Hosts, an unexpected Force,
Break from the Bowels of the Fatal Horse.
Within the Gates, proud *Sinon* throws about
The Flames, and Foes for entrance press without,
445   With thousand others, whom I fear to name,
More than from *Argos*, or *Mycenæ* came.
To sev'ral Posts their Parties they divide;
Some block the narrow Streets, some scour the wide.
The bold they kill, th' unwary they surprise;
450   Who fights finds Death, and Death finds him who flies.
The Warders of the Gate but scarce maintain
Th' unequal Combat, and resist in vain.
I heard; and Heav'n, that well born Souls inspires,
Prompts me, thro' lifted Swords, and rising Fires
455   To run, where clashing Arms and Clamour calls,
And rush undaunted to defend the Walls.
Ripheus and *Iph'tus* by my side engage,
For Valour one Renown'd, and one for Age.
Dymas and *Hypanis* by Moonlight knew
460   My Motions, and my Meen, and to my Party drew;
With young *Choræbus*, who by Love was led
To win Renown, and fair *Cassandra*'s Bed;
And lately brought his Troops to *Priam*'s aid:
Forewarn'd in vain, by the Prophetic Maid.
465   Whom, when I saw, resolv'd in Arms to fall,
And that one Spirit animated all;

Brave Souls, said I, but Brave, alas! in vain:
Come, finish what our Cruel Fates ordain.
You see the desp'rate state of our Affairs;
470   And Heav'ns protecting Pow'rs are deaf to Pray'rs.
The passive Gods behold the *Greeks* defile
Their Temples, and abandon to the Spoil
Their own Abodes: we, feeble few, conspire
To save a sinking Town, involv'd in Fire.
475   Then let us fall, but fall amidst our Foes,
Despair of Life, the Means of living shows.
So bold a Speech incourag'd their desire
Of Death, and added fuel to their Fire.
      As hungry Wolves, with raging appetite,
480   Scour thro' the Fields, nor fear the Stormy Night;
Their Whelps at home expect the promis'd Food,
And long to temper their dry Chaps in Blood:
So rush'd we forth at once, resolv'd to die,
Resolv'd in Death the last Extreams to try.
485   We leave the narrow Lanes behind, and dare ⎫
Th' unequal Combat in the publick Square: ⎬
Night was our Friend, our Leader was Despair. ⎭
What Tongue can tell the Slaughter of that Night?
What Eyes can weep the Sorrows and Affright!
490   An ancient and imperial City falls,
The Streets are fill'd with frequent Funerals:
Houses and Holy Temples float in Blood,
And hostile Nations make a common Flood.
Not only *Trojans* fall, but in their turn,
495   The vanquish'd Triumph, and the Victors mourn.
Ours take new Courage from Despair and Night;
Confus'd the Fortune is, confus'd the Fight.
All parts resound with Tumults, Plaints, and Fears,
And grisly Death in sundry shapes appears.
500   *Androgeos* fell among us, with his Band,
Who thought us *Grecians* newly come to Land:
From whence, said he, my Friends this long delay?
You loiter, while the Spoils are born away:
Our Ships are laden with the *Trojan* Store,
505   And you like Truants come too late ashore.

He said, but soon corrected his Mistake,
Found, by the doubtful Answers which we make:
Amaz'd, he wou'd have shun'd th' unequal Fight,
But we, more num'rous, intercept his flight.
510   As when some Peasant in a bushy Brake,
Has with unwary Footing press'd a Snake;
He starts aside, astonish'd, when he spies ⎫
His rising Crest, blue Neck, and rowling Eyes; ⎬
So from our Arms, surpriz'd *Androgeos* flies. ⎭
515   In vain; for him and his we compass'd round, ⎫
Possess'd with Fear, unknowing of the Ground; ⎬
And of their Lives an easie Conquest found. ⎭
Thus Fortune on our first Endeavour smil'd:
Chorœbus then, with youthful Hopes beguil'd,
520   Swoln with Success, and of a daring Mind,
This new Invention fatally design'd.
My Friends, said he, since Fortune shows the way,
'Tis fit we shou'd th' auspicious Guide obey.
For what has she these *Grecian* Arms bestow'd,
525   But their Destruction, and the *Trojans* good?
Then change we Shields, and their Devices bear,
Let Fraud supply the want of Force in War.
They find us Arms. This said, himself he dress'd ⎫
In dead *Androgeos*'s Spoils, his upper Vest, ⎬
530   His painted Buckler, and his plumy Crest. ⎭
Thus *Ripheus*, *Dymas*, all the *Trojan* Train
Lay down their own Attire, and strip the slain.
Mix'd with the *Greeks*, we go with ill Presage,
Flatter'd with hopes to glut our greedy Rage:
535   Unknown, assaulting whom we blindly meet,
And strew, with *Grecian* Carcasses, the Street.
Thus while their stragling Parties we defeat,
Some to the Shoar and safer Ships retreat:
And some oppress'd with more ignoble Fear,
540   Remount the hollow Horse, and pant in secret there.
    But ah! what use of Valour can be made,
When Heav'ns propitious Pow'rs refuse their Aid!
Behold the royal Prophetess, the Fair
Cassandra, drag'd by her dishevel'd Hair;

545 Whom not *Minerva*'s Shrine, nor sacred Bands,
In safety cou'd protect from sacrilegious Hands:
On Heav'n she cast her Eyes, she sigh'd, she cry'd,
('Twas all she cou'd) her tender Arms were ty'd.
So sad a Sight *Choræbus* cou'd not bear,
550 But fir'd with Rage, distracted with Despair;
Amid the barb'rous Ravishers he flew:
Our Leader's rash Example we pursue.
But storms of Stones, from the proud Temple's height,
Pour down, and on our batter'd Helms alight:
555 We from our Friends receiv'd this fatal Blow,
Who thought us *Grecians*, as we seem'd in show.
They aim at the mistaken Crests, from high,
And ours beneath the pond'rous Ruin lie.
Then, mov'd with Anger and Disdain, to see
560 Their Troops dispers'd, the Royal Virgin free:
The *Grecians* rally, and their Pow'rs unite;
With Fury charge us, and renew the Fight.
The Brother-Kings with *Ajax* join their force,
And the whole Squadron of *Thessalian* Horse.
565   Thus, when the Rival Winds their Quarrel try,
Contending for the Kingdom of the Skie;
South, East, and West, on airy Coursers born,
The Whirlwind gathers, and the Woods are torn:
Then *Nereus* strikes the deep, the Billows rise,
570 And, mix'd with Ooze and Sand, pollute the Skies.
The Troops we squander'd first, again appear
From sev'ral Quarters, and enclose the Rear.
They first observe, and to the rest betray
Our diff'rent Speech; our borrow'd Arms survey.
575 Oppress'd with odds, we fall; *Choræbus* first,
At *Pallas*'s Altar, by *Peneleus* pierc'd.
Then *Ripheus* follow'd, in th' unequal Fight;
Just of his Word, observant of the right;
Heav'n thought not so: *Dymas* their Fate attends,
580 With *Hypanis*, mistaken by their Friends.
Nor *Pantheus*, thee, thy Mitre nor the Bands
Of awful *Phœbus*, sav'd from impious Hands.
Ye *Trojan* Flames your Testimony bear,
What I perform'd, and what I suffer'd there:

585   No Sword avoiding in the fatal Strife,
      Expos'd to Death, and prodigal of Life.
      Witness, ye Heav'ns! I live not by my Fault,
      I strove to have deserv'd the Death I sought.
      But when I cou'd not fight, and wou'd have dy'd,
590   Born off to distance by the growing Tide,
      Old *Iphitus* and I were hurry'd thence,
      With *Pelias* wounded, and without Defence.
      New Clamors from th' invested Palace ring;
      We run to die, or disengage the King.
595   So hot th' Assault, so high the Tumult rose,
      While ours defend, and while the *Greeks* oppose;
      As all the *Dardan* and *Argolick* Race
      Had been contracted in that narrow Space:
      Or as all *Ilium* else were void of Fear,
600   And Tumult, War, and Slaughter only there.
      Their Targets in a Tortoise cast, the Foes
      Secure advancing, to the Turrets rose:
      Some mount the scaling Ladders, some more bold
      Swerve upwards, and by Posts and Pillars hold:
605   Their left hand gripes their Bucklers, in th' ascent,
      While with the right they seise the Battlement.
      From their demolish'd Tow'rs the *Trojans* throw
      Huge heaps of Stones, that falling, crush the Foe:
      And heavy Beams, and Rafters from the sides,
610   (Such Arms their last necessity provides:)
      And gilded Roofs come tumbling from on high,
      The marks of State, and ancient Royalty.
      The Guards below, fix'd in the Pass, attend
      The Charge undaunted, and the Gate defend.
615   Renew'd in Courage with recover'd Breath,
      A second time we ran to tempt our Death:
      To clear the Palace from the Foe, succeed
      The weary living, and revenge the dead.
      A Postern-door, yet unobserv'd and free,
620   Join'd by the length of a blind Gallery,
      To the King's Closet led; a way well known
      To *Hector*'s Wife, while *Priam* held the Throne:
      Through which she brought *Astyanax*, unseen,
      To chear his Grandsire, and his Grandsire's Queen.

625 Through this we pass, and mount the Tow'r, from whence
With unavailing Arms the *Trojans* make defence.
From this the trembling King had oft descry'd
The *Grecian* Camp, and saw their Navy ride.
Beams from its lofty height with Swords we hew;
630 Then wrenching with our hands, th' Assault renew.
And where the Rafters on the Columns meet,
We push them headlong with our Arms and Feet:
The Lightning flies not swifter than the Fall;
Nor Thunder louder than the ruin'd Wall:
635 Down goes the top at once; the *Greeks* beneath
Are piecemeal torn, or pounded into Death.
Yet more succeed, and more to death are sent;
We cease not from above, nor they below relent.
Before the Gate stood *Pyrrhus*, threat'ning loud,
640 With glitt'ring Arms conspicuous in the Crowd.
So shines, renew'd in Youth, the crested Snake,
Who slept the Winter in a thorny Brake:
And casting off his Slough, when Spring returns,
Now looks aloft, and with new Glory burns:
645 Restor'd with pois'nous Herbs, his ardent sides
Reflect the Sun, and rais'd on Spires he rides:
High o're the Grass, hissing he rowls along,
And brandishes by fits his forky Tongue.
Proud *Periphas*, and fierce *Automedon*,
650 His Father's Charioteer, together run
To force the Gate: The *Scyrian* Infantry
Rush on in Crowds, and the barr'd Passage free.
Ent'ring the Court, with Shouts the Skies they rend,
And flaming Firebrands to the Roofs ascend.
655 Himself, among the foremost, deals his Blows,
And with his Axe repeated Stroaks bestows
On the strong Doors: then all their Shoulders ply,
'Till from the Posts the brazen Hinges fly.
He hews apace, the double Bars at length
660 Yield to his Ax, and unresisted Strength.
A mighty Breach is made; the Rooms conceal'd
Appear, and all the Palace is reveal'd.
The Halls of Audience, and of publick State,
And where the lonely Queen in secret sate.

665   Arm'd Souldiers now by trembling Maids are seen,
       With not a Door, and scarce a Space between.
       The House is fill'd with loud Laments and Cries,
       And Shrieks of Women rend the vaulted skies.
       The fearful Matrons run from place to place,
670   And kiss the Thresholds, and the Posts embrace.
       The fatal work inhuman *Pyrrhus* plies,
       And all his Father sparkles in his Eyes.
       Nor Bars, nor fighting Guards his force sustain;
       The Bars are broken, and the Guards are slain:
675   In rush the *Greeks*, and all the Apartments fill;
       Those few Defendants whom they find, they kill.
       Not with so fierce a Rage, the foaming Flood
       Roars, when he finds his rapid Course withstood:
       Bears down the Dams with unresisted sway,
680   And sweeps the Cattle and the Cots away.
       These Eyes beheld him, when he march'd between
       The Brother-Kings: I saw th' unhappy Queen,
       The hundred Wives, and where old *Priam* stood,
       To stain his hallow'd Altar with his Blood.
685   The fifty Nuptial Beds: (such Hopes had he,
       So large a Promise of a Progeny.)
       The Posts of plated Gold, and hung with Spoils,
       Fell the Reward of the proud Victor's Toils.
       Where e're the raging Fire had left a space,
690   The *Grecians* enter, and possess the Place.
       Perhaps you may of *Priam*'s Fate enquire.
       He, when he saw his Regal Town on fire,
       His ruin'd Palace, and his ent'ring Foes,
       On ev'ry side inevitable woes;
695   In Arms, disus'd, invests his Limbs decay'd
       Like them, with Age; a late and useless aid.
       His feeble shoulders scarce the weight sustain: ⎫
       Loaded, not arm'd, he creeps along, with pain; ⎬
       Despairing of Success; ambitious to be slain! ⎭
700   Uncover'd but by Heav'n, there stood in view
       An Altar; near the hearth a Lawrel grew;
       Dodder'd with Age, whose Boughs encompass round
       The Household Gods, and shade the holy Ground.

Here *Hecuba*, with all her helpless Train
705 Of Dames, for shelter sought, but sought in vain.
Driv'n like a Flock of Doves along the skie,
Their Images they hugg, and to their Altars fly.
The Queen, when she beheld her trembling Lord,
And hanging by his side a heavy Sword,
710 What Rage, she cry'd, has seiz'd my Husband's mind;
What Arms are these, and to what use design'd?
These times want other aids: were *Hector* here,
Ev'n *Hector* now in vain, like *Priam* wou'd appear.
With us, one common shelter thou shalt find,
715 Or in one common Fate with us be join'd.
She said, and with a last Salute embrac'd
The poor old Man, and by the Lawrel plac'd.
Behold *Polites*, one of *Priam*'s Sons,
Pursu'd by *Pyrrhus*, there for safety runs.
720 Thro Swords, and Foes, amaz'd and hurt, he flies
Through empty Courts, and open Galleries:
Him *Pyrrhus*, urging with his Lance, pursues;
And often reaches, and his thrusts renews.
The Youth transfix'd, with lamentable Cries
725 Expires, before his wretched Parent's Eyes.
Whom, gasping at his feet, when *Priam* saw,
The Fear of Death gave place to Nature's Law.
And shaking more with Anger, than with Age,
The Gods, said He, requite thy brutal Rage:
730 As sure they will, Barbarian, sure they must,
If there be Gods in Heav'n, and Gods be just:
Who tak'st in Wrongs an insolent delight;
With a Son's death t' infect a Father's sight.
Not He, whom thou and lying Fame conspire
735 To call thee his; Nor He, thy vaunted Sire,
Thus us'd my wretched Age: The Gods he fear'd,
The Laws of Nature and of Nations heard.
He chear'd my Sorrows, and for Sums of Gold
The bloodless Carcass of my *Hector* sold.
740 Pity'd the Woes a Parent underwent,
And sent me back in safety from his Tent.
     This said, his feeble hand a Javelin threw,
Which flutt'ring, seem'd to loiter as it flew:

Just, and but barely, to the Mark it held,
745   And faintly tinckl'd on the Brazen Shield.
        Then *Pyrrhus* thus: Go thou from me to Fate;
      And to my Father my foul deeds relate.
      Now dye: with that he dragg'd the trembling Sire,
      Slidd'ring through clotter'd Blood, and holy Mire,
750   (The mingl'd Paste his murder'd Son had made,) ⎫
      Haul'd from beneath the violated Shade;   ⎬
      And on the Sacred Pile, the Royal Victim laid. ⎭
      His right Hand held his bloody Fauchion bare:
      His left he twisted in his hoary Hair:
755   Then, with a speeding Thrust, his Heart he found: ⎫
      The lukewarm Blood came rushing through the Wound, ⎬
      And sanguine Streams distain'd the sacred Ground. ⎭
      Thus *Priam* fell: and shar'd one common Fate
      With *Troy* in Ashes, and his ruin'd State:
760   He, who the Scepter of all *Asia* sway'd,
      Whom Monarchs like Domestick Slaves obey'd,
      On the bleak Shoar now lies th' abandon'd King,
      *A headless Carcass, and a nameless thing.
        Then, not before, I felt my crudled Blood
765   Congeal with Fear; my Hair with horror stood:
      My Father's Image fill'd my pious Mind;
      Lest equal Years might equal Fortune find.
      Again I thought on my forsaken Wife;
      And trembl'd for my Son's abandon'd Life.
770   I look'd about; but found my self alone:
      Deserted at my need, my Friends were gone.
      Some spent with Toil, some with Despair oppress'd,
      Leap'd headlong from the Heights; the Flames consum'd
            the rest.
      Thus, wand'ring in my way, without a Guide,
775   The graceless *Helen* in the Porch I spy'd
      Of *Vesta*'s Temple: there she lurk'd alone;
      Muffled she sate, and what she cou'd, unknown:
      But, by the Flames, that cast their Blaze around,
      That common Bane of *Greece* and *Troy*, I found.

* *This whole line is taken from Sir John Denham.*

780 For *Ilium* burnt, she dreads the *Trojan* Sword; ⎤
      More dreads the Vengeance of her injur'd Lord; ⎬
      Ev'n by those Gods, who refug'd her, abhorr'd. ⎦
      Trembling with Rage, the Strumpet I regard;
      Resolv'd to give her Guilt the due reward.

785 Shall she triumphant sail before the Wind,
      And leave in Flames, unhappy *Troy* behind?
      Shall she, her Kingdom and her Friends review,
      In State attended with a Captive Crew;
      While unreveng'd the good old *Priam* falls,

790 And *Grecian* Fires consume the *Trojan* Walls?
      For this the *Phrygian* Fields, and *Xanthian* Flood
      Were swell'd with Bodies, and were drunk with Blood?
      'Tis true a Souldier can small Honour gain:
      And boast no Conquest from a Woman slain:

795 Yet shall the Fact not pass without Applause,
      Of Vengeance taken in so just a Cause.
      The punish'd Crime shall set my Soul at ease:
      And murm'ring Manes of my Friends appease.
      Thus while I rave, a gleam of pleasing Light ⎤

800 Spread o're the Place, and shining Heav'nly bright, ⎬
      My Mother stood reveal'd before my Sight. ⎦
      Never so radiant did her Eyes appear;
      Not her own Star confess'd a light so clear.
      Great in her Charms, as when on Gods above

805 She looks, and breaths her self into their Love.
      She held my Hand, the destin'd Blow to break:
      Then from her rosie Lips began to speak.
      My Son, from whence this Madness, this neglect
      Of my Commands, and those whom I protect?

810 Why this unmanly Rage? Recall to mind
      Whom you forsake, what Pledges leave behind.
      Look if your helpless Father yet survive;
      Or if *Ascanius*, or *Creusa* live.
      Around your House the greedy *Grecians* err; ⎤

815 And these had perish'd in the nightly War, ⎬
      But for my Presence and protecting Care. ⎦
      Not *Helen*'s Face, nor *Paris* was in fault;
      But by the Gods was this Destruction brought.

Now cast your Eyes around; while I dissolve
820 The Mists and Films that Mortal Eyes involve:
Purge from your sight the Dross, and make you see
The Shape of each avenging Deity.
Enlightn'd thus, my just Commands fulfill;
Nor fear Obedience to your Mother's Will.
825 Where yon disorder'd heap of Ruin lies,
Stones rent from Stones, where Clouds of Dust arise,
Amid that smother, *Neptune* holds his place:
Below the Wall's foundation drives his Mace:
And heaves the Building from the solid Base.
830 Look where, in Arms, Imperial *Juno* stands,
Full in the *Scæan* Gate, with loud Commands;
Urging on Shore the tardy *Grecian* Bands.
See *Pallas*, of her snaky Buckler proud,
Bestrides the Tow'r, refulgent through the Cloud:
835 See *Jove* new Courage to the Foe supplies,
And Arms against the Town, the partial Deities.
Haste hence, my Son; this fruitless Labour end:
Haste where your trembling Spouse, and Sire attend:
Haste, and a Mother's Care your Passage shall befriend.
840 She said: and swiftly vanish'd from my Sight,
Obscure in Clouds, and gloomy Shades of Night.
I look'd, I listen'd; dreadful Sounds I hear;
And the dire Forms of hostile Gods appear.
Troy sunk in Flames I saw, nor could prevent;
845 And *Ilium* from its old Foundations rent.
Rent like a Mountain Ash, which dar'd the Winds;
And stood the sturdy Stroaks of lab'ring Hinds:
About the Roots the cruel Ax resounds,
The Stumps are pierc'd, with oft repeated Wounds.
850 The War is felt on high, the nodding Crown
Now threats a Fall, and throws the leafy Honours down.
To their united Force it yields, though late;
And mourns with mortal Groans th' approaching Fate:
The Roots no more their upper load sustain;
855 But down she falls, and spreads a ruin thro' the Plain.
  Descending thence, I scape through Foes, and Fire:
Before the Goddess, Foes and Flames retire.

Arriv'd at home, he for whose only sake,
Or most for his, such Toils I undertake,
860   The good *Anchises*, whom, by timely Flight,
I purpos'd to secure on *Ida*'s height,
Refus'd the Journey: Resolute to die,
And add his Fun'rals to the fate of *Troy*:
Rather than Exile and old Age sustain.
865   Go you, whose Blood runs warm in ev'ry Vein:
Had Heav'n decreed that I shou'd Life enjoy,
Heav'n had decreed to save unhappy *Troy*.
'Tis sure enough, if not too much for one;
Twice to have seen our *Ilium* overthrown.
870   Make haste to save the poor remaining Crew;
And give this useless Corps a long Adieu.
These weak old Hands suffice to stop my Breath:
At least the pitying Foes will aid my Death,
To take my Spoils: and leave my Body bare:
875   As for my Sepulchre let Heav'n take Care.
'Tis long since I, for my Cœlestial Wife,
Loath'd by the Gods, have drag'd a lingring Life:
Since ev'ry Hour and Moment I expire,
Blasted from Heav'n by *Jove*'s avenging Fire.
880   This oft repeated, he stood fix'd to die:
My self, my Wife, my Son, my Family,   }
Intreat, pray, beg, and raise a doleful Cry. }
What, will he still persist, on Death resolve,
And in his Ruin all his House involve!
885   He still persists, his Reasons to maintain;
Our Pray'rs, our Tears, our loud Laments are vain.
      Urg'd by Despair, again I go to try
The fate of Arms, resolv'd in Fight to die.
What hope remains, but what my Death must give?
890   Can I without so dear a Father live?
You term it Prudence, what I Baseness call:
Cou'd such a Word from such a Parent fall?
If Fortune please, and so the Gods ordain,   }
That nothing shou'd of ruin'd *Troy* remain: }
895   And you conspire with Fortune, to be slain; }
The way to Death is wide, th' Approaches near:
For soon relentless *Pyrrhus* will appear,

Reeking with *Priam*'s Blood: The wretch who slew ⎫
The Son (inhuman) in the Father's view, ⎪
900   And then the Sire himself, to the dire Altar drew. ⎭

    O Goddess Mother, give me back to fate;
Your Gift was undesir'd, and came too late.
Did you for this, unhappy me convey
Through Foes and Fires to see my House a Prey?
905   Shall I, my Father, Wife, and Son, behold
Welt'ring in Blood, each others Arms infold?
Haste, gird my Sword, tho' spent, and overcome:
'Tis the last Summons to receive our Doom.
I hear thee, Fate, and I obey thy Call:
910   Not unreveng'd the Foe shall see my Fall.
Restore me to the yet unfinish'd Fight:
My Death is wanting to conclude the Night.
Arm'd once again, my glitt'ring Sword I wield, ⎫
While th' other hand sustains my weighty Shield: ⎬
915   And forth I rush to seek th' abandon'd Field. ⎭
I went; but sad *Creusa* stop'd my way,
And cross the Threshold in my Passage lay;
Embrac'd my Knees; and when I wou'd have gone
Shew'd me my feeble Sire, and tender Son.
920   If Death be your design, at least, said she,
Take us along, to share your Destiny.
If any farther hopes in Arms remain,
This Place, these Pledges of your Love, maintain.
To whom do you expose your Father's Life,
925   Your Son's, and mine, your now forgotten Wife!
While thus she fills the House with clam'rous Cries,
Our Hearing is diverted by our Eyes.
For while I held my Son, in the short space,
Betwixt our Kisses and our last Embrace;
930   Strange to relate, from young *Julus* Head ⎫
A lambent Flame arose, which gently spread ⎬
Around his Brows, and on his Temples fed. ⎭
Amaz'd, with running Water we prepare
To quench the sacred Fire, and shake his Hair;
935   But old *Anchises*, vers'd in Omens, rear'd
His Hands to Heav'n, and this Request preferr'd.

If any Vows, Almighty *Jove*, can bend
Thy Will, if Piety can Pray'rs commend,
Confirm the glad Presage which thou art pleas'd to send.

940   Scarce had he said, when, on our left, we hear
A peal of ratling Thunder rowl in Air:
There shot a streaming Lamp along the Sky,
Which on the winged Lightning seem'd to fly;
From o're the Roof the blaze began to move;

945   And trailing vanish'd in th' *Idean* Grove.
It swept a path in Heav'n, and shone a Guide;
Then in a steaming stench of Sulphur dy'd.
    The good old Man with suppliant Hands implor'd
The Gods protection, and their Star ador'd.

950   Now, now, said he, my Son, no more delay,
I yield, I follow where Heav'n shews the way.
Keep (O my Country Gods) our dwelling Place,
And guard this Relick of the *Trojan* Race:
This tender Child; these Omens are your own;

955   And you can yet restore the ruin'd Town.
At least accomplish what your Signs foreshow:
I stand resign'd, and am prepar'd to go.
    He said; the crackling Flames appear on high,
And driving Sparkles dance along the Sky.

960   With *Vulcan*'s rage the rising Winds conspire;
And near our Palace rowl the flood of Fire.
Haste, my dear Father, ('tis no time to wait,)
And load my Shoulders with a willing Fraight.
What e're befalls, your Life shall be my care,

965   One Death, or one Deliv'rance we will share.
My Hand shall lead our little Son; and you
My faithful Consort, shall our Steps pursue.
Next, you my Servants, heed my strict Commands:
Without the Walls a ruin'd Temple stands;

970   To *Ceres* hallow'd once; a Cypress nigh
Shoots up her venerable Head on high;
By long Religion kept: there bend your Feet;
And in divided Parties let us meet.
Our Country Gods, the Relicks, and the Bands,

975   Hold you, my Father, in your guiltless Hands:

In me 'tis impious holy things to bear,
Red as I am with Slaughter, new from War:
'Till in some living Stream I cleanse the Guilt
Of dire Debate, and Blood in Battel spilt.
980 Thus, ord'ring all that Prudence cou'd provide,
I cloath my Shoulders with a Lion's Hide;
And yellow Spoils: Then, on my bending Back,
The welcome load of my dear Father take.
While on my better Hand *Ascanius* hung,
985 And with unequal Paces tript along.
Creusa kept behind: by choice we stray
Through ev'ry dark and ev'ry devious Way.
I, who so bold and dauntless just before,
The *Grecian* Darts and shock of Lances bore,
990 At ev'ry Shadow now am seiz'd with Fear:
Not for my self, but for the Charge I bear,
Till near the ruin'd Gate arriv'd at last,
Secure, and deeming all the Danger past;
A frightful noise of trampling Feet we hear;
995 My Father looking through the Shades, with fear,
Cry'd out, haste, haste my Son, the Foes are nigh;
Their Swords, and shining Armour I descry.
Some hostile God, for some unknown Offence,
Had sure bereft my Mind of better Sence:
1000 For while through winding Ways I took my Flight;
And sought the shelter of the gloomy Night;
Alas! I lost *Creusa*: hard to tell
If by her fatal Destiny she fell,
Or weary sate, or wander'd with affright;
1005 But she was lost for ever to my sight.
I knew not, or reflected, 'till I meet
My Friends, at *Ceres* now deserted Seat:
We met: not one was wanting, only she
Deceiv'd her Friends, her Son, and wretched me.
1010 What mad expressions did my Tongue refuse!
Whom did I not of Gods or Men accuse!
This was the fatal Blow, that pain'd me more
Than all I felt from ruin'd *Troy* before.
Stung with my Loss, and raving with Despair,
1015 Abandoning my now forgotten Care,

Of Counsel, Comfort, and of Hope bereft,
My Sire, my Son, my Country Gods, I left.
In shining Armour once again I sheath
My Limbs, not feeling Wounds, nor fearing Death.
1020 Then headlong to the burning Walls I run,
And seek the Danger I was forc'd to shun.
I tread my former Tracks: through Night explore
Each Passage, ev'ry Street I cross'd before.
All things were full of Horrour and Affright,
1025 And dreadful ev'n the silence of the Night.
Then, to my Father's House I make repair,
With some small Glimps of hope to find her there:
Instead of her the cruel *Greeks* I met;
The house was fill'd with Foes, with Flames beset.
1030 Driv'n on the wings of Winds, whole sheets of Fire,
Through Air transported, to the Roofs aspire.
From thence to *Priam*'s Palace I resort;
And search the Citadel, and desart Court.
Then, unobserv'd, I pass by *Juno*'s Church;
1035 A guard of *Grecians* had possess'd the Porch:
There *Phœnix* and *Ulysses* watch the Prey:
And thither all the Wealth of *Troy* convey.
The Spoils which they from ransack'd Houses brought;
And golden Bowls from burning Altars caught.
1040 The Tables of the Gods, the Purple Vests;
The People's Treasure, and the Pomp of Priests.
A ranck of wretched Youths, with pinion'd Hands,
And captive Matrons in long Order stands.
Then, with ungovern'd Madness, I proclaim,
1045 Through all the silent Streets, *Creusa*'s Name.
Creusa still I call: At length she hears;
And suddain, through the Shades of Night appears:
Appears, no more *Creusa*, nor my Wife:
But a pale Spectre, larger than the Life.
1050 Aghast, astonish'd, and struck dumb with Fear,
I stood; like Bristles rose my stiffen'd Hair.
Then thus the Ghost began to sooth my Grief:
Nor Tears, nor Cries can give the dead Relief;
Desist, my much lov'd Lord, t' indulge your Pain:
1055 You bear no more than what the Gods ordain.

My Fates permit me not from hence to fly;
Nor he, the great Comptroller of the Sky.
Long wandring Ways for you the Pow'rs decree:
On Land hard Labors, and a length of Sea.
1060   Then, after many painful Years are past,
On *Latium*'s happy Shore you shall be cast:
Where gentle *Tiber* from his Bed beholds
The flow'ry Meadows, and the feeding Folds.
There end your Toils: And there your Fates provide
1065   A quiet Kingdom, and a Royal Bride:
There Fortune shall the *Trojan* Line restore;
And you for lost *Creusa* weep no more.
Fear not that I shall watch with servile Shame,
Th' imperious Looks of some proud *Grecian* Dame:
1070   Or, stooping to the Victor's Lust, disgrace
My Goddess Mother, or my Royal Race.
And now, farewell: the Parent of the Gods
Restrains my fleeting Soul in her Abodes:
I trust our common Issue to your Care.
1075   She said: And gliding pass'd unseen in Air.
I strove to speak, but Horror ty'd my Tongue; ⎫
And thrice about her Neck my Arms I flung; ⎬
And thrice deceiv'd, on vain Embraces hung. ⎭
Light as an empty Dream at break of Day,
1080   Or as a blast of Wind, she rush'd away.
   Thus, having pass'd the Night in fruitless Pain,
I, to my longing Friends, return again.
Amaz'd th' augmented Number to behold,
Of Men, and Matrons mix'd, of young and old:
1085   A wretched Exil'd Crew together brought,
With Arms appointed, and with Treasure fraught.
Resolv'd, and willing under my Command,
To run all hazards both of Sea and Land.
The Morn began, from *Ida*, to display
1090   Her rosy Cheeks, and *Phosphor* led the day;
Before the Gates the *Grecians* took their Post:
And all pretence of late Relief was lost.
I yield to Fate, unwillingly retire;
And loaded, up the Hill convey my Sire.

THE THIRD BOOK OF THE ÆNEIS

The Argument

Æneas proceeds in his Relation: He gives an Account of the Fleet with which he sail'd, and the Success of his first Voyage to Thrace*; from thence he directs his Course to* Delos*, and asks the Oracle what place the Gods had appointed for his Habitation? By a mistake of the Oracle's Answer, he settles in* Crete*; his Household Gods give him the true sense of the Oracle, in a Dream. He follows their advice, and makes the best of his way for* Italy*: He is cast on several Shores, and meets with very surprising Adventures, 'till at length he lands on* Sicily*; where his Father* Anchises *dies. This is the place which he was sailing from, when the Tempest rose and threw him upon the* Carthaginian *Coast.*

When Heav'n had overturn'd the *Trojan* State,
And *Priam*'s Throne, by too severe a Fate:
When ruin'd *Troy* became the *Grecians* Prey,
And *Ilium*'s lofty Tow'rs in Ashes lay:
5 Warn'd by Cœlestial Omens, we retreat,
To seek in foreign Lands a happier Seat.
Near old *Antandros*, and at *Ida*'s foot,
The Timber of the sacred Groves we cut:
And build our Fleet; uncertain yet to find
10 What place the Gods for our Repose assign'd.
Friends daily flock; and scarce the kindly Spring
Began to cloath the Ground, and Birds to sing;
When old *Anchises* summon'd all to Sea:
The Crew, my Father and the Fates obey.
15 With Sighs and Tears I leave my native Shore,
And empty Fields, where *Ilium* stood before.
My Sire, my Son, our less, and greater Gods,
All sail at once; and cleave the briny Floods.

Against our Coast appears a spacious Land,
20 Which once the fierce *Lycurgus* did command:
Thracia the Name; the People bold in War;
Vast are their Fields, and Tillage is their Care.
A hospitable Realm while Fate was kind;
With *Troy* in friendship and Religion join'd.
25 I land; with luckless Omens, then adore
Their Gods, and draw a Line along the Shore:
I lay the deep Foundations of a Wall;
And *Enos*, nam'd from me, the City call.
To *Dionæan Venus* Vows are paid, ⎫
30 And all the Pow'rs that rising Labours aid; ⎬
A Bull on *Jove*'s Imperial Altar laid. ⎭
Not far, a rising Hillock stood in view;
Sharp Myrtles, on the sides, and Cornels grew.

There, while I went to crop the Silvan Scenes,
35   And shade our Altar with their leafy Greens;
I pull'd a Plant; (with horror I relate
A Prodigy so strange, and full of Fate.)
The rooted Fibres rose; and from the Wound,
Black bloody Drops distill'd upon the Ground.
40   Mute, and amaz'd, my Hair with Terrour stood;
Fear shrunk my Sinews, and congeal'd my Blood.
Man'd once again, another Plant I try;
That other gush'd with the same sanguine Dye.
Then, fearing Guilt, for some Offence unknown,
45   With Pray'rs and Vows the *Driads* I attone:
With all the Sisters of the Woods, and most
The God of Arms, who rules the *Thracian* Coast:
That they, or he, these Omens wou'd avert;
Release our Fears, and better signs impart.
50   Clear'd, as I thought, and fully fix'd at length
To learn the Cause, I tug'd with all my Strength;
I bent my knees against the Ground; once more
The violated Myrtle ran with Gore.
Scarce dare I tell the Sequel: From the Womb
55   Of wounded Earth, and Caverns of the Tomb,
A Groan, as of a troubled Ghost, renew'd
My Fright, and then these dreadful Words ensu'd.
Why dost thou thus my bury'd Body rend?
O spare the Corps of thy unhappy Friend!
60   Spare to pollute thy pious Hands with Blood:
The Tears distil not from the wounded Wood;
But ev'ry drop this living Tree contains,
Is kindred Blood, and ran in *Trojan* Veins:
O fly from this unhospitable Shore,
65   Warn'd by my Fate; for I am *Polydore*!
Here loads of Lances, in my Blood embru'd,
Again shoot upward, by my Blood renew'd.
    My faultring Tongue, and shiv'ring Limbs declare
My Horror, and in Bristles rose my Hair.
70   When *Troy* with *Grecian* Arms was closely pent, ⎫
Old *Priam*, fearful of the Wars Event,   ⎬
This hapless *Polydore* to *Thracia* sent.   ⎭

Loaded with Gold, he sent his Darling, far ⎫
From Noise and Tumults, and destructive War: ⎬
75 Committed to the faithless Tyrant's Care.   ⎭
Who, when he saw the Pow'r of *Troy* decline,
Forsook the weaker, with the strong to join.
Broke ev'ry Bond of Nature, and of Truth;
And murder'd, for his Wealth, the Royal Youth.
80 O sacred Hunger of pernicious Gold,
What bands of Faith can impious Lucre hold!
Now, when my Soul had shaken off her Fears,
I call my Father, and the *Trojan* Peers:
Relate the Prodigies of Heav'n; require
85 What he commands, and their Advice desire.
All vote to leave that execrable Shore,
Polluted with the Blood of *Polydore*.
But e're we sail, his Fun'ral Rites prepare;
Then, to his Ghost, a Tomb and Altars rear,
90 In mournful Pomp the Matrons walk the round: ⎫
With baleful Cypress, and blue Fillets crown'd; ⎬
With Eyes dejected, and with Hair unbound.   ⎭
Then Bowls of tepid Milk and Blood we pour,
And thrice invoke the Soul of *Polydore*.
95   Now when the raging Storms no longer reign;
But Southern Gales invite us to the Main;
We launch our Vessels, with a prosp'rous Wind;
And leave the Cities and the Shores behind.
     An Island in th' *Ægean* Main appears:
100 *Neptune* and wat'ry *Doris* claim it theirs.
It floated once, till *Phœbus* fix'd the sides
To rooted Earth, and now it braves the Tides.
Here, born by friendly Winds, we come ashore, ⎫
With needful ease our weary Limbs restore;   ⎬
105 And the Sun's Temple, and his Town adore.   ⎭
     Anius the Priest, and King, with Lawrel crown'd,
His hoary Locks with purple Fillets bound.
Who saw my Sire the *Delian* Shore ascend,
Came forth with eager haste to meet his Friend.
110 Invites him to his Palace; and in sign
Of ancient Love, their plighted Hands they join.

Then to the Temple of the God I went;
And thus, before the Shrine, my Vows present.
Give, O *Thymbræus*, give a resting place,
115   To the sad Relicks of the *Trojan* Race:
A Seat secure, a Region of their own,
A lasting Empire, and a happier Town.
Where shall we fix, where shall our Labours end,
Whom shall we follow, and what Fate attend?
120   Let not my Pray'rs a doubtful Answer find,
But in clear Auguries unveil thy Mind.
Scarce had I said, He shook the Holy Ground: ⎫
The Lawrels, and the lofty Hills around: ⎬
And from the *Tripos* rush'd a bellowing Sound. ⎭
125   Prostrate we fell; confess'd the present God,
Who gave this Answer from his dark Abode.
Undaunted Youths, go seek that Mother Earth
From which your Ancestors derive their Birth.
The Soil that sent you forth, her Ancient Race,
130   In her old Bosom, shall again embrace.
Through the wide World th' *Æneian* House shall reign,
And Childrens Children shall the Crown sustain.
Thus *Phœbus* did our future Fates disclose;
A mighty Tumult, mix'd with Joy, arose.
135   All are concern'd to know what place the God
Assign'd, and where determin'd our abode.
My Father, long revolving in his Mind,
The Race and Lineage of the *Trojan* Kind,
Thus answer'd their demands: Ye Princes, hear
140   Your pleasing Fortune; and dispel your fear.
The fruitful Isle of *Crete* well known to Fame,
Sacred of old to *Jove*'s Imperial Name,
In the mid Ocean lies, with large Command;
And on its Plains a hundred Cities stand.
145   Another *Ida* rises there; and we
From thence derive our *Trojan* Ancestry.
From thence, as 'tis divulg'd by certain Fame,
To the *Rhœtean* Shores old *Teucrus* came.
There fix'd, and there the Seat of Empire chose,
150   E're *Ilium* and the *Trojan* Tow'rs arose.

In humble Vales they built their soft abodes:
Till *Cybele*, the Mother of the Gods,
With tinckling Cymbals charm'd th' *Idean* Woods.
She, secret Rites and Ceremonies taught,
155   And to the Yoke, the salvage Lions brought.
Let us the Land, which Heav'n appoints, explore;
Appease the Winds, and seek the *Gnossian* Shore.
If *Jove* assists the passage of our Fleet,
The third propitious dawn discovers *Creet*.
160   Thus having said, the Sacrifices laid
On smoking Altars, to the Gods He paid.
A Bull, to *Neptune* an Oblation due,
Another Bull to bright *Apollo* slew:
A milk white Ewe the Western Winds to please;
165   And one cole black to calm the stormy Seas.
E're this, a flying Rumour had been spread,
That fierce *Idomeneus* from *Crete* was fled;
Expell'd and exil'd; that the Coast was free
From Foreign or Domestick Enemy:
170   We leave the *Delian* Ports, and put to Sea.
By *Naxos*, fam'd for Vintage, make our way:
Then green *Donysa* pass; and Sail in sight
Of *Paros* Isle, with Marble Quarries white.
We pass the scatter'd Isles of *Cyclades*;
175   That, scarce distinguish'd, seem to stud the Seas.
The shouts of Sailors double near the shores;
They stretch their Canvass, and they ply their Oars.
All hands aloft, for *Creet* for *Creet* they cry,
And swiftly through the foamy Billows fly.
180   Full on the promis'd Land at length we bore,
With Joy descending on the *Cretan* Shore.
With eager haste a rising Town I frame,
Which from the *Trojan Pergamus* I name:
The Name it self was grateful; I exhort
185   To found their Houses, and erect a Fort.
Our Ships are haul'd upon the yellow strand,
The Youth begin to Till the labour'd Land.
And I my self new Marriages promote,
Give Laws: and Dwellings I divide by Lot.

190   When rising Vapours choak the wholesom Air,
       And blasts of noisom Winds corrupt the Year:
       The Trees, devouring Caterpillers burn:
       Parch'd was the Grass, and blited was the Corn.
       Nor scape the Beasts: for *Syrius* from on high, ⎫
195   With pestilential Heat infects the Sky: ⎬
       My Men, some fall, the rest in Feavers fry.   ⎭
       Again my Father bids me seek the Shore
       Of sacred *Delos*; and the God implore:
       To learn what end of Woes we might expect,
200   And to what Clime, our weary Course direct.
          'Twas Night, when ev'ry Creature, void of Cares,
       The common gift of balmy Slumber shares:
       The Statues of my Gods, (for such they seem'd)
       Those Gods whom I from flaming *Troy* redeem'd,
205   Before me stood; Majestically bright,
       Full in the Beams of *Phœbe*'s entring light.
       Then thus they spoke; and eas'd my troubled Mind:
       What from the *Delian* God thou go'st to find,
       He tells thee here; and sends us to relate:
210   Those Pow'rs are we, Companions of thy Fate,
       Who from the burning Town by thee were brought;
       Thy Fortune follow'd, and thy safety wrought.
       Through Seas and Lands, as we thy Steps attend,
       So shall our Care thy Glorious Race befriend.
215   An ample Realm for thee thy Fates ordain;
       A Town, that o're the conquer'd World shall reign.
       Thou, mighty Walls for mighty Nations build;
       Nor let thy weary Mind to labours yield:
       But change thy Seat; for not the *Delian* God,
220   Nor we, have giv'n thee *Crete* for our Abode.
       A Land there is, *Hesperia* call'd of old,
       The Soil is fruitful, and the Natives bold.
       Th' *Oenotrians* held it once; by later Fame,
       Now call'd *Italia* from the Leader's Name.
225   *Jasius* there, and *Dardanus* were born:
       From thence we came, and thither must return.
       Rise, and thy Sire with these glad Tidings greet;
       Search *Italy*, for *Jove* denies thee *Creet*.
       Astonish'd at their Voices, and their sight,
230   (Nor were they Dreams, but Visions of the Night;

I saw, I knew their Faces, and descry'd
In perfect View, their Hair with Fillets ty'd:)
I started from my Couch, a clammy Sweat
On all my Limbs, and shiv'ring Body sate.
235 To Heav'n I lift my Hands with pious haste,
And sacred Incense in the Flames I cast.
Thus to the Gods their perfect Honours done,
More chearful to my good old Sire I run:
And tell the pleasing News; in little space
240 He found his Error, of the double Race.
Not, as before he deem'd, deriv'd from *Creet*;
No more deluded by the doubtful Seat.
Then said, O Son, turmoil'd in *Trojan* Fate;
Such things as these *Cassandra* did relate.
245 This Day revives within my mind, what she
Foretold of *Troy* renew'd in *Italy*;
And *Latian* Lands: but who cou'd then have thought, ⎫
That *Phrygian* Gods to *Latium* should be brought; ⎬
Or who believ'd what mad *Cassandra* taught?   ⎭
250 Now let us go, where *Phœbus* leads the way:
He said, and we with glad Consent obey.
Forsake the Seat; and leaving few behind,
We spread our sails before the willing Wind.
Now from the sight of Land, our Gallies move,
255 With only Seas around, and Skies above.
When o're our Heads, descends a burst of Rain;
And Night, with sable Clouds involves the Main:
The ruffling Winds the foamy Billows raise:
The scatter'd Fleet is forc'd to sev'ral Ways:
260 The face of Heav'n is ravish'd from our Eyes,
And in redoubl'd Peals the roaring Thunder flies.
Cast from our Course, we wander in the Dark;
No Stars to guide, no point of Land to mark.
Ev'n *Palinurus* no distinction found
265 Betwixt the Night and Day; such Darkness reign'd around.
Three starless Nights the doubtful Navy strays
Without Distinction, and three Sunless days.
The fourth renews the Light, and from our Shrowds
We view a rising Land like distant Clouds:
270 The Mountain tops confirm the pleasing Sight;
And curling Smoke ascending from their Height.

The Canvas falls; their Oars the Sailors ply;
From the rude strokes the whirling Waters fly.
At length I land upon the *Strophades*;
275   Safe from the danger of the stormy Seas:
Those Isles are compass'd by th' *Ionian* Main;
The dire Abode where the foul *Harpies* reign:
Forc'd by the winged Warriors to repair
To their old Homes, and leave their costly Fare.
280   Monsters more fierce, offended Heav'n ne're sent
From Hell's Abyss, for Human Punishment.
With Virgin-faces, but with Wombs obscene, ⎫
Foul Paunches, and with Ordure still unclean: ⎬
With Claws for Hands, and Looks for ever lean. ⎭
285   We landed at the Port; and soon beheld
Fat Herds of Oxen graze the flow'ry Field:
And wanton Goats without a Keeper stray'd:
With Weapons we the welcome Prey invade:
Then call the Gods, for Partners of our Feast:
290   And *Jove* himself the chief invited Guest.
We spread the Tables, on the greensword Ground:
We feed with Hunger, and the Bowls go round.
When from the Mountain tops, with hideous Cry,
And clatt'ring Wings, the hungry Harpies fly:
295   They snatch the Meat; defiling all they find:
And parting leave a loathsom Stench behind.
Close by a hollow Rock, again we sit;
New dress the Dinner, and the Beds refit:
Secure from Sight, beneath a pleasing Shade;
300   Where tufted Trees a Native Arbour made.
Again the Holy Fires on Altars burn:
And once again the rav'nous Birds return:
Or from the dark Recesses where they ly,
Or from another Quarter of the Sky.
305   With filthy Claws their odious Meal repeat,
And mix their loathsom Ordures with their Meat.
I bid my Friends for Vengeance then prepare;
And with the Hellish Nation wage the War.
They, as commanded, for the Fight provide,
310   And in the Grass their glitt'ring Weapons hide:

Then, when along the crooked Shoar we hear
Their clatt'ring Wings, and saw the Foes appear;
Misenus sounds a charge: We take th' Alarm;
And our strong hands with Swords and Bucklers arm.
315　In this new kind of Combat, all employ
Their utmost Force, the Monsters to destroy.
In vain; the fated Skin is proof to Wounds:
And from their Plumes the shining Sword rebounds.
At length rebuff'd, they leave their mangled Prey,
320　And their stretch'd Pinions to the Skies display.
Yet one remain'd, the Messenger of Fate; ⎫
High on a craggy Cliff *Celæno* sate, ⎬
And thus her dismal Errand did relate. ⎭
What, not contented with our Oxen slain, ⎫
325　Dare you with Heav'n an impious War maintain, ⎬
And drive the Harpies from their Native Reign? ⎭
Heed therefore what I say; and keep in mind
What *Jove* decrees, what *Phœbus* has design'd:
And I, the Fury's Queen, from both relate:
330　You seek th' *Italian* Shores, foredoom'd by Fate:
Th' *Italian* Shores are granted you to find:
And a safe Passage to the Port assign'd,
But know, that e're your promis'd Walls you build,
My Curses shall severely be fulfill'd.
335　Fierce Famine is your Lot, for this Misdeed,
Reduc'd to grind the Plates on which you feed.
She said; and to the neigh'bring Forest flew:
Our Courage fails us, and our Fears renew.
Hopeless to win by War, to Pray'rs we fall:
340　And on th' offended Harpies humbly call.
And whether Gods, or Birds obscene they were,
Our Vows for Pardon, and for Peace prefer.
But old *Anchises*, off'ring Sacrifice,
And lifting up to Heav'n his Hands, and Eyes;
345　Ador'd the greater Gods: Avert, said he, ⎫
These Omens, render vain this Prophecy: ⎬
And from th' impending Curse, a Pious People free. ⎭
Thus having said, he bids us put to Sea; ⎫
We loose from Shore our Haulsers, and obey: ⎬
350　And soon with swelling sails, pursue the wat'ry Way. ⎭

Amidst our course *Zacynthian* Woods appear;
And next by rocky *Neritos* we steer:
We fly from *Ithaca*'s detested Shore,
And curse the Land which dire *Ulysses* bore.

355   At length *Leucates* cloudy top appears;
And the Sun's Temple, which the Sailor fears.
Resolv'd to breath a while from Labour past, ⎤
Our crooked Anchors from the Prow we cast; ⎬
And joyful to the little City haste. ⎦

360   Here safe beyond our Hopes, our Vows we pay
To *Jove*, the Guide and Patron of our way.
The Customs of our Country we pursue;
And *Trojan* Games on *Actian* Shores renew.
Our Youth, their naked Limbs besmear with Oyl;

365   And exercise the Wrastlers noble Toil.
Pleas'd to have sail'd so long before the Wind;
And left so many *Grecian* Towns behind.
The Sun had now fulfill'd his Annual Course,
And *Boreas* on the Seas display'd his Force:

370   I fix'd upon the Temples lofty Door,
The brazen Shield which vanquish'd *Abas* bore:
The Verse beneath, my Name and Action speaks,
These Arms, *Æneas* took from Conqu'ring *Greeks*.
Then I command to weigh; the Seamen ply

375   Their sweeping Oars, the smokeing Billows fly.
The sight of high *Phæacia* soon we lost:
And skim'd along *Epirus* rocky Coast.
Then to *Chaonia*'s Port our Course we bend,
And landed, to *Buthrotus* heights ascend.

380   Here wond'rous things were loudly blaz'd by Fame;
How *Helenus* reviv'd the *Trojan* Name;
And raign'd in *Greece*: That *Priam*'s captive Son
Succeeded *Pyrrhus* in his Bed and Throne.
And fair *Andromache*, restor'd by Fate,

385   Once more was happy in a *Trojan* Mate.
I leave my Gallies riding in the Port;
And long to see the new *Dardanian* Court.
By chance, the mournful Queen, before the Gate,
Then solemniz'd her former Husband's Fate.

390   Green Altars rais'd of Turf, with Gifts she Crown'd; ⎫
      And sacred Priests in order stand around;   ⎬
      And thrice the Name of hapless *Hector* sound.   ⎭
      The Grove it self resembles *Ida*'s Wood;
      And *Simois* seem'd the well dissembl'd Flood.

395   But when, at nearer distance, she beheld
      My shining Armour, and my *Trojan* Shield;
      Astonish'd at the sight, the vital Heat
      Forsakes her Limbs, her Veins no longer beat:
      She faints, she falls, and scarce recov'ring strength,
400   Thus, with a falt'ring Tongue, she speaks at length.
         Are you alive, O Goddess born! she said,
      Or if a Ghost, then where is *Hector*'s Shade?
      At this, she cast a loud and frightful Cry:
      With broken words, I made this brief Reply.

405   All of me that remains, appears in sight,
      I live; if living be to loath the Light.
      No Phantome; but I drag a wretched life;
      My Fate resembling that of *Hector*'s Wife.
      What have you suffer'd since you lost your Lord,
410   By what strange blessing are you now restor'd!
      Still are you *Hector*'s, or is *Hector* fled,
      And his Remembrance lost in *Pyrrhus* Bed?
      With Eyes dejected, in a lowly tone,
      After a modest pause, she thus begun.

415   Oh only happy Maid of *Priam*'s Race,
      Whom death deliver'd from the Foes embrace!
      Commanded on *Achilles* Tomb to die,   ⎫
      Not forc'd, like us, to hard Captivity: ⎬
      Or in a haughty Master's Arms to lie.   ⎭
420   In *Grecian* Ships unhappy we were born:
      Endur'd the Victor's Lust, sustain'd the Scorn:
      Thus I submitted to the lawless pride
      Of *Pyrrhus*, more a Handmaid than a Bride.
      Cloy'd with Possession, He forsook my Bed,
425   And *Helen*'s lovely Daughter sought to wed.
      Then me, to *Trojan Helenus* resign'd:
      And his two Slaves in equal Marriage join'd.
      Till young *Orestes*, pierc'd with deep despair,   ⎫
      And longing to redeem the promis'd Fair,   ⎬
430   Before *Appollo*'s Altar slew the Ravisher.   ⎭

By *Pyrrhus* death the Kingdom we regain'd:
At least one half with *Helenus* remain'd;
Our part, from *Chaon*, He *Chaonia* calls:
And names, from *Pergamus*, his rising Walls.
435 But you, what Fates have landed on our Coast,
What Gods have sent you, or what Storms have tost?
Does young *Ascanius* life and health enjoy,
Sav'd from the Ruins of unhappy *Troy*!
O tell me how his Mothers loss he bears,
440 What hopes are promis'd from his blooming years, }
How much of *Hector* in his Face appears?
She spoke: and mix'd her Speech with mournful Cries:
And fruitless Tears came trickling from her Eyes.
At length her Lord descends upon the Plain;
445 In Pomp, attended with a num'rous Train:
Receives his Friends, and to the City leads;
And Tears of Joy amidst his Welcome sheds.
Proceeding on, another *Troy* I see;
Or, in less compass, *Troy*'s Epitome.
450 A Riv'let by the name of *Xanthus* ran:
And I embrace the *Scæan* Gate again.
My Friends in Portico's were entertain'd;
And Feasts and Pleasures through the City reign'd.
The Tables fill'd the spacious Hall around:
455 And Golden Bowls with sparkling Wine were crown'd.
Two days we pass'd in mirth, till friendly Gales,
Blown from the South, supply'd our swelling Sails.
Then to the Royal Seer I thus began:
O thou who know'st beyond the reach of Man,
460 The Laws of Heav'n, and what the Stars decree, }
Whom *Phœbus* taught unerring Prophecy, }
From his own Tripod, and his holy Tree: }
Skill'd in the wing'd Inhabitants of Air,
What Auspices their notes, and flights declare:
465 O say; for all Religious Rites portend
A happy Voyage, and a prosp'rous End:
And ev'ry Pow'r and Omen of the Sky,
Direct my Course for destin'd *Italy*:
But only dire *Celæno*, from the Gods,
470 A dismal Famine fatally fore-bodes:

O say what Dangers I am first to shun:
What Toils to Vanquish, and what Course to run.
    The Prophet first with Sacrifice adores
The greater Gods; their Pardon then implores:
475   Unbinds the Fillet from his holy Head; ⎫
To *Phœbus* next, my trembling Steps he led: ⎬
Full of religious Doubts and awful dread. ⎭
Then with his God possess'd, before the Shrine,
These words proceeded from his Mouth Divine.
480   O Goddess-born, (for Heav'n's appointed Will,
With greater Auspices of good than ill,
Fore-shows thy Voyage, and thy course directs;
Thy Fates conspire, and *Jove* himself protects:)
Of many things, some few I shall explain, ⎫
485   Teach thee to shun the dangers of the Main, ⎬
And how at length the promis'd Shore to gain. ⎭
The rest the Fates from *Helenus* conceal;
And *Juno*'s angry Pow'r forbids to tell.
First then, that happy Shore, that seems so nigh, ⎫
490   Will far from your deluded Wishes fly: ⎬
Long tracts of Seas divide your hopes from *Italy*. ⎭
For you must cruise along *Sicilian* Shoars;
And stem the Currents with your struggling Oars:
Then round th' *Italian* Coast your Navy steer;
495   And after this to *Circe*'s Island veer.
And last, before your new Foundations rise,
Must pass the *Stygian* Lake, and view the neather Skies.
Now mark the Signs of future Ease and Rest;
And bear them safely treasur'd in thy Breast.
500   When in the shady Shelter of a Wood,
And near the Margin of a gentle Flood,
Thou shalt behold a Sow upon the Ground,
With thirty sucking young encompass'd round;
The Dam and Off-spring white as falling Snow: ⎫
505   These on thy City shall their Name bestow: ⎬
And there shall end thy Labours and thy Woe. ⎭
Nor let the threatned Famine fright thy Mind,
For *Phœbus* will assist; and Fate the way will find.
Let not thy Course to that ill Coast be bent,
510   Which fronts from far th' *Epirian* Continent;

Those parts are all by Grecian Foes possess'd:
The salvage *Locrians* here the Shores infest:
There fierce *Idomeneus* his City builds,
And guards with Arms the *Salentinian* Fields.
515 And on the Mountains brow *Petilia* stands,
Which *Philoctetes* with his Troops commands.
Ev'n when thy Fleet is landed on the Shore,
And Priests with holy Vows the Gods adore;
Then with a Purple Veil involve your Eyes,
520 Lest hostile Faces blast the Sacrifice.
These Rites and Customs to the rest commend;
That to your Pious Race they may descend.
  When parted hence, the Wind that ready waits
For *Sicily*, shall bear you to the Streights:
525 Where proud *Pelorus* opes a wider way,
Tack to the Larboord, and stand off to Sea:
Veer Star-board Sea and Land. Th' *Italian* Shore,
And fair *Sicilia*'s Coast were one, before
An Earthquake caus'd the Flaw, the roaring Tides
530 The Passage broke, that Land from Land divides:
And where the Lands retir'd, the rushing Ocean rides.
Distinguish'd by the Streights, on either hand,
Now rising Cities in long order stand;
And fruitful Fields: (So much can Time invade
535 The mouldring Work, that beauteous Nature made.)
Far on the right, her Dogs foul *Scylla* hides:
Charibdis roaring on the left presides;
And in her greedy Whirl-pool sucks the Tides:
Then Spouts them from below; with Fury driv'n,
540 The Waves mount up, and wash the face of Heav'n.
But *Scylla* from her Den, with open Jaws,
The sinking Vessel in her Eddy draws;
Then dashes on the Rocks: A Human Face,
And Virgin Bosom, hides her Tails disgrace.
545 Her Parts obscene below the Waves descend,
With Dogs inclos'd; and in a Dolphin end.
Tis safer, then, to bear aloof to Sea,
And coast *Pachynus*, though with more delay;
Than once to view mishappen *Scylla* near,
550 And the loud yell of watry Wolves to hear.

Besides, if Faith to *Helenus* be due,
And if Prophetick *Phœbus* tell me true;
Do not this Precept of your Friend forget;
Which therefore more than once I must repeat.
555 Above the rest, great *Juno*'s Name adore:
Pay Vows to *Juno*; *Juno*'s Aid implore.
Let Gifts be to the mighty Queen design'd;
And mollify with Pray'rs her haughty Mind.
Thus, at the length, your Passage shall be free,
560 And you shall safe descend on *Italy*.
Arriv'd at *Cumæ*, when you view the Flood
Of black *Avernus*, and the sounding Wood,
The mad prophetick *Sibyl* you shall find,
Dark in a Cave, and on a Rock reclin'd.
565 She sings the Fates, and in her frantick Fitts,
The Notes and Names inscrib'd, to Leafs commits.
What she commits to Leafs, in order laid,
Before the Caverns Entrance are display'd:
Unmov'd they lie, but if a blast of Wind
570 Without, or Vapours issue from behind,
The leafs are born aloft in liquid Air,
And she resumes no more her Museful Care:
Nor gathers from the Rocks her scatter'd Verse;
Nor sets in order what the Winds disperse.
575 Thus, many not succeeding, most upbraid ⎫
The Madness of the visionary Maid; ⎬
And with loud Curses leave the mystick Shade. ⎭
      Think it not loss of time a while to stay;
Though thy Companions chide thy long delay:
580 Tho' summon'd to the Seas, tho' pleasing Gales
Invite thy Course, and stretch thy swelling Sails.
But beg the sacred Priestess to relate
With willing Words, and not to write thy Fate.
The fierce *Italian* People she will show; ⎫
585 And all thy Wars, and all thy Future Woe; ⎬
And what thou may'st avoid, and what must undergo. ⎭
She shall direct thy Course, instruct thy Mind;
And teach thee how the happy Shores to find.
This is what Heav'n allows me to relate: ⎫
590 Now part in Peace; pursue thy better Fate, ⎬
And raise, by strength of Arms, the *Trojan* State. ⎭

This, when the Priest with friendly Voice declar'd,
He gave me Licence, and rich Gifts prepar'd:
Bounteous of Treasure, he supply'd my want
595   With heavy Gold, and polish'd Elephant.
Then *Dodonæan* Caldrons put on Board,
And ev'ry Ship with Sums of Silver stor'd.
A trusty Coat of Mail to me he sent,
Thrice chain'd with Gold, for Use and Ornament:
600   The Helm of *Pyrrhus* added to the rest,
That flourish'd with a Plume and waving Crest.
Nor was my Sire forgotten, nor my Friends:
And large Recruits he to my Navy sends;
Men, Horses, Captains, Arms, and Warlike Stores:
605   Supplies new Pilots, and new sweeping Oars.
Mean time, my Sire commands to hoist our Sails;
Lest we shou'd lose the first auspicious Gales.
The Prophet bless'd the parting Crew: and last,
With Words like these, his ancient Friend embrac'd.
610   Old happy Man, the Care of Gods above,
Whom Heav'nly *Venus* honour'd with her Love,
And twice preserv'd thy Life, when *Troy* was lost;
Behold from far the wish'd *Ausonian* Coast:
There land; but take a larger Compass round;
615   For that before is all forbidden Ground.
The Shore that *Phœbus* has design'd for you,
At farther distance lies, conceal'd from view.
Go happy hence, and seek your new Abodes;
Bless'd in a Son, and favour'd by the Gods:
620   For I with useless words prolong your stay;
When Southern Gales have summon'd you away.
    Nor less the Queen our parting thence deplor'd;
Nor was less bounteous than her *Trojan* Lord.
A noble Present to my Son she brought,
625   A Robe with Flow'rs on Golden Tissue wrought;
A *Phrygian* Vest; and loads, with Gifts beside
Of precious Texture, and of *Asian* Pride.
Accept, she said, these Monuments of Love;
Which in my Youth with happier Hands I wove:
630   Regard these Trifles for the Giver's sake;
'Tis the last Present *Hector*'s Wife can make.

Thou call'st my lost *Astyanax* to mind:
In thee his Features, and his Form I find.
His Eyes so sparkled with a lively Flame;
635   Such were his Motions, such was all his Frame;
And ah! had Heav'n so pleas'd, his Years had been the
            same.
        With Tears I took my last adieu, and said,
Your Fortune, happy pair, already made,
Leaves you no farther Wish: My diff'rent state,
640   Avoiding one, incurs another Fate.
To you a quiet Seat the Gods allow,
You have no Shores to search, no Seas to plow,
Nor Fields of flying *Italy* to chase:
(Deluding Visions, and a vain Embrace!)
645   You see another *Simois*, and enjoy
The labour of your Hands, another *Troy*;
With better Auspice than her ancient Tow'rs:
And less obnoxious to the *Grecian* Pow'rs.
If e're the Gods, whom I with Vows adore,
650   Conduct my Steps to *Tiber*'s happy Shore:
If ever I ascend the *Latian* Throne,
And build a City I may call my own,
As both of us our Birth from *Troy* derive,
So let our Kindred Lines in Concord live:
655   And both in Acts of equal Friendship strive.
Our Fortunes, good or bad, shall be the same,
The double *Troy* shall differ but in Name:
That what we now begin, may never end;
But long, to late Posterity descend.
660   Near the *Ceraunean* Rocks our Course we bore:
(The shortest passage to th' *Italian* shore:)
Now had the Sun withdrawn his radiant Light,
And hills were hid in dusky Shades of Night:
We land; and on the bosom of the Ground
665   A safe Retreat, and a bare *Lodging* found;
Close by the Shore we lay; the Sailors keep
Their watches, and the rest securely sleep.
The Night proceeding on with silent pace,
Stood in her noon; and view'd with equal Face,
670   Her steepy rise, and her declining Race.

Then wakeful *Palinurus* rose, to spie
The face of Heav'n, and the Nocturnal Skie; }
And listen'd ev'ry breath of Air to try:
Observes the Stars, and notes their sliding Course,
675 The *Pleiads*, *Hyads*, and their wat'ry force;
And both the Bears is careful to behold;
And bright *Orion* arm'd with burnish'd Gold.
Then when he saw no threat'ning Tempest Nigh,
But a sure promise of a settled Skie;
680 He gave the Sign to weigh; we break our sleep;
Forsake the pleasing Shore, and plow the Deep.
And now the rising Morn, with rosie light
Adorns the Skies, and puts the Stars to flight:
When we from far, like bluish Mists, descry
685 The Hills, and then the Plains of *Italy*.
Achates first pronounc'd the Joyful Sound;
Then *Italy* the chearful Crew rebound.
My Sire *Anchises* crown'd a Cup with Wine:
And off'ring, thus implor'd the Pow'rs Divine.
690 Ye Gods, presiding over Lands and Seas,
And you who raging Winds and Waves appease,
Breath on our swelling Sails a prosp'rous Wind:
And smooth our Passage to the Port assign'd.
The gentle Gales their flagging force renew;
695 And now the happy Harbour is in view.
Minerva's Temple then salutes our sight;
Plac'd, as a Land-mark, on the Mountains height:
We furl our Sails, and turn the Prows to shore;
The curling Waters round the Galleys roar:
700 The Land lies open to the raging East,
Then, bending like a Bow, with Rocks compress'd,
Shuts out the Storms; the Winds and Waves complain,
And vent their malice on the Cliffs in vain.
The Port lies hid within; on either side
705 Two Tow'ring Rocks the narrow mouth divide.
The Temple, which aloft we view'd before,
To distance flies, and seems to shun the Shore.
Scarce landed, the first Omens I beheld
Were four white Steeds that crop'd the flow'ry Field.

710 War, War is threaten'd from this Forreign Ground,
     (My Father cry'd) where warlike Steeds are found.
     Yet, since reclaim'd to Chariots they submit,
     And bend to stubborn Yokes, and champ the Bitt,
     Peace may succeed to War. Our way we bend
715 To *Pallas*, and the sacred Hill ascend.
     There, prostrate to the fierce *Virago* pray;
     Whose Temple was the Land-Mark of our way.
     Each with a *Phrygian* Mantle veil'd his Head; ⎤
     And all Commands of *Helenus* obey'd;   ⎬
720 And pious Rites to *Grecian Juno* paid.   ⎦
     These dues perform'd, we stretch our Sails, and stand
     To Sea, forsaking that suspected Land.
     From hence *Tarentum*'s Bay appears in view;
     For *Hercules* renown'd, if Fame be true.
725 Just opposite, *Lacinian Juno* stands;
     Caulonian Tow'rs and *Scylacæan* Strands,
     For Shipwrecks fear'd: Mount *Ætna* thence we spy,
     Known by the smoaky Flames which Cloud the Skie.
     Far off we hear the Waves, with surly sound
730 Invade the Rocks, the Rocks their groans rebound.
     The Billows break upon the sounding Strand;
     And rowl the rising Tide, impure with Sand.
     Then thus *Anchises*, in Experience old,
     'Tis that *Charibdis* which the Seer foretold:
735 And those the promis'd Rocks; bear off to Sea:
     With haste the frighted Mariners obey.
     First *Palinurus* to the Larboor'd veer'd;
     Then all the Fleet by his Example steer'd.
     To Heav'n aloft on ridgy Waves we ride;
740 Then down to Hell descend, when they divide.
     And thrice our Gallies knock'd the stony ground, ⎤
     And thrice the hollow Rocks return'd the sound, ⎬
     And thrice we saw the Stars, that stood with dews⎟
          around.   ⎦
     The flagging Winds forsook us, with the Sun;
745 And weary'd, on *Cyclopean* Shores we run.
     The Port capacious, and secure from Wind,
     Is to the foot of thundring *Etna* joyn'd.

By turns a pitchy Cloud she rowls on high;
By turns hot Embers from her entrails fly;
750   And flakes of mounting Flames, that lick the Skie.
Oft from her Bowels massy Rocks are thrown,
And shiver'd by the force come piece-meal down.
Oft liquid Lakes of burning Sulphur flow,
Fed from the fiery Springs that boil below.
755   *Enceladus* they say, transfix'd by *Jove*,
With blasted Limbs came tumbling from above:
And, where he fell, th' Avenging Father drew
This flaming Hill, and on his Body threw:
As often as he turns his weary sides,
760   He shakes the solid Isle, and smoke the Heavens hides.
In shady Woods we pass the tedious Night,
Where bellowing Sounds and Groans our Souls affright.
Of which no Cause is offer'd to the sight.
For not one Star was kindled in the Skie;
765   Nor cou'd the Moon her borrow'd Light supply:
For misty Clouds involv'd the Firmament;
The Stars were muffled, and the Moon was pent.
Scarce had the rising Sun the day reveal'd;
Scarce had his heat the pearly dews dispell'd;
770   When from the Woods there bolts, before our sight,
Somewhat, betwixt a Mortal and a Spright.
So thin, so ghastly meager, and so wan,
So bare of flesh, he scarce resembled Man.
This thing, all tatter'd, seem'd from far t' implore,
775   Our pious aid, and pointed to the Shore.
We look behind; then view his shaggy Beard;
His Cloaths were tagg'd with Thorns, and Filth his Limbs
        besmear'd:
The rest, in Meen, in habit, and in Face,
Appear'd a *Greek* and such indeed he was.
780   He cast on us, from far, a frightfull view,
Whom soon for *Trojans* and for Foes he knew:
Stood still, and paus'd; then all at once began
To stretch his Limbs, and trembled as he ran.
Soon as approach'd, upon his Knees he falls,
785   And thus with Tears and Sighs for pity calls.
Now by the Pow'rs above, and what we share
From Nature's common Gift, this vital Air,

O *Trojans* take me hence: I beg no more,
But bear me far from this unhappy Shore.
790 'Tis true I am a *Greek*, and farther own,
Among your Foes besieg'd th' Imperial Town;
For such Demerits if my death be due,
No more for this abandon'd life I sue:
This only Favour let my Tears obtain,
795 To throw me headlong in the rapid Main:
Since nothing more than Death my Crime demands,
I die content, to die by human Hands.
He said, and on his Knees my Knees embrac'd,
I bad him boldly tell his Fortune past;
800 His present State, his Lineage and his Name;
Th' occasion of his Feats, and whence he came.
The good *Anchises* rais'd him with his Hand;
Who, thus encourag'd, answer'd our Demand:
From *Ithaca* my Native Soil I came
805 To *Troy*, and *Achæmenides* my Name.
Me, my poor Father, with *Ulysses* sent;
(Oh had I stay'd, with Poverty content!)
But fearful for themselves, my Country-men
Left me forsaken in the *Cyclop*'s Den.
810 The Cave, though large, was dark, the dismal Flore
Was pav'd with mangled Limbs and putrid Gore.
Our monstrous Host, of more than Human Size,
Erects his Head, and stares within the Skies.
Bellowing his Voice, and horrid is his Hue.
815 Ye Gods, remove this Plague from Mortal View!
The Joynts of slaughter'd Wretches are his Food:
And for his Wine he quaffs the streaming Blood.
These Eyes beheld, when with his spacious Hand
He seiz'd two Captives of our *Grecian* Band;
820 Stretch'd on his Back, he dash'd against the Stones
Their broken Bodies, and their crackling Bones:
With spouting Blood the Purple Pavement swims,
While the dire Glutton grinds the trembling Limbs.
    Not unreveng'd, *Ulysses* bore their Fate,
825 Nor thoughtless of his own unhappy State:
For, gorg'd with Flesh, and drunk with Human Wine,
While fast asleep the Giant lay supine;

Snoaring aloud, and belching from his Maw
His indigested Foam, and Morsels raw:
830   We pray, we cast the Lots, and then surround
The monstrous Body, stretch'd along the Ground:
Each, as he cou'd approach him, lends a hand
To bore his Eyeball with a flaming Brand:
Beneath his frowning Forehead lay his Eye,
835   (For only one did the vast Frame supply;)
But that a Globe so large, his Front it fill'd,
Like the Sun's disk, or like a *Grecian* Shield.
The Stroke succeeds; and down the Pupil bends;
This Vengeance follow'd for our slaughter'd Friends.
840   But haste, unhappy Wretches, haste to fly;
Your Cables cut, and on your Oars rely.
Such, and so vast as *Polypheme* appears,
A hundred more this hated Island bears:
Like him in Caves they shut their woolly Sheep,
845   Like him, their Herds on tops of Mountains keep;
Like him, with mighty Strides, they stalk from Steep to
      Steep.
And now three Moons their sharpen'd Horns renew,
Since thus in Woods and Wilds, obscure from view,
I drag my loathsom Days with mortal Fright;
850   And in deserted Caverns lodge by Night.
Oft from the Rocks a dreadful Prospect see,
Of the huge *Cyclops*, like a walking Tree:
From far I hear his thund'ring Voice resound;
And trampling Feet that shake the solid Ground.
855   Cornels, and salvage Berries of the Wood,
And Roots and Herbs have been my meagre Food.
   While all around my longing Eyes I cast,
I saw your happy Ships appear at last.
On those I fix'd my hopes, to these I run,
860   'Tis all I ask this cruel Race to shun:
What other Death you please your selves, bestow.
Scarce had he said, when on the Mountain's brow,
We saw the Giant-Shepherd stalk before
His following Flock, and leading to the Shore.
865   A monstrous Bulk, deform'd, depriv'd of Sight,
His Staff a trunk of Pine, to guide his steps aright.

His pondrous Whistle from his Neck descends; ⎫
His woolly Care their pensive Lord attends: ⎬
This only Solace his hard Fortune sends. ⎭

870   Soon as he reach'd the Shore, and touch'd the Waves,
From his bor'd Eye the gutt'ring Blood he laves:
He gnash'd his Teeth and groan'd; thro' Seas he strides,
And scarce the topmost billows touch'd his sides.
    Seiz'd with a sudden Fear, we run to Sea,
875   The Cables cut, and silent haste away:
The well deserving Stranger entertain;
Then, buckling to the Work, our Oars divide the Main.
The Giant harken'd to the dashing sound:
But when our Vessels out of reach he found,
880   He strided onward; and in vain essay'd
Th' *Ionian* Deep, and durst no farther wade.
With that he roar'd aloud; the dreadful Cry ⎫
Shakes Earth, and Air, and Seas; the Billows fly ⎬
Before the bellowing Noise, to distant *Italy*. ⎭
885   The neighb'ring *Ætna* trembling all around;
The winding Caverns eccho to the sound.
His brother *Cyclops* hear the yelling Roar;
And, rushing down the Mountains, crowd the Shoar:
We saw their stern distorted looks, from far,
890   And one ey'd Glance, that vainly threatned War.
A dreadful Council, with their heads on high;
The misty Clouds about their Foreheads fly:
Not yielding to the tow'ring Tree of *Jove*;
Or tallest Cypress of *Diana*'s Grove.
895   New Pangs of mortal Fear our Minds assail, ⎫
We tug at ev'ry Oar, and hoist up ev'ry Sail; ⎬
And take th' Advantage of the friendly Gale. ⎭
Forewarn'd by *Helenus*, we strive to shun
Charibdis Gulph, nor dare to *Scylla* run.
900   An equal Fate on either side appears;
We, tacking to the left, are free from Fears.
For from *Pelorus* Point, the North arose,
And drove us back where swift *Pantagias* flows.
His Rocky Mouth we pass; and make our Way
905   By *Thapsus*, and *Megara*'s winding Bay;

This Passage *Achæmenides* had shown,
Tracing the Course which he before had run.
    Right o're-against *Plemmyrium*'s watry Strand,
There lies an Isle once call'd th' *Ortygian* Land:
910 *Alpheus*, as Old Fame reports, has found
From *Greece* a secret Passage under-ground:
By Love to beauteous *Arethusa* led,
And mingling here, they rowl in the same Sacred Bed.
As *Helenus* enjoyn'd, we next adore
915 *Diana*'s Name, Protectress of the Shore.
With prosp'rous Gales we pass the quiet Sounds
Of still *Elorus* and his fruitful Bounds.
Then doubling Cape *Pachynus*, we survey
The rocky Shore extended to the Sea.
920 The Town of *Camarine* from far we see;
And fenny Lake undrain'd by Fates decree.
In sight of the *Geloan* Fields we pass,
And the large Walls, where mighty *Gela* was:
Then *Agragas* with lofty Summets crown'd;
925 Long for the Race of warlike Steeds renown'd:
We pass'd *Selinus*, and the Palmy Land,
And widely shun the *Lilybæan* Strand,
Unsafe, for secret Rocks, and moving Sand.
At length on Shore the weary Fleet arriv'd;
930 Which *Drepanum*'s unhappy Port receiv'd.
Here, after endless Labours, often tost
By raging Storms, and driv'n on ev'ry Coast,
My dear, dear Father, spent with Age I lost.
Ease of my Cares, and Solace of my Pain,
935 Sav'd through a thousand Toils, but sav'd in vain:
The Prophet, who my future Woes reveal'd,
Yet this, the greatest and the worst, conceal'd.
And dire *Celæno*, whose foreboding Skill
Denounc'd all else, was silent of this Ill:
940 This my last Labour was. Some friendly God,
From thence convey'd us to your blest Abode.
    Thus to the listning Queen, the Royal Guest
His wand'ring Course, and all his Toils express'd;
And here concluding, he retir'd to rest.

THE FOURTH BOOK OF THE ÆNEIS

The Argument

Dido *discovers to her Sister her Passion for* Æneas, *and her thoughts of Marrying him. She prepares a Hunting-Match for his Entertainment.* Juno *by* Venus's *consent raises a Storm, which separates the Hunters, and drives* Æneas *and* Dido *into the same Cave, where their Marriage is suppos'd to be compleated.* Jupiter *dispatches* Mercury *to* Æneas, *to warn him from* Carthage; Æneas *secretly prepares for his Voyage:* Dido *finds out his Design, and to put a stop to it, makes use of her own, and her Sister's Entreaties, and discovers all the variety of Passions that are incident to a neglected Lover: When nothing wou'd prevail upon him, she contrives her own Death, with which this Book concludes.*

But anxious Cares already seiz'd the Queen:
She fed within her Veins a Flame unseen:
The Heroe's Valour, Acts, and Birth inspire
Her Soul with Love, and fann the secret Fire.
His Words, his Looks imprinted in her Heart, 5
Improve the Passion, and increase the Smart.
Now, when the Purple Morn had chas'd away
The dewy Shadows, and restor'd the Day;
Her Sister first, with early Care she sought,
And thus in mournful Accents eas'd her Thought. 10
My dearest *Anna*, what new Dreams affright
My lab'ring Soul; what Visions of the Night
Disturb my Quiet, and distract my Breast,
With strange Ideas of our *Trojan* Guest?
His Worth, his Actions, and Majestick Air, 15
A Man descended from the Gods declare:
Fear ever argues a degenerate kind,
His Birth is well asserted by his Mind.
Then what he suffered, when by Fate betray'd,
What brave Attempts for falling *Troy* he made! 20
Such were his Looks, so gracefully he spoke,
That were I not resolv'd against the Yoke
Of hapless Marriage; never to be curs'd
With second Love, so fatal was my first;
To this one Error I might yield again: 25
For since *Sichæus* was untimely slain,
This onely Man, is able to subvert
The fix'd Foundations of my stubborn Heart.
And to confess my Frailty, to my shame,
Somewhat I find within, if not the same, 30 }
Too like the Sparkles of my former flame. }
But first let yawning Earth a Passage rend;
And let me through the dark Abyss descend;

First let avenging *Jove*, with Flames from high, ⎫
35   Drive down this Body, to the neather Sky, ⎬
Condemn'd with Ghosts in endless Night to lye; ⎭
Before I break the plighted Faith I gave; ⎫
No; he who had my Vows, shall ever have; ⎬
For whom I lov'd on Earth, I worship in the Grave. ⎭
40   She said; the Tears ran gushing from her Eyes,
And stop'd her Speech: her Sister thus replies.
O dearer than the vital Air I breath,
Will you to Grief your blooming Years bequeath?
Condemn'd to wast in Woes, your lonely Life,
45   Without the Joys of Mother, or of Wife.
Think you these Tears, this pompous Train of Woe,
Are known, or valu'd by the Ghosts below?
I grant, that while your Sorrows yet were green,
It well became a Woman, and a Queen,
50   The Vows of *Tyrian* Princes to neglect,
To scorn *Hyarbas*, and his Love reject;
With all the *Lybian* Lords of mighty Name,
But will you fight against a pleasing Flame!
This little Spot of Land, which Heav'n bestows,
55   On ev'ry side is hemm'd with warlike Foes:
Getulian Cities here are spread around;
And fierce *Numidians* there your Frontiers bound;
Here lies a barren Wast of thirsty Land,
And there the *Syrtes* raise the moving Sand:
60   *Barcæan* Troops besiege the narrow Shore;
And from the Sea *Pigmalion* threatens more.
Propitious Heav'n, and gracious *Juno*, lead
This wand'ring Navy to your needful Aid:
How will your Empire spread, your City rise
65   From such an Union, and with such Allies!
Implore the Favour of the Pow'rs above;
And leave the Conduct of the rest to Love.
Continue still your hospitable way,
And still invent occasions of their stay;
70   'Till Storms, and Winter Winds, shall cease to threat,
And Plancks and Oars, repair their shatter'd Fleet.
     These Words, which from a Friend, and Sister came, ⎫
With ease resolv'd the Scruples of her Fame; ⎬
And added Fury to the kindled Flame. ⎭

75   Inspir'd with Hope, the Project they pursue;
      On ev'ry Altar Sacrifice renew;
      A chosen Ewe of two Years old they pay
      To *Ceres*, *Bacchus*, and the God of Day:
      Preferring *Juno*'s Pow'r: For *Juno* ties
80   The Nuptial Knot, and makes the Marriage Joys.
      The beauteous Queen before her Altar stands,
      And holds the Golden Goblet in her Hands:
      A milk-white Heifer she with Flow'rs adorns,
      And pours the ruddy Wine betwixt her Horns;
85   And while the Priests with Pray'r the Gods invoke,
      She feeds their Altars with *Sabæan* Smoke.
      With hourly Care the Sacrifice renews,
      And anxiously the panting Entrals Views.
      What Priestly Rites, alas! what Pious Art,
90   What Vows avail to cure a bleeding Heart!
      A gentle Fire she feeds within her Veins;
      Where the soft God secure in silence reigns.
          Sick with desire, and seeking him she loves,
      From Street to Street, the raving *Dido* roves.
95   So when the watchful Shepherd, from the Blind,
      Wounds with a random Shaft the careless Hind;
      Distracted with her pain she flies the Woods,
      Bounds o're the Lawn, and seeks the silent Floods;
      With fruitless Care; for still the fatal Dart
100   Sticks in her side; and ranckles in her Heart.
      And now she leads the *Trojan* Chief, along
      The lofty Walls, amidst the busie Throng;
      Displays her *Tyrian* Wealth, and rising Town,
      Which Love, without his Labour, makes his own.
105   This Pomp she shows to tempt her wand'ring Guest;
      Her falt'ring Tongue forbids to speak the rest.
      When Day declines and Feasts renew the Night,
      Still on his Face she feeds her famish'd sight;
      She longs again to hear the Prince relate
110   His own Adventures, and the *Trojan* Fate:
      He tells it o're and o're; but still in vain;
      For still she begs to hear it, once again.
      The Hearer on the Speaker's Mouth depends;
      And thus the Tragick Story never ends.

115   Then, when they part, when *Phœbe*'s paler Light
       Withdraws, and falling Stars to Sleep invite,
       She last remains, when ev'ry Guest is gone,
       Sits on the Bed he press'd, and sighs alone;
       Absent, her absent Heroe sees and hears;
120   Or in her Bosom young *Ascanius* bears:
       And seeks the Father's Image in the Child,
       If Love by Likeness might be so beguil'd.
          Mean time the rising Tow'rs are at a stand:
       No Labours exercise the youthful Band:
125   Nor use of Arts, nor Toils of Arms they know;
       The Mole is left unfinish'd to the Foe.
       The Mounds, the Works, the Walls, neglected lye,
       Short of their promis'd heigth that seem'd to threat the
          Sky.
          But when Imperial *Juno*, from above,
130   Saw *Dido* fetter'd in the Chains of Love;
       Hot with the Venom, which her Veins inflam'd,
       And by no sense of Shame to be reclaim'd:
       With soothing Words to *Venus* she begun.
       High Praises, endless Honours you have won,
135   And mighty Trophees with your worthy Son:
       Two Gods a silly Woman have undone.
       Nor am I ignorant, you both suspect
       This rising City, which my Hands erect:
       But shall Cœlestial Discord never cease?
140   'Tis better ended in a lasting Peace.
       You stand possess'd of all your Soul desir'd;
       Poor *Dido* with consuming Love is fir'd:
       Your *Trojan* with my *Tyrian* let us join, ⎫
       So *Dido* shall be yours, *Æneas* mine: ⎬
145   One common Kingdom, one united Line. ⎭
       Elisa shall a *Dardan* Lord obey,
       And lofty *Carthage* for a Dow'r convey.
       Then *Venus*, who her hidden Fraud descry'd, ⎫
       (Which wou'd the Scepter of the World, misguide ⎬
150   To *Lybian* Shores,) thus artfully reply'd, ⎭
       Who but a Fool, wou'd Wars with *Juno* chuse,
       And such Alliance, and such Gifts refuse?

If Fortune with our joint Desires comply:
The Doubt is all from *Jove*, and Destiny.
155   Lest he forbid, with absolute Command,
To mix the People in one common Land.
Or will the *Trojan*, and the *Tyrian* Line,
In lasting Leagues, and Sure Succession join?
But you, the Partner of his Bed and Throne,
160   May move his Mind; my Wishes are your own.
Mine, said Imperial *Juno*, be the Care; ⎫
Time urges, now, to perfect this Affair: ⎬
Attend my Counsel, and the Secret share. ⎭
When next the Sun his rising Light displays,
165   And guilds the World below, with Purple Rays;
The Queen, *Æneas*, and the *Tyrian* Court,
Shall to the shady Woods, for Silvan Game, resort.
There, while the Huntsmen pitch their Toils around,
And cheerful Horns, from Side to Side, resound;
170   A Pitchy Cloud shall cover all the Plain
With Hail, and Thunder, and tempestuous Rain:
The fearful Train shall take their speedy Flight,
Dispers'd, and all involv'd in gloomy Night:
One Cave a grateful Shelter shall afford
175   To the fair Princess and the *Trojan* Lord.
I will my self, the bridal Bed prepare,
If you, to bless the Nuptials, will be there:
So shall their Loves be crown'd with due Delights,
And *Hymen* shall be present at the Rites.
180   The Queen of Love consents, and closely smiles
At her vain Project, and discover'd Wiles.
    The rosy Morn was risen from the Main,
And Horns and Hounds awake the Princely Train:
They issue early through the City Gate,
185   Where the more wakeful Huntsmen ready wait,
With Nets, and Toils, and Darts, beside the force
Of *Spartan* Dogs, and swift *Massylian* Horse.
The *Tyrian* Peers, and Officers of State,
For the slow Queen, in Anti-Chambers wait:
190   Her lofty Courser, in the Court below,
(Who his Majestick Rider seems to know,)

Proud of his Purple Trappings, paws the Ground;
And champs the Golden Bitt; and spreads the Foam
  around.
The Queen at length appears: On either Hand
195 The brawny Guards in Martial order stand.
A flow'rd Cymarr, with Golden Fringe she wore;
And at her Back a Golden Quiver bore:
Her flowing Hair, a Golden Caul restrains;
A golden Clasp, the *Tyrian* Robe sustains.
200 Then young *Ascanius*, with a sprightly Grace,
Leads on the *Trojan* Youth to view the Chace.
But far above the rest in beauty shines
The great *Æneas*, when the Troop he joins:
Like fair *Apollo*, when he leaves the frost
205 Of wintry *Xanthus*, and the *Lycian* Coast;
When to his Native *Delos* he resorts,
Ordains the Dances, and renews the Sports:
Where painted *Scythians*, mix'd with *Cretin* Bands,
Before the joyful Altars join their Hands.
210 Himself, on *Cynthus* walking, sees below
The merry Madness of the sacred Show.
Green Wreaths of Bays his length of Hair inclose,
A Golden Fillet binds his awful brows:
His Quiver sounds: Not less the Prince is seen
215 In manly Presence, or in lofty Meen.
    Now had they reach'd the Hills, and storm'd the Seat
Of salvage Beasts, in Dens, their last Retreat;
The Cry pursues the Mountain-Goats; they bound
From Rock to Rock, and keep the craggy Ground:
220 Quite otherwise the Stags, a trembling Train, ⎫
In Herds unsingl'd, scour the dusty Plain; ⎬
And a long Chace, in open view, maintain. ⎭
The glad *Ascanius*, as his Courser guides,
Spurs through the Vale; and these and those outrides.
225 His Horses flanks and sides are forc'd to feel
The clanking lash, and goring of the Steel.
Impatiently he views the feeble Prey,
Wishing some Nobler Beast to cross his way.
And rather wou'd the tusky Boar attend,
230 Or see the tawny Lyon downward bend.

Mean time, the gath'ring Clouds obscure the Skies;
From Pole to Pole the forky Lightning flies;
The ratling Thunders rowl; and *Juno* pours
A wintry Deluge down; and sounding Show'rs.
235 The Company dispers'd, to Coverts ride,
And seek the homely Cotts, or Mountains hollow side.
The rapid Rains, descending from the Hills,
To rowling Torrents raise the creeping Rills.
The Queen and Prince, as Love or Fortune guides,
240 One common Cavern in her Bosom hides.
Then first the trembling Earth the signal gave;
And flashing Fires enlighten all the Cave:
Hell from below, and *Juno* from above,
And howling Nymphs, were conscious to their Love.
245 From this ill Omen'd Hour, in Time arose
Debate and Death, and all succeeding Woes.

　　　The Queen whom sense of Honour cou'd not move
No longer made a Secret of her Love;
But call'd it Marriage, by that specious Name,
250 To veil the Crime and sanctifie the Shame.
　　　The loud Report through *Lybian* Cities goes;
Fame, the great Ill, from small beginnings grows.
Swift from the first; and ev'ry Moment brings
New Vigour to her flights, new Pinions to her wings.
255 Soon grows the Pygmee to Gygantic size;
Her Feet on Earth, her Forehead in the Skies:
Inrag'd against the Gods, revengeful Earth
Produc'd her last of the *Titanian* birth.
Swift is her walk, more swift her winged hast:
260 A monstrous Fantom, horrible and vast;
As many Plumes as raise her lofty flight,
So many piercing Eyes inlarge her sight:
Millions of opening Mouths to Fame belong,
And ev'ry Mouth is furnish'd with a Tongue:
265 And round with listning Ears the flying Plague is hung.
She fills the peaceful Universe with Cries;
No Slumbers ever close her wakeful Eyes.
By Day from lofty Tow'rs her Head she shews;
And spreads through trembling Crowds disastrous News.

270 With Court Informers haunts, and Royal Spyes,
Things done relates, not done she feigns; and mingles
        Truth with Lyes.
Talk is her business; and her chief delight
To tell of Prodigies, and cause affright.
She fills the Peoples Ears with *Dido*'s Name;
275 Who, lost to Honour, and the sense of Shame,
Admits into her Throne and Nuptial Bed
A wandring Guest, who from his Country fled:
Whole days with him she passes in delights;
And wastes in Luxury long Winter Nights.
280 Forgetful of her Fame, and Royal Trust;
Dissolv'd in Ease, abandon'd to her Lust.
    The Goddess widely spreads the loud Report;
And flies at length to King *Hyarba*'s Court.
When first possess'd with this unwelcome News,
285 Whom did he not of Men and Gods accuse!
This Prince, from ravish'd *Garamantis* born,
A hundred Temples did with Spoils adorn,
In *Ammon*'s Honour, his Cœlestial Sire;
A hundred Altars fed, with wakeful Fire:
290 And through his vast Dominions, Priests ordain'd,
Whose watchful Care these holy Rites maintain'd.
The Gates and Columns were with Garlands crown'd,
And Blood of Victim Beasts enrich the Ground.
    He, when he heard a Fugitive cou'd move
295 The *Tyrian* Princess, who disdain'd his Love,
His Breast with Fury burn'd, his Eyes with Fire;
Mad with Despair, impatient with Desire.
Then on the Sacred Altars pouring Wine,
He thus with Pray'rs implor'd his Sire divine.
300 Great *Jove*, propitious to the *Moorish* Race,
Who feast on painted Beds, with Off'rings grace
Thy Temples, and adore thy Pow'r Divine
With Blood of Victims, and with sparkling Wine:
Seest thou not this? or do we fear in vain
305 Thy boasted Thunder, and thy thoughtless Reign?
Do thy broad Hands the forky Lightnings lance,
Thine are the Bolts, or the blind work of Chance?

A wandring Woman builds, within our State,
A little Town, bought at an easie Rate;
310   She pays me Homage, and my Grants allow,
A narrow space of *Lybian* Lands to plough.
Yet scorning me, by Passion blindly led,
Admits a banish'd *Trojan* to her Bed:
And now this other *Paris*, with his Train
315   Of conquer'd Cowards, must in *Affrick* reign!
(Whom, what they are, their Looks and Garb confess;
Their Locks with Oil perfum'd, their *Lydian* dress:)
He takes the Spoil, enjoys the Princely Dame;
And I, rejected I, adore an empty Name.

320   His Vows, in haughty Terms, he thus preferr'd,
And held his Altar's Horns; the mighty Thund'rer heard,
Then cast his Eyes on *Carthage*, where he found
The lustful Pair, in lawless pleasure drown'd.
Lost in their Loves, insensible of Shame;
325   And both forgetful of their better Fame.
He calls *Cyllenius*; and the God attends;
By whom his menacing Command he sends.
Go, mount the Western Winds, and cleave the Skie;
Then, with a swift descent, to *Carthage* fly:
330   There find the *Trojan* Chief, who wastes his Days
In sloathful Riot, and inglorious Ease.
Nor minds the future City, giv'n by Fate;
To him this Message from my Mouth relate.
Not so, fair *Venus* hop'd, when twice she won
335   Thy Life with Pray'rs; nor promis'd such a Son.
Hers was a Heroe, destin'd to command
A Martial Race; and rule the *Latian* Land.
Who shou'd his ancient Line from *Teucer* draw;
And, on the conquer'd World, impose the Law.
340   If Glory cannot move a Mind so mean,
Nor future Praise, from fading Pleasure wean,
Yet why shou'd he defraud his Son of Fame;
And grudge the *Romans* their Immortal Name!
What are his vain Designs! what hopes he more,
345   From his long ling'ring on a hostile Shore?
Regardless to redeem his Honour lost,
And for his Race to gain th' *Ausonian* Coast!

Bid him with speed the *Tyrian* Court forsake;
With this Command the slumb'ring Warrior wake.
350   *Hermes* obeys; with Golden Pinions binds
His flying Feet, and mounts the Western Winds:
And whether o're the Seas or Earth he flies,
With rapid Force, they bear him down the Skies.
But first he grasps within his awful Hand,
355 The mark of Sov'raign Pow'r, his Magick Wand:
With this, he draws the Ghosts from hollow Graves,
With this he drives them down the *Stygian* Waves;
With this he seals in Sleep, the wakeful sight;
And Eyes, though Clos'd in Death restores to Light.
360 Thus arm'd, the God begins his Airy Race;
And drives the racking Clouds along the liquid Space.
Now sees the Tops of *Atlas*, as he flies;
Whose brawny Back supports the Starry Skies:
Atlas, whose Head with Piny Forests crown'd,
365 Is beaten by the Winds; with foggy Vapours bound.
Snows hide his Shoulders; from beneath his Chin
The Founts of Rolling Streams their Race begin:
A beard of Ice on his large Breast depends:
Here pois'd upon his Wings, the God descends:
370 Then, rested thus, he from the tow'ring height
Plung'd downward, with precipitated Flight:
Lights on the Seas, and skims along the Flood:
As Water-fowl, who seek their fishy Food,
Less, and yet less, to distant Prospect show,
375 By turns they dance aloft, and dive below:
Like these, the steerage of his Wings he plies;
And near the surface of the Water flies.
'Till having pass'd the Seas, and cross'd the Sands,
He clos'd his Wings, and stoop'd on *Lybian* Lands:
380 Where Shepherds once were hous'd in homely sheds,
Now Tow'rs within the Clouds, advance their Heads.
Arriving there, he found the *Trojan* Prince,
New Ramparts raising for the Town's defence:
A Purple Scarf, with Gold Imbroider'd o're,
385 (Queen *Dido*'s Gift) about his Waste he wore;
A Sword with glitt'ring Gems diversify'd,
For Ornament, not use, hung idly by his side.

Then thus, with winged Words, the God began;
(Resuming his own Shape) degenerate Man,
390   Thou Woman's Property, what mak'st thou here,
These foreign Walls, and *Tyrian* Tow'rs to rear?
Forgetful of thy own? All pow'rful *Jove*,
Who sways the World below, and Heav'n above,
Has sent me down, with this severe Command:
395   What means thy ling'ring in the *Lybian* Land?
If Glory cannot move a Mind so mean,
Nor future Praise, from flitting Pleasure wean,
Regard the Fortunes of thy rising Heir;
The promis'd Crown let young *Ascanius* wear.
400   To whom th' *Ausonian* Scepter, and the State
Of *Rome*'s Imperial Name, is ow'd by Fate.
So spoke the God; and speaking took his flight,
Involv'd in Clouds; and vanish'd out of sight.

    The Pious Prince was seiz'd with sudden Fear;
405   Mute was his Tongue, and upright stood his Hair:
Revolving in his Mind the stern Command,
He longs to fly, and loaths the charming Land.
What shou'd he say, or how shou'd he begin,
What Course, alas! remains, to steer between
410   Th' offended Lover, and the Pow'rful Queen!
This way, and that, he turns his anxious Mind,
And all Expedients tries, and none can find:
Fix'd on the Deed, but doubtful of the Means;
After long thought to this Advice he leans.
415   Three Chiefs he calls, commands them to repair
The Fleet, and ship their Men with silent Care:
Some plausible Pretence he bids them find,
To colour what in secret he design'd.
Himself, mean time, the softest Hours wou'd chuse,
420   Before the Love-sick Lady heard the News.
And move her tender Mind, by slow degrees,
To suffer what the Sov'raign Pow'r decrees:
Jove will inspire him, when, and what to say:
They hear with Pleasure, and with haste obey.

425   But soon the Queen perceives the thin Disguise;
(What Arts can blind a jealous Woman's Eyes!)

She was the first to find the secret Fraud,
Before the fatal News was blaz'd abroad.
Love, the first Motions of the Lover hears,
430   Quick to presage, and ev'n in Safety fears.
Nor impious Fame was wanting to report }
The Ships repair'd; the *Trojans* thick Resort, }
And purpose to forsake the *Tyrian* Court. }
Frantick with Fear, impatient of the Wound,
435   And impotent of Mind, she roves the City round.
Less wild the *Bacchanalian* Dames appear, }
When, from afar, their nightly God they hear, }
And houl about the Hills, and shake the wreathy Spear. }
At length she finds the dear perfidious Man;
440   Prevents his form'd Excuse, and thus began.
Base and ungrateful, cou'd you hope to fly,
And undiscover'd scape a Lover's Eye!
Nor cou'd my Kindness your Compassion move,
Nor plighted Vows, nor dearer bands of Love!
445   Or is the Death of a despairing Queen
Not worth preventing, though too well foreseen?
Ev'n when the Wintry Winds command your stay,
You dare the Tempests, and defie the Sea.
False, as you are, suppose you were not bound
450   To Lands unknown, and foreign Coasts to sound;
Were *Troy* restor'd, and *Priam*'s happy Reign,
Now durst you tempt for *Troy*, the raging Main?
See, whom you fly; am I the Foe you shun;
Now by those holy Vows, so late begun,
455   By this right Hand, (since I have nothing more
To challenge, but the Faith you gave before;)
I beg you by these Tears too truly shed,
By the new Pleasures of our Nuptial Bed;
If ever *Dido*, when you most were kind,
460   Were pleasing in your Eyes, or touch'd your Mind;
By these my Pray'rs, if Pray'rs may yet have Place,
Pity the Fortunes of a falling Race.
For you I have provok'd a Tyrant's Hate,
Incens'd the *Lybian*, and the *Tyrian* State;
465   For you alone I suffer in my Fame;
Bereft of Honour, and expos'd to Shame:

Whom have I now to trust, (ungrateful Guest,)
That only Name remains of all the rest!
What have I left, or whither can I fly;
470   Must I attend *Pygmalion*'s Cruelty!
Or till *Hyarba* shall in Triumph lead
A Queen, that proudly scorn'd his proffer'd Bed!
Had you deferr'd, at least, your hasty Flight,
And left behind some Pledge of our delight,
475   Some Babe to bless the Mother's mournful sight;
Some young *Æneas*, to supply your place;
Whose Features might express his Father's Face;
I should not then complain to live bereft
Of all my Husband, or be wholly left.

480   Here paus'd the Queen; unmov'd he holds his Eyes,
By *Jove*'s Command; nor suffer'd Love to rise,
Tho' heaving in his Heart; and thus at length, replies.
Fair Queen, you never can enough repeat
Your boundless Favours, or I own my Debt;
485   Nor can my Mind forget *Eliza*'s Name,
While vital Breath inspires this Mortal Frame.
This, only let me speak in my Defence,
I never hop'd a secret Flight from hence:
Much less pretended to the Lawful Claim
490   Of Sacred Nuptials, or, a Husband's Name.
For if indulgent Heav'n would leave me free,
And not submit my Life to Fate's Decree,
My Choice would lead me to the *Trojan* Shore,
Those Reliques to review, their Dust adore;
495   And *Priam*'s ruin'd Palace to restore.
But now the *Delphian Oracle* Commands;
And Fate invites me to the *Latian* Lands.
That is the promis'd Place to which I steer,
And all my Vows are terminated there.
500   If you, a *Tyrian*, and a Stranger born,
With Walls and Tow'rs a *Lybian* Town adorn;
Why may not we, like you, a Foreign Race,
Like you seek shelter in a Foreign Place?
As often as the Night obscures the Skies
505   With humid Shades, or twinkling Stars arise,

Anchises angry Ghost in Dreams appears;
Chides my delay, and fills my Soul with fears:
And young *Ascanius* justly may complain,
Of his defrauded Fate, and destin'd Reign.
510   Ev'n now the Herald of the Gods appear'd,
Waking I saw him, and his Message heard.
From *Jove* he came commission'd, Heav'nly bright
With Radiant Beams, and manifest to Sight.
The Sender and the Sent, I both attest,
515   These Walls he enter'd, and those Words Express'd.
Fair Queen, oppose not what the Gods command;
Forc'd by my Fate, I leave your happy Land.
     Thus, while he spoke, already She began,
With sparkling Eyes, to view the guilty Man:
520   From Head to Foot survey'd his Person o're,
Nor longer these outrageous Threats forbore.
False as thou art, and more than false, forsworn;
Not sprung from Noble Blood, nor Goddess-born,
But hewn from hardned Entrails of a Rock;
525   And rough *Hyrcanian* Tygers gave thee suck.
Why shou'd I fawn, what have I worse to fear? ⎤
Did he once look, or lent a list'ning Ear; ⎬
Sigh'd when I sob'd, or shed one kindly Tear? ⎦
All Symptoms of a base Ungrateful Mind,
530   So foul, that which is worse, 'tis hard to find.
Of Man's Injustice, why shou'd I complain?
The Gods, and *Jove* himself behold in vain
Triumphant Treason, yet no Thunder flies: ⎤
Nor *Juno* views my Wrongs with equal Eyes; ⎬
535   Faithless is Earth, and faithless are the Skies! ⎦
Justice is fled, and Truth is now no more;
I sav'd the Shipwrack'd Exile on my Shore:
With needful Food his hungry *Trojans* fed;
I took the Traytor to my Throne and Bed:
540   Fool that I was — 'tis little to repeat
The rest, I stor'd and Rigg'd his ruin'd Fleet.
I rave, I rave: A God's Command he pleads,
And makes Heav'n accessary to his Deeds.
Now *Lycian* Lotts, and now the *Delian* God;
545   Now *Hermes* is employ'd from *Jove*'s abode,

To warn him hence; as if the peaceful State
Of Heav'nly Pow'rs were touch'd with Humane Fate!
But go; thy flight no longer I detain;
Go seek thy promis'd Kingdom through the Main:
550 Yet if the Heav'ns will hear my Pious Vow,
The faithless Waves, not half so false as thou;
Or secret Sands, shall Sepulchers afford
To thy proud Vessels, and their perjur'd Lord.
Then shalt thou call on injur'd *Dido*'s Name;
555 *Dido* shall come, in a black Sulph'ry flame;
When Death has once dissolv'd her Mortal frame. }
Shall smile to see the Traitor vainly weep,
Her angry Ghost arising from the Deep,
Shall haunt thee wakeing, and disturb thy Sleep. }
560 At least my Shade thy Punishment shall know;
And Fame shall spread the pleasing News below.
    Abruptly here she stops: Then turns away
Her loathing Eyes, and shuns the sight of Day.
Amaz'd he stood, revolving in his Mind
565 What Speech to frame, and what Excuse to find.
Her fearfull Maids their fainting Mistress led;
And softly laid her on her Iv'ry Bed.
    But good *Æneas*, tho' he much desir'd
To give that Pity, which her Grief requir'd,
570 Tho' much he mourn'd, and labour'd with his Love,
Resolv'd at length, obeys the Will of *Jove*:
Reviews his Forces; they with early Care
Unmoor their Vessels, and for Sea prepare.
The Fleet is soon afloat, in all its Pride:
575 And well calk'd Gallies in the Harbour ride.
Then Oaks for Oars they fell'd; or as they stood,
Of its green Arms despoil'd the growing Wood.
Studious of Flight: The Beach is cover'd o're
With *Trojan* Bands that blacken all the Shore:
580 On ev'ry side are seen, descending down,
Thick swarms of Souldiers loaden from the Town.
Thus, in Battalia, march embody'd Ants,
Fearefull of Winter, and of future Wants,
T' invade the Corn, and to their Cells convey
585 The plunder'd Forrage of their yellow Prey.

The sable Troops, along the narrow Tracks,
Scarce bear the weighty Burthen on their Backs:
Some set their Shoulders to the pond'rous Grain;
Some guard the Spoil, some lash the lagging Train;
590   All ply their sev'ral Tasks, and equal Toil sustain.
What Pangs the tender Breast of *Dido* tore,
When, from the Tow'r, she saw the cover'd Shore,
And heard the Shouts of Sailors from afar,
Mix'd with the Murmurs of the wat'ry War?
595   All pow'rful Love, what Changes canst thou cause
In Human Hearts, subjected to thy Laws!
Once more her haughty Soul the Tyrant bends;
To Pray'rs and mean Submissions she descends.
No female Arts or Aids she left untry'd,
600   Nor Counsels unexplor'd, before she dy'd.
Look, *Anna*, look; the *Trojans* crowd to Sea,
They spread their Canvass, and their Anchors weigh.
The shouting Crew, their Ships with Garlands bind;
Invoke the Sea-Gods, and invite the Wind.
605   Cou'd I have thought this threatning Blow so near,
My tender Soul had been forewarn'd to bear.
But do not you my last Request deny,
With yon perfidious Man your Int'rest try;
And bring me News, if I must live or die.
610   You are his Fav'rite, you alone can find
The dark recesses of his inmost Mind:
In all his trusted Secrets you have part,
And know the soft Approaches to his Heart.
Haste then, and humbly seek my haughty Foe;
615   Tell him, I did not with the *Grecians* go;
Nor did my Fleet against his Friends employ,
Nor swore the Ruin of unhappy *Troy*.
Nor mov'd with Hands prophane his Father's Dust;
Why should he then reject a suit so just!
620   Whom does he shun, and whither would he fly;
Can he this last, this only Pray'r deny!
Let him at least his dang'rous Flight delay,
Wait better Winds, and hope a calmer Sea.
The Nuptials he disclaims I urge no more;
625   Let him pursue the promis'd *Latian* Shore.

A short delay is all I ask him now,
A pause of Grief; an interval from Woe:
'Till my soft Soul be temper'd to sustain
Accustom'd Sorrows, and inur'd to Pain.
630　If you in Pity grant this one Request,
My Death shall glut the Hatred of his Brest.
This mournful message, Pious *Anna* bears,
And seconds, with her own, her Sister's Tears:
But all her Arts are still employ'd in vain;
635　Again she comes, and is refus'd again.
His harden'd Heart nor Pray'rs nor Threatnings move;
Fate, and the God, had stop'd his Ears to Love.

As when the Winds their airy Quarrel try;
Justling from ev'ry quarter of the Sky;
640　This way and that, the Mountain Oak they bend,
His Boughs they shatter, and his Branches rend;
With Leaves, and falling Mast, they spread the Ground,
The hollow Vallies eccho to the Sound:
Unmov'd, the Royal Plant their Fury mocks;
645　Or shaken, clings more closely to the Rocks:
Far as he shoots his tow'ring Head on high,
So deep in Earth his fix'd Foundations lie.
No less a Storm the *Trojan* Heroe bears; ⎫
Thick Messages and loud Complaints he hears; ⎬
650　And bandy'd Words, still beating on his Ears. ⎭
Sighs, Groans and Tears, proclaim his inward Pains,
But the firm purpose of his Heart remains.

The wretched Queen, pursu'd by cruel Fate,
Begins at length the light of Heav'n to hate:
655　And loaths to live: Then dire Portents she sees,
To hasten on the death her Soul decrees.
Strange to relate: For when before the Shrine
She pours, in Sacrifice, the Purple Wine,
The Purple Wine is turn'd to putrid Blood:
660　And the white offer'd Milk, converts to Mud.
This dire Presage, to her alone reveal'd,
From all, and ev'n her Sister, she conceal'd.
A Marble Temple stood within the Grove,
Sacred to Death, and to her murther'd Love;

665   That honour'd Chappel she had hung around
      With snowy Fleeces, and with Garlands crown'd:
      Oft, when she visited this lonely Dome,
      Strange Voices issu'd from her Husband's Tomb:
      She thought she heard him summon her away;
670   Invite her to his Grave; and chide her stay.
      Hourly 'tis heard, when with a bodeing Note
      The solitary Screech-Owl strains her Throat:
      And on a Chimney's top, or Turret's height,
      With Songs obscene, disturbs the Silence of the Night.
675   Besides, old Prophecies augment her Fears;
      And stern *Æneas* in her Dreams appears,
      Disdainful as by Day: She seems alone,
      To wander in her Sleep, thro' ways unknown,
      Guidless and dark: or, in a Desart Plain,
680   To seek her Subjects, and to seek in vain.
      Like *Pentheus*, when distracted with his Fear,
      He saw two Suns, and double *Thebes* appear:
      Or mad *Orestes*, when his Mother's Ghost
      Full in his Face, infernal Torches tost;
685   And shook her snaky locks: He shuns the sight,
      Flies o're the Stage, surpris'd with mortal fright;
      The Furies guard the Door; and intercept his flight.
         Now, sinking underneath a load of Grief,
      From Death alone, she seeks her last Relief:
690   The Time and Means, resolv'd within her Breast,
      She to her mournful Sister, thus address'd.
      (Dissembling hope, her cloudy front she clears,
      And a false Vigour in her Eyes appears.)
      Rejoyce she said, instructed from above,
695   My Lover I shall gain, or lose my Love.
      Nigh rising *Atlas*, next the falling Sun,
      Long tracts of *Æthiopian* Climates run:
      There, a *Massylian* Priestess I have found,
      Honour'd for Age; for Magick Arts renown'd:
700   Th' *Hesperian* Temple was her trusted Care;
      'Twas she supply'd the wakeful Dragons Fare.
      She Poppy-Seeds in Honey taught to steep;
      Reclaim'd his Rage; and sooth'd him into sleep.

She watch'd the Golden Fruit; her Charms unbind
705   The Chains of Love; or fix them on the Mind.
She stops the Torrents, leaves the Channel dry;
Repels the Stars; and backward bears the Sky.
The yawning Earth rebellows to her Call;
Pale Ghosts ascend; and Mountain Ashes fall.
710   Witness, ye Gods, and thou my better part,
How loth I am to try this impious Art!
Within the secret Court, with silent Care,
Erect a lofty Pile, expos'd in Air:
Hang on the topmost part, the *Trojan* Vest;
715   Spoils, Arms, and Presents of my faithless Guest.
Next, under these, the Bridal Bed be plac'd,
Where I my Ruin in his Arms embrac'd:
All Relicks of the Wretch are doom'd to Fire;
For so the Priestess, and her Charms require.
720   Thus far she said, and farther Speech forbears:
A Mortal Paleness in her Face appears:
Yet, the mistrustless *Anna*, could not find ⎫
The secret Fun'ral, in these Rites design'd; ⎬
Nor thought so dire a Rage possess'd her Mind. ⎭
725   Unknowing of a Train conceal'd so well,
She fear'd no worse than when *Sichæus* fell:
Therefore obeys. The fatal Pile they rear,
Within the secret Court, expos'd in Air.
The cloven Holms and Pines are heap'd on high;
730   And Garlands on the hollow Spaces lye.
Sad Cypress, Vervain, Eugh, compose the Wreath;
And ev'ry baleful green denoting Death.
The Queen, determin'd to the fatal Deed, ⎫
The Spoils and Sword he left, in order spread: ⎬
735   And the Man's Image on the Nuptial Bed. ⎭
      And now (the sacred Altars plac'd around) ⎫
The Priestess enters, with her Hair unbound, ⎬
And thrice invokes the Pow'rs below the Ground. ⎭
Night, *Erebus* and *Chaos* she proclaims,
740   And threefold *Hecat*, with her hundred Names,
And three *Diana*'s: next she sprinkles round,
With feign'd *Avernian* Drops, the hallow'd ground;

Culls hoary Simples, found by *Phœbe*'s Light,
With brazen Sickles reap'd at Noon of Night.
745   Then mixes baleful Juices in the Bowl:
And cuts the Forehead of a new-born Fole;
Robbing the Mother's love. The destin'd Queen
Observes, assisting at the Rites obscene:
A leaven'd Cake in her devoted Hands
750   She holds, and next the highest Altar stands:
One tender Foot was shod, her other bare;
Girt was her gather'd Gown, and loose her Hair.
Thus dress'd, she summon'd with her dying Breath,
The Heav'ns and Planets conscious of her Death:
755   And ev'ry Pow'r, if any rules above,
Who minds, or who revenges injur'd Love.
      'Twas dead of Night, when weary Bodies close
Their Eyes in balmy Sleep, and soft Repose:
The Winds no longer whisper through the Woods,
760   Nor murm'ring Tides disturb the gentle Floods.
The Stars in silent order mov'd around,
And Peace, with downy wings, was brooding on the ground.
The Flocks and Herds, and parti-colour'd Fowl,
Which haunt the Woods, or swim the weedy Pool;
765   Stretch'd on the quiet Earth securely lay,
Forgetting the past Labours of the day.
All else of Nature's common Gift partake;
Unhappy *Dido* was alone awake.
Nor Sleep nor Ease the Furious Queen can find,
770   Sleep fled her Eyes, as Quiet fled her mind.
Despair, and Rage, and Love, divide her heart;
Despair, and Rage had some, but Love the greater part.
      Then thus she said within her secret Mind:
What shall I do, what Succour can I find!
775   Become a Supplyant to *Hyarba*'s Pride,
And take my turn, to Court and be deny'd!
Shall I with this ungrateful *Trojan* go,
Forsake an Empire, and attend a Foe?
Himself I refug'd, and his Train reliev'd;
780   Tis true; but am I sure to be receiv'd?
Can Gratitude in *Trojan* Souls have place?
Laomedon still lives in all his Race!

Then, shall I seek alone the Churlish Crew,
Or with my Fleet their flying Sails pursue?
785　What force have I but those, whom scarce before
I drew reluctant from their Native Shore?
Will they again Embark at my desire,
Once more sustain the Seas, and quit their second *Tyre*?
Rather with Steel thy guilty Breast invade,
790　And take the Fortune thou thy self hast made.
Your pity, Sister, first seduc'd my Mind;
Or seconded too well, what I design'd.
These dear-bought Pleasures had I never known,
Had I continu'd free, and still my own;
795　Avoiding Love; I had not found Despair:
But shar'd with Salvage Beasts the Common Air.
Like them a lonely life I might have led,
Not mourn'd the Living, nor disturb'd the Dead.
These Thoughts she brooded in her anxious Breast;
800　On board, the *Trojan* found more easie rest.
Resolv'd to sail, in Sleep he pass'd the Night;
And order'd all things for his early flight.

　　To whom once more the winged God appears; ⎫
His former Youthfull Meen and Shape he wears, ⎬
805　And with this new alarm invades his Ears. ⎭
Sleep'st thou, O Goddess born! and can'st thou drown
Thy needful Cares, so near a Hostile Town?
Beset with Foes; nor hear'st the Western Gales
Invite thy passage, and Inspire thy sails?
810　She harbours in her Heart a furious hate;
And thou shalt find the dire Effects too late;
Fix'd on Revenge, and Obstinate to die:
Haste swiftly hence, while thou hast pow'r to fly.
The Sea with Ships will soon be cover'd o're,
815　And blazing Firebrands kindle all the Shore.
Prevent her rage, while Night obscures the Skies;
And sail before the purple Morn arise.
Who knows what Hazards thy Delay may bring?
Woman's a various and a changeful Thing.
820　Thus *Hermes* in the Dream; then took his flight,
Aloft in Air unseen; and mix'd with Night.

Twice warn'd by the Cœlestial Messenger,
The Pious Prince arose with hasty fear:
Then rowz'd his drowsie Train without delay,
825   Haste to your banks; your crooked Anchors weigh;
And spread your flying Sails, and stand to Sea.
A God commands; he stood before my sight;
And urg'd us once again to speedy flight.
O sacred Pow'r, what Pow'r so e're thou art,
830   To thy bless'd Orders I resign my heart:
Lead thou the way; protect thy *Trojan* Bands;
And prosper the Design thy Will Commands.
He said, and drawing forth his flaming Sword,
His thund'ring Arm divides the many twisted Cord:
835   An emulating Zeal inspires his Train;
They run, they snatch; they rush into the main.
With headlong haste they leave the desert Shores,
And brush the liquid Seas with lab'ring Oars.
Aurora now had left her Saffron Bed,
840   And beams of early Light the Heav'ns o'respread,
When from a Tow'r the Queen, with wakeful Eyes,
Saw Day point upward from the rosie Skies:
She look'd to Seaward, but the Sea was void,
And scarce in ken the sailing Ships descry'd:
845   Stung with despight, and furious with despair,
She struck her trembling Breast, and tore her Hair.
And shall th' ungrateful Traytor go, she said,
My Land forsaken, and my Love betray'd?
Shall we not Arm, not rush from ev'ry Street,
850   To follow, sink, and burn his perjur'd Fleet?
Haste, haul my Gallies out, pursue the Foe:
Bring flaming Brands, set sail, and swiftly row.
What have I said? where am I? Fury turns
My Brain; and my distemper'd Bosom burns.
855   Then, when I gave my Person and my Throne,
This Hate, this Rage, had been more timely shown.
See now the promis'd Faith, the vaunted Name,
The Pious Man, who, rushing through the Flame,
Preserv'd his Gods; and to the *Phrygian* Shore
860   The Burthen of his feeble Father bore!

I shou'd have torn him piece-meal; strow'd in Floods
His scatter'd Limbs, or left expos'd in Woods:
Destroy'd his Friends and Son; and from the Fire
Have set the reeking Boy before the Sire.
865   Events are doubtful, which on Battels wait;
Yet where's the doubt, to Souls secure of Fate!
My *Tyrians*, at their injur'd Queen's Command,
Had toss'd their Fires amid the *Trojan* Band:
At once extinguish'd all the faithless Name;
870   And I my self, in vengeance of my Shame,
Had fall'n upon the Pile to mend the Fun'ral Flame.
Thou Sun, who view'st at once the World below,
Thou *Juno*, Guardian of the Nuptial Vow,
Thou *Hecat*, hearken from thy dark abodes;
875   Ye Furies, Fiends, and violated Gods,
All Pow'rs invok'd with *Dido*'s dying breath,
Attend her Curses, and avenge her death.
If so the Fates ordain, and *Jove* commands,
Th' ungrateful Wretch should find the *Latian* Lands,
880   Yet let a Race untam'd, and haughty Foes,
His peaceful Entrance with dire Arms oppose;
Oppress'd with Numbers in th' unequal Field,
His Men discourag'd, and himself expell'd,
Let him for Succour sue from place to place,
885   Torn from his Subjects, and his Son's embrace:
First let him see his Friends in Battel slain;
And their untimely Fate lament in vain:
And when, at length, the cruel War shall cease;
On hard Conditions may he buy his Peace.
890   Nor let him then enjoy supreme Command;
But fall untimely, by some hostile Hand:
And lie unbury'd on the barren Sand.
These are my Pray'rs, and this my dying Will:
And you my *Tyrians* ev'ry Curse fulfill.
895   Perpetual Hate, and mortal Wars proclaim,
Against the Prince, the People, and the Name.
These grateful Off'rings on my Grave bestow;
Nor League, nor Love, the Hostile Nations know:
Now, and from hence in ev'ry future Age,
900   When Rage excites your Arms, and Strength supplies the

Rise some Avenger of our *Lybian* Blood,
With Fire and Sword pursue the perjur'd Brood:
Our Arms, our Seas, our Shores, oppos'd to theirs,
And the same hate descend on all our Heirs.

905   This said, within her anxious Mind she weighs
The Means of cutting short her odious Days.
Then to *Sicheus*'s Nurse, she briefly said,
(For when she left her Country, hers was dead)
Go *Barce*, call my Sister; let her Care
910 The solemn Rites of Sacrifice prepare:
The Sheep, and all th' attoneing Off'rings bring;
Sprinkling her Body from the Crystal Spring
With living Drops: then let her come, and thou
With sacred Fillets, bind thy hoary Brow.
915 Thus will I pay my Vows, to *Stygian Jove*;
And end the Cares of my disastrous Love.
Then cast the *Trojan* Image on the Fire;
And as that burns, my Passion shall expire.

      The Nurse moves onward, with officious Care,
920 And all the speed her aged Limbs can bear.
But furious *Dido*, with dark Thoughts involv'd,
Shook at the mighty Mischief she resolv'd.
With livid Spots distinguish'd was her Face,
Red were her rowling Eyes, and discompos'd her Pace:
925 Ghastly she gaz'd, with Pain she drew her Breath,
And Nature shiver'd at approaching Death.

      Then swiftly to the fatal place she pass'd;
And mounts the Fun'ral Pile, with furious haste.
Unsheaths the Sword the *Trojan* left behind,
930 (Not for so dire an Enterprise design'd,)
But when she view'd the Garments loosely spred,
Which once he wore, and saw the conscious Bed,
She paus'd, and, with a Sigh, the Robes embrac'd; ⎫
Then on the Couch her trembling Body cast,   ⎬
935 Repress'd the ready Tears, and spoke her last. ⎭
Dear Pledges of my Love, while Heav'n so pleas'd,
Receive a Soul, of Mortal Anguish eas'd:
My fatal Course is finish'd; and I go
A glorious Name, among the Ghosts below.

940 A lofty City by my Hands is rais'd;
    Pygmalion punish'd, and my Lord appeas'd.
    What cou'd my Fortune have afforded more,
    Had the false *Trojan* never touch'd my Shore!
    Then kiss'd the Couch; and must I die, she said
945 And unreveng'd; 'tis doubly to be dead!
    Yet ev'n this Death with Pleasure I receive;
    On any Terms, 'tis better than to live.
    These Flames, from far, may the false *Trojan* view;
    These boding Omens his base flight pursue.
950 She said, and struck: Deep enter'd in her side
    The piercing Steel, with reeking Purple dy'd:
    Clog'd in the Wound the cruel Weapon stands;
    The spouting Blood came streaming on her Hands.
    Her sad Attendants saw the deadly Stroke,
955 And with loud Cries the sounding Palace shook.
    Distracted from the fatal sight they fled;
    And thro' the Town the dismal Rumour spread.
    First from the frighted Court, the Yell began,
    Redoubled thence from House to House it ran:
960 The groans of Men, with Shrieks, Laments, and Cries
    Of mixing Women, mount the vaulted Skies.
    Not less the Clamour, than if ancient *Tyre*,
    Or the new *Carthage*, set by Foes on Fire,
    The rowling Ruin, with their lov'd Abodes,
965 Involv'd the blazing Temples of their Gods.
    Her Sister hears, and, furious with Despair,
    She beats her Breast, and rends her yellow Hair:
    And calling on *Eliza*'s Name aloud,
    Runs breathless to the Place, and breaks the Crowd.
970 Was all that Pomp of Woe for this prepar'd,
    These Fires, this Fun'ral Pile, these Altars rear'd;
    Was all this Train of Plots contriv'd, said she,
    All only to deceive unhappy me?
    Which is the worst, didst thou in Death pretend
975 To scorn thy Sister, or delude thy Friend!
    Thy summon'd Sister, and thy Friend had come:
    One Sword had serv'd us both, one common Tomb.
    Was I to raise the Pile, the Pow'rs invoke,
    Not to be present at the fatal Stroke?

980   At once thou hast destroy'd thy self and me;
       Thy Town, thy Senate, and thy Colony!
       Bring Water, bathe the Wound; while I in death
       Lay close my Lips to hers; and catch the flying Breath.
       This said, she mounts the Pile with eager haste;
985   And in her Arms the gasping Queen embrac'd:
       Her Temples chaf'd; and her own Garments tore
       To stanch the streaming Blood, and cleanse the Gore.
       Thrice *Dido* try'd to raise her drooping Head,
       And fainting thrice, fell grov'ling on the Bed.
990   Thrice op'd her heavy Eyes, and sought the Light, ⎫
       But having found it, sicken'd at the sight;   ⎬
       And clos'd her Lids at last, in endless Night.   ⎭
       Then *Juno*, grieving that she shou'd sustain
       A Death so ling'ring, and so full of Pain;
995   Sent *Iris* down, to free her from the Strife
       Of lab'ring Nature, and dissolve her Life.
       For since she dy'd, not doom'd by Heav'ns Decree,
       Or her own Crime; but Human Casualty;
       And rage of Love, that plung'd her in Despair,
1000   The Sisters had not cut the topmost Hair;
       Which *Proserpine*, and they can only know;
       Nor made her sacred to the Shades below.
       Downward the various Goddess took her flight;
       And drew a thousand Colours from the Light:
1005   Then stood above the dying Lover's Head,
       And said, I thus devote thee to the dead.
       This Off'ring to th' Infernal Gods I bear: ⎫
       Thus while she spoke, she cut the fatal Hair;   ⎬
       The strugling Soul was loos'd; and Life dissolv'd in Air. ⎭

THE FIFTH BOOK OF THE ÆNEIS

The Argument

Æneas *setting sail from* Africk, *is driven by a Storm on the Coasts of* Sicily: *Where he is Hospitably receiv'd by his Friend* Acestes, *King of part of the Island, and Born of* Trojan *Parentage. He applies himself to celebrate the Memory of his Father with Divine Honours: And accordingly institutes Funeral Games, and appoints Prizes for those who shou'd Conquer in them. While the Ceremonies were performing,* Juno *sends* Iris *to perswade the* Trojan *Women to burn the Ships, who upon her Instigation, set fire to them, which burnt four, and would have consum'd the rest, had not* Jupiter, *by a miraculous Shower extinguish'd it. Upon this* Æneas *by the Advice of one of his Generals, and a Vision of his Father, builds a City for the Women, Old Men, and others, who were either unfit for War, or weary of the Voyage, and sails for* Italy: Venus *procures of* Neptune *a safe Voyage for him and all his Men, excepting only his Pilot* Palinurus, *who is unfortunately lost.*

Mean time the *Trojan* cuts his wat'ry way,
Fix'd on his Voyage, thro' the curling Sea:
Then, casting back his Eyes, with dire Amaze,
Sees on the *Punic* Shore the mounting Blaze.
5   The Cause unknown; yet his presaging Mind,
The Fate of *Dido* from the Fire divin'd:
He knew the stormy Souls of Woman-kind:
What secret Springs their eager Passions move,
How capable of Death for injur'd Love.
10 Dire Auguries from hence the *Trojans* draw;
'Till neither Fires, nor shining Shores they saw.
Now Seas and Skies, their Prospect only bound;
An empty space above, a floating Field around.
But soon the Heav'ns with shadows were o'respread;
15 A swelling Cloud hung hov'ring o're their Head:
Livid it look'd, (the threatning of a Storm;)
Then Night and Horror Ocean's Face deform.
The Pilot, *Palinurus*, cry'd aloud,
What Gusts of Weather from that gath'ring Cloud
20 My Thoughts presage; e're yet the Tempest roars,
Stand to your Tackle, Mates, and stretch your Oars;
Contract your swelling Sails, and luff to Wind:
The frighted Crew perform the Task assign'd.
Then, to his fearless Chief, not Heav'n, said he,
25 Tho' *Jove* himself shou'd promise *Italy*,
Can stem the Torrent of this raging Sea.
Mark how the shifting Winds from West arise,
And what collected Night involves the Skies!
Nor can our shaken Vessels live at Sea,
30 Much less against the Tempest force their way;
'Tis Fate diverts our Course; and Fate we must obey.
Not far from hence, if I observ'd aright
The southing of the Stars, and Polar Light,

Sicilia lies; whose hospitable Shores
35   In safety we may reach with strugling Oars.
Æneas then reply'd, too sure I find,
We strive in vain against the Seas, and Wind:
Now shift your Sails: What place can please me more
Than what you promise, the *Sicilian* Shore;
40   Whose hallow'd Earth *Anchises* Bones contains,
And where a Prince of *Trojan* Lineage reigns?
The Course resolv'd, before the Western Wind
They scud amain; and make the Port assign'd.
    Mean time *Acestes*, from a lofty Stand,
45   Beheld the Fleet descending on the Land;
And not unmindful of his ancient Race,
Down from the Cliff he ran with eager Pace;
And held the Heroe in a strict Embrace.
Of a rough *Lybian* Bear the Spoils he wore;
50   And either Hand a pointed Jav'lin bore.
His Mother was a Dame of *Dardan* Blood;
His Sire *Crinisus*, a *Sicilian* Flood;
He welcomes his returning Friends ashore
With plenteous Country Cates; and homely Store.
55   Now, when the following Morn had chas'd away
The flying Stars, and light restor'd the Day,
Æneas call'd the *Trojan* Troops around;
And thus bespoke them from a rising Ground.
Off-spring of Heav'n, Divine *Dardanian* Race,
60   The Sun revolving thro' th' Etherial Space,
The shining Circle of the Year has fill'd,
Since first this Isle my Father's Ashes held:
And now the rising Day renews the Year,
(A Day for ever sad, for ever dear,)
65   This wou'd I celebrate with Annual Games,
With Gifts on Altars pil'd, and holy Flames,
Tho banish'd to *Getulia*'s barren Sands,
Caught on the *Grecian* Seas, or hostile Lands:
But since this happy Storm our Fleet has driv'n
70   (Not, as I deem, without the Will of Heav'n,)
Upon these friendly Shores, and flow'ry Plains,
Which hide *Anchises*, and his blest Remains;

Let us with Joy perform his Honours due;
And pray for prosp'rous Winds, our Voyage to renew.
75   Pray, that in Towns, and Temples of our own,
The Name of great *Anchises* may be known;
And yearly Games may spread the Gods renown.
Our Sports, *Acestes* of the *Trojan* Race,
With Royal Gifts, ordain'd, is pleas'd to grace:
80   Two Steers on ev'ry Ship the King bestows;
His Gods and ours, shall share your equal Vows.
Besides, if nine days hence, the rosy Morn
Shall with unclouded Light the Skies adorn,
That Day with solemn Sports I mean to grace;
85   Light Gallies on the Seas, shall run a wat'ry Race.
Some shall in Swiftness for the Goal contend,
And others try the twanging Bow to bend:
The strong with Iron Gauntlets arm'd shall stand,
Oppos'd in Combat on the yellow Sand.
90   Let all be present at the Games prepar'd;
And joyful Victors wait the Just Reward.
But now assist the Rites, with Garlands crown'd;
He said, and first his Brows with Myrtle bound.
Then *Helymus*, by his Example led,
95   And old *Acestes*, each adorn'd his Head;
Thus, young *Ascanius*, with a sprightly Grace,
His Temples ty'd, and all the *Trojan* Race.
   Æneas then advanc'd amidst the Train,
By thousands follow'd thro' the flowry Plain,
100 To great *Anchises* Tomb: Which when he found,
He pour'd to *Bacchus*, on the hallow'd Ground,
Two Bowls of sparkling Wine, of Milk two more,
And two from offer'd Bulls of Purple Gore.
With Roses then the Sepulchre he strow'd;
105 And thus, his Father's Ghost bespoke aloud.
Hail, O ye Holy Manes; hail again
Paternal Ashes, now review'd in vain!
The Gods permitted not, that you, with me,
Shou'd reach the promis'd Shores of *Italy*;
110 Or *Tiber*'s Flood, what Flood so e're it be.
Scarce had he finish'd, when, with speckled Pride,
A Serpent from the Tomb began to glide;

His hugy Bulk on sev'n high Volumes roll'd;
Blue was his breadth of Back, but streak'd with scaly Gold:
115   Thus riding on his Curls, he seem'd to pass
A rowling Fire along; and singe the Grass.
More various Colours thro' his Body run,
Than *Iris* when her Bow imbibes the Sun;
Betwixt the rising Altars, and around,
120   The sacred Monster shot along the Ground;
With harmless play amidst the Bowls he pass'd;
And with his lolling Tongue assay'd the Taste:
Thus fed with Holy Food, the wond'rous Guest
Within the hollow Tomb retir'd to rest.
125   The Pious Prince, surpris'd at what he view'd,
The Fun'ral Honours with more Zeal renew'd:
Doubtful if this the Place's Genius were,
Or Guardian of his Father's Sepulchre.
Five Sheep, according to the Rites, he slew;
130   As many Swine, and Steers of Sable Hue;
New gen'rous Wine he from the Goblets pour'd,
And call'd his Fathers Ghost, from Hell restor'd.
The glad Attendants in long Order come,
Off'ring their Gifts at great *Anchises* Tomb:
135   Some add more Oxen, some divide the Spoil, ⎫
Some place the Chargers on the grassy Soil; ⎬
Some blow the Fires and offer'd Entrails broil. ⎭
      Now came the Day desir'd; the Skies were bright
With rosy Lustre of the rising Light:
140   The bord'ring People, rowz'd by sounding Fame
Of *Trojan* Feasts, and great *Acestes* Name;
The crowded Shore with Acclamations fill,
Part to behold, and part to prove their Skill.
And first the Gifts in Publick view they place,
145   Green Lawrel Wreaths, and Palm, (the Victors grace:)
Within the Circle, Arms and Tripods lye; ⎫
Ingotts of Gold, and Silver, heap'd on high; ⎬
And Vests embroider'd of the *Tyrian* dye. ⎭
The Trumpet's clangor then the Feast proclaims;
150   And all prepare for their appointed Games.
Four Gallies first which equal Rowers bear,
Advanc'ing, in the wat'ry Lists appear.

The speedy Dolphin, that out-strips the Wind,
Bore *Mnestheus*, Author of the *Memmian* kind:
155   *Gyas*, the vast *Chymæra*'s Bulk commands,
Which rising like a tow'ring City stands:
Three *Trojans* tug at ev'ry lab'ring Oar;   }
Three Banks in three degrees the Sailors bore;
Beneath their Sturdy Stroaks the Billows roar.
160   *Sergestus*, who began the *Sergian* Race,
In the great *Centaur* took the leading Place:
Cloanthus on the Sea-green *Scylla* stood;
From whom *Cluentius* draws his *Trojan* Blood.

      Far in the Sea, against the foaming Shoar,
165   There stands a Rock; the raging Billows roar
Above his Head in Storms; but when 'tis clear,
Uncurl their ridgy Backs, and at his Foot appear.
In Peace below the gentle Waters run;
The Cormorants above, lye Basking in the Sun.
170   On this the Heroe fix'd an Oak in sight,
The mark to guide the Mariners aright.
To bear with this, the Seamen stretch their Oars;
Then round the rock they steer, and seek the former Shoars.
The Lots decide their place; above the rest,
175   Each Leader shining in his *Tyrian* Vest:
The common Crew, with Wreaths of Poplar Boughs,
Their Temples crown, and shade their sweaty Brows.
Besmear'd with Oil, their naked Shoulders shine;
All take their Seats, and wait the sounding sign.
180   They gripe their Oars, and ev'ry panting Breast
Is rais'd by turns with Hope, by turns with Fear depress'd.
The clangor of the Trumpet gives the Sign;
At once they start, advancing in a Line:
With shouts the Sailors rend the starry Skys,   }
185   Lash'd with their Oars, the smoaky Billows rise;
Sparkles the briny Main, and the vex'd Ocean fries.
Exact in time, with equal Stroaks they row;   }
At once the brushing Oars, and brazen prow
Dash up the sandy Waves, and ope the Depths below.
190   Not fiery Coursers, in a Chariot Race,
Invade the Field with half so swift a Pace.

Not the fierce Driver with more Fury lends
The sounding Lash; and, e're the Stroke descends,
Low to the Wheels his pliant Body bends.

195 The partial Crowd their Hopes and Fears divide;
And aid, with eager shouts the favour'd Side.
Cries, Murmurs, Clamours, with a mixing Sound,
From Woods to Woods, from Hills to Hills rebound.

　　Amidst the loud Applauses of the Shore,

200 *Gyas* out-strip'd the rest, and sprung before;
Cloanthus, better mann'd, pursu'd him fast;
But his o're-masted Gally check'd his Haste.
The *Centaur*, and the Dolphin, brush the brine
With equal Oars, advancing in a Line:

205 And now the mighty *Centaur* seems to lead,
And now the speedy Dolphin gets a head:
Now Board to Board the rival Vessels row;
The Billows lave the Skies, and Ocean groans below.
They reach'd the Mark; proud *Gyas* and his Train,

210 In Triumph rode the Victors of the Main:
But steering round, he charg'd his Pilot stand
More close to Shore and skim along the Sand.
Let others bear to Sea. *Menætes* heard,
But secret shelves too cautiously he fear'd:

215 And fearing, sought the Deep; and still aloof he steer'd.
With louder Cries the Captain call'd again;
Bear to the rocky Shore, and shun the Main.
He spoke, and speaking at his stern he saw
The bold *Cloanthus* near the Shelvings draw;

220 Betwixt the mark and him the *Scylla* stood,
And in a closer Compass plow'd the Flood,
He pass'd the Mark; and wheeling got before;
Gyas blasphem'd the Gods, devoutly swore,
Cry'd out for Anger, and his Hair he tore.

225 Mindless of others Lives, (so high was grown
His rising Rage,) and careless of his own:
The trembling Dotard to the Deck he drew,
Then hoisted up, and over-board he threw,
This done he seiz'd the Helm; his Fellows cheer'd;

230 Turn'd short upon the Shelfs, and madly steer'd.

Hardly his Head, the plunging Pilot rears,
Clog'd with his Cloaths, and cumber'd with his Years:
Now dropping wet, he climbs the Cliff with Pain;
The Crowd that saw him fall, and float again,
235 Shout from the distant Shore; and loudly laught,
To see his heaving Breast disgorge the briny Draught.
The following Centaur, and the Dolphin's Crew,
Their vanish'd hopes of Victory renew:
While *Gyas* lags, they kindle in the Race,
240 To reach the Mark; *Sergesthus* takes the place:
Mnestheus pursues; and while around they wind,
Comes up, not half his Gally's length behind.
Then, on the Deck amidst his Mates appear'd,
And thus their drooping Courages he cheer'd.
245 My Friends, and *Hector*'s Followers heretofore;
Exert your Vigour, tug the lab'ring Oar;
Stretch to your Stroaks, my still unconquer'd Crew,
Whom from the flaming Walls of *Troy* I drew.
In this, our common Int'rest, let me find
250 That strength of Hand, that courage of the Mind,
As when you stem'd the strong *Malæan* Flood,
And o're the *Syrtes* broken Billows row'd.
I seek not now the foremost Palm to gain; ⎫
Tho yet – But ah, that haughty Wish is vain! ⎬
255 Let those enjoy it whom the Gods ordain. ⎭
But to be last, the Lags of all the Race,
Redeem your selves and me from that Disgrace.
Now one and all, they tug amain; they row
At the full stretch, and shake the Brazen Prow.
260 The Sea beneath 'em sinks; their lab'ring sides
Are swell'd, and Sweat runs gutt'ring down in Tides.
Chance aids their daring with unhop'd Success;
Sergesthus, eager with his Beak, to press
Betwixt the Rival Gally and the Rock;
265 Shuts up th' unwieldy Centaur in the Lock.
The Vessel struck, and with the dreadful shock
Her Oars she shiver'd, and her Head she broke.
The trembling Rowers from their Banks arise,
And anxious for themselves renounce the Prize.

270   With Iron Poles they heave her off the Shores;
And gather, from the Sea, their floating Oars.
The Crew of *Mnestheus*, with elated Minds,
Urge their Success, and call the willing Winds:
Then ply their Oars, and cut their liquid way;
275   In larger Compass on the roomy Sea.
As when the Dove her Rocky Hold forsakes,
Rowz'd in a Fright, her sounding Wings she shakes
The Cavern rings with clatt'ring; out she flies,
And leaves her Callow Care, and cleaves the Skies;
280   At first she flutters; but at length she springs,
To smoother flight, and shoots upon her Wings:
So *Mnestheus* in the *Dolphin* cuts the Sea,
And flying with a force, that force assists his Way.
Sergesthus in the *Centaur* soon he pass'd,
285   Wedg'd in the Rocky Sholes, and sticking fast.
In vain the Victor he with Cries implores,
And practices to row with shatter'd Oars.
Then *Mnestheus* bears with *Gyas*, and out-flies:
The Ship without a Pilot yields the Prize.
290   Unvanquish'd *Scylla* now alone remains;
Her he pursues; and all his vigour strains.
Shouts from the fav'ring Multitude arise,
Applauding Eccho to the Shouts replies;
Shouts, Wishes, and Applause run ratling through the
    Skies.
295   These Clamours with disdain the *Scylla* heard;
Much grudg'd the Praise, but more the rob'd Reward:
Resolv'd to hold their own, they mend their pace;
All obstinate to dye, or gain the Race.
Rais'd with Success, the *Dolphin* swiftly ran,
300   (For they can Conquer who believe they can:)
Both urge their Oars, and Fortune both supplies;
And both, perhaps had shar'd an equal Prize;
When to the Seas *Cloanthus* holds his Hands,
And Succour from the Watry Pow'rs Demands:
305   Gods of the liquid Realms, on which I row,
If giv'n by you, the Lawrel bind my Brow,
Assist to make me guilty of my Vow.

A Snow-white Bull shall on your Shore be slain,
His offer'd Entrails cast into the Main;
310 And ruddy Wine from Golden Goblets thrown,
Your grateful Gift and my Return shall own.
The Quire of Nymphs, and *Phorcus* from below,
With Virgin *Panopea*, heard his Vow;
And old *Portunus*, with his breadth of Hand,
315 Push'd on, and sped the Gally to the Land.
Swift as a Shaft, or winged Wind, she flies;
And darting to the Port, obtains the Prize.
The Herald summons all, and then proclaims
Cloanthus Conqu'ror of the Naval Games.
320 The Prince with Lawrel crowns the Victor's Head,
And three fat Steers are to his Vessel led;
The Ships Reward: with gen'rous Wine beside;
And Sums of Silver, which the Crew divide.
The Leaders are distinguish'd from the rest;
325 The Victor honour'd with a nobler Vest:
Where Gold and Purple strive in equal Rows;
And Needle-work its happy Cost bestows.
There, *Ganymede* is wrought with living Art,
Chasing thro' *Ida*'s Groves the trembling Hart:
330 Breathless he seems, yet eager to pursue;
When from aloft, descends in open view,
The Bird of *Jove*; and sowsing on his Prey,
With crooked Tallons bears the Boy away.
In vain, with lifted Hands, and gazing Eyes, ⎫
335 His Guards behold him soaring thro' the Skies; ⎬
And Dogs pursue his Flight, with imitated Cries. ⎭
Mnestheus the second Victor was declar'd;
And summon'd there, the second Prize he shar'd.
A Coat of Mail, which brave *Demoleus* bore; ⎫
340 More brave *Æneas* from his Shoulders tore; ⎬
In single Combat on the *Trojan* Shore. ⎭
This was ordain'd for *Mnestheus* to possess;
In War for his Defence; for Ornament in Peace.
Rich was the Gift, and glorious to behold;
345 But yet so pond'rous with its Plates of Gold,
That scarce two Servants cou'd the Weight sustain; ⎫
Yet, loaded thus, *Demoleus* o're the Plain ⎬
Pursu'd, and lightly seiz'd the *Trojan* Train. ⎭

The Third succeeding to the last Reward,
350 Two goodly Bowls of Massy Silver shar'd;
With Figures prominent, and richly wrought:
And two Brass Caldrons from *Dodona* brought.
    Thus, all rewarded by the Heroe's hands,
Their conqu'ring Temples bound with Purple Bands.
355 And now *Sergesthus*, clearing from the Rock,
Brought back his Gally shatter'd with the shock.
Forlorn she look'd, without an aiding Oar;
And howted, by the Vulgar, made to Shoar.
As when a Snake, surpris'd upon the Road,
360 Is crush'd athwart her Body by the load
Of heavy Wheels; or with a Mortal Wound
Her Belly bruis'd, and trodden to the Ground:
In vain, with loosen'd curls, she crawls along,
Yet fierce above, she brandishes her Tongue:
365 Glares with her Eyes, and bristles with her Scales,
But groveling in the Dust; her parts unsound she trails.
So slowly to the Port the *Centaur* tends,
But what she wants in Oars, with Sails amends:
Yet, for his Gally sav'd, the grateful Prince,
370 Is pleas'd th' unhappy Chief to recompence.
Pholoe, the *Cretan* Slave, rewards his Care,
Beauteous her self, with lovely Twins, as fair.
    From thence his way the *Trojan* Heroe bent,
Into the neighb'ring Plain, with Mountains pent;
375 Whose sides were shaded with surrounding Wood:
Full in the midst of this fair Vally stood
A Native Theatre, which rising slow,
By just degrees, o're-look'd the Ground below.
High on a Sylvan Throne the Leader sate;
380 A num'rous Train attend in Solemn State;
Here those, that in the rapid Course delight,
Desire of Honour, and the Prize invite.
The Rival Runners, without Order stand,
The *Trojans*, mix'd with the *Sicilian* Band.
385 First *Nisus*, with *Euryalus*, appears,
Euryalus a Boy of blooming Years;
With sprightly Grace, and equal Beauty crown'd:
Nisus, for Friendship to the Youth, renown'd.

Diores, next, of *Priam*'s Royal Race,
390   Then *Salius*, join'd with *Patron* took their Place:
But *Patron* in *Arcadia* had his Birth,
And *Salius* his, from *Acarnanian* Earth.
Then two *Sicilian* Youths, the Names of these
Swift *Helymus*, and lovely *Panopes*:
395   Both jolly Huntsmen, both in Forests bred,
And owning old *Acestes* for their Head.
With sev'ral others of Ignobler Name;
Whom Time has not deliver'd o're to Fame.
     To these the Heroe thus his Thoughts explain'd,
400   In Words, which gen'ral Approbation gain'd.
One common Largess is for all design'd:
The Vanquish'd and the Victor shall be join'd.
Two Darts of polish'd Steel, and *Gnosian* Wood,
A Silver'd studded Ax alike bestow'd.
405   The foremost three have Olive Wreaths decreed;
The first of these obtains a stately Steed
Adorn'd with Trappings; and the next in Fame,
The Quiver of an *Amazonian* Dame;
With feather'd *Thracian* Arrows well supply'd, ⎫
410   A Golden Belt shall gird his Manly side; ⎬
Which with a sparkling Diamond shall be ty'd: ⎭
The third this *Grecian* Helmet shall content.
He said; to their appointed Base they went:
With beating Hearts th' expected Sign receive,
415   And starting all at once, the Barrier leave.
Spread out, as on the winged Winds, they flew,
And seiz'd the distant Goal with greedy view.
Shot from the Crowd, swift *Nisus* all o're-pass'd;
Nor Storms, nor Thunder, equal half his haste.
420   The next, but tho' the next, yet far dis-join'd,
Came *Salius*, and *Euryalus* behind;
Then *Helymus*, whom young *Diores* ply'd,
Step after Step, and almost Side by Side:
His Shoulders pressing, and in longer Space,
425   Had won, or left at least a dubious Race.
     Now spent, the Goal they almost reach at last;
When eager *Nisus*, hapless in his hast,

Slip'd first, and slipping, fell upon the Plain,
Soak'd with the Blood of Oxen, newly slain:
430 The careless Victor had not mark'd his way;
But treading where the treach'rous Puddle lay,
His Heels flew up; and on the grassy Floor,
He fell, besmear'd with Filth, and Holy Gore.
Not mindless then, *Euryalus*, of thee,
435 Nor of the Sacred Bonds of Amity;
He strove th' immediate Rival's hope to cross;
And caught the Foot of *Salius* as he rose:
So *Salius* lay extended on the Plain;
Euryalus springs out, the Prize to gain;
440 And leaves the Crowd; applauding Peals attend
The Victor to the Goal, who vanquish'd by his Friend.
Next *Helymus*, and then *Diores* came;
By two Misfortunes made the third in Fame.
    But *Salius* enters; and, exclaiming loud
445 For justice, deafens, and disturbs the Crowd:
Urges his Cause may in the Court be heard;
And pleads the Prize is wrongfully conferr'd.
But Favour for *Euryalus* appears;
His blooming Beauty, with his tender Tears,
450 Had brib'd the Judges for the promis'd Prize;
Besides *Diores* fills the Court with Cry's,
Who vainly reaches at the last Reward,
If the first Palm on *Salius* be conferr'd.
Then thus the Prince; let no Disputes arise:
455 Where Fortune plac'd it, I award the Prize.
But Fortune's Errors give me leave to mend,
At least to pity my deserving Friend.
He said, and from among the Spoils, he draws,
(Pond'rous with shaggy Main, and Golden Paws)
460 A Lyon's Hide; to *Salius* this he gives:
Nisus, with Envy sees the Gift, and grieves.
If such Rewards to vanquish'd Men are due,
He said, and Falling is to rise by you,
What Prize may *Nisus* from your Bounty claim,
465 Who merited the first Rewards and Fame?
In falling, both an equal Fortune try'd;
Wou'd Fortune for my Fall so well provide!

With this he pointed to his Face, and show'd
His Hands, and all his Habit smear'd with Blood.
470   Th' indulgent Father of the People smil'd;
And caus'd to be produc'd an ample Shield;
Of wond'rous Art by *Didymaon* wrought,
Long since from *Neptune*'s Bars in Triumph brought.
This giv'n to *Nisus*; he divides the rest;
475   And equal Justice, in his Gifts, express'd.
The Race thus ended, and Rewards bestow'd;
Once more the Prince bespeaks th' attentive Crowd.
If there be here, whose dauntless Courage dare,
In Gauntlet fight, with Limbs and Body bare,
480   His Opposite sustain in open view,
Stand forth the Champion; and the Games renew.
Two Prizes I propose, and thus divide,
A Bull with gilded Horns, and Fillets ty'd,
Shall be the Portion of the conqu'ring Chief:
485   A Sword and Helm shall chear the Loser's Grief.
     Then haughty *Dares* in the Lists appears;
Stalking he strides, his Head erected bears:
His nervous Arms the weighty Gauntlet weild;
And loud Applauses echo thro' the Field.
490   *Dares* alone, in Combat us'd to stand
The match of mighty *Paris* hand to hand;
The same, at *Hector*'s Fun'rals undertook
Gygantick *Butes*, of th' *Amician* Stock;
And by the Stroak of his resistless Hand,
495   Stretch'd the vast Bulk upon the yellow Sand.
Such *Dares* was; and such he strod along,
And drew the Wonder of the gazing Throng.
His brawny Back, and ample Breast he shows; ⎫
His lifted Arms around his Head he throws; ⎬
500   And deals, in whistling Air, his empty Blows. ⎭
His Match is sought; but thro' the trembling Band,
Not one dares answer to the proud Demand.
Presuming of his Force, with sparkling Eyes,
Already he devours the promis'd Prize.
505   He claims the Bull with awless Insolence;
And having seiz'd his Horns, accosts the Prince.

If none my matchless Valour dares oppose,
How long shall *Dares* wait his dastard Foes?
Permit me, Chief, permit without Delay,
510   To lead this uncontended Gift away.
The Crowd assents; and, with redoubled Cries,
For the proud Challenger demands the Prize.
    Acestes, fir'd with just Disdain, to see
The Palm usurp'd without a Victory;
515   Reproach'd *Entellus* thus, who sate beside,
And heard, and saw unmov'd, the *Trojan*'s Pride:
Once, but in vain, a Champion of Renown,
So tamely can you bear the ravish'd Crown?
A Prize in triumph born before your sight,
520   And shun for fear the danger of the Fight?
Where is our *Eryx* now, the boasted Name,
The God who taught your thund'ring Arm the Game;
Where now your baffled Honour, where the Spoil
That fill'd your House, and Fame that fill'd our Isle?
525   *Entellus*, thus: My Soul is still the same;
Unmov'd with Fear, and mov'd with Martial Fame:
But my chill Blood is curdled in my Veins;
And scarce the Shadow of a Man remains.
Oh, cou'd I turn to that fair Prime again,
530   That Prime, of which this Boaster is so vain,
The Brave who this decrepid Age defies,
Shou'd feel my force, without the promis'd Prize.
He said, and rising at the Word, he threw
Two pond'rous Gauntlets down, in open view:
535   Gauntlets, which *Eryx* wont in Fight to wield,
And sheath his Hands with in the listed Field.
With Fear and Wonder seiz'd, the Crowd beholds
The Gloves of Death, with sev'n distinguish'd folds,
Of tough Bull Hides; the space within is spread
540   With Iron, or with loads of heavy Lead.
Dares himself was daunted at the sight,
Renounc'd his Challenge, and refus'd to fight.
Astonish'd at their weight the Heroe stands,
And poiz'd the pond'rous Engins in his hands.
545   What had your wonder, said *Entellus*, been,
Had you the Gauntlets of *Alcides* seen,
Or view'd the stern debate on this unhappy Green!

These which I bear, your Brother *Eryx* bore,
Still mark'd with batter'd Brains, and mingled Gore.
550   With these he long sustain'd th' *Herculean* Arm;
And these I weilded while my Blood was warm:
This languish'd Frame, while better Spirits fed,
E're Age unstrung my Nerves, or Time o'resnow'd my
            Head.
But if the Challenger these Arms refuse,
555   And cannot weild their weight, or dare not use;
If great *Æneas*, and *Acestes* joyn
In his Request, these Gauntlets I resign:
Let us with equal Arms perform the Fight,
And let him leave to Fear, since I resign my Right.
560   This said, *Entellus* for the Strife prepares;
Strip'd of his quilted Coat, his Body bares:
Compos'd of mighty Bones and Brawn, he stands,
A goodly tow'ring Object on the Sands.
Then just *Æneas* equal Arms supply'd,
565   Which round their Shoulders to their Wrists they ty'd.
Both on the tiptoe stand, at full extent,
Their Arms aloft, their Bodies inly bent;
Their Heads from aiming Blows they bear a far;
With clashing Gauntlets then provoke the War.
570   One on his Youth and pliant Limbs relies;
One on his Sinews, and his Gyant size.
The last is stiff with Age, his Motion slow,
He heaves for Breath, he staggers to and fro;   ⎫
And Clouds of issuing Smoak his Nostrils loudly blow. ⎬
                                                                                 ⎭
575   Yet equal in Success, they ward, they strike;
Their ways are diff'rent, but their Art alike.
Before, behind, the blows are dealt; around
Their hollow sides the ratling Thumps resound.
A Storm of Strokes, well meant, with fury flies,
580   And errs about their Temples, Ears, and Eyes.
Nor always errs; for oft the Gauntlet draws
A sweeping stroke, along the crackling Jaws.
Heavy with Age, *Entellus* stands his Ground,
But with his warping Body wards the Wound.
585   His Hand, and watchful Eye keep even pace;
While *Dares* traverses, and shifts his place.

And like a Captain, who beleaguers round,
Some strong built Castle, on a rising Ground,
Views all th' approaches with observing Eyes, ⎤
590   This, and that other part, in vain he tries; ⎬
And more on Industry, than Force relies. ⎦
With Hands on high, *Entellus* threats the Foe; ⎤
But *Dares* watch'd the Motion from below, ⎬
And slip'd aside, and shun'd the long descending Blow. ⎦
595   *Entellus* wasts his Forces on the Wind;
And thus deluded of the Stroke design'd,
Headlong, and heavy fell: his ample Breast,
And weighty Limbs, his ancient Mother press'd.
So falls a hollow Pine, that long had stood
600   On *Ida*'s height, or *Erymanthus* Wood,
Torn from the Roots: the diff'ring Nations rise,
And Shouts, and mingl'd Murmurs, rend the Skies.
Acestes runs, with eager haste, to raise
The fall'n Companion of his youthful Days:
605   Dauntless he rose, and to the Fight return'd:
With shame his glowing Cheeks, his Eyes with fury burn'd.
Disdain, and conscious Virtue fir'd his Breast;
And with redoubled Force his Foe he press'd.
He lays on load with either Hand, amain,
610   And headlong drives the *Trojan* o'er the Plain.
Nor stops, nor stays; nor rest, nor Breath allows, ⎤
But Storms of Strokes descend about his Brows; ⎬
A ratling Tempest, and a Hail of Blows. ⎦
But now the Prince, who saw the wild increase ⎤
615   Of Wounds, commands the Combatants to cease: ⎬
And bounds *Entellus* Wrath, and bids the Peace. ⎦
First to the *Trojan* spent with Toil he came,
And sooth'd his Sorrow for the suffer'd Shame.
What Fury seiz'd my Friend, the Gods, said he,
620   To him propitious, and averse to thee,
Have giv'n his Arm superior Force to thine;
'Tis Madness to contend with Strength Divine.
The Gauntlet Fight thus ended, from the Shore,
His faithful Friends unhappy *Dares* bore:
625   His Mouth and Nostrils, pour'd a Purple Flood;
And pounded Teeth, came rushing with his Blood.

Faintly he stagger'd thro the hissing Throng;
And hung his Head, and trail'd his Legs along.
The Sword and Casque, are carry'd by his Train;
630   But with his Foe the Palm and Ox remain.
     The Champion, then, before *Æneas* came,
Proud of his Prize; but prouder of his Fame;
O Goddess-born, and you *Dardanian* Host,
Mark with Attention, and forgive my Boast:
635   Learn what I was, by what remains; and know
From what impending Fate, you sav'd my Foe.
Sternly he spoke; and then confronts the Bull; ⎫
And, on his ample Forehead, aiming full,   ⎬
The deadly Stroke descending, pierc'd the Skull. ⎭
640   Down drops the Beast; nor needs a second Wound:
But sprawls in pangs of Death; and spurns the Ground.
Then, thus: In *Dares* stead I offer this;
Eryx, accept a nobler Sacrifice:
Take the last Gift my wither'd Arms can yield,
645   Thy Gauntlets I resign; and here renounce the Field.
     This done, *Æneas* orders, for the close,
The strife of Archers, with contending Bows.
The Mast, *Sergesthus* shatter'd Gally bore,
With his own Hands, he raises on the Shore.
650   A flutt'ring Dove upon the Top they tye,
The living Mark, at which their Arrows fly.
The rival Archers in a Line advance;
Their turn of Shooting to receive from Chance.
A Helmet holds their Names: The Lots are drawn,
655   On the first Scroll was read *Hippocoon*:
The People shout; upon the next was found
Young *Mnestheus*, late with Naval Honours crownd.
The third contain'd *Eurytion*'s Noble Name,
Thy Brother, *Pandarus*, and next in Fame:
660   Whom *Pallas* urg'd the Treaty to confound,
And send among the *Greeks* a feather'd Wound.
Acestes in the bottom, last remain'd;
Whom not his Age from Youthful Sports restrain'd.
Soon, all with Vigour bend their trusty Bows,
665   And from the Quiver each his Arrow chose,

Hippocoon's was the first: with forceful sway
It flew, and, whizzing, cut the liquid way:
Fix'd in the Mast the feather'd Weapon stands,
The fearful Pidgeon flutters in her Bands;
670   And the Tree trembled: and the shouting Cries
Of the pleas'd People, rend the vaulted Skies.
Then *Mnestheus* to the head his Arrow drove, ⎫
With lifted Eyes; and took his Aim above; ⎬
But made a glancing Shot, and miss'd the Dove. ⎭
675   Yet miss'd so narrow, that he cut the Cord
Which fasten'd, by the Foot, the flitting Bird.
The Captive thus releas'd, away she flies,
And beats with clapping Wings, the yielding Skies.
His Bow already bent, *Eurytion* stood,
680   And having first invok'd his Brother God,
His winged Shaft with eager haste he sped;
The fatal Message reach'd her as she fled:
She leaves her Life aloft, she strikes the Ground;
And renders back the Weapon in the Wound.
685   *Acestes* grudging at his Lot, remains,
Without a Prize to gratifie his Pains.
Yet shooting upward, sends his Shaft, to show
An Archer's Art, and boast his twanging Bow.
The featherd Arrow gave a dire Portent;
690   And latter Augures judge from this Event.
Chaf'd by the speed, it fir'd; and as it flew,
A Trail of following Flames, ascending drew:
Kindling they mount; and mark the shiny Way: ⎫
Across the Skies as falling Meteors play, ⎬
695   And vanish into Wind; or in a Blaze decay. ⎭
The *Trojans* and *Sicilians* wildly stare:
And trembling, turn their Wonder into Pray'r.
The *Dardan* Prince put on a smiling Face,
And strain'd *Acestes* with a close Embrace:
700   Then hon'ring him with Gifts above the rest,
Turn'd the bad Omen, nor his Fears confess'd.
The Gods, said he, this Miracle have wrought;
And order'd you the Prize without the Lot.
Accept this Goblet rough with figur'd Gold,
705   Which *Thracian Cisseus* gave my Sire of old:

This Pledge of ancient Amity receive,
Which to my second Sire I justly give.
He said, and with the Trumpets chearful sound,
Proclaim'd him Victor, and with Lawrel crown'd.
710   Nor good *Eurytion* envy'd him the Prize;
Tho' he transfix'd the Pidgeon in the Skies.
Who cut the Line, with second Gifts was grac'd;
The third was his, whose Arrow pierc'd the Mast.
The Chief, before the Games were wholly done,
715   Call'd *Periphantes*, Tutor to his Son;
And whisper'd thus; with speed *Ascanius* find,
And if his Childish Troop be ready join'd;
On Horse-back let him grace his Grandsire's Day,
And lead his Equals arm'd, in just Array.
720   He said, and calling out, the Cirque he clears;
The Crowd withdrawn, an open Plain appears.
And now the Noble Youths, of Form Divine,
Advance before their Fathers, in a Line:
The Riders grace the Steeds; the Steeds with Glory
      shine.
725   Thus marching on, in Military Pride,
Shouts of Applause resound from side to side.
Their Casques, adorn'd with Lawrel Wreaths, they wear.
Each brandishing aloft a Cornel Spear.
Some at their Backs their guilded Quivers bore;
730   Their Chains of burnish'd Gold hung down before.
Three graceful Troops they form'd upon the Green;
Three graceful Leaders at their Head were seen;
Twelve follow'd ev'ry Chief, and left a Space between.
The first young *Priam* led, a lovely Boy,
735   Whose Grandsire was th' unhappy King of *Troy*:
His Race in after times was known to Fame,
New Honours adding to the *Latian* Name;
And well the Royal Boy his *Thracian* Steed became.
White were the Fetlocks of his Feet before;
740   And on his Front a snowy Star he bore:
Then beauteous *Atys*, with *Iulus* bred,
Of equal Age, the second Squadron led.
The last in order, but the first in place,
First in the lovely Features of his Face;

745   Rode fair *Ascanius* on a fiery Steed,
       Queen *Dido*'s Gift, and of the *Tyrian* breed.
       Sure Coursers for the rest the King ordains;
       With Golden Bitts adorn'd, and Purple Reins.
       The pleas'd Spectators peals of Shouts renew;
750   And all the Parents in the Children view:
       Their Make, their Motions, and their sprightly Grace;
       And Hopes and Fears alternate in their Face.
       Th' unfledg'd Commanders, and their Martial Train,
       First make the Circuit of the sandy Plain,
755   Around their Sires: And at th' appointed Sign,
       Drawn up in beauteous Order form a Line:
       The second Signal sounds; the Troop divides,
       In three distinguish'd parts, with three distinguish'd Guides.
       Again they close, and once again dis-join;
760   In Troop to Troop oppos'd, and Line to Line.
       They meet, they wheel, they throw their Darts afar
       With harmless Rage, and well dissembled War.
       Then in a round the mingl'd Bodies run;
       Flying they follow, and pursuing shun.
765   Broken they break, and rallying, they renew
       In other Forms the Military shew.
       At last, in order, undiscern'd they join;
       And march together, in a friendly Line.
       And, as the *Cretan* Labyrinth of old,
770   With wand'ring Wave, and many a winding fold,
       Involv'd the weary Feet, without redress,
       In a round Error, which deny'd recess;
       So fought the *Trojan* Boys in warlike Play,
       Turn'd, and return'd, and still a diff'rent way.
775   Thus Dolphins, in the Deep, each other chase,
       In Circles, when they swim around the wat'ry Race.
       This Game, these Carousels *Ascanius* taught;
       And, building *Alba*, to the *Latins* brought.
       Shew'd what he learn'd: The *Latin* Sires impart,
780   To their succeeding Sons, the graceful Art:
       From these Imperial *Rome* receiv'd the Game;
       Which *Troy*, the Youths the *Trojan* Troop, they name.

Thus far the sacred Sports they celebrate:
But Fortune soon resum'd her ancient hate.
785   For while they pay the dead his Annual dues,
Those envy'd Rites *Saturnian Juno* views.
And sends the Goddess of the various bow,
To try new Methods of Revenge below:
Supplies the Winds to wing her Airy way;
790   Where in the Port secure the Navy lay.
Swiftly fair *Iris* down her Arch descends;
And undiscern'd her fatal Voyage ends.
She saw the gath'ring Crowd; and gliding thence,
The desart Shore, and Fleet without defence.
795   The *Trojan* Matrons on the Sands alone,
With Sighs and Tears, *Anchises* death bemoan.
Then, turning to the Sea their weeping Eyes,
Their pity to themselves, renews their Cries.
Alas! said one, what Oceans yet remain
800   For us to sail; what Labours to sustain!
All take the Word; and with a gen'ral groan,
Implore the Gods for Peace; and Places of their own.
The Goddess, great in Mischief, views their pains;
And in a Woman's Form her heav'nly Limbs restrains.
805   In Face and Shape, old *Beroe* she became, ⎫
Doriclus Wife, a venerable Dame; ⎬
Once bless'd with Riches, and a Mother's Name. ⎭
Thus chang'd, amidst the crying Crowd she ran,
Mix'd with the Matrons, and these words began.
810   O wretched we, whom not the *Grecian* Pow'r,
Nor Flames destroy'd, in *Troy*'s unhappy hour!
O wretched we, reserv'd by Cruel Fate,
Beyond the Ruins of the sinking State!
Now sev'n revolving Years are wholly run,
815   Since this improsp'rous Voyage we begun:
Since toss'd from Shores to Shores, from Lands to Lands,
Inhospitable Rocks and barren Sands;
Wand'ring in Exile, through the stormy Sea,
We search in vain for flying *Italy*.
820   Now Cast by Fortune on this kindred Land, ⎫
What shou'd our Rest, and rising Walls withstand, ⎬
Or hinder here to fix our banish'd Band? ⎭

O, Country lost, and Gods redeem'd in vain,
If still in endless Exile we remain!
825 Shall we no more the *Trojan* Walls renew,
Or Streams of some dissembl'd *Simois* view!
Haste, joyn with me, th' unhappy Fleet consume:
Cassandra bids, and I declare her doom.
In sleep I saw her; she supply'd my hands,
830 (For this I more than dreamt) with flaming Brands:
With these, said she, these wand'ring Ships destroy; ⎫
These are your fatal Seats, and this your *Troy*. ⎬
Time calls you now, the precious Hour employ. ⎭
Slack not the good Presage, while Heav'n inspires
835 Our Minds to dare, and gives the ready Fires.
See *Neptune*'s Altars minister their Brands;
The God is pleas'd; the God supplies our hands.
Then, from the Pile, a flaming Fire she drew,
And, toss'd in Air, amidst the Gallies threw.
840 Wrap'd in a maze, the Matrons wildly stare:
Then *Pyrgo*, reverenc'd for her hoary Hair,
Pyrgo, the Nurse of *Priam*'s num'rous Race,
No *Beroe* this, tho she belies her Face:
What Terrours from her frowning Front arise;
845 Behold a Goddess in her ardent Eyes!
What Rays around her heav'nly Face are seen,
Mark her Majestick Voice, and more than mortal Meen!
Beroe but now I left; whom pin'd with pain,
Her Age and Anguish from these Rites detain.
850 She said; the Matrons, seiz'd with new Amaze,
Rowl their malignant Eyes, and on the Navy gaze.
They fear, and hope, and neither part obey:
They hope the fated Land, but fear the fatal Way.
The Goddess, having done her Task below,
855 Mounts up on equal Wings, and bends her painted Bow.
Struck with the sight, and seiz'd with Rage Divine;
The Matrons prosecute their mad Design:
They shriek aloud, they snatch, with Impious Hands,
The food of Altars, Fires, and flaming Brands.
860 Green Boughs, and Saplings, mingled in their haste;
And smoaking Torches on the Ships they cast.

The Flame, unstop'd at first, more Fury gains;
And *Vulcan* rides at large with loosen'd Reins:
Triumphant to the painted Sterns he soars,
865   And seizes in his way, the Banks, and crackling Oars.
Eumelus was the first, the News to bear,
While yet they crowd the Rural Theatre.
Then what they hear, is witness'd by their Eyes;
A storm of Sparkles, and of Flames arise.
870   *Ascanius* took th' Alarm, while yet he led
His early Warriors on his prancing Steed.
And spurring on, his Equals soon o'repass'd,
Nor cou'd his frighted Friends reclaim his haste.
Soon as the Royal Youth appear'd in view,
875   He sent his Voice before him as he flew;
What Madness moves you, Matrons, to destroy
The last Remainders of unhappy *Troy*!
Not hostile Fleets, but your own hopes you burn,
And on your Friends, your fatal Fury turn.
880   Behold your own *Ascanius*: while he said, ⎫
He drew his glitt'ring Helmet from his Head; ⎬
In which the Youths to sportful Arms he led. ⎭
By this, *Æneas* and his Train appear;
And now the Women, seiz'd with Shame and Fear,
885   Dispers'd, to Woods and Caverns take their Flight;
Abhor their Actions, and avoid the Light:
Their Friends acknowledge, and their Error find;
And shake the Goddess from their alter'd Mind.
        Not so the raging Fires their Fury cease;
890   But lurking in the Seams, with seeming Peace,
Work on their way, amid the smouldring Tow,
Sure in Destruction, but in Motion slow.
The silent Plague, thro' the green Timber eats,
And vomits out a tardy Flame, by fits.
895   Down to the Keels, and upward to the Sails,
The Fire descends, or mounts; but still prevails:
Nor Buckets pour'd, nor strength of Human Hand,
Can the victorious Element withstand.
        The Pious Heroe rends his Robe, and throws
900   To Heav'n his Hands, and with his Hands his Vows.

O *Jove*, he cry'd, if Pray'rs can yet have place;
If thou abhorr'st not all the *Dardan* Race;
If any spark of Pity still remain;
If Gods are Gods, and not invok'd in vain;
905   Yet spare the Relicks of the *Trojan* Train.
Yet from the Flames our burning Vessels free:
Or let thy Fury fall alone on me.
At this devoted Head thy Thunder throw,
And send the willing Sacrifice below.
910   Scarce had he said, when Southern Storms arise,
From Pole to Pole, the forky Lightning flies;
Loud ratling shakes the Mountains, and the Plain:
Heav'n bellies downward, and descends in Rain.
Whole Sheets of Water from the Clouds are sent,
915   Which hissing thro' the Planks, the Flames prevent:
And stop the fiery Pest: Four Ships alone
Burn to the wast; and for the Fleet attone.
        But doubtful thoughts the Hero's Heart divide;
If he should still in *Sicily* reside,
920   Forgetful of his Fates; or tempt the Main,
In hope the promis'd *Italy* to gain.
Then *Nautes*, old, and wise, to whom alone
The Will of Heav'n, by *Pallas* was fore-shown;
Vers'd in Portents, experienc'd and inspir'd,
925   To tell Events, and what the Fates requir'd:
Thus while he stood, to neither part inclin'd,
With chearful Words reliev'd his lab'ring Mind.
O Goddess-born, resign'd in ev'ry state,
With Patience bear, with Prudence push your Fate.
930   By suff'ring well, our Fortune we subdue;
Fly when she frowns, and when she calls pursue.
Your Friend *Acestes* is of *Trojan* Kind,
To him disclose the Secrets of your Mind:
Trust in his Hands your old and useless Train,
935   Too num'rous for the Ships which yet remain:
The feeble, old, indulgent of their Ease,
The Dames who dread the Dangers of the Seas,
With all the dastard Crew, who dare not stand
The shock of Battle with your Foes by Land;

940   Here you may build a common Town for all;
      And from *Acestes* name, *Acesta* call.
      The Reasons, with his Friend's Experience join'd,
      Encourag'd much, but more disturb'd his Mind.
      'Twas dead of Night; when to his slumb'ring Eyes,
945   His Father's Shade descended from the Skies;
      And thus he spoke: O more than vital Breath
      Lov'd while I liv'd, and dear ev'n after Death;
      O Son, in various Toils and Troubles tost,
      The King of Heav'n employs my careful Ghost
950   On his Commands; the God who sav'd from Fire
      Your flaming Fleet, and heard your just desire:
      The wholsom Counsel of your Friend receive;
      And here, the Coward Train, and Women leave:
      The chosen Youth, and those who nobly dare,
955   Transport; to tempt the Dangers of the War.
      The stern *Italians* will their Courage try;
      Rough are their Manners, and their Minds are high.
      But first to *Pluto*'s Palace you shall go,
      And seek my Shade among the blest below.
960   For not with impious Ghosts my Soul remains, ⎫
      Nor suffers, with the Damn'd, perpetual Pains; ⎬
      But breaths the living Air of soft *Elysian* Plains. ⎭
      The chast *Sybilla* shall your steps convey;
      And Blood of offer'd Victims free the way.
965   There shall you know what Realms the Gods assign;
      And learn the Fates and Fortunes of your Line.
      But now, farewel; I vanish with the Night;   ⎫
      And feel the blast of Heav'ns approaching Light: ⎬
      He said, and mix'd with Shades, and took his airy flight. ⎭
970   Whither so fast, the filial Duty cry'd,
      And why, ah why, the wish'd Embrace deny'd!
      He said, and rose: as holy Zeal inspires
      He rakes hot Embers, and renews the Fires.
      His Country Gods and *Vesta*, then adores
975   With Cakes and Incense; and their Aid implores.
      Next, for his Friends, and Royal Host he sent,
      Reveal'd his Vision and the Gods intent,
      With his own Purpose: All, without delay,
      The Will of *Jove*, and his Desires obey.

980 They list with Women each degenerate Name,
     Who dares not hazard Life, for future Fame.
     These they cashier; the brave remaining few,
     Oars, Banks, and Cables half consum'd renew.
     The Prince designs a City with the Plough;
985 The Lots their sev'ral Tenements allow.
     This part is nam'd from *Ilium*, that from *Troy*;
     And the new King ascends the Throne with Joy.
     A chosen Senate from the People draws;
     Appoints the Judges, and ordains the Laws.
990 Then on the top of *Eryx*, they begin
     A rising Temple to the *Paphian* Queen:
     Anchises, last, is honour'd as a God,   ⎫
     A Priest is added, annual Gifts bestow'd;   ⎬
     And Groves are planted round his blest Abode.   ⎭
995 Nine days they pass in Feasts, their Temples crown'd;
     And fumes of Incense in the Fanes abound.
     Then, from the South arose a gentle Breeze,
     That curl'd the smoothness of the glassy Seas:
     The rising Winds, a ruffling Gale afford,
1000 And call the merry Marriners aboard.
         Now loud Laments along the Shores resound,
     Of parting Friends in close Embraces bound.
     The trembling Women, the degenerate Train,
     Who shun'd the frightful Dangers of the Main;
1005 Ev'n those desire to sail, and take their share
     Of the rough Passage, and the promis'd War.
     Whom Good *Æneas* chears; and recommends
     To their new Master's Care, his fearful Friends.
     On *Eryx* Altars three fat Calves he lays;   ⎫
1010 A Lamb new fall'n to the stormy Seas;   ⎬
     Then slips his Haulsers, and his Anchors weighs. ⎭
     High on the Deck, the Godlike Heroe stands;
     With Olive crown'd; a Charger in his Hands;
     Then cast the reeking Entrails in the brine,
1015 And pour'd the Sacrifice of Purple Wine.
     Fresh Gales arise, with equal Strokes they vye,
     And brush the buxom Seas, and o're the Billows fly.
         Mean time the Mother-Goddess, full of Fears,
     To *Neptune* thus address'd, with tender Tears.

1020 The Pride of *Jove*'s Imperious Queen, the Rage,
The malice which no Suff'rings can asswage,
Compel me to these Pray'rs: Since neither Fate,
Nor Time, nor Pity, can remove her hate.
Ev'n *Jove* is thwarted by his haughty Wife;
1025 Still vanquish'd, yet she still renews the Strife.
As if 'twere little to consume the Town
Which aw'd the World; and wore th' Imperial Crown:
She prosecutes the Ghost of *Troy* with Pains;
And gnaws, ev'n to the Bones, the last Remains.
1030 Let her the Causes of her Hatred tell;
But you can witness its Effects too well.
You saw the Storm she rais'd on *Lybian* Floods,
That mix'd the mounting Billows with the Clouds.
When, bribing *Eolus*, she shook the Main,
1035 And mov'd Rebellion in your wat'ry Reign.
With Fury she possess'd the *Dardan* Dames;
To burn their Fleet with execrable Flames.
And forc'd *Æneas*, when his Ships were lost,
To leave his Foll'wers on a Foreign Coast.
1040 For what remains, your Godhead I implore;
And trust my Son to your protecting Pow'r.
If neither *Jove*'s, nor Fate's decree withstand,
Secure his Passage to the *Latian* Land.
    Then thus the mighty Ruler of the Main,
1045 What may not *Venus* hope, from *Neptune*'s Reign?
My Kingdom claims your Birth: My late Defence
Of your indanger'd Fleet, may claim your Confidence.
Nor less by Land than Sea, my Deeds declare,
How much your lov'd *Æneas* is my Care.
1050 Thee *Xanthus*, and thee *Simois* I attest:
Your *Trojan* Troops, when proud *Achilles* press'd,
And drove before him headlong on the Plain,   ⎫
And dash'd against the Walls the trembling Train, ⎬
When Floods were fill'd with bodies of the slain: ⎭
1055 When Crimson *Xanthus*, doubtful of his way,   ⎫
Stood up on ridges to behold the Sea;   ⎬
New heaps came tumbling in, and choak'd his way: ⎭
When your *Æneas* fought, but fought with odds
Of Force unequal, and unequal Gods;

1060 I spread a Cloud before the Victor's sight,
Sustain'd the vanquish'd, and secur'd his flight.
Ev'n then secur'd him, when I sought with joy
The vow'd destruction of ungrateful *Troy*.
My Will's the same: Fair Goddess fear no more,
1065 Your Fleet shall safely gain the *Latian* Shore:
Their lives are giv'n; one destin'd Head alone
Shall perish, and for Multitudes attone.
Thus having arm'd with Hopes her anxious Mind,
His finny Team *Saturnian Neptune* join'd.
1070 Then, adds the foamy Bridle to their Jaws;
And to the loosen'd Reins permits the Laws.
High on the Waves his Azure Car he guides, ⎫
Its Axles thunder, and the Sea subsides; ⎬
And the smooth Ocean rowls her silent Tides. ⎭
1075 The Tempests fly before their Father's face,
Trains of inferiour Gods his Triumph grace;
And Monster Whales before their Master play,
And Quires of Tritons crowd the wat'ry way.
The Martial'd Pow'rs, in equal Troops divide, ⎫
1080 To right and left: the Gods his better side ⎬
Inclose, and on the worse the Nymphs and Nereids ride. ⎭
    Now smiling Hope, with sweet Vicissitude,
Within the Hero's Mind, his Joys renew'd.
He calls to raise the Masts, the Sheats display; ⎫
1085 The Chearful Crew with diligence obey; ⎬
They scud before the Wind, and sail in open Sea. ⎭
A Head of all the Master Pilot steers,
And as he leads, the following Navy veers.
The Steeds of Night had travell'd half the Sky,
1090 The drowzy Rowers on their Benches lye;
When the soft God of Sleep, with easie flight,
Descends, and draws behind a trail of Light.
Thou *Palinurus* art his destin'd Prey;
To thee alone he takes his fatal way.
1095 Dire Dreams to thee, and Iron Sleep he bears;
And lighting on thy Prow, the Form of *Phorbas* wears.
Then thus the Traytor God began his Tale: ⎫
The Winds, my Friend, inspire a pleasing gale; ⎬
The Ships, without thy Care, securely sail. ⎭

1100 Now steal an hour of sweet Repose; and I
      Will take the Rudder, and thy room supply.
      To whom the yauning Pilot, half asleep;
      Me dost thou bid to trust the treach'rous Deep!
      The Harlot-smiles of her dissembling Face,
1105 And to her Faith commit the *Trojan* Race?
      Shall I believe the *Syren* South again,
      And, oft betray'd, not know the Monster Main?
      He said, his fasten'd hands the Rudder keep,
      And fix'd on Heav'n, his Eyes repel invading Sleep.
1110 The God was wroth, and at his Temples threw
      A Brand in *Lethe* dip'd, and drunk with *Stygian* Dew:
      The Pilot, vanquish'd by the Pow'r Divine,
      Soon clos'd his swimming Eyes, and lay supine.
      Scarce were his Limbs extended at their length,
1115 The God, insulting with superiour Strength,
      Fell heavy on him, plung'd him in the Sea,
      And, with the Stern, the Rudder tore away.
      Headlong he fell, and strugling in the Main,
      Cry'd out for helping hands, but cry'd in vain:
1120 The Victor Dæmon mounts obscure in Air;
      While the Ship sails without the Pilot's care.
      On *Neptune*'s Faith the floating Fleet relies; ⎫
      But what the Man forsook, the God supplies; ⎬
      And o're the dang'rous Deep secure the Navy flies. ⎭
1125 Glides by the Syren's Cliffs, a shelfy Coast,
      Long infamous for Ships, and Sailors lost;
      And white with Bones: Th' impetuous Ocean roars;
      And Rocks rebellow from the sounding Shores.
      The watchful Heroe felt the knocks; and found
1130 The tossing Vessel sail'd on shoaly Ground.
      Sure of his Pilot's loss, he takes himself
      The Helm, and steers aloof, and shuns the Shelf.
      Inly he griev'd; and groaning from the Breast,
      Deplor'd his Death; and thus his Pain express'd:
1135 For Faith repos'd on Seas, and on the flatt'ring Sky,
      Thy naked Corps is doom'd, on Shores unknown to lye.

THE SIXTH BOOK OF THE ÆNEIS

The Argument

*The Sibyl foretels Æneas the Adventures he should meet with in Italy.
She attends him to Hell; describing to him the various Scenes of that
Place, and conducting him to his Father Anchises. Who instructs
him in those sublime Mysteries of the Soul of the World, and the
Transmigration: And shews him that glorious Race of Heroes, which
was to descend from him, and his Posterity.*

He said, and wept: Then spread his Sails before ⎫
The Winds, and reach'd at length the *Cuman* Shore: ⎬
Their Anchors drop'd, his Crew the Vessels moor. ⎭
They turn their Heads to Sea; their Sterns to Land;
And greet with greedy Joy th' *Italian* Strand.
Some strike from clashing Flints their fiery Seed;
Some gather Sticks, the kindled Flames to feed:
Or search for hollow Trees, and fell the Woods,
Or trace thro Valleys the discover'd Floods.
Thus, while their sev'ral Charges they fulfil,
The Pious Prince ascends the sacred Hill
Where *Phœbus* is ador'd; and seeks the Shade,
Which hides from sight, his venerable Maid.
Deep in a Cave the Sibyl makes abode;
Thence full of Fate returns, and of the God.
Thro *Trivia*'s Grove they walk; and now behold,
And enter now, the Temple roof'd with Gold.
When *Dedalus*, to fly the *Cretan* Shore,
His heavy Limbs on jointed Pinions bore,
(The first who sail'd in Air,) 'tis sung by Fame, ⎫
To the *Cumæan* Coast at length he came; ⎬
And, here alighting, built this costly Frame. ⎭
Inscrib'd to *Phœbus*, here he hung on high
The steerage of his Wings, that cut the Sky:
Then o're the lofty Gate his Art emboss'd
Androgeos Death, and Off'rings to his Ghost.
Sev'n Youths from *Athens* yearly sent, to meet
The Fate appointed by revengeful *Creet*.
And next to those the dreadful Urn was plac'd,
In which the destin'd Names, by Lots were cast:
The mournful Parents stand around in Tears;
And rising *Creet* against their Shore appears.

There too, in living Sculpture, might be seen
The mad Affection of the *Cretan* Queen:
35   Then how she cheats her bellowing Lover's Eye:
The rushing leap, the doubtful Progeny,
The lower part a Beast, a Man above,
The Monument of their polluted Love.
Nor far from thence he grav'd the wond'rous Maze;
40   A thousand Doors, a thousand winding Ways;
Here dwells the Monster, hid from Human View,
Not to be found, but by the faithful Clue:
'Till the kind Artist, mov'd with Pious Grief,
Lent to the loving Maid this last Relief.
45   And all those erring Paths describ'd so well,
That *Theseus* conquer'd, and the Monster fell.
Here hapless *Icarus* had found his part;
Had not the Father's Grief restrain'd his Art.
He twice assay'd to cast his Son in Gold;
50   Twice from his Hands he drop'd the forming Mould.
All this with wond'ring Eyes *Æneas* view'd:
Each varying Object his Delight renew'd.
Eager to read the rest, *Achates* came,
And by his side the mad divining Dame;
55   The Priestess of the God, *Deiphobe* her Name.
Time suffers not, she said, to feed your Eyes
With empty Pleasures: haste the Sacrifice.
Sev'n Bullocks yet unyok'd, for *Phœbus* chuse,
And for *Diana* sev'n unspotted Ewes.
60   This said, the Servants urge the Sacred Rites;
While to the Temple she the Prince invites.
A spacious Cave, within its farmost part,
Was hew'd and fashion'd by laborious Art
Thro' the Hills hollow sides: before the place,
65   A hundred Doors a hundred Entries grace:
As many Voices issue; and the sound
Of Sibyl's Words as many times rebound.
Now to the Mouth they come: Aloud she cries,
This is the time, enquire your Destinies.
70   He comes, behold the God! Thus while she said,
(And shiv'ring at the sacred Entry staid)

Her Colour chang'd, her Face was not the same,
And hollow Groans from her deep Spirit came.
Her Hair stood up; convulsive Rage possess'd
75 Her trembling Limbs, and heav'd her lab'ring Breast.
Greater than Human Kind she seem'd to look:
And with an Accent, more than Mortal, spoke.
Her staring Eyes with sparkling Fury rowl;
When all the God came rushing on her Soul.
80 Swiftly she turn'd, and foaming as she spoke,
Why this Delay, she cry'd; the Pow'rs invoke.
Thy Pray'rs alone can open this abode,
Else vain are my Demands, and dumb the God.
She said no more: The trembling *Trojans* hear;
85 O're-spread with a damp Sweat, and holy Fear.
The Prince himself, with awful Dread possess'd,
His Vows to great *Apollo* thus address'd.
Indulgent God, propitious Pow'r to *Troy*,
Swift to relieve, unwilling to destroy;
90 Directed by whose Hand, the *Dardan* Dart
Pierc'd the proud *Grecian*'s only Mortal part:
Thus far, by Fates Decrees, and thy Commands,
Through ambient Seas, and thro' devouring Sands,
Our exil'd Crew has sought th' *Ausonian* Ground:
95 And now, at length, the flying Coast is found.
Thus far the Fate of *Troy*, from place to place,
With Fury has pursu'd her wand'ring Race:
Here cease ye Pow'rs, and let your Vengeance end,
Troy is no more, and can no more offend.
100 And thou, O sacred Maid, inspir'd to see
Th' Event of things in dark Futurity;
Give me, what Heav'n has promis'd to my Fate,
To conquer and command the *Latian* State:
To fix my wand'ring Gods; and find a place
105 For the long Exiles of the *Trojan* Race.
Then shall my grateful Hands a Temple rear
To the twin Gods, with Vows and solemn Pray'r;
And Annual Rites, and Festivals, and Games,
Shall be perform'd to their auspicious Names.
110 Nor shalt thou want thy Honours in my Land,
For there thy faithful Oracles shall stand,

Preserv'd in Shrines: and ev'ry Sacred Lay,
Which, by thy Mouth, *Apollo* shall convey.
All shall be treasur'd, by a chosen Train
115   Of holy Priests, and ever shall remain.
But, oh! commit not thy prophetick Mind
To flitting Leaves, the sport of ev'ry Wind:
Lest they disperse in Air our empty Fate:
Write not, but, what the Pow'rs ordain, relate.
120   Strugling in vain, impatient of her Load,
And lab'ring underneath the pond'rous God,
The more she strove to shake him from her Breast,
With more, and far superior Force he press'd:
Commands his Entrance, and without Controul,
125   Usurps her Organs, and inspires her Soul.
Now, with a furious Blast, the hundred Doors
Ope of themselves; a rushing Wirlwind roars
Within the Cave; and Sibyl's Voice restores.
        Escap'd the Dangers of the wat'ry Reign,
130   Yet more, and greater Ills, by Land remain.
The Coast so long desir'd, (nor doubt th' Event)
Thy Troops shall reach, but having reach'd, repent.
Wars, horrid Wars I view; a field of Blood;
And *Tyber* rolling with a Purple Flood.
135   *Simois* nor *Xanthus* shall be wanting there;
A new *Achilles* shall in Arms appear:
And he, too, Goddess-born: fierce *Juno*'s Hate,
Added to hostile Force, shall urge thy Fate.
To what strange Nations shalt not thou resort,
140   Driv'n to sollicite Aid at ev'ry Court!
The Cause the same which *Ilium* once oppress'd,
A foreign Mistress, and a foreign Guest.
But thou, secure of Soul, unbent with Woes,
The more thy Fortune frowns, the more oppose.
145   The dawnings of thy Safety, shall be shown,
From whence thou least shalt hope, a *Grecian* Town.
        Thus, from the dark Recess, the Sibyl spoke,
And the resisting Air the Thunder broke;
The Cave rebellow'd; and the Temple shook.
150   Th' ambiguous God who rul'd her lab'ring Breast,
In these mysterious Words his Mind exprest:
Some Truths reveal'd, in Terms involv'd the rest.

At length her Fury fell; her foaming ceas'd,
And, ebbing in her Soul, the God decreas'd.
155   Then thus the Chief: no Terror to my view,
No frightful Face of Danger can be new.
Inur'd to suffer, and resolv'd to dare,
The Fates, without my Pow'r, shall be without my Care.
This let me crave, since near your Grove the Road ⎫
160   To Hell lies open, and the dark Abode, ⎬
Which *Acheron* surrounds, th' innavigable Flood: ⎭
Conduct me thro' the Regions void of Light,
And lead me longing to my Father's sight.
For him, a thousand Dangers I have sought; ⎫
165   And, rushing where the thickest *Grecians* fought, ⎬
Safe on my Back the sacred Burthen brought. ⎭
He, for my sake, the raging Ocean try'd, ⎫
And Wrath of Heav'n; my still auspicious Guide, ⎬
And bore beyond the strength decrepid Age supply'd. ⎭
170   Oft since he breath'd his last, in dead of Night,
His reverend Image stood before my sight;
Enjoin'd to seek below, his holy Shade;
Conducted there, by your unerring aid.
But you, if pious Minds by Pray'rs are won,
175   Oblige the Father, and protect the Son.
Yours is the Pow'r; nor *Proserpine* in vain
Has made you Priestess of her nightly Reign.
If *Orpheus*, arm'd with his enchanting Lyre,
The ruthless King with Pity could inspire;
180   And from the Shades below redeem his Wife:
If *Pollux*, off'ring his alternate Life,
Cou'd free his Brother; and can daily go
By turns aloft, by turns descend below:
Why name I *Theseus*, or his greater Friend,
185   Who trod the downward Path, and upward cou'd ascend!
Not less than theirs, from *Jove* my Lineage came:
My Mother greater, my Descent the same.
So pray'd the *Trojan* Prince; and while he pray'd
His Hand upon the holy Altar laid.
190   Then thus reply'd the Prophetess Divine:
O Goddess-born! of Great *Anchises* Line;
The Gates of Hell are open Night and Day;
Smooth the Descent, and easie is the Way:

But, to return, and view the chearful Skies;
195　In this the Task, and mighty Labour lies.
　　To few great *Jupiter* imparts this Grace:
　　And those of shining Worth, and Heav'nly Race.
　　Betwixt those Regions, and our upper Light,
　　Deep Forrests, and impenetrable Night
200　Possess the middle space: Th' Infernal Bounds
　　Cocytus, with his sable Waves, surrounds.
　　But if so dire a Love your Soul invades;
　　As twice below to view the trembling Shades;
　　If you so hard a Toil will undertake,
205　As twice to pass th' innavigable Lake;
　　Receive my Counsel. In the Neighb'ring Grove
　　There stands a Tree; the Queen of *Stygian Jove*
　　Claims it her own; thick Woods, and gloomy Night,
　　Conceal the happy Plant from Humane sight.
210　One Bough it bears; but, wond'rous to behold;
　　The ductile Rind, and Leaves, of Radiant Gold:
　　This, from the vulgar Branches must be torn,
　　And to fair *Proserpine*, the Present born:
　　E're leave be given to tempt the neather Skies:　⎫
215　The first thus rent, a second will arise;　　　　 ⎬
　　And the same Metal the same room supplies.　　 ⎭
　　Look round the Wood, with lifted Eyes, to see
　　The lurking Gold upon the fatal Tree:
　　Then rend it off, as holy Rites command:
220　The willing Metal will obey thy Hand,
　　Following with ease, if, favour'd by thy Fate,
　　Thou art foredoom'd to view the *Stygian* State:
　　If not, no labour can the Tree constrain:
　　And strength of stubborn Arms, and Steel are vain.
225　Besides, you know not, while you here attend
　　Th' unworthy Fate of your unhappy Friend:
　　Breathless he lies: And his unbury'd Ghost,
　　Depriv'd of Fun'ral Rites, pollutes your Host.
　　Pay first his Pious Dues: And for the dead,
230　Two sable Sheep around his Herse be led.
　　Then, living Turfs upon his Body lay;　　　⎫
　　This done, securely take the destin'd Way,　 ⎬
　　To find the Regions destitute of Day.　　　 ⎭

　　　She said: and held her Peace. *Æneas* went ⎫
235　Sad from the Cave, and full of Discontent;　⎬
　　　Unknowing whom the sacred Sibyl meant. ⎭
　　　Achates, the Companion of his Breast,
　　　Goes grieving by his side; with equal Cares oppress'd.
　　　Walking, they talk'd, and fruitlessly divin'd
240　What Friend, the Priestess by those Words design'd.
　　　But soon they found an Object to deplore:
　　　Misenus lay extended on the Shore.
　　　Son of the God of Winds; none so renown'd,
　　　The Warrior Trumpet in the Field to sound:
245　With breathing Brass to kindle fierce Alarms;
　　　And rouze to dare their Fate, in honourable Arms.
　　　He serv'd great *Hector*; and was ever near;
　　　Not with his Trumpet only, but his Spear.
　　　But, by *Pelides* Arms, when *Hector* fell,
250　He chose *Æneas*, and he chose as well.
　　　Swoln with Applause, and aiming still at more,
　　　He now provokes the Sea Gods from the Shore;
　　　With Envy *Triton* heard the Martial sound,
　　　And the bold Champion, for his Challenge, drown'd.
255　Then cast his mangled Carcass on the Strand:
　　　The gazing Crowd around the Body stand.
　　　All weep, but most *Æneas* mourns his Fate;
　　　And hastens to perform the Funeral state.
　　　In Altar-wise, a stately Pile they rear;
260　The Basis broad below, and top advanc'd in Air.
　　　An ancient Wood, fit for the Work design'd,
　　　(The shady Covert of the Salvage Kind)
　　　The *Trojans* found: The sounding Ax is ply'd:
　　　Firs, Pines, and Pitch-Trees, and the tow'ring Pride
265　Of Forest Ashes, feel the fatal Stroke:
　　　And piercing Wedges cleave the stubborn Oak.
　　　Huge Trunks of Trees, fell'd from the steepy Crown
　　　Of the bare Mountains, rowl with Ruin down.
　　　Arm'd like the rest the *Trojan* Prince appears:
270　And, by his pious Labour, urges theirs.
　　　Thus while he wrought, revolving in his Mind,
　　　The ways to compass what his Wish design'd,

He cast his Eyes upon the gloomy Grove;
And then with Vows implor'd the Queen of Love.
275   O may thy Pow'r, propitious still to me,
Conduct my steps to find the fatal Tree,
In this deep Forest; since the Sibyl's Breath
Foretold, alas! too true, *Misenus* Death.
Scarce had he said, when full before his sight ⎫
280   Two Doves, descending from their Airy Flight, ⎬
Secure upon the grassy Plain alight. ⎭
He knew his Mother's Birds: And thus he pray'd:
Be you my Guides, with your auspicious Aid:
And lead my Footsteps, till the Branch be found,
285   Whose glitt'ring Shadow guilds the sacred Ground:
And thou, great Parent! With Cœlestial Care,
In this Distress, be present to my Pray'r.
Thus having said, he stop'd: With watchful sight,
Observing still the motions of their Flight.
290   What course they took, what happy Signs they shew. ⎫
They fed, and flutt'ring by degrees, withdrew ⎬
Still farther from the Place; but still in view. ⎭
Hopping, and flying, thus they led him on
To the slow Lake; whose baleful Stench to shun,
295   They wing'd their Flight aloft; then, stooping low,
Perch'd on the double Tree, that bears the golden Bough.
Thro' the green Leafs the glitt'ring Shadows glow;
As on the sacred Oak, the wintry Misleto:
Where the proud Mother views her precious Brood;
300   And happier Branches, which she never sow'd.
Such was the glitt'ring; such the ruddy Rind,
And dancing Leaves, that wanton'd in the Wind.
He seiz'd the shining Bough with griping hold;
And rent away, with ease, the ling'ring Gold.
305   Then, to the Sibyl's Palace bore the Prize. ⎫
Mean time, the *Trojan* Troops, with weeping Eyes, ⎬
To dead *Misenus* pay his Obsequies. ⎭
First, from the Ground, a lofty Pile they rear,
Of Pitch-trees, Oaks, and Pines, and unctuous Firr:
310   The Fabrick's Front with Cypress Twigs they strew;
And stick the sides with Boughs of baleful Yough.

The topmost part, his glitt'ring Arms adorn;
Warm Waters, then, in brazen Caldrons born,
Are pour'd to wash his Body, Joint by Joint:
315   And fragrant Oils the stiffen'd Limbs anoint.
With Groans and Cries *Misenus* they deplore:
Then on a Bier, with Purple cover'd o're,
The breathless Body, thus bewail'd, they lay: ⎫
And fire the Pile, their Faces turn'd away: ⎬
320   (Such reverend Rites their Fathers us'd to pay.) ⎭
Pure Oyl, and Incense, on the Fire they throw:
And Fat of Victims, which his Friends bestow.
These Gifts, the greedy Flames to Dust devour;
Then, on the living Coals, red Wine they pour:
325   And last, the Relicks by themselves dispose;
Which in a brazen Urn the Priests inclose.
Old *Chorineus* compass'd thrice the Crew;
And dip'd an Olive Branch in holy dew;
Which thrice he sprinkl'd round; and thrice aloud
330   Invok'd the dead, and then dismiss'd the Crowd.
    But good *Æneas* order'd on the Shore ⎫
A stately Tomb; whose top a Trumpet bore: ⎬
A Souldier's Fauchion, and a Sea-man's Oar. ⎭
Thus was his Friend interr'd: And deathless Fame
335   Still to the lofty Cape consigns his Name.
    These Rites perform'd, the Prince, without delay,
Hastes to the neather World, his destin'd Way.
Deep was the Cave; and downward as it went
From the wide Mouth, a rocky rough Descent;
340   And here th' access a gloomy Grove defends;
And there th' unnavigable Lake extends.
O're whose unhappy Waters, void of Light,
No Bird presumes to steer his Airy Flight;
Such deadly Stenches from the depth arise,
345   And steaming Sulphur, that infects the Skies.
From hence the *Grecian* Bards their Legends make,
And give the name *Avernus* to the Lake.
Four sable Bullocks, in the Yoke untaught,
For Sacrifice the pious Heroe brought.
350   The Priestess pours the Wine betwixt their Horns:
Then cuts the curling Hair; that first Oblation burns.

Invoking *Hecate* hither to repair;
(A pow'rful Name in Hell, and upper Air.)
The sacred Priests with ready Knives bereave
355   The Beasts of Life; and in full Bowls receive
The streaming Blood: A Lamb to Hell and Night,
(The sable Wool without a streak of white)
Æneas offers: And, by Fates decree,
A barren Heifar, *Proserpine* to thee.
360   With Holocausts he *Pluto*'s Altar fills:
Sev'n brawny Bulls with his own Hand he kills:
Then on the broiling Entrails Oyl he pours;
Which, ointed thus, the raging Flame devours.
Late, the Nocturnal Sacrifice begun;
365   Nor ended, 'till the next returning Sun.
Then Earth began to bellow, Trees to dance;
And howling Dogs in glimm'ring Light advance;
E're *Hecate* came: Far hence be Souls prophane,
The Sibyl cry'd, and from the Grove abstain.
370   Now, *Trojan*, take the way, thy Fates afford:
Assume thy Courage, and unsheath thy Sword.
She said, and pass'd along the gloomy Space:
The Prince pursu'd her Steps with equal pace.

Ye Realms, yet unreveal'd to Human sight,
375   Ye Gods, who rule the Regions of the Night,
Ye gliding Ghosts, permit me to relate
The mystick Wonders of your silent State.

Obscure they went thro dreery Shades, that led
Along the waste Dominions of the dead:
380   Thus wander Travellers in Woods by Night,
By the Moon's doubtful, and malignant Light:
When *Jove* in dusky Clouds involves the Skies;
And the faint Crescent shoots by fits before their Eyes.

Just in the Gate, and in the Jaws of Hell,
385   Revengeful Cares, and sullen Sorrows dwell;
And pale Diseases, and repining Age;
Want, Fear, and Famine's unresisted rage.
Here Toils, and Death, and Death's half-brother, Sleep,
Forms terrible to view, their Centry keep:
390   With anxious Pleasures of a guilty Mind,
Deep Frauds before, and open Force behind:

The Furies Iron Beds, and Strife that shakes
Her hissing Tresses, and unfolds her Snakes.
Full in the midst of this infernal Road,
395   An Elm displays her dusky Arms abroad;
The God of Sleep there hides his heavy Head:
And empty Dreams on ev'ry Leaf are spread.
Of various Forms unnumber'd Specters more;
Centaurs, and double Shapes, besiege the Door:
400   Before the Passage horrid *Hydra* stands,
And *Briareus* with all his hundred Hands:
Gorgons, *Geryon* with his triple Frame;
And vain *Chimæra* vomits empty Flame.
The Chief unsheath'd his shining Steel, prepar'd,
405   Tho seiz'd with sudden Fear, to force the Guard.
Offring his brandish'd Weapon at their Face;
Had not the Sibyl stop'd his eager Pace,
And told him what those empty Fantomes were;
Forms without Bodies, and impassive Air.
410   Hence to deep *Acheron* they take their way;
Whose troubled Eddies, thick with Ooze and Clay,
Are whirl'd aloft, and in *Cocytus* lost:
There *Charon* stands, who rules the dreary Coast:
A sordid God; down from his hoary Chin
415   A length of Beard descends; uncomb'd, unclean:
His Eyes, like hollow Furnaces on Fire:
A Girdle, foul with grease, binds his obscene Attire.
He spreads his Canvas, with his Pole he steers;
The Freights of flitting Ghosts in his thin Bottom bears.
420   He look'd in Years; yet in his Years were seen
A youthful Vigour, and Autumnal green.
An Airy Crowd came rushing where he stood;
Which fill'd the Margin of the fatal Flood.
Husbands and Wives, Boys and unmarry'd Maids;
425   And mighty Heroes more Majestick Shades.
And Youths, intomb'd before their Fathers Eyes,
With hollow Groans, and Shrieks, and feeble Cries:
Thick as the Leaves in Autumn strow the Woods:
Or Fowls, by Winter forc'd, forsake the Floods,
430   And wing their hasty flight to happier Lands: ⎫
Such, and so thick, the shiv'ring Army stands: ⎬
And press for passage with extended hands. ⎭

Now these, now those, the surly Boatman bore:
The rest he drove to distance from the Shore.
435   The Heroe, who beheld with wond'ring Eyes,
The Tumult mix'd with Shrieks, Laments, and Cries;
Ask'd of his Guide, what the rude Concourse meant?
Why to the Shore the thronging People bent?
What Forms of Law, among the Ghosts were us'd?
440   Why some were ferry'd o're, and some refus'd?
    Son of *Anchises*, Offspring of the Gods,
The Sibyl said; you see the *Stygian* Floods,
The Sacred Stream, which Heav'n's Imperial State
Attests in Oaths, and fears to violate.
445   The Ghosts rejected, are th' unhappy Crew
Depriv'd of Sepulchers, and Fun'ral due.
The Boatman *Charon*; those, the bury'd host,
He Ferries over to the Farther Coast.
Nor dares his Transport Vessel cross the Waves,
450   With such whose Bones are not compos'd in Graves.
A hundred years they wander on the Shore,
At length, their Pennance done, are wafted o're.
The *Trojan* Chief his forward pace repress'd;
Revolving anxious Thoughts within his Breast.
455   He saw his Friends, who whelm'd beneath the Waves,
Their Fun'ral Honours claim'd, and ask'd their quiet
        Graves.
The lost *Leucaspis* in the Crowd he knew;
And the brave Leader of the *Lycian* Crew:
Whom, on the *Tyrrhene* Seas, the Tempests met;
460   The Sailors master'd, and the Ship o'reset.
Amidst the Spirits *Palinurus* press'd;
Yet fresh from life; a new admitted Guest.
Who, while he steering view'd the Stars, and bore
His Course from *Affrick*, to the *Latian* Shore,
465   Fell headlong down. The *Trojan* fix'd his view;
And scarcely through the gloom the sullen Shadow knew.
Then thus the Prince. What envious Pow'r, O Friend,
Brought your lov'd Life to this disastrous end?
For *Phœbus*, ever true in all he said,
470   Has, in your fate alone, my Faith betray'd?

The God foretold you shou'd not die, before
You reach'd, secure from Seas, th' *Italian* Shore?
Is this th' unerring Pow'r? The Ghost reply'd,
Nor *Phœbus* flatter'd, nor his Answers ly'd;
475   Nor envious Gods have sent me to the Deep:
But while the Stars, and course of Heav'n I keep,
My weary'd Eyes were seiz'd with fatal sleep.
I fell; and with my weight, the Helm constrain'd,
Was drawn along, which yet my gripe retain'd.
480   Now by the Winds, and raging Waves, I swear,
Your Safety, more than mine, was then my Care:
Lest, of the Guide bereft, the Rudder lost,
Your Ship shou'd run against the rocky Coast.
Three blust'ring Nights, born by the Southern blast,
485   I floated; and discover'd Land at last:
High on a Mounting Wave, my head I bore:
Forcing my Strength, and gath'ring to the Shore:
Panting, but past the danger, now I seiz'd
The Craggy Cliffs, and my tyr'd Members eas'd:
490   While, cumber'd with my dropping Cloaths, I lay,
The cruel Nation, covetous of Prey,
Stain'd with my Blood th' unhospitable Coast:
And now, by Winds and Waves, my lifeless Limbs are tost.
Which O avert, by yon Etherial Light
495   Which I have lost, for this eternal Night:
Or if by dearer tyes you may be won,
By your dead Sire, and by your living Son,
Redeem from this Reproach, my wand'ring Ghost;
Or with your Navy seek the *Velin* Coast:
500   And in a peaceful Grave my Corps compose:
Or, if a nearer way your Mother shows,
Without whose Aid, you durst not undertake
This frightful Passage o're the *Stygian* Lake;
Lend to this Wretch your Hand, and waft him o're
505   To the sweet Banks of yon forbidden Shore.
Scarce had he said, the Prophetess began;
What Hopes delude thee, miserable Man?
Think'st thou thus unintomb'd to cross the Floods,
To view the Furies, and Infernal Gods;
510   And visit, without leave, the dark abodes?

Attend the term of long revolving Years:
Fate, and the dooming Gods, are deaf to Tears.
This Comfort of thy dire Misfortune take;
The Wrath of Heav'n, inflicted for thy sake,
515   With Vengeance shall pursue th' inhumane Coast.
Till they propitiate thy offended Ghost,
And raise a Tomb, with Vows, and solemn Pray'r;
And *Palinurus* name the Place shall bear.
This calm'd his Cares: sooth'd with his future Fame;
520   And pleas'd to hear his propagated Name.
    Now nearer to the *Stygian* Lake they draw:
Whom from the Shore, the surly Boatman saw:
Observ'd their Passage thro' the shady Wood;
And mark'd their near Approaches to the Flood:
525   Then thus he call'd aloud, inflam'd with Wrath;
Mortal, what e're, who this forbidden Path
In Arms presum'st to tread, I charge thee stand,
And tell thy Name, and Buis'ness in the Land.
Know this, the Realm of Night; the *Stygian* Shore:
530   My Boat conveys no living Bodies o're:
Nor was I pleas'd great *Theseus* once to bear;
Who forc'd a Passage with his pointed Spear;
Nor strong *Alcides*, Men of mighty Fame;
And from th' immortal Gods their Lineage came.
535   In Fetters one the barking Porter ty'd,
And took him trembling from his Sov'raign's side: }
Two sought by Force to seize his beauteous Bride.
To whom the Sibyl thus, compose thy Mind:
Nor Frauds are here contriv'd, nor Force design'd.
540   Still may the Dog the wand'ring Troops constrain   }
Of Airy Ghosts; and vex the guilty Train;
And with her grisly Lord his lovely Queen remain.
The *Trojan* Chief, whose Lineage is from *Jove*,   }
Much fam'd for Arms, and more for filial Love,
545   Is sent to seek his Sire, in your *Elisian* Grove.
If neither Piety, nor Heav'ns Command,
Can gain his Passage to the *Stygian* Strand,
This fatal Present shall prevail, at least;
Then shew'd the shining Bough, conceal'd within her
     Vest.

550 No more was needful: for the gloomy God
    Stood mute with Awe, to see the Golden Rod:
    Admir'd the destin'd Off'ring to his Queen;
    (A venerable Gift so rarely seen.)
    His Fury thus appeas'd, he puts to Land:
555 The Ghosts forsake their Seats, at his Command:
    He clears the Deck, receives the mighty Freight,
    The leaky Vessel groans beneath the weight.
    Slowly he sails; and scarcely stems the Tides:
    The pressing Water pours within her sides.
560 His Passengers at length are wafted o're;
    Expos'd in muddy Weeds, upon the miry Shore.
    No sooner landed, in his Den they found
    The triple Porter of the *Stygian* Sound:
    Grim *Cerberus*; who soon began to rear
565 His crested Snakes, and arm'd his bristling Hair.
    The prudent Sibyl had before prepar'd
    A Sop, in Honey steep'd, to charm the Guard.
    Which, mix'd with pow'rful Drugs, she cast before
    His greedy grinning Jaws, just op'd to roar:
570 With three enormous Mouths he gapes; and streight,
    With Hunger prest, devours the pleasing Bait.
    Long draughts of Sleep his monstrous Limbs enslave;
    He reels, and falling, fills the spacious Cave.
    The Keeper charm'd, the Chief without Delay
575 Pass'd on, and took th' irremeable way.
    Before the Gates, the Cries of Babes new born,
    Whom Fate had from their tender Mothers torn,
    Assault his Ears: Then those, whom Form of Laws
    Condemn'd to die, when Traitors judg'd their Cause.
580 Nor want they Lots, nor Judges to review
    The wrongful Sentence, and award a new.
    Minos, the strict Inquisitor, appears;
    And Lives and Crimes, with his Assessors, hears.
    Round, in his Urn, the blended Balls he rowls;
585 Absolves the Just, and dooms the Guilty Souls.
    The next in Place, and Punishment, are they
    Who prodigally throw their Souls away.
    Fools, who repining at their wretched State,
    And loathing anxious life, suborn'd their Fate.

590 With late Repentance, now they would retrieve
The Bodies they forsook, and wish to live.
Their Pains and Poverty desire to bear,
To view the Light of Heav'n, and breath the vital Air:
But Fate forbids; the *Stygian* Floods oppose;
595 And, with nine circling Streams, the captive Souls inclose.
    Not far from thence, the mournful Fields appear;
So call'd, from Lovers that inhabit there.
The Souls, whom that unhappy Flame invades,
In secret Solitude, and Myrtle Shades,
600 Make endless Moans, and pining with Desire,
Lament too late, their unextinguish'd Fire.
Here *Procris*, *Eryphile* here, he found
Baring her Breast, yet bleeding with the Wound
Made by her Son. He saw *Pasiphae* there,
605 With *Phædra*'s Ghost, a foul incestuous pair;
There *Laodamia*, with *Evadne* moves:
Unhappy both; but loyal in their Loves.
Cæneus, a Woman once, and once a Man;
But ending in the Sex she first began.
610 Not far from these *Phœnician Dido* stood;
Fresh from her Wound, her Bosom bath'd in Blood.
Whom, when the *Trojan* Heroe hardly knew,
Obscure in Shades, and with a doubtful view,
(Doubtful as he who runs thro' dusky Night,
615 Or thinks he sees the Moon's uncertain Light:)
With Tears he first approach'd the sullen Shade;
And, as his Love inspir'd him, thus he said.
Unhappy Queen! then is the common breath
Of Rumour true, in your reported Death,
620 And I, alas, the Cause! by Heav'n, I vow,
And all the Pow'rs that rule the Realms below,
Unwilling I forsook your friendly State:
Commanded by the Gods, and forc'd by Fate.
Those Gods, that Fate, whose unresisted Might }
625 Have sent me to these Regions, void of Light, }
Thro' the vast Empire of eternal Night. }
Nor dar'd I to presume, that, press'd with Grief,
My Flight should urge you to this dire Relief.

Stay, stay your Steps, and listen to my Vows:
630 'Tis the last Interview that Fate allows!
In vain he thus attempts her Mind to move,
With Tears and Pray'rs, and late repenting Love.
Disdainfully she look'd; then turning round,
But fix'd her Eyes unmov'd upon the Ground.
635 And, what he says, and swears, regards no more
Than the deaf Rocks, when the loud Billows roar.
But whirl'd away, to shun his hateful sight,
Hid in the Forest, and the Shades of Night.
Then sought *Sicheus*, thro' the shady Grove,
640 Who answer'd all her Cares, and equal'd all her Love.
Some pious Tears the pitying Heroe paid;
And follow'd with his Eyes the flitting Shade.
Then took the forward Way, by Fate ordain'd,
And, with his Guide, the farther Fields attain'd;
645 Where, sever'd from the rest, the Warrior Souls
       remain'd.
Tideus he met, with *Meleager*'s Race;
The Pride of Armies, and the Souldier's Grace;
And pale *Adrastus* with his ghastly Face.
Of *Trojan* Chiefs he view'd a numerous Train:
650 All much lamented, all in Battel slain.
Glaucus and *Medon*, high above the rest,
Antenor's Sons, and *Ceres* sacred Priest:
And proud *Ideus*, *Priam*'s Charioteer;
Who shakes his empty Reins, and aims his Airy Spear.
655 The gladsome Ghosts, in circling Troops, attend,
And with unweary'd Eyes behold their Friend.
Delight to hover near; and long to know
What buis'ness brought him to the Realms below.
    But *Argive* Chiefs, and *Agamemnon*'s Train,
660 When his refulgent Arms flash'd thro' the shady Plain,
Fled from his well known Face, with wonted Fear,
As when his thund'ring Sword, and pointed Spear,
Drove headlong to their Ships, and glean'd the routed
       Reer.
They rais'd a feeble Cry, with trembling Notes:
665 But the weak Voice deceiv'd their gasping Throats.

Here *Priam*'s Son, *Deiphobus*, he found:
Whose Face and Limbs were one continu'd Wound.
Dishonest, with lop'd Arms, the Youth appears:
Spoil'd of his Nose, and shorten'd of his Ears.
670   He scarcely knew him, striving to disown
His blotted Form, and blushing to be known.
And therefore first began. O *Teucer*'s Race,
Who durst thy Faultless Figure thus deface?
What heart cou'd wish, what Hand inflict this dire
    Disgrace?
675   'Twas fam'd, that in our last and fatal Night,
Your single Prowess long sustain'd the Fight:
Till tir'd, not forc'd, a glorious Fate you chose:
And fell upon a Heap of slaughter'd Foes.
But in remembrance of so brave a Deed,
680   A Tomb, and Fun'ral Honours I decreed:
Thrice call'd your *Manes*, on the *Trojan* Plains:
The place your Armour, and your Name retains.
Your Body too I sought; and had I found,
Design'd for Burial in your Native Ground.
685   The Ghost reply'd, your Piety has paid
All needful Rites, to rest my wand'ring Shade:
But cruel Fate, and my more cruel Wife,
To *Grecian* swords betray'd my sleeping Life.
These are the Monuments of *Helen*'s Love:
690   The Shame I bear below, the Marks I bore above.
You know in what deluding Joys we past
The Night, that was by Heav'n decreed our last.
For when the fatal Horse, descending down,
Pregnant with Arms, o'rewhelm'd th' unhappy Town;
695   She feign'd Nocturnal Orgyes: left my Bed,
And, mix'd with *Trojan* Dames, the Dances led.
Then, waving high her Torch, the Signal made,
Which rouz'd the *Grecians* from their Ambuscade.
With Watching overworn, with Cares opprest,
700   Unhappy I had laid me down to rest;
And heavy Sleep my weary Limbs possess'd.
Mean time my worthy Wife, our Arms mislay'd;
And from beneath my head my Sword convey'd:

The Door unlatch'd; and with repeated calls,
705 Invites her former Lord within my walls.
Thus in her Crime her confidence she plac'd:
And with new Treasons wou'd redeem the past.
What need I more, into the Room they ran;
And meanly murther'd a defenceless Man.
710 *Ulysses*, basely born, first led the way:
Avenging Pow'rs! with Justice if I pray,
That Fortune be their own another day.

      But answer you; and in your turn relate,
What brought you, living, to the *Stygian* State?
715 Driv'n by the Winds and Errors of the Sea,
Or did you Heav'ns Superior Doom obey?
Or tell what other Chance conducts your way?
To view, with Mortal Eyes, our dark Retreats,
Tumults and Torments of th' Infernal Seats?
720 While thus, in talk, the flying Hours they pass,
The Sun had finish'd more than half his Race:
And they, perhaps, in Words and Tears had spent
The little time of stay, which Heav'n had lent.
But thus the Sibyl chides their long delay;
725 Night rushes down, and headlong drives the Day:
'Tis here, in different Paths, the way divides:
The right, to *Pluto*'s Golden Palace guides:
The left to that unhappy Region tends,
Which to the depth of *Tartarus* descends;
730 The Seat of Night profound, and punish'd Fiends.
Then thus *Deiphobus*: O Sacred Maid!
Forbear to chide; and be your Will Obey'd:
Lo to the secret Shadows I retire,
To pay my Penance 'till my Years expire.
735 Proceed Auspicious Prince, with Glory Crownd,
And born to better Fates than I have found.
He said; and while he said, his Steps he turn'd
To Secret Shadows; and in silence Mourn'd.
The Heroe, looking on the left, espy'd
740 A lofty Tow'r, and strong on ev'ry side
With treble Walls, which *Phlegethon* surrounds,
Whose fiery Flood the burning Empire bounds:
And press'd betwixt the Rocks, the bellowing noise
      resounds.

Wide is the fronting Gate, and rais'd on high
745   With Adamantine Columns, threats the Sky.
Vain is the force of Man, and Heav'ns as vain,
To crush the Pillars which the Pile sustain.
Sublime on these a Tow'r of Steel is rear'd;
And dire *Tisiphone* there keeps the Ward.
750   Girt in her sanguine Gown, by Night and Day,
Observant of the Souls that pass the downward way:
From hence are heard the Groans of Ghosts, the pains
Of sounding Lashes, and of dragging Chains.
The *Trojan* stood astonish'd at their Cries;
755   And ask'd his Guide, from whence those Yells arise?
And what the Crimes and what the Tortures were,
And loud Laments that rent the liquid Air?
She thus reply'd: The chast and holy Race,
Are all forbidden this polluted Place.
760   But *Hecate*, when she gave to rule the Woods, ⎫
Then led me trembling thro' these dire Abodes: ⎬
And taught the Tortures of th' avenging Gods. ⎭
These are the Realms of unrelenting Fate:
And awful *Rhadamanthus* rules the State.
765   He hears and judges each committed Crime;
Enquires into the Manner, Place, and Time.
The conscious Wretch must all his Acts reveal:
Loath to confess, unable to conceal:
From the first Moment of his vital Breath,
770   To his last Hour of unrepenting Death.
Straight, o're the guilty Ghost, the Fury shakes ⎫
The sounding Whip, and brandishes her Snakes: ⎬
And the pale Sinner, with her Sisters, takes. ⎭
Then, of it self, unfolds th' Eternal Door:
775   With dreadful Sounds the brazen Hinges roar.
You see, before the Gate, what stalking Ghost
Commands the Guard, what Centries keep the Post:
More formidable *Hydra* stands within;
Whose Jaws with Iron Teeth severely grin.
780   The gaping Gulph, low to the Centre lies;
And twice as deep as Earth is distant from the Skies.
The Rivals of the Gods, the *Titan* Race,
Here sing'd with Lightning, rowl within th' unfathom'd
        space.

Here lye th' *Alœan* Twins, (I saw them both)
785   Enormous Bodies, of Gigantick Growth;
Who dar'd in Fight the Thund'rer to defy;
Affect his Heav'n, and force him from the Sky.
Salmoneus, suff'ring cruel Pains, I found,
For emulating *Jove*; the ratling Sound
790   Of Mimick Thunder, and the glitt'ring Blaze
Of pointed Lightnings, and their forky Rays.
Through *Elis*, and the *Grecian* Towns he flew:
Th' audacious Wretch four fiery Coursers drew:
He wav'd a Torch aloft, and, madly vain,
795   Sought Godlike Worship from a Servile Train.
Ambitious Fool, with horny Hoofs to pass
O're hollow Arches, of resounding Brass;
To rival Thunder, in its rapid Course:
And imitate inimitable Force.
800   But he, the King of Heav'n, obscure on high,
Bar'd his red Arm, and launching from the Sky
His writhen Bolt, not shaking empty Smoak,
Down to the deep Abyss the flaming Felon strook.
There *Tityus* was to see; who took his Birth
805   From Heav'n, his Nursing from the foodful Earth.
Here his Gygantic Limbs, with large Embrace,
Infold nine Acres of Infernal Space.
A rav'nous Vulture in his open'd side,
Her crooked Beak and cruel Tallons try'd:
810   Still for the growing Liver dig'd his Breast;
The growing Liver still supply'd the Feast.
Still are his Entrails fruitful to their Pains:
Th' immortal Hunger lasts, th' immortal Food remains.
Ixion and *Perithous* I cou'd name;
815   And more *Thessalian* Chiefs of mighty Fame.
High o're their Heads a mould'ring Rock is plac'd,
That promises a fall, and shakes at ev'ry Blast.
They lye below, on Golden Beds display'd,
And genial Feasts, with Regal Pomp, are made.
820   The Queen of Furies by their sides is set;
And snatches from their Mouths th' untasted Meat.
Which, if they touch, her hissing Snakes she rears:
Tossing her Torch, and thund'ring in their Ears.

Then they, who Brothers better Claim disown,
825   Expel their Parents, and usurp the Throne;
Defraud their Clients, and to Lucre sold,
Sit brooding on unprofitable Gold:
Who dare not give, and ev'n refuse to lend
To their poor Kindred, or a wanting Friend:
830   Vast is the Throng of these; nor less the Train
Of lustful Youths, for foul Adultry slain.
Hosts of Deserters, who their Honour sold,
And basely broke their Faith for Bribes of Gold:
All these within the Dungeon's depth remain:
835   Despairing Pardon, and expecting Pain.
Ask not what Pains; nor farther seek to know
Their Process, or the Forms of Law below.
Some rowl a weighty Stone; some laid along,
And bound with burning Wires, on Spokes of Wheels are
     hung.
840   Unhappy *Theseus*, doom'd for ever there,
Is fix'd by Fate on his Eternal Chair:
And wretched *Phlegias* warns the World with Cries; ⎫
(Cou'd Warning make the World more just or wise,) ⎬
Learn Righteousness, and dread th' avenging Deities. ⎭
845   To Tyrants others have their Country sold,
Imposing Foreign Lords, for Foreign Gold:
Some have old Laws repeal'd, new Statutes made;
Not as the People pleas'd, but as they paid.
With Incest some their Daughters Bed prophan'd,
850   All dar'd the worst of Ills, and what they dar'd, attain'd.
Had I a hundred Mouths, a hundred Tongues,
And Throats of Brass, inspir'd with Iron Lungs,
I could not half those horrid Crimes repeat:
Nor half the Punishments those Crimes have met.
855   But let us haste our Voyage to pursue;
The Walls of *Pluto*'s Palace are in view.
The Gate, and Iron Arch above it, stands
On *Anvils*, labour'd by the *Cyclops* Hands.
Before our farther way the Fates allow,
860   Here must we fix on high the Golden Bough.
She said, and thro' the gloomy Shades they past,
And chose the middle Path: Arriv'd at last,

The Prince, with living Water, sprinkl'd o're
His Limbs, and Body; then approach'd the Door.
865 Possess'd the Porch, and on the Front above
He fix'd the fatal Bough, requir'd by *Pluto*'s Love.
These Holy Rites perform'd, they took their Way,
Where long extended Plains of Pleasure lay.
The verdant Fields with those of Heav'n may vye;
870 With *Æther* vested, and a Purple Sky:
The blissful Seats of Happy Souls below:
Stars of their own, and their own Suns they know.
Their Airy Limbs in Sports they exercise,
And, on the Green, contend the Wrestler's Prize.
875 Some, in Heroick Verse, divinely sing;
Others in artful Measures lead the ring.
The *Thracian* Bard, surrounded by the rest,
There stands conspicuous in his flowing Vest.
His flying Fingers, and harmonious Quill,
880 Strike sev'n distinguish'd Notes, and sev'n at once they
    fill.
Here found they *Tucer*'s old Heroick Race;
Born better times and happier Years to grace.
Assaracus and *Ilus* here enjoy
Perpetual Fame, with him who founded *Troy*.
885 The Chief beheld their Chariots from afar;
Their shining Arms, and Coursers train'd to War:
Their Lances fix'd in Earth, their Steeds around,
Free from their Harness, graze the flow'ry Ground.
The love of Horses which they had, alive,
890 And care of Chariots, after Death survive.
Some chearful Souls, were feasting on the Plain;
Some did the Song, and some the Choir maintain
Beneath a Laurel Shade, where mighty *Po*
Mounts up to Woods above, and hides his Head below.
895 Here Patriots live, who, for their Countries good,
In fighting Fields, were prodigal of Blood:
Priests of unblemish'd Lives here make Abode;
And Poets worthy their inspiring God:
And searching Wits, of more Mechanick parts,
900 Who grac'd their Age with new invented Arts.

Those who, to worth, their Bounty did extend;
And those who knew that Bounty to commend.
The Heads of these with holy Fillets bound;
And all their Temples were with Garlands crown'd.
905   To these the Sibyl thus her Speech address'd: ⎫
And first, to him surrounded by the rest;   ⎬
Tow'ring his Height, and ample was his Breast; ⎭
Say happy Souls, Divine *Musæus* say,
Where lives *Anchises*, and where lies our Way
910 To find the Heroe, for whose only sake
We sought the dark Abodes, and cross'd the bitter Lake?
To this the Sacred Poet thus reply'd;
In no fix'd place the Happy Souls reside.
In Groves we live; and lie on mossy Beds
915 By Crystal Streams, that murmur through the Meads:
But pass yon easie Hill, and thence descend,
The Path conducts you to your Journeys end.
This said, he led them up the Mountains brow, ⎫
And shews them all the shining Fields below;   ⎬
920 They wind the Hill, and thro' the blissful Meadows go. ⎭
But old *Anchises*, in a flow'ry Vale,
Review'd his muster'd Race; and took the Tale.
Those Happy Spirits, which ordain'd by Fate,
For future Beings, and new Bodies wait.
925 With studious Thought observ'd th' illustrious Throng;
In Nature's Order as they pass'd along.
Their Names, their Fates, their Conduct, and their Care,
In peaceful Senates, and successful War.
He, when *Æneas* on the Plain appears,
930 Meets him with open Arms, and falling Tears.
Welcome, he said, the God's undoubted Race, ⎫
O long expected to my dear Embrace;   ⎬
Once more 'tis giv'n me to behold your Face! ⎭
The Love, and Pious Duty which you pay,
935 Have pass'd the Perils of so hard a way.
'Tis true, computing times, I now believ'd
The happy Day approach'd; nor are my Hopes deceiv'd.
What lengths of Lands, what Oceans have you pass'd,
What Storms sustain'd, and on what Shores been cast?

940 How have I fear'd your Fate! But fear'd it most,
     When Love assail'd you, on the *Lybian* Coast.
     To this, the Filial Duty thus replies; ⎫
     Your sacred Ghost, before my sleeping Eyes, ⎬
     Appear'd; and often urg'd this painful Enterprise. ⎭
945 After long tossing on the *Tyrrhene* Sea,
     My Navy rides at Anchor in the Bay.
     But reach your Hand, oh Parent Shade, nor shun
     The dear Embraces of your longing Son!
     He said; and falling Tears his Face bedew:
950 Then thrice, around his Neck, his Arms he threw;
     And thrice the flitting Shaddow slip'd away;
     Like Winds, or empty Dreams that fly the Day.
     Now in a secret Vale, the *Trojan* sees ⎫
     A sep'rate Grove, thro' which a gentle Breeze ⎬
955 Plays with a passing Breath, and whispers thro' the ⎭
         Trees.
     And just before the Confines of the Wood,
     The gliding *Lethe* leads her silent Flood.
     About the Boughs an Airy Nation flew,
     Thick as the humming Bees, that hunt the golden Dew;
960 In Summer's heat, on tops of Lillies feed,
     And creep within their Bells, to suck the balmy Seed.
     The winged Army roams the Field around;
     The Rivers and the Rocks remurmur to the sound.
     Æneas wondring stood: Then ask'd the Cause,
965 Which to the Stream the Crowding People draws.
     Then thus the Sire. The Souls that throng the Flood
     Are those, to Whom, by Fate, are other Bodies ow'd:
     In *Lethe*'s Lake they long Oblivion tast;
     Of future Life secure, forgetful of the Past.
970 Long has my Soul desir'd this time, and place,
     To set before your sight your glorious Race.
     That this presaging Joy may fire your Mind,
     To seek the Shores by Destiny design'd.
     O Father, can it be, that Souls sublime,
975 Return to visit our Terrestrial Clime?
     And that the Gen'rous Mind, releas'd by Death,
     Can Covet lazy Limbs, and Mortal Breath?

Anchises then, in order, thus begun
To clear those Wonders to his Godlike Son.
980 Know first, that Heav'n, and Earth's compacted Frame,
And flowing Waters, and the starry Flame,
And both the Radiant Lights, one Common Soul
Inspires, and feeds, and animates the whole.
This Active Mind infus'd through all the Space,
985 Unites and mingles with the mighty Mass.
Hence Men and Beasts the Breath of Life obtain;
And Birds of Air, and Monsters of the Main.
Th' Etherial Vigour is in all the same,
And every Soul is fill'd with equal Flame:
990 As much as Earthy Limbs, and gross allay }
Of Mortal Members, subject to decay, }
Blunt not the Beams of Heav'n and edge of Day. }
From this course Mixture of Terrestrial parts,
Desire, and Fear, by turns possess their Hearts:
995 And Grief, and Joy: Nor can the groveling Mind, }
In the dark Dungeon of the Limbs confin'd, }
Assert the Native Skies; or own its heavenly Kind. }
Nor Death it self can wholly wash their Stains;
But long contracted Filth, even in the Soul remains.
1000 The Reliques of inveterate Vice they wear;
And Spots of Sin obscene, in ev'ry Face appear.
For this are various Penances enjoyn'd;
And some are hung to bleach, upon the Wind;
Some plung'd in Waters, others purg'd in Fires,
1005 Till all the Dregs are drain'd; and all the Rust expires:
All have their *Manes*, and those *Manes* bear: }
The few, so cleans'd to these Abodes repair: }
And breath, in ample Fields, the soft *Elysian* Air. }
Then are they happy, when by length of time
1010 The Scurf is worn away, of each committed Crime.
No Speck is left, of their habitual Stains;
But the pure Æther of the Soul remains.
But, when a Thousand rowling Years are past,
(So long their Punishments and Penance last;)
1015 Whole Droves of Minds are, by the driving God,
Compell'd to drink the deep *Lethæan* Flood:

In large forgetful draughts to steep the Cares
Of their past Labours, and their Irksom Years.
That, unrememb'ring of its former Pain,
1020   The Soul may suffer mortal Flesh again.
Thus having said; the Father Spirit, leads
The Priestess and his Son through Swarms of Shades.
And takes a rising Ground, from thence to see
The long Procession of his Progeny.
1025   Survey (pursu'd the Sire) this airy Throng;
As, offer'd to thy view, they pass along.
These are th' *Italian* Names, which Fate will join
With ours, and graff upon the *Trojan* Line.
Observe the Youth who first appears in sight;
1030   And holds the nearest Station to the Light:
Already seems to snuff the vital Air;
And leans just forward, on a shining Spear,
Silvius is he: thy last begotten Race;
But first in order sent, to fill thy place,
1035   An *Alban* Name; but mix'd with *Dardan* Blood;
Born in the Covert of a shady Wood:
Him fair *Lavinia*, thy surviving Wife,
Shall breed in Groves, to lead a solitary Life.
In *Alba* he shall fix his Royal Seat:
1040   And, born a King, a Race of Kings beget.
Then *Procas*, Honour of the *Trojan* Name,
Capys, and *Numitor*, of endless Fame.
A second *Silvius* after these appears;
Silvius Æneas, for thy Name he bears.
1045   For Arms and Justice equally renown'd;
Who, late restor'd, in *Alba* shall be crown'd.
How great they look, how vig'rously they wield
Their weighty Lances, and sustain the Shield!
But they, who crown'd with Oaken Wreaths appear,
1050   Shall *Gabian* Walls, and strong *Fidena* rear:
Nomentum, *Bola*, with *Pometia*, found;
And raise *Colatian* Tow'rs on Rocky Ground.
All these shall then be Towns of mighty Fame;
Tho' now they lye obscure; and Lands without a Name.
1055   See *Romulus* the great, born to restore
The Crown that once his injur'd Grandsire wore.

This Prince, a Priestess of your Blood shall bear;
And like his Sire in Arms he shall appear.
Two rising Crests his Royal Head adorn;
1060 Born from a God, himself to Godhead born.
His Sire already signs him for the Skies,
And marks the Seat amidst the Deities.
Auspicious Chief! thy Race in times to come
Shall spread the Conquests of Imperial *Rome*.
1065 *Rome* whose ascending Tow'rs shall Heav'n invade;
Involving Earth and Ocean in her Shade.
High as the Mother of the Gods in place;
And proud, like her, of an Immortal Race.
Then when in Pomp she makes the *Phrygian* round;
1070 With Golden Turrets on her Temples crown'd:
A hundred Gods her sweeping Train supply;
Her Offspring all, and all command the Sky.
Now fix your Sight, and stand intent, to see
Your *Roman* Race, and *Julian* Progeny.
1075 The mighty *Cæsar* waits his vital Hour;
Impatient for the World, and grasps his promis'd Pow'r.
But next behold the Youth of Form Divine,
Cæsar himself, exalted in his Line;
Augustus, promis'd oft, and long foretold, ⎫
1080 Sent to the Realm that *Saturn* rul'd of old; ⎬
Born to restore a better Age of Gold. ⎭
Affrick, and *India*, shall his Pow'r obey, ⎫
He shall extend his propagated Sway, ⎬
Beyond the Solar Year; without the starry Way. ⎭
1085 Where *Atlas* turns the rowling Heav'ns around;
And his broad shoulders with their Lights are crown'd.
At his fore-seen Approach, already quake
The *Caspian* Kingdoms, and *Mæotian* Lake.
Their Seers behold the Tempest from afar;
1090 And threatning Oracles denounce the War.
Nile hears him knocking at his sev'nfold Gates;
And seeks his hidden Spring, and fears his Nephew's Fates.
Nor *Hercules* more Lands or Labours knew,
Not tho' the brazen-footed Hind he slew;
1095 Freed *Erymanthus* from the foaming Boar,
And dip'd his Arrows in *Lernæan* Gore.

Nor *Bacchus*, turning from his *Indian* War,
By Tygers drawn triumphant in his Car,
From *Nisus* top descending on the Plains;
1100   With curling Vines around his purple Reins.
And doubt we yet thro' Dangers to pursue
The Paths of Honour, and a Crown in view?
But what's the Man, who from afar appears,
His Head with Olive crown'd, his Hand a Censer bears?
1105   His hoary Beard, and holy Vestments bring
His lost Idea back: I know the *Roman* King.
He shall to peaceful *Rome* new Laws ordain:
Call'd from his mean abode, a Scepter to sustain.
Him, *Tullus* next in Dignity succeeds;
1110   An active Prince, and prone to Martial Deeds.
He shall his Troops for fighting Fields prepare,
Disus'd to Toils, and Triumphs of the War.
By dint of Sword his Crown he shall increase;
And scour his Armour from the Rust of Peace.
1115   Whom *Ancus* follows, with a fawning Air;
But vain within, and proudly popular.
Next view the *Tarquin* Kings: Th' avenging Sword
Of *Brutus*, justly drawn, and *Rome* restor'd.
He first renews the Rods, and Axe severe;
1120   And gives the Consuls Royal Robes to wear.
His Sons, who seek the Tyrant to sustain,
And long for Arbitrary Lords again,
With Ignominy scourg'd, in open sight,
He dooms to Death deserv'd; asserting Publick Right.
1125   Unhappy Man, to break the Pious Laws
Of Nature, pleading in his Children's Cause!
Howe're the doubtful Fact is understood,   ⎫
'Tis Love of Honour, and his Country's good: ⎬
The Consul, not the Father, sheds the Blood. ⎭
1130   Behold *Torquatus* the same Track pursue;
And next, the two devoted *Decij* view.
The *Drusian* Line, *Camillus* loaded home
With Standards well redeem'd, and foreign Foes o'recome.
The Pair you see in equal Armour shine;
1135   (Now, Friends below, in close Embraces joyn:

But when they leave the shady Realms of Night,
And, cloath'd in Bodies, breath your upper Light,)
With mortal Hate each other shall pursue:
What Wars, what Wounds, what Slaughter shall ensue!
1140 From *Alpine* Heights the Father first descends; ⎫
His Daughter's Husband in the Plain attends: ⎬
His Daughter's Husband arms his Eastern Friends. ⎭
Embrace again, my Sons, be Foes no more:
Nor stain your Country with her Childrens Gore.
1145 And thou, the first, lay down thy lawless claim;
Thou, of my Blood, who bear'st the *Julian* Name.
Another comes, who shall in Triumph ride;
And to the Capitol his Chariot guide;
From conquer'd *Corinth*, rich with *Grecian* Spoils.
1150 And yet another, fam'd for Warlike Toils,
On *Argos* shall impose the *Roman* Laws:
And, on the *Greeks*, revenge the *Trojan* Cause:
Shall drag in Chains their *Achillæan* Race; ⎫
Shall vindicate his Ancestors Disgrace: ⎬
1155 And *Pallas*, for her violated Place.   ⎭
Great *Cato* there, for Gravity renown'd,
And conqu'ring *Cossus* goes with Lawrels crown'd.
Who can omit the *Gracchi*, who declare
The *Scipio*'s Worth, those Thunderbolts of War,
1160 The double Bane of *Carthage*? Who can see,
Without esteem for virtuous Poverty,
Severe *Fabritius*, or can cease t' admire
The Ploughman Consul in his Course Attire!
Tir'd as I am, my Praise the *Fabij* claim;
1165 And thou great Heroe, greatest of thy Name;
Ordain'd in War to save the sinking State,
And, by Delays, to put a stop to Fate!
Let others better mold the running Mass ⎫
Of Mettals, and inform the breathing Brass; ⎬
1170 And soften into Flesh a Marble Face: ⎭
Plead better at the Bar; describe the Skies,
And when the Stars descend, and when they rise.
But, *Rome*, 'tis thine alone, with awful sway, ⎫
To rule Mankind; and make the World obey; ⎬
1175 Disposing Peace, and War, thy own Majestick Way. ⎭

To tame the Proud, the fetter'd Slave to free;
These are Imperial Arts, and worthy thee.
He paus'd: And while with wondr'ing Eyes they view'd
The passing Spirits, thus his Speech renew'd.
1180　See great *Marcellus*! how, untir'd in Toils,
He moves with Manly grace, how rich with Regal Spoils!
He, when his Country, (threaten'd with Alarms,)
Requires his Courage, and his Conqu'ring Arms,
Shall more than once the *Punic* Bands affright:
1185　Shall kill the *Gaulish* King in single Fight:
Then, to the Capitol in Triumph move,
And the third Spoils shall grace *Feretrian Jove*.
Æneas, here, beheld of Form Divine
A Godlike Youth, in glitt'ring Armour shine:
1190　With great *Marcellus* keeping equal pace;
But gloomy were his Eyes, dejected was his Face:
He saw, and, wond'ring, ask'd his airy Guide,
What, and of whence was he, who press'd the Hero's side?
His Son, or one of his Illustrious Name,
1195　How like the former, and almost the same:
Observe the Crowds that compass him around;
All gaze, and all admire, and raise a shouting sound:
But hov'ring Mists around his Brows are spread,
And Night, with sable Shades, involves his Head.
1200　Seek not to know (the Ghost reply'd with Tears)
The Sorrows of thy Sons, in future Years.
This Youth (the blissful Vision of a day)
Shall just be shown on Earth, and snatch'd away.
The Gods too high had rais'd the *Roman* State;
1205　Were but their Gifts as permanent as great.
What groans of Men shall fill the *Martian* Field!
How fierce a Blaze his flaming Pile shall yield!
What Fun'ral Pomp shall floating *Tiber* see,
When, rising from his Bed, he views the sad Solemnity!
1210　No Youth shall equal hopes of Glory give:
No Youth afford so great a Cause to grieve.
The *Trojan* Honour, and the *Roman* Boast;
Admir'd when living, and Ador'd when lost!
Mirror of ancient Faith in early Youth!
1215　Undaunted Worth, Inviolable Truth!

No Foe unpunish'd in the fighting Field,
Shall dare thee Foot to Foot, with Sword and Shield.
Much less, in Arms, oppose thy matchless Force,
When thy sharp Spurs shall urge thy foaming Horse.
1220   Ah, cou'dst thou break through Fates severe Decree,
A new *Marcellus* shall arise in thee!
Full Canisters of fragrant Lillies bring,
Mix'd with the Purple Roses of the Spring:
Let me with Fun'ral Flowers his Body strow;
1225   This Gift which Parents to their Children owe,
This unavailing Gift, as least I may bestow!
Thus having said, He led the Heroe round
The confines of the blest *Elysian* Ground.
Which, when *Anchises* to his Son had shown,
1230   And fir'd his Mind to mount the promis'd Throne,
He tells the future Wars, ordain'd by Fate;
The Strength and Customs of the *Latian* State:
The Prince, and People: And fore-arms his Care
With Rules, to push his Fortune, or to bear.
1235   Two Gates the silent House of Sleep adorn;
Of polish'd Iv'ry this, that of transparent Horn:
True Visions thro' transparent Horn arise;
Thro' polish'd Iv'ry pass deluding Lies.
Of various things discoursing as he pass'd,
1240   *Anchises* hither bends his Steps at last.
Then, through the Gate of Iv'ry, he dismiss'd
His valiant Offspring, and Divining Guest.
Streight to the Ships *Æneas* took his way;
Embarq'd his Men, and skim'd along the Sea:
1245   Still Coasting, till he gain'd *Cajeta*'s Bay.
At length on Oozy ground his Gallies moor:
Their Heads are turn'd to Sea, their Sterns to Shoar.

THE SEVENTH BOOK OF THE ÆNEIS

The Argument

King Latinus *entertains* Æneas, *and promises him his only Daughter,* Lavinia, *the Heiress of his Crown.* Turnus *being in Love with her, favour'd by her Mother, and stir'd up by* Juno, *and* Alecto, *breaks the Treaty which was made, and engages in his Quarrel,* Mezentius, Camilla, Messapus, *and many other of the Neighbouring Princes; whose Forces and the Names of their Commanders are here particularly related.*

And thou, O Matron of Immortal Fame!
Here Dying, to the Shore hast left thy Name:
Cajeta still the place is call'd from thee,
The Nurse of great *Eneas* Infancy.
Here rest thy Bones in rich *Hesperia*'s Plains,
Thy Name ('tis all a Ghost can have) remains.

   Now, when the Prince her Fun'ral Rites had paid,
He plough'd the *Tyrrhene* Seas with Sails display'd.
From Land a gentle Breeze arose by Night, }
Serenely shone the Stars, the Moon was bright, }
And the Sea trembled with her Silver Light. }
Now near the Shelves of *Circe*'s Shores they run,
(*Circe* the rich, the Daughter of the Sun)
A dang'rous Coast: The Goddess wasts her Days
In joyous Songs, the Rocks resound her Lays:
In spinning, or the Loom, she spends the Night,
And Cedar Brands supply her Father's Light.
From hence were heard, (rebellowing to the Main,)
The Roars of Lyons that refuse the Chain,
The Grunts of Bristled Boars, and Groans of Bears,
And Herds of Howling Wolves that stun the Sailors Ears.
These from their Caverns, at the close of Night,
Fill the sad Isle with Horror and Affright.
Darkling they mourn their Fate, whom *Circe*'s Pow'r
(That watch'd the Moon, and Planetary Hour)
With Words and wicked Herbs, from Human Kind
Had alter'd, and in Brutal Shapes confin'd.
With Monsters, lest the *Trojans* pious Host
Shou'd bear, or touch upon th' inchanted Coast;
Propitious *Neptune* steer'd their Course by Night,
With rising Gales, that sped their happy Flight.
Supply'd with these, they skim the sounding Shore,
And hear the swelling Surges vainly roar.

Now when the rosie Morn began to rise,
35   And wav'd her Saffron Streamer thro' the Skies;
When *Thetis* blush'd in Purple, not her own,
And from her Face the breathing Winds were blown:
A sudden Silence sat upon the Sea,
And sweeping Oars, with Strugling, urge their Way.
40   The *Trojan*, from the Main beheld a Wood,
Which thick with Shades, and a brown Horror, stood:
Betwixt the Trees the *Tyber* took his Course,
With Whirlpools dimpl'd; and with downward Force
That drove the Sand along, he took his Way,
45   And rowl'd his yellow Billows to the Sea.
About him, and above, and round the Wood,
The Birds that haunt the Borders of his Flood;
That bath'd within, or bask'd upon his side,
To tuneful Songs their narrow Throats apply'd.
50   The Captain gives Command, the joyful Train
Glide thro' the gloomy Shade, and leave the Main.
Now, *Erato*, thy Poet's Mind inspire,
And fill his Soul with thy Cœlestial Fire.
Relate what *Latium* was, her ancient Kings:
55   Declare the past, and present State of things,
When first the *Trojan* Fleet *Ausonia* sought;
And how the Rivals lov'd, and how they fought.
These are my Theme, and how the War began,
And how concluded by the Godlike Man.
60   For I shall sing of Battels, Blood and Rage,
Which Princes, and their People did engage:
And haughty Souls, that mov'd with mutual Hate,
In fighting Fields pursu'd and found their Fate:
That rouz'd the *Tyrrhene* Realm with loud Alarms,
65   And peaceful *Italy* involv'd in Arms.
A larger Scene of Action is display'd,
And, rising hence, a greater Work is weigh'd.
Latinus old and mild, had long possess'd
The *Latian* Scepter, and his People bless'd:
70   His Father *Faunus*: a *Laurentian* Dame
His Mother, fair *Marica* was her Name.
But *Faunus* came from *Picus*, *Picus* drew
His Birth from *Saturn*, if Records be true.

Thus King *Latinus*, in the third Degree,
75 Had *Saturn* Author of his Family.
But this old peaceful Prince, as Heav'n decreed,
Was bless'd with no Male Issue to succeed:
His Sons in blooming Youth were snatch'd by Fate;
One only Daughter heir'd the Royal State.
80 Fir'd with her Love, and with Ambition led,
The neighb'ring Princes court her nuptial Bed.
Among the Crowd, but far above the rest,
Young *Turnus* to the Beauteous Maid address'd.
Turnus, for high Descent, and graceful Meen,
85 Was first, and favour'd by the *Latian* Queen:
With him she strove to joyn *Lavinia*'s Hand:
But dire Portants the purpos'd Match withstand.
      Deep in the Palace, of long Growth there stood
A Lawrels Trunk, a venerable Wood;
90 Where Rites Divine were paid; whose holy Hair
Was kept, and cut with superstitious Care.
This Plant *Latinus*, when his Town he wall'd,
Then found, and from the Tree *Laurentum* call'd:
And last in Honour of his new Abode,
95 He vow'd the Lawrel, to the Lawrel's God.
It happen'd once, (a boding Prodigy,)
A swarm of Bees, that cut the liquid Sky,
Unknown from whence they took their airy flight,
Upon the topmost Branch in Clouds alight:
100 There, with their clasping Feet together clung,
And a long Cluster from the Lawrel hung.
An ancient Augur prophesy'd from hence:
Behold on *Latian* Shores a foreign Prince!
From the same parts of Heav'n his Navy stands, ⎫
105 To the same parts on Earth: his Army lands; ⎬
The Town he conquers, and the Tow'r commands. ⎭
Yet more, when fair *Lavinia* fed the Fire
Before the Gods, and stood beside her Sire;
Strange to relate, the Flames, involv'd in Smoke
110 Of Incense, from the sacred Altar broke;
Caught her dishevell'd Hair, and rich Attire;
Her Crown and Jewels crackled in the Fire:

From thence the fuming Trail began to spread,
And lambent Glories danc'd about her Head.
115   This new Portent the Seer with Wonder views;
Then pausing, thus his Prophecy renews.
The Nymph who scatters flaming Fires around,
Shall shine with Honour, shall her self be crown'd:
But, caus'd by her irrevocable Fate,
120   War shall the Country waste, and change the State.
Latinus, frighted with this dire Ostent,
For Counsel to his Father *Faunus* went:
And sought the Shades renown'd for Prophecy,
Which near *Albunea*'s sulph'rous Fountain lye.
125   To these the *Latian*, and the *Sabine* Land
Fly, when distress'd, and thence Relief demand.
The Priest on Skins of Off'rings takes his Ease;
And nightly Visions in his Slumber sees:
A swarm of thin aerial Shapes appears,
130   And, flutt'ring round his Temples, deafs his Ears:
These he consults, the future Fates to know,
From Pow'rs above, and from the Fiends below.
Here, for the Gods advice, *Latinus* flies,
Off'ring a hundred Sheep for Sacrifice:
135   Their wooly Fleeces, as the Rites requir'd,
He laid beneath him, and to Rest retir'd.
No sooner were his Eyes in Slumber bound,
When, from above, a more than Mortal Sound
Invades his Ears; and thus the Vision spoke: ⎫
140   Seek not, my Seed, in *Latian* Bands to Yoke ⎬
Our fair *Lavinia*, nor the Gods provoke. ⎭
A foreign Son upon the Shore descends,
Whose Martial Fame from Pole to Pole extends.
His Race in Arms, and Arts of Peace renown'd, ⎫
145   Not *Latium* shall contain, nor *Europe* bound: ⎬
'Tis theirs what e're the Sun surveys around. ⎭
These answers in the silent Night receiv'd,
The King himself divulg'd, the Land believ'd:
The Fame through all the Neighb'ring Nations flew,
150   When now the *Trojan* Navy was in view.
Beneath a shady Tree the Heroe spread ⎫
His Table on the Turf, with Cakes of Bread; ⎬
And, with his Chiefs, on Forest Fruits he fed. ⎭

They sate, and (not without the God's Command)
155   Their homely Fare dispatch'd; the hungry Band
Invade their Trenchers next, and soon devour,
To mend the scanty Meal, their Cakes of Flow'r.
Ascanius this observ'd, and, smiling, said,
See, we devour the Plates on which we fed.
160   The Speech had Omen, that the *Trojan* Race
Shou'd find Repose, and this the Time and Place.
Æneas took the Word, and thus replies;
(Confessing Fate with Wonder in his Eyes)
All hail, O Earth! all hail my houshold Gods,
165   Behold the destin'd place of your Abodes!
For thus *Anchises* prophecy'd of old,
And this our fatal place of Rest foretold.
'When on a Foreign Shore, instead of Meat,
'By Famine forc'd, your Trenchers you shall eat;
170   'Then Ease your weary *Trojans* will attend:
'And the long Labours of your Voyage end.
'Remember on that happy Coast to build:
'And with a Trench inclose the fruitful Field.'
This was that Famine, this the fatal place,
175   Which ends the Wand'ring of our exil'd Race.
Then, on to Morrow's Dawn, your Care employ, ⎤
To search the Land, and where the Cities lye,   ⎬
And what the Men; but give this Day to Joy.   ⎦
Now pour to *Jove*, and after *Jove* is blest,
180   Call great *Anchises* to the Genial Feast:
Crown high the Goblets with a chearful Draught;
Enjoy the present Hour, adjourn the future Thought.
Thus having said, the Heroe bound his Brows.
With leafy Branches, then perform'd his Vows:
185   Adoring first the Genius of the Place;
Then Earth, the Mother of the Heav'nly Race;
The Nymphs, and native Godheads yet unknown,
And Night, and all the Stars that guild her Sable Throne.
And ancient *Cybel*, and *Idæan Jove*;
190   And last his Sire below, and Mother Queen above.
Then Heav'ns high Monarch thundred thrice aloud;
And thrice he shook aloft, a Golden Cloud.

Soon thro' the joyful Camp a Rumor flew,
The time was come their City to renew:
195   Then ev'ry Brow with chearful Green is crown'd,
The Feasts are doubl'd, and the Bowls go round.
   When next the rosie Morn disclos'd the Day,
The Scouts to sev'ral parts divide their Way,
To learn the Natives Names, their Towns, explore
200   The Coasts, and Trendings of the crooked Shore:
Here *Tyber* flows, and here *Numicus* stands,
Here warlike *Latins* hold the happy Lands.
   The Pious Chief, who sought by peaceful Ways,
To found his Empire, and his Town to raise;
205   A hundred Youths from all his Train selects,
And to the *Latian* Court their Course directs:
(The spacious Palace where their Prince resides;)
And all their heads with Wreaths of Olive hides.
They go commission'd to require a Peace;
210   And carry Presents to procure Access.
Thus while they speed their Pace, the Prince designs
His new elected Seat, and draws the Lines:
The *Trojans* round the Place a Rampire cast,
And Palisades about the Trenches plac'd.
215   Mean time the Train, proceeding on their way,
From far the Town, and lofty Tow'rs survey:
At length approach the Walls: without the Gate
They see the Boys, and *Latian* Youth debate
The Martial Prizes on the dusty Plain;
220   Some drive the Cars, and some the Coursers rein:
Some bend the stubborn Bow for Victory;
And some with Darts their active Sinews try.
A posting Messenger dispatch'd from hence,
Of this fair Troop advis'd their aged Prince;
225   That foreign Men, of mighty Stature came;
Uncouth their Habit, and unknown their Name.
The King ordains their entrance, and ascends
His Regal Seat, surrounded by his Friends.
The Palace built by *Picus*, vast and Proud, ⎤
230   Supported by a hundred Pillars stood: ⎬
And round incompass'd with a rising Wood. ⎦
The Pile o'relooked the Town, and drew the sight;
Surpriz'd at once with Reverence and Delight.

There Kings receiv'd the Marks of Sov'raign Pow'r:
235 In State the Monarchs march'd, the Lictors bore
Their Awful Axes, and the Rods before.
Here the Tribunal stood, the House of Pray'r;
And here the sacred Senators repair:
All at large Tables, in long order set,
240 A Ram their Off'ring, and a Ram their Meat.
Above the Portal, Carv'd in Cedar Wood,
Plac'd in their Ranks, their Godlike Grandsires stood.
Old *Saturn*, with his crooked Scythe, on high;
And *Italus*, that led the Colony:
245 And ancient *Janus*, with his double Face,
And Bunch of Keys, the Porter of the place.
There good *Sabinus*, planter of the Vines,
On a short Pruning-hook his Head reclines:
And studiously surveys his gen'rous Wines.
250 Then Warlike Kings, who for their Country fought,
And honourable Wounds from Battel brought.
Around the Posts hung Helmets, Darts, and Spears;
And Captive Chariots, Axes, Shields, and Bars,
And broken Beaks of Ships, the Trophies of their Wars.
255 Above the rest, as Chief of all the Band,
Was *Picus* plac'd, a Buckler in his hand;
His other wav'd a long divining Wand.
Girt in his Gabin Gown the Heroe sate:
Yet could not with his Art avoid his Fate.
260 For *Circe* long had lov'd the Youth in vain,
Till Love, refus'd, converted to Disdain:
Then mixing pow'rful Herbs, with Magic Art,
She chang'd his Form, who cou'd not change his heart.
Constrain'd him in a Bird, and made him fly,
265 With party-colour'd Plumes; a Chattring Pye.
In this high Temple, on a Chair of State,
The Seat of Audience, old *Latinus* sate;
Then gave admission to the *Trojan* Train,
And thus, with pleasing accents, he began.
270 Tell me, ye *Trojans*, for that Name you own;
Nor is your Course upon our Coasts unknown;
Say what you seek, and whither were you bound?
Were you by stress of Weather cast a-ground?

Such dangers as on Seas are often seen,
275   And oft befall to miserable Men?
Or come, your Shipping in our Ports to lay,
Spent and disabl'd in so long a way?
Say what you want, the *Latians* you shall find
Not forc'd to goodness, but by Will inclin'd:
280   For since the time of *Saturn*'s holy Reign,
His Hospitable Customs we retain.
I call to mind, but (Time the Tale has worn,)
Th' *Arunci* told; that *Dardanus*, tho' born
On *Latian* Plains, yet sought the *Phrygian* Shore,
285   And *Samothracia*, *Samos* call'd before:
From *Tuscan Coritum* he claim'd his Birth,
But after, when exempt from Mortal Earth,
From thence ascended to his kindred Skies,
A God, and as a God augments their Sacrifice.
290   He said. *Ilioneus* made this Reply,
O King, of *Faunus* Royal Family!
Nor Wint'ry Winds to *Latium* forc'd our way,
Nor did the Stars our wand'ring Course betray.
Willing we sought your Shores, and hither bound,
295   The Port so long desir'd, at length we found.
From our sweet Homes and ancient Realms expell'd;
Great as the greatest that the Sun beheld.
The God began our Line, who rules above,
And as our Race, our King descends from *Jove*:
300   And hither are we come, by his Command,
To crave Admission in your happy Land.
How dire a Tempest, from *Mycenæ* pour'd,
Our Plains, our Temples, and our Town devour'd;
What was the Waste of War, what fierce Alarms
305   Shook *Asia*'s Crown with *Europæan* Arms;
Ev'n such have heard, if any such there be,
Whose Earth is bounded by the frozen Sea:
And such as born beneath the burning Sky,
And sultry Sun betwixt the Tropicks lye.
310   From that dire Deluge, through the wat'ry Waste,
Such length of Years, such various Perils past:
At last escap'd, to *Latium* we repair,
To beg what you without your Want may spare; ⎫
The common Water, and the common Air. ⎭

315 Sheds which our selves will build, and mean abodes,
    Fit to receive and serve our banish'd Gods.
    Nor our Admission shall your Realm disgrace,
    Nor length of time our Gratitude efface.
    Besides, what endless Honour you shall gain
320 To save and shelter *Troy*'s unhappy Train.
    Now, by my Sov'raign, and his Fate I swear,
    Renown'd for Faith in Peace, for Force in War;
    Oft our Alliance other Lands desir'd,
    And what we seek of you, of us requir'd.
325 Despise not then, that in our Hands we bear
    These Holy Boughs, and sue with Words of Pray'r.
    Fate and the Gods, by their supreme Command,
    Have doom'd our Ships to see the *Latian* Land.
    To these abodes our Fleet *Apollo* sends;
330 Here *Dardanus* was born, and hither tends:
    Where *Thuscan Tyber* rowls with rapid Force,
    And where *Numicus* opes his Holy Source.
    Besides our Prince presents, with his Request,
    Some small Remains of what his Sire possess'd.
335 This Golden Charger, snatch'd from burning *Troy*,
    Anchises did in Sacrifice employ:
    This Royal Robe, and this *Tiara* wore
    Old *Priam*, and this Golden Scepter bore
    In full Assemblies, and in solemn Games;
340 These Purple Vests were weav'd by *Darden* Dames.
        Thus while he spoke *Latinus* rowld around
    His Eyes, and fix'd a while upon the Ground.
    Intent he seem'd, and anxious in his Brest;
    Not by the Scepter mov'd, or Kingly Vest:
345 But pond'ring future Things of wond'rous Weight;
    Succession, Empire, and his Daughter's Fate:
    On these he mus'd within his thoughtful Mind;
    And then revolv'd what *Faunus* had divin'd.
    This was the Foreign Prince, by Fate decreed
350 To share his Scepter, and *Lavinia*'s Bed:
    This was the Race, that sure Portents foreshew
    To sway the World, and Land and Sea subdue.
    At length he rais'd his chearful Head, and spoke:
    The Pow'rs, said he, the Pow'rs we both invoke,

355 To you, and yours, and mine, propitious be,
     And firm our Purpose with their Augury.
     Have what you ask; your Presents I receive,
     Land where, and when you please, with ample Leave:
     Partake and use my Kingdom as your own;
360 All shall be yours, while I command the Crown.
     And if my wish'd Alliance please your King,
     Tell him he shou'd not send the Peace, but bring:
     Then let him not a Friend's Embraces fear;
     The Peace is made when I behold him here.
365 Besides this Answer, tell my Royal Guest,
     I add to his Commands, my own Request:
     One only Daughter heirs my Crown and State,
     Whom, not our Oracles, nor Heav'n, nor Fate,
     Nor frequent Prodigies permit to join
370 With any Native of th' *Ausonian* Line.
     A foreign Son-in-Law shall come from far,
     (Such is our Doom) a Chief renown'd in War:
     Whose Race shall bear aloft the *Latian* Name,
     And through the conquer'd World diffuse our Fame.
375 Himself to be the Man the Fates require,
     I firmly judge, and what I judge, desire.
     He said, and then on each bestow'd a Steed;
     Three hundred Horses, in high Stables fed,
     Stood ready, shining all, and smoothly dress'd;
380 Of these he chose the fairest and the best,
     To mount the *Trojan* Troop; at his Command,
     The Steeds caparison'd with Purple stand;
     With Golden Trappings, glorious to behold,
     And champ betwixt their Teeth the foaming Gold.
385 Then to his absent Guest the King decreed
     A pair of Coursers born of Heavenly Breed:
     Who from their Nostrils breath'd Etherial Fire;
     Whom *Circe* stole from her Cœlestial Sire:
     By substituting Mares, produc'd on Earth,
390 Whose Wombs conceiv'd a more than Mortal Birth.
     These draw the Chariot which *Latinus* sends;
     And the rich Present to the Prince commends.
     Sublime on stately Steeds the *Trojans* born,
     To their expecting Lord with Peace return.

395 But jealous *Juno*, from *Pachynus* height,
As she from *Argos* took her airy Flight, }
Beheld, with envious Eyes, this hateful Sight. }
She saw the *Trojan*, and his joyful Train
Descend upon the Shore, desert the Main;
400 Design a Town, and with unhop'd Success
Th' Embassadors return with promis'd Peace.
Then pierc'd with Pain, she shook her haughty Head,
Sigh'd from her inward Soul; and thus she said.
O hated Off-spring of my *Phrygian* Foes!
405 O Fates of *Troy*, which *Juno*'s Fates oppose!
Cou'd they not fall unpity'd, on the Plain,
But slain revive, and taken, scape again?
When execrable *Troy* in Ashes lay,
Thro' Fires, and Swords, and Seas, they forc'd their Way.
410 Then vanquish'd *Juno* must in vain contend,
Her Rage disarm'd, her Empire at an end.
Breathless and tir'd, is all my Fury spent,
Or does my glutted Spleen at length relent?
As if 'twere little from their Town to chase,
415 I thro' the Seas pursu'd their exil'd Race:
Ingag'd the Heav'ns, oppos'd the Stormy Main;
But Billows roar'd, and Tempests rag'd in vain.
What have my *Scylla*'s and my *Sirtes* done,
When these they overpass, and those they shun?
420 On *Tyber*'s Shores they land, secure of Fate,
Triumphant o'er the Storms and *Juno*'s Hate.
Mars cou'd in mutual Blood the *Centaurs* bath,
And *Jove* himself gave way to *Cynthia*'s Wrath:
Who sent the tusky Boar to *Calydon*:
425 What great Offence had either People done?
But I, the Consort of the Thunderer,
Have wag'd a long and unsuccessful War:
With various Arts and Arms in vain have toil'd,
And by a Mortal Man at length am foil'd.
430 If native Pow'r prevail not, shall I doubt
To seek for needful Succour from without:
If *Jove* and Heav'n my just Desires deny,
Hell shall the Pow'r of Heav'n and *Jove* supply.

Grant that the Fates have firm'd, by their Decree,
435   The *Trojan* Race to reign in *Italy*;
At least I can defer the Nuptial Day,
And with protracted Wars the Peace delay:
With Blood the dear Alliance shall be bought;
And both the People near Destruction brought.
440   So shall the Son-in-Law, and Father join,
With Ruin, War, and Waste of either Line.
O fatal Maid! thy Marriage is endow'd
With *Phrygian*, *Latian*, and *Rutulian* Blood!
Bellona leads thee to thy Lover's Hand,   ⎫
445   Another Queen brings forth another Brand;   ⎬
To burn with foreign Fires another Land!   ⎭
A second *Paris*, diff'ring but in Name,
Shall fire his Country with a second Flame.
      Thus having said, she sinks beneath the Ground,
450   With furious haste, and shoots the *Stygian* Sound;
To rowze *Alecto* from th' Infernal Seat
Of her dire Sisters, and their dark Retreat.
This Fury, fit for her Intent, she chose;
One who delights in Wars, and Human Woes.
455   Ev'n *Pluto* hates his own mishapen Race:
Her Sister-Furies fly her hideous Face:
So frightful are the Forms the Monster takes,
So fierce the Hissings of her speckled Snakes.
Her *Juno* finds, and thus inflames her Spight:
460   O Virgin Daughter of Eternal Night,
Give me this once thy Labour, to sustain
My Right, and execute my just disdain.
Let not the *Trojans*, with a feign'd Pretence
Of proffer'd Peace, delude the *Latian* Prince:
465   Expel from *Italy* that odious Name,
And let not *Juno* suffer in her Fame.
'Tis thine to ruin Realms, o'return a State,   ⎫
Betwixt the dearest Friends to raise Debate;   ⎬
And kindle kindred Blood to mutual Hate.   ⎭
470   Thy Hand o're Towns the fun'ral Torch displays,
And forms a thousand Ills ten thousand Ways.
Now shake from out thy fruitful Breast, the Seeds
Of Envy, Discord, and of Cruel Deeds:
Confound the Peace establish'd, and prepare

475   Their Souls to Hatred, and their Hands to War.
       Smear'd as she was with black *Gorgonean* Blood,
       The Fury sprang above the *Stygian* Flood:
       And on her wicker Wings, sublime through Night,
       She to the *Latian* Palace took her Flight.
480   There sought the Queen's Apartment, stood before
       The peaceful Threshold, and besieg'd the Door.
       Restless *Amata* lay, her swelling Breast   ⎫
       Fir'd with Disdain for *Turnus* dispossest,   ⎬
       And the new Nuptials of the *Trojan* Guest.   ⎭
485   From her black bloody Locks the Fury shakes
       Her darling Plague, the Fav'rite of her Snakes:
       With her full Force she threw the pois'nous Dart,
       And fix'd it deep within *Amatas* Heart.
       That thus envenom'd she might kindle Rage,
490   And sacrifice to Strife her House and Husbands Age.
       Unseen, unfelt; the fiery Serpent skims
       Betwixt her Linnen, and her naked Limbs.
       His baleful Breath inspiring, as he glides,
       Now like a Chain around her Neck he rides;
495   Now like a Fillet to her Head repairs,
       And with his Circling Volumes folds her Hairs.
       At first the silent Venom slid with ease,
       And seiz'd her cooler Senses by degrees;
       Then e're th' infected Mass was fir'd too far,
500   In Plaintive Accents she began the War:
       And thus bespoke her Husband; Shall, she said,
       A wandring Prince enjoy *Lavinia*'s Bed?
       If Nature plead not in a Parent's Heart,
       Pity my Tears, and pity her Desert:
505   I know, my dearest Lord, the time will come,
       You wou'd, in vain, reverse your Cruel doom:
       The faithless Pirate soon will set to Sea,
       And bear the Royal Virgin far away!
       A Guest like him, a *Trojan* Guest before,   ⎫
510   In shew of friendship, sought the *Spartan* Shore; ⎬
       And ravish'd *Helen* from her Husband bore.   ⎭
       Think on a King's inviolable Word;
       And think on *Turnus*, her once plighted Lord:
       To this false Foreigner you give your Throne,
515   And wrong a Friend, a Kinsman, and a Son.

Resume your ancient Care; and if the God
Your Sire, and you, resolve on Foreign Blood:
Know all are Foreign, in a larger Sense,
Not born your Subjects, or deriv'd from hence.
520   Then if the Line of *Turnus* you retrace;
He springs from *Inachus* of *Argive* Race.
But when she saw her Reasons idly spent,
And cou'd not move him from his fix'd Intent;
She flew to rage; for now the Snake possess'd
525   Her vital parts, and poison'd all her Breast;
She raves, she runs with a distracted pace,
And fills, with horrid howls, the publick Place.
And, as young Striplings whip the Top for sport,
On the smooth Pavement of an empty Court;
530   The wooden Engine flies and whirls about,
Admir'd, with Clamours, of the Beardless rout;
They lash aloud, each other they provoke,
And lend their little Souls at ev'ry stroke:
Thus fares the Queen, and thus her fury blows
535   Amidst the Crowd, and kindles as she goes.
Nor yet content, she strains her Malice more,
And adds new ills to those contriv'd before:
She flies the Town, and mixing with a throng
Of madding Matrons, bears the Bride along:
540   Wand'ring through Woods and Wilds, and devious ways,
And with these Arts the *Trojan* Match delays.
She feign'd the Rites of *Bacchus*! cry'd aloud,
And to the Buxom God the Virgin vow'd.
Evoe, O *Bacchus* thus began the Song,
545   And *Evoe*! answer'd all the Female Throng:
O Virgin! worthy thee alone, she cry'd;
O worthy thee alone, the Crew reply'd.
For thee she feeds her Hair, she leads thy Dance,
And with thy winding Ivy wreaths her Lance.
550   Like fury seiz'd the rest; the progress known,
All seek the Mountains, and forsake the Town:
All Clad in Skins of Beasts the Jav'lin bear, ⎫
Give to the wanton Winds their flowing Hair: ⎬
And shrieks and showtings rend the suff'ring Air. ⎭
555   The Queen, her self, inspir'd with Rage Divine,

Shook high above her head a flaming Pine:
Then rowl'd her haggar'd Eyes around the throng,
And sung, in *Turnus* Name, the Nuptial Song:
Io ye *Latian* Dames, if any here
560 Hold, your unhappy Queen, *Amata*, dear;
If there be here, she said, who dare maintain
My Right, nor think the Name of Mother vain:
Unbind your Fillets, loose your flowing Hair,
And *Orgies*, and Nocturnal Rites prepare.
565 *Amata*'s Breast the Fury thus invades,
And fires with Rage, amid the Silvan Shades.
Then when she found her Venom spread so far,
The Royal House embroil'd in Civil War:
Rais'd on her dusky Wings she cleaves the Skies,
570 And seeks the Palace where young *Turnus* lies.
His Town, as Fame reports, was built of old
By *Danae*, pregnant with Almighty Gold:
Who fled her Father's Rage, and with a Train ⎫
Of following *Argives*, thro' the stormy Main, ⎬
575 Driv'n by the *Southern* Blasts, was fated here to reign. ⎭
      'Twas *Ardua* once, now *Ardea*'s Name it bears:
Once a fair City, now consum'd with Years.
Here in his lofty Palace *Turnus* lay,
Betwixt the Confines of the Night and Day,
580 Secure in Sleep: The Fury laid aside ⎫
Her Looks and Limbs, and with new methods try'd, ⎬
The foulness of th' infernal Form to hide. ⎭
Prop'd on a Staff, she takes a trembling Meen,
Her Face is furrow'd, and her Front obscene:
585 Deep dinted Wrinckles on her Cheek she draws,
Sunk are her Eyes, and toothless are her Jaws:
Her hoary Hair with holy Fillets bound,
Her Temples with an Olive Wreath are crown'd.
Old *Calibe*, who kept the sacred Fane ⎫
590 Of *Juno*, now she seem'd, and thus began, ⎬
Appearing in a Dream, to rouze the careless Man. ⎭
Shall *Turnus* then such endless Toil sustain,
In fighting Fields, and conquer Towns in vain:
Win, for a *Trojan* Head to wear the Prize,
595 Usurp thy Crown, enjoy thy Victories?

The Bride and Scepter which thy Blood has bought,
The King transfers, and Foreign Heirs are sought:
Go now, deluded Man, and seek again
New Toils, new Dangers on the dusty Plain.
600 Repel the *Tuscan* Foes, their City seize,
Protect the *Latians* in luxurious Ease.
This Dream all-pow'rful *Juno* sends, I bear
Her mighty Mandates, and her Words you hear.
Haste, arm your *Ardeans*, issue to the Plain,
605 With Fate to friend, assault the *Trojan* Train:
Their thoughtless Chiefs, their painted Ships that lye
In *Tyber*'s Mouth, with Fire and Sword destroy.
The *Latian* King, unless he shall submit,
Own his old Promise, and his new forget;
610 Let him, in Arms, the Pow'r of *Turnus* prove,
And learn to fear whom he disdains to Love.
For such is Heav'ns Command. The youthful Prince
With Scorn reply'd, and made this bold Defence.
You tell me, Mother, what I knew before,
615 The *Phrygian* Fleet is landed on the Shore:
I neither fear, nor will provoke the War;
My Fate is *Juno*'s most peculiar Care.
But Time has made you dote, and vainly tell
Of Arms imagin'd, in your lonely Cell:
620 Go, be the Temple and the Gods your Care,
Permit to Men the Thought of Peace and War.
      These haughty Words *Alecto*'s Rage provoke,
And frighted *Turnus* trembled as she spoke,
Her Eyes grow stiffen'd, and with Sulphur burn,
625 Her hideous Looks, and hellish Form return:
Her curling Snakes, with Hissings fill the place,
And open all the Furies of her Face:
Then, darting Fire from her malignant Eyes,   ⎫
She cast him backward as he strove to rise,   ⎬
630 And, ling'ring, sought to frame some new Replies. ⎭
High on her Head she rears two twisted Snakes, ⎫
Her Chains she rattles, and her Whip she shakes; ⎬
And churning bloody Foam, thus loudly speaks.   ⎭
Behold whom Time has made to dote, and tell
635 Of Arms, imagin'd in her lonely Cell:

Behold the Fates Infernal Minister;
War, Death, Destruction, in my Hand I bear.
      Thus having said, her smould'ring Torch impress'd,
With her full Force, she plung'd into his Breast.
640   Aghast he wak'd, and, starting from his Bed,
Cold Sweat, in clammy Drops, his Limbs o'respread.
Arms, Arms, he cries, my Sword and Shield prepare;
He breaths Defiance, Blood, and Mortal War.
So when with crackling Flames a Cauldron fries,
645   The bubling Waters from the Bottom rise:
Above the Brims they force their fiery way;
Black Vapours climb aloft, and cloud the Day.
      The Peace polluted thus, a chosen Band
He first commissions to the *Latian* Land;
650   In threatning Embassy: Then rais'd the rest,
To meet in Arms th' intruding *Trojan* Guest:
To force the Foes from the *Lavinian* Shore,
And *Italy*'s indanger'd Peace restore.
Himself alone, an equal Match he boasts,
655   To fight the *Phrygian* and *Ausonian* Hoasts.
The Gods invok'd, the *Rutuli* prepare
Their Arms, and warm each other to the War.
His Beauty these, and those his blooming Age,
The rest his House, and his own Fame ingage.
660   While *Turnus* urges thus his Enterprise;
The *Stygian* Fury to the *Trojans* flies:
New Frauds invents, and takes a steepy Stand,
Which overlooks the Vale with wide Command;
Where fair *Ascanius*, and his youthful Train,
665   With Horns and Hounds a hunting Match ordain, }
And pitch their Toils around the shady Plain.
The Fury fires the Pack; they snuff, they vent,
And feed their hungry Nostrils with the Scent.
'Twas of a well grown Stag, whose Antlers rise
670   High o're his Front, his Beams invade the Skies:
From this light Cause, th' Infernal Maid prepares
The Country Churls to Mischief, Hate, and Wars.
      The stately Beast, the Two *Tyrrheidæ* bred,
Snatch'd from his Dam, and the tame Youngling fed.

675   Their Father *Tyrrheus* did his Fodder bring,
        Tyrrheus, chief Ranger to the *Latian* King:
        Their Sister *Silvia* cherish'd with her Care
        The little Wanton, and did Wreaths prepare
        To hang his budding Horns: with Ribbons ty'd
680   His tender Neck, and comb'd his silken Hide;
        And bath'd his Body. Patient of Command,
        In time he grew, and growing us'd to Hand.
        He waited at his Master's Board for Food;
        Then sought his salvage Kindred in the Wood:
685   Where grazing all the Day, at Night he came
        To his known Lodgings, and his Country Dame.
           This household Beast, that us'd the Woodland Grounds,
        Was view'd at first by the young Hero's Hounds;
        As down the Stream he swam, to seek Retreat
690   In the cool Waters, and to quench his Heat.
        Ascanius young, and eager of his Game,
        Soon bent his Bow, uncertain in his Aim:
        But the dire Fiend the fatal Arrow guides,
        Which pierc'd his Bowels thro' his panting sides.
695   The bleeding Creature issues from the Floods,
        Possess'd with Fear, and seeks his known abodes;
        His old familiar Hearth, and household Gods.
        He falls, he fills the House with heavy Groans,
        Implores their Pity, and his Pain bemoans.
700   Young *Silvia* beats her Breast, and cries aloud
        For Succour, from the clownish Neighbourhood:
        The Churls assemble; for the Fiend, who lay
        In the close Woody Covert, urg'd their way.
        One with a Brand, yet burning from the Flame;
705   Arm'd with a knotty Club, another came:
        What e're they catch or find, without their Care,
        Their Fury makes an Instrument of War.
        Tyrrheus, the Foster-Father of the Beast,
        Then clench'd a Hatchet in his horny Fist:
710   But held his Hand from the descending Stroke,
        And left his Wedge within the cloven Oak,
        To whet their Courage, and their Rage provoke.
        And now the Goddess, exercis'd in Ill,
        Who watch'd an Hour to work her impious Will,

715 Ascends the Roof, and to her crooked Horn,
 Such as was then by *Latian* Shepherds born,
 Adds all her Breath, the Rocks and Woods around,
 And Mountains, tremble at th' infernal Sound.
 The Sacred Lake of *Trivia* from afar, ⎫
720 The *Veline* Fountains, and sulphureous *Nar*, ⎬
 Shake at the baleful Blast, the Signal of the War. ⎭
 Young Mothers wildly stare, with Fear possess'd,
 And strain their helpless Infants to their Breast.
  The Clowns, a boist'rous, rude, ungovern'd Crew,
725 With furious haste to the loud Summons flew.
 The Pow'rs of *Troy* then issuing on the Plain,
 With fresh Recruits their youthful Chief sustain:
 Not theirs a raw and unexperienc'd Train,
 But a firm Body of embattel'd Men.
730 At first, while Fortune favour'd neither side,
 The Fight with Clubs and burning Brands was try'd:
 But now, both Parties reinforc'd, the Fields
 Are bright with flaming Swords and brazen Shields.
 A shining Harvest either Host displays,
735 And shoots against the Sun with equal Rays.
  Thus when a black-brow'd Gust begins to rise, ⎫
 White Foam at first on the curl'd Ocean fries; ⎬
 Then roars the Main, the Billows mount the Skies: ⎭
 'Till by the Fury of the Storm full blown,
740 The muddy Bottom o're the Clouds is thrown.
  First *Almon* falls, old *Tyrrheus* eldest Care,
 Pierc'd with an Arrow from the distant War:
 Fix'd in his Throat the flying Weapon stood,
 And stop'd his Breath, and drank his vital Blood.
745 Huge Heaps of slain around the Body rise;
 Among the rest, the rich *Galesus* lyes:
 A good old Man, while Peace he preach'd in vain,
 Amidst the Madness of th' unruly Train:
 Five Heards, five bleating Flocks his Pastures fill'd,
750 His Lands a hundred Yoke of Oxen till'd.
 Thus, while in equal Scales their Fortune stood,
 The Fury bath'd them in each others Blood.
 Then having fix'd the Fight, exulting flies,
 And bears fulfill'd her Promise to the Skies.

755   To *Juno* thus she speaks; Behold, 'tis done,
The Blood already drawn, the War begun;
The discord is compleat, nor can they cease
The dire Debate, nor you command the Peace.
Now since the *Latian* and the *Trojan* Brood
760   Have tasted Vengeance, and the Sweets of Blood;
Speak, and my Pow'r shall add this Office more:
The Neighb'ring Nations of th' *Ausonian* Shore
Shall hear the dreadful Rumour, from afar,
Of arm'd Invasion, and embrace the War.
765   Then *Juno* thus; The grateful Work is done,
The Seeds of Discord sow'd, the War begun:
Frauds, Fears, and Fury have Possess'd the State,
And fix'd the Causes of a lasting Hate:
A bloody *Hymen* shall th' Alliance join
770   Betwixt the *Trojan* and *Ausonian* Line:
But thou with Speed to Night and Hell repair,
For not the Gods, nor angry *Jove* will bear
Thy lawless wand'ring walks, in upper Air.
Leave what remains to me. *Saturnia* said:
775   The sullen Fiend her sounding Wings display'd;
Unwilling left the Light, and sought the neather Shade.
    In midst of *Italy*, well known to Fame,
There lies a Lake, *Amsanctus* is the Name,
Below the lofty Mounts: On either side
780   Thick Forrests, the forbidden Entrance hide:
Full in the Centre of the sacred Wood
An Arm arises of the *Stygian* Flood;
Which, breaking from beneath with bellowing sound,
Whirls the black Waves and rattling Stones around.
785   Here *Pluto* pants for Breath from out his Cell,
And opens wide the grinning Jaws of Hell.
To this Infernal Lake the Fury flies;
Here hides her hated Head, and frees the lab'ring Skies.
Saturnian Juno now, with double Care,
790   Attends the fatal Process of the War.
The Clowns return'd, from Battel bear the slain,
Implore the Gods, and to their King complain.
The Corps of *Almon* and the rest are shown,
Shrieks, Clamours, Murmurs fill the frighted Town.

795   Ambitious *Turnus* in the Press appears,
      And, aggravating Crimes, augments their Fears:
      Proclaims his Private Injuries aloud,
      A Solemn Promise made, and disavow'd;
      A foreign Son is sought, and a mix'd Mungril Brood.

800   Then they, whose Mothers, frantick with their Fear,
      In Woods and Wilds the Flags of *Bacchus* bear,
      And lead his Dances with dishevelled hair,
      Increase the Clamour, and the War demand,
      (Such was *Amata*'s Interest in the Land)

805   Against the Public Sanctions of the Peace,
      Against all Omens of their ill Success;
      With Fates averse, the Rout in Arms resort,
      To Force their Monarch, and insult the Court.
      But like a Rock unmov'd, a Rock that braves

810   The rageing Tempest and the rising Waves,
      Prop'd on himself he stands: His solid sides
      Wash off the Sea-weeds, and the sounding Tides:
      So stood the Pious Prince unmov'd: and long
      Sustain'd the madness of the noisie Throng.

815   But when he found that *Juno*'s Pow'r prevail'd,
      And all the Methods of cool Counsel fail'd,
      He calls the Gods to witness their offence,
      Disclaims the War, asserts his Innocence.
      Hurry'd by Fate, he cries, and born before

820   A furious Wind, we leave the faithful Shore:
      O more than Madmen! you your selves shall bear
      The guilt of Blood, and Sacrilegious War:
      Thou, *Turnus*, shalt attone it by thy Fate,
      And pray to Heav'n for Peace, but pray too late.

825   For me, my stormy Voyage at an end,
      I to the Port of Death securely tend.
      The Fun'ral Pomp which to your Kings you pay,
      Is all I want, and all you take away.
      He said no more, but in his Walls confin'd,

830   Shut out the Woes which he too well divin'd:
      Nor with the rising Storm wou'd vainly strive,
      But left the Helm, and let the Vessel drive.
      A solemn Custom was observ'd of old,
      Which *Latium* held, and now the *Romans* hold;

835   Their Standard, when in fighting Fields they rear
    Against the fierce *Hircanians*, or declare
    The *Scythian*, *Indian*, or *Arabian* War:
    Or from the boasting *Parthians* wou'd regain
    Their Eagles lost in *Carrhæ*'s bloody Plain:
840   Two Gates of Steel (the Name of *Mars* they bear)
    And still are worship'd with religious Fear;
    Before his Temple stand: The dire abode,
    And the fear'd Issues of the furious God,
    Are fenc'd with Brazen Bolts; without the Gates,
845   The wary Guardian *Janus* doubly waits.
    Then, when the sacred Senate votes the Wars,
    The *Roman* Consul their Decree declares,
    And in his Robes the sounding Gates unbars.
    The Youth in Military Shouts arise,
850   And the loud Trumpets break the yielding Skies.
    These Rites of old by Sov'raign Princes us'd,
    Were the King's Office, but the King refus'd.
    Deaf to their Cries, nor wou'd the Gates unbar
    Of sacred Peace, or loose th' imprison'd War:
855   But hid his Head, and, safe from loud Alarms,
    Abhor'd the wicked Ministry of Arms.
    Then Heav'ns Imperious Queen shot down from high;
    At her Approach the Brazen Hinges fly,
    The Gates are forc'd, and ev'ry falling Bar,
860   And like a Tempest issues out the War.
    The peaceful Cities of th' *Ausonian* Shore,
    Lull'd in their Ease, and undisturb'd before;
    Are all on Fire, and some with studious Care,
    Their restiff Steeds in sandy Plains prepare:
865   Some their soft Limbs in painful Marches try,
    And War is all their Wish, and Arms the gen'ral Cry.
    Part scour the rusty Shields with Seam, and part
    New grind the blunted Ax, and point the Dart:
    With Joy they view the waving Ensigns fly,
870   And hear the Trumpet's Clangor pierce the Sky.
    Five Cities forge their Arms: th' *Atinian* Pow'rs,
    Antemnæ, *Tybur* with her lofty Tow'rs,
    Ardea the proud, the *Crustumerian* Town:
    All these of old were places of Renown.

875 Some hammer Helmets for the fighting Field,
Some twine young Sallows to support the Shield;
The Croslet some, and some the Cuishes mould,
With Silver plated, and with ductile Gold.
The rustick Honours of the Scythe and Share,
880 Give place to Swords and Plumes, the Pride of War.
Old Fauchions are new temper'd in the Fires:
The sounding Trumpet ev'ry Soul inspires.
The word is giv'n, with eager Speed they lace
The shining Head-piece, and the Shield embrace.
885 The neighing Steeds are to the Chariot ty'd,
The trusty Weapon sits on ev'ry side.
      And now the mighty Labour is begun,
Ye Muses open all your *Helicon.*
Sing you the Chiefs that sway'd th' *Ausonian* Land,
890 Their Arms, and Armies under their Command:
What Warriours in our ancient Clime were bred,
What Souldiers follow'd, and what Heroes led.
For well you know, and can record alone,
What Fame to future times conveys but darkly down.
895   *Mezentius* first appear'd upon the Plain,
Scorn sate upon his Brows, and sour Disdain;
Defying Earth and Heav'n: *Etruria* lost,
He brings to *Turnus*'s Aid his baffled Host.
The charming *Lausus,* full of youthful Fire,
900 Rode in the Rank, and next his sullen Sire:
To *Turnus* only second in the Grace
Of Manly Meen, and features of the Face.
A skilful Horseman, and a Huntsman bred,
With Fates averse a thousand Men he led:
905 His Sire unworthy of so brave a Son;
Himself well worthy of a happier Throne.
      Next *Aventinus* drives his Chariot round
The *Latian* Plains, with Palms and Lawrels crown'd.
Proud of his Steeds he smoaks along the Field,
910 His Father's *Hydra* fills the ample Shield.
A hundred Serpents hiss about the Brims;
The Son of *Hercules* he justly seems,
By his broad Shoulders and Gigantick Limbs.

Of Heav'nly part, and part of Earthly Blood,
915   A mortal Woman mixing with a God.
For strong *Alcides*, after he had slain
The triple *Geryon*, drove from conquer'd *Spain*
His captive Herds, and thence in Triumph led;
On *Tuscan Tyber*'s flow'ry Banks they fed.
920   Then on Mount *Aventine*, the Son of *Jove*
The Priestess *Rhea* found, and forc'd to Love.
    For Arms his Men long Piles and Jav'lins bore,
And Poles with pointed Steel their Foes in Battel gore.
Like *Hercules* himself, his Son appears,
925   In Salvage Pomp: a Lyon's Hide he wears;
About his Shoulders hangs the shaggy Skin,
The Teeth, and gaping Jaws severely grin.
Thus like the God his Father, homely drest,
He strides into the Hall, a horrid Guest.
930   Then two Twin-Brothers from fair *Tybur* came,
(Which from their Brother *Tyburs* took the Name,)
Fierce *Coras*, and *Catillus*, void of Fear,
Arm'd *Argive* Horse they led, and in the Front appear.
Like Cloud-born *Centaurs*, from the Mountain's height,
935   With rapid Course descending to the Fight;
They rush along, the ratling Woods give way,
The Branches bend before their sweepy Sway.
    Nor was *Præneste*'s Founder wanting there,
Whom Fame reports the Son of *Mulciber*:
940   Found in the Fire, and foster'd in the Plains; ⎤
A Shepherd and a King at once he reigns,   ⎬
And leads to *Turnus* Aid his Country Swains. ⎦
His own *Præneste* sends a chosen Band,
With those who plough *Saturnia*'s *Gabine* Land:
945   Besides the Succour which cold *Anien* yields,
The Rocks of *Hernicus*, and dewy Fields;
Anagnia fat, and Father *Amasene*,
A num'rous Rout, but all of naked Men:
Nor Arms they wear, nor Swords and Bucklers wield,
950   Nor drive the Chariot thro' the dusty Field:
But whirle from Leathern Slings huge Balls of Lead;
And Spoils of yellow Wolves adorn their Head:
The Left Foot naked, when they march to fight,
But in a Bull's raw Hide they sheath the Right.

955   *Messapus* next, (great *Neptune* was his Sire)
    Secure of Steel, and fated from the Fire;
    In Pomp appears: And with his Ardour warms
    A heartless Train, unexercis'd in Arms:
    The just *Faliscans* he to Battel brings,
960   And those who live where Lake *Ciminia* springs;
    And where *Feronia*'s Grove and Temple stands,
    Who till *Fescennian* or *Flavinian* Lands:
    All these in order march, and marching sing
    The warlike Actions of their Sea-born King.
965   Like a long Team of Snowy Swans on high,
    Which clap their Wings, and cleave the liquid Sky,
    When homeward from their wat'ry Pastures born,
    They sing, and *Asia*'s Lakes their Notes return.
    Not one who heard their Musick from afar,
970   Wou'd think these Troops an Army train'd to War:
    But Flocks of Fowl, that when the Tempests roar,
    With their hoarse gabling seek the silent Shoar.
       Then *Clausus* came, who led a num'rous Band
    Of Troops embody'd, from the *Sabine* Land:
975   And in himself alone, an Army brought,
    'Twas he the noble *Claudian* Race begot:
    The *Claudian* Race, ordain'd, in times to come,
    To share the Greatness of Imperial *Rome*.
    He led the *Cures* forth of old Renown,
980   *Mutuscans* from their Olive-bearing Town;
    And all th' *Eretian* Pow'rs: Besides a Band
    That follow'd from *Velinum*'s dewy Land:
    And *Amiternian* Troops, of mighty Fame,
    And Mountaineers, that from *Severus* came.
985   And from the craggy Cliffs of *Tetrica*,   ⎫
    And those where yellow *Tyber* takes his way, ⎬
    And where *Himella*'s wanton Waters play.   ⎭
    Casperia sends her Arms, with those that lye
    By *Fabaris*, and fruitful *Foruli*:
990   The warlike Aids of *Horta* next appear,
    And the cold *Nursians* come to close the Reer:
    Mix'd with the Natives born of *Latine* Blood,
    Whom *Allia* washes with her fatal Flood.
    Not thicker Billows beat the *Lybian* Main,
995   When pale *Orion* sets in wint'ry Rain;

Not thicker Harvests on rich *Hermus* rise,
Or *Lycian* Fields, when *Phœbus* burns the Skies;
Than stand these Troops: Their Bucklers ring around,
Their Trampling turns the Turf, and shakes the solid
    Ground.

1000   High in his Chariot then *Halesus* came,
A Foe by Birth to *Troy*'s unhappy Name:
From *Agamemnon* born; to *Turnus* Aid,
A thousand Men the youthful Heroe led;
Who till the *Massick* Soil, for Wine renown'd,
1005 And fierce *Auruncans* from their Hilly Ground:
And those who live by *Sidicinian* Shores,
And where, with shoaly Foords *Vulturnus* roars;
Cales and *Osca*'s old Inhabitants,
And rough *Saticulans* inur'd to Wants:
1010 Light demi-Launces from afar they throw,
Fasten'd with Leathern Thongs to gaul the Foe.
Short crooked Swords in closer Fight they wear,
And on their warding Arm light Bucklers bear.

      Nor *Oebalus*, shalt thou be left unsung,
1015 From Nymph *Semethis* and old *Telon* sprung:
Who then in *Teleboan Capri* reign'd,
But that short Isle th' ambitious Youth disdain'd;
And o're *Campania* stretch'd his ample Sway;
Where swelling *Sarnus* seeks the *Tyrrhene* Sea:
1020 O're *Batulum*, and where *Abella* sees,
From her high Tow'rs, the Harvest of her Trees.
And these (as was the *Teuton* use of old)
Wield Brazen Swords, and Brazen Bucklers hold:
Sling weighty Stones when from afar they fight;
1025 Their Casques are Cork, a Covering thick and light.
Next these in Rank, the warlike *Ufens* went,
And led the Mountain Troops that *Nursia* sent.
The rude *Equicolæ* his Rule obey'd,
Hunting their Sport, and Plund'ring was their Trade.
1030 In Arms they plough'd, to Battel still prepar'd;
Their Soil was barren, and their Hearts were hard.

    Umbro the Priest the proud *Marrubians* led, ⎫
By King *Archippus* sent to *Turnus* aid;   ⎬
And peaceful Olives crown'd his hoary head.   ⎭

1035 His Wand and holy Words, the Viper's rage,
And venom'd wound of Serpents, cou'd asswage.
He, when he pleas'd with powerful Juice to steep
Their Temples, shut their Eyes in pleasing Sleep.
But vain were *Marsian* Herbs, and Magick Art,
1040 To cure the Wound giv'n by the *Dardan* Dart.
Yet his untimely Fate, th' *Angitian* Woods
In sighs remurmur'd, to the *Fucine* Floods.
The Son of fam'd *Hippolitus* was there;
Fam'd as his Sire, and as his Mother fair.
1045 Whom in *Egerian* Groves *Aricia* bore,
And nurs'd his Youth along the Marshy Shore:
Where great *Diana*'s peaceful Altars flame,
In fruitful Fields, and *Virbius* was his Name.
Hippolitus, as old Records have said,
1050 Was by his Stepdam sought to share her Bed:
But when no Female Arts his Mind cou'd move,
She turn'd to furious Hate her impious Love.
Torn by Wild Horses on the sandy Shore,
Another's Crimes th' unhappy Hunter bore; ⎫
1055 Glutting his Father's Eyes with guiltless gore. ⎬
But chast *Diana*, who his death deplor'd,
With *Æsculapian* Herbs his life restor'd.
Then *Jove* who saw from high, with just disdain,
The dead inspir'd with Vital Breath again,
1060 Struck to the Center with his flaming Dart
Th' unhappy Founder of the Godlike Art.
But *Trivia* kept in secret Shades alone,
Her care, *Hippolitus*, to Fate unknown;
And call'd him *Virbius* in th' *Egerian* Grove:
1065 Where then he liv'd obscure, but safe from *Jove*.
For this, from *Trivia*'s Temple and her Wood, ⎫
Are Coursers driv'n, who shed their Master's Blood; ⎬
Affrighted by the Monsters of the Flood. ⎭
His Son, the Second *Virbius*, yet retain'd
1070 His Father's Art, and Warrior Steeds he rein'd.
Amid the Troops, and like the leading God,
High o're the rest in Arms the Graceful *Turnus* rode:
A triple Pile of Plumes his Crest adorn'd,
On which with belching Flames *Chimæra* burn'd:

1075   The more the kindled Combat, rises high'r,
The more with fury burns the blazing Fire.
Fair *Io* grac'd his Shield, but *Io* now
With Horns exalted stands, and seems to lowe:
(A noble charge) her Keeper by her side,
1080   To watch her Walks his hundred Eyes apply'd.
And on the Brims her Sire, the wat'ry God,
Rowl'd from a Silver Urn his Crystal Flood.
A Cloud of Foot succeeds, and fills the Fields
With Swords and pointed Spears, and clatt'ring Shields;
1085   Of *Argives*, and of old *Sicanian* Bands,
And those who Plow the rich *Rutulian* Lands;
Auruncan Youth and those *Sacrana* yields,
And the proud *Labicans* with painted Shields.
And those who near *Numician* Streams reside, ⎫
1090   And those whom *Tyber*'s holy Forests hide; ⎬
Or *Circes* Hills from the main Land divide. ⎭
Where *Ufens* glides along the lowly Lands,
Or the black Water of *Pomptina* stands.
Last from the *Volscians* fair *Camilla* came;
1095   And led her warlike Troops, a Warriour Dame:
Unbred to Spinning, in the Loom unskill'd,
She chose the nobler *Pallas* of the Field.
Mix'd with the first, the fierce *Virago* fought,
Sustain'd the Toils of Arms, the Danger sought:
1100   Outstrip'd the Winds in speed upon the Plain,
Flew o're the Fields, nor hurt the bearded Grain:
She swept the Seas, and as she skim'd along,
Her flying Feet unbath'd on Billows hung.
Men, Boys, and Women stupid with Surprise,
1105   Where e're she passes, fix their wond'ring Eyes:
Longing they look, and gaping at the Sight,
Devour her o're and o're with vast Delight.
Her Purple Habit sits with such a Grace
On her smooth Shoulders, and so suits her Face:
1110   Her Head with Ringlets of her Hair is crown'd,
And in a Golden Caul the Curls are bound.
She shakes her Myrtle Jav'lin: And, behind,
Her *Lycian* Quiver dances in the Wind.

THE EIGHTH BOOK OF THE ÆNEIS

The Argument

The War being now begun, both the Generals make all possible Preparations. Turnus *sends to* Diomedes. Æneas *goes in Person to beg Succours from* Evander *and the* Tuscans. Evander *receives him kindly, furnishes him with Men, and sends his Son* Pallas *with him.* Vulcan, *at the Request of* Venus, *makes Arms for her Son* Æneas, *and draws on his Shield the most memorable Actions of his Posterity.*

When *Turnus* had assembled all his Pow'rs;
His Standard planted on *Laurentum*'s Tow'rs;
When now the sprightly Trumpet, from afar,
Had giv'n the Signal of approaching War,
5   Had rouz'd the neighing Steeds to scour the Fields,
While the fierce Riders clatter'd on their Shields,
Trembling with Rage, the *Latian* Youth prepare
To join th' Allies, and headlong rush to War.
Fierce *Ufens*, and *Messapus*, led the Crowd;
10 With bold *Mezentius*, who blasphem'd aloud.
These, thro' the Country took their wasteful Course;
The Fields to forage, and to gather Force.
Then *Venulus* to *Diomede* they send,
To beg his Aid *Ausonia* to defend:
15 Declare the common Danger; and inform
The *Grecian* Leader of the growing Storm:
Æneas landed on the *Latian* Coast,
With banish'd Gods, and with a baffled Hoast;
Yet now aspir'd to Conquest of the State;
20 And claim'd a Title from the Gods and Fate.
What num'rous Nations in his Quarrel came,
And how they spread his formidable Name:
What he design'd, what Mischief might arise,
If fortune favour'd his first Enterprise,
25 Was left for him to weigh: whose equal Fears,
And common Interest was involv'd in theirs.
While *Turnus* and th' Allies thus urge the War, ⎫
The *Trojan* floating in a Flood of Care,   ⎬
Beholds the Tempest which his Foes prepare.   ⎭
30 This way and that he turns his anxious Mind;
Thinks, and rejects the Counsels he design'd.
Explores himself in vain in ev'ry part,
And gives no rest to his distracted Heart.

So when the Sun by Day, or Moon by Night,
35   Strike, on the polish'd Brass their trembling Light,
The glitt'ring Species here and there divide;
And cast their dubious Beams from side to side:
Now on the Walls, now on the Pavement play,
And to the Cieling flash the glaring Day.
40   'Twas Night: And weary Nature lul'd asleep
The Birds of Air, and Fishes of the Deep;
And Beasts, and Mortal Men: The *Trojan* Chief ⎫
Was laid on *Tyber*'s Banks, oppress'd with Grief, ⎬
And found in silent Slumber late Relief. ⎭
45   Then, thro' the Shadows of the Poplar Wood,
Arose the Father of the *Roman* Flood;
An Azure Robe was o're his Body spread,
A Wreath of shady Reeds adorn'd his Head:
Thus, manifest to Sight, the God appear'd,
50   And with these pleasing Words his Sorrow chear'd.
Undoubted Off-spring of Etherial Race,
O long expected in this promis'd Place,
Who, thro' the Foes, hast born thy banish'd Gods,
Restor'd them to their Hearths, and old Abodes;
55   This is thy Happy Home! The Clime where Fate
Ordains thee to restore the *Trojan* State.
Fear not, the War shall end in lasting Peace;
And all the Rage of haughty *Juno* cease.
And that this nightly Vision may not seem
60   Th' Effect of Fancy, or an idle Dream,
A Sow beneath an Oak shall lye along;
All white her self, and white her thirty Young.
When thirty rowling Years have run their Race,
Thy Son, *Ascanius*, on this empty Space,
65   Shall build a Royal Town, of lasting Fame;
Which from this Omen shall receive the Name.
Time shall approve the Truth: For what remains,
And how with sure Success to crown thy Pains,
With Patience next attend. A banish'd Band,
70   Driv'n with *Evander* from th' *Arcadian* Land,
Have planted here: and plac'd on high their Walls;
Their Town the Founder, *Palanteum* calls:

Deriv'd from *Pallas*, his great Grandsire's Name:
But the fierce *Latians* old Possession claim:
75   With War infesting the new Colony;
These make thy Friends, and on their Aid rely.
To thy free Passage I submit my Streams:
Wake Son of *Venus* from thy pleasing Dreams;
And, when the setting Stars are lost in Day,
80   To *Juno*'s Pow'r thy just Devotion pay.
With Sacrifice the wrathful Queen appease;
Her Pride at length shall fall, her Fury cease;
When thou return'st victorious from the War,
Perform thy Vows to me with grateful Care.
85   The God am I, whose yellow Water flows
Around these Fields, and fattens as it goes:
Tyber my Name: among the rowling Floods,
Renown'd on Earth, esteem'd among the Gods.
This is my certain Seat: In Times to come,
90   My Waves shall wash the Walls of mighty *Rome*.
He said; and plung'd below, while yet he spoke:
His Dream *Æneas* and his Sleep forsook.
He rose, and looking up, beheld the Skies
With Purple blushing, and the Day arise.
95   Then, Water in his hollow Palm he took,
From *Tyber*'s Flood; and thus the Pow'rs bespoke.
Laurentian Nymphs, by whom the Streams are fed,
And Father *Tyber*, in thy sacred Bed
Receive *Æneas*; and from Danger keep.
100   Whatever Fount, whatever holy deep,
Conceals thy wat'ry Stores; where e're they rise,
And, bubling from below, salute the Skies:
Thou King of horned Floods, whose plenteous Urn
Suffices Fatness to the fruitful Corn,
105   For this thy kind Compassion of our Woes,
Shalt share my Morning Song, and Ev'ning Vows.
But, oh! be present to thy Peoples Aid;
And firm the gracious promise thou hast made.
Thus having said, two Gallies, from his Stores,
110   With Care he chuses; Mans, and fits with Oars.
Now on the Shore the fatal Swine is found:
Wond'rous to tell; she lay along the Ground:

Her well fed Offspring at her Udders hung;
She white her self, and white her thirty young;
115 *Æneas* takes the Mother, and her Brood,
And all on *Juno*'s Altar are bestow'd.
The foll'wing Night, and the succeeding Day,
Propitious *Tyber* smooth'd his wat'ry Way:
He rowl'd his River back; and pois'd he stood;
120 A gentle Swelling, and a peaceful Flood.
The *Trojans* mount their Ships; they put from Shore,
Born on the Waves, and scarcely dip an Oar.
Shouts from the Land give Omen to their Course;
And the pitch'd Vessells glide with easie Force.
125 The Woods and Waters, wonder at the Gleam
Of Shields, and painted Ships, that stem the Stream.
One Summer's Night, and one whole Day they pass,
Betwixt the green-wood Shades; and cut the liquid Glass.
The fiery Sun had finish'd half his Race;
130 Look'd back, and doubted in the middle Space:
When they from far beheld the rising Tow'rs,
The Tops of Sheds, and Shepherds lowly Bow'rs:
Thin as they stood, which, then of homely Clay,
Now rise in Marble, from the *Roman* Sway.
135 These Cots, (*Evanders* Kingdom, mean and poor)
The *Trojan* saw, and turn'd his Ships to Shore.
'Twas on a solemn Day: Th' *Arcadian* States,
The King and Prince without the City Gates,
Then paid their Off'rings in a sacred Grove,
140 To *Hercules*, the Warrior Son of *Jove*.
Thick Clowds of rowling Smoke involve the Sky's;
And Fat of Entrails on his Altar fry's.
  But when they saw the Ships that stemm'd the Flood,
And glitter'd thro' the Covert of the Wood,
145 They rose with Fear; and left th' unfinish'd Feast:
'Till dauntless *Pallas* reassur'd the rest,
To pay the Rites. Himself without delay
A Jav'lin seiz'd, and singly took his Way.
Then gain'd a rising Ground; and call'd from far.
150 Resolve me, Strangers, whence, and what you are;
Your Buis'ness here; and bring you Peace or War?

High on the Stern, *Æneas* took his Stand,
And held a Branch of Olive in his Hand;
While thus he spoke. The *Phrygians* Arms you see;
155   Expell'd from *Troy*, provok'd in *Italy*
By *Latian* Foes, with War unjustly made:
At first affianc'd, and at last betray'd.
This Message bear: The *Trojans* and their Chief
Bring holy Peace; and beg the King's Relief.
160   Struck with so great a Name, and all on fire,
The Youth Replies, Whatever you require,
Your Fame exacts: Upon our Shores descend,
A welcome Guest, and what you wish, a Friend.
He said; and downward hasting to the Strand,
165   Embrac'd the Stranger Prince, and join'd his Hand.
Conducted to the Grove, *Æneas* broke
The silence first, and thus the King bespoke.
Best of the *Greeks*, to whom, by Fates Command,
I bear these peaceful Branches in my hand;
170   Undaunted I approach you; though I know
Your Birth is *Grecian*, and your Land my Foe:
From *Atreus* tho' your ancient Lineage came;
And both the Brother Kings your Kindred claim:
Yet, my self-conscious Worth, your high Renown,
175   Your Vertue, through the Neighb'ring Nations blown,
Our Fathers mingl'd Blood, *Appollo*'s Voice,
Have led me hither, less by Need than Choice.
Our Founder *Dardanus*, as Fame has sung,
And *Greeks* acknowledge, from *Electra* sprung:
180   *Electra* from the Loins of *Atlas* came;
Atlas whose Head sustains the Starry Frame.
Your Sire is *Mercury*; whom long before
On cold *Cyllene*'s top fair *Maja* bore.
Maja the fair, on Fame if we rely,
185   Was *Atlas* Daughter, who sustains the Sky.
Thus from one common Source our Streams divide:
Ours is the *Trojan*, yours th' *Arcadian* side.
Rais'd by these Hopes, I sent no News before:
Nor ask'd your leave, nor did your Faith implore; }
190   But come, without a Pledg, my own Ambassador. }

The same *Rutulians*, who with Arms pursue
The *Trojan* Race, are equal Foes to you.
Our Host expell'd, what farther Force can stay
The Victor Troops from Universal Sway?
195   Then will they stretch their Pow'r athwart the Land;
And either Sea from side to side command.
Receive our offer'd Faith: and give us thine;
Ours is a gen'rous, and experienc'd Line:
We want not Hearts, nor Bodies for the War;
200   In Council cautious, and in Fields we dare.
He said; and while he spoke, with piercing Eyes,
Evander view'd the Man with vast surprize.
Pleas'd with his Action, ravish'd with his Face,
Then answer'd briefly, with a Royal grace.
205   O Valiant Leader of the *Trojan* Line,
In whom the Features of thy Father shine;
How I recall *Anchises*, how I see
His Motions, Meen, and all my Friend in thee!
Long tho it be, 'tis fresh within my Mind,
210   When *Priam*, to his Sister's Court design'd
A welcome Visit, with a friendly stay;
And, through th' *Arcadian* Kingdom took his way.
Then, past a Boy, the callow Down began
To shade my Chin, and call me first a Man.
215   I saw the shining Train, with vast delight,
And *Priam*'s goodly Person pleas'd my sight:
But great *Anchises*, far above the rest,
With awful Wonder fir'd my Youthful Breast.
I long'd to join, in Friendship's holy Bands,
220   Our mutual Hearts, and plight our mutual Hands.
I first accosted him: I su'd, I sought,
And, with a loving force, to *Pheneus* brought.
He gave me, when at length constrain'd to go,
A *Lycian* Quiver, and a *Gnossian* Bow:
225   A Vest embroyder'd, glorious to behold,
And two rich Bridles, with their Bits of Gold; }
Which my Son's Coursers in obedience hold. }
The League you ask I offer, as your Right:
And when to Morrow's Sun reveals the Light,

230   With swift Supplies you shall be sent away: ⎤
      Now celebrate, with us, this solemn Day: ⎬
      Whose Holy Rites admit no long Delay. ⎦
      Honour our Annual Feast; and take your Seat
      With friendly Welcome, at a homely Treat.

235   Thus having said, the Bowls (remov'd for Fear)
      The Youths replac'd; and soon restor'd the Chear.
      On sods of Turf he set the Souldiers round;
      A Maple Throne, rais'd higher from the Ground,
      Receiv'd the *Trojan* Chief: And o're the Bed,

240   A Lyon's shaggy Hide for Ornament they spread.
      The Loaves were serv'd in Canisters; the Wine ⎤
      In Bowls, the Priest renew'd the Rites Divine: ⎬
      Broil'd Entrails are their Food; and Beefs continu'd ⎥
           Chine. ⎦
      But, when the Rage of Hunger was repress'd,

245   Thus spoke *Evander* to his Royal Guest.
      These Rites, these Altars, and this Feast, O King,
      From no vain Fears, or Superstition spring:
      Or blind Devotion, or from blinder Chance;
      Or heady Zeal, or brutal Ignorance:

250   But, sav'd from Danger, with a grateful Sence,
      The Labours of a God we recompence.
      See, from afar, yon Rock that mates the Sky;
      About whose Feet such heaps of Rubbish lye:
      Such indigested Ruin; bleak and bare,

255   How desart now it stands, expos'd in Air!
      'Twas once a Robber's Den; inclos'd around
      With living Stone, and deep beneath the Ground.
      The Monster *Cacus*, more than half a Beast,
      This Hold, impervious to the Sun, possess'd.

260   The Pavement ever foul with humane Gore;
      Heads, and their mangled Members, hung the Door.
      Vulcan this Plague begot: And, like his Sire,
      Black Clouds he belch'd, and flakes of livid Fire.
      Time, long expected, eas'd us of our Load:

265   And brought the needful presence of a God.
      Th' avenging force of *Hercules*, from *Spain*, ⎤
      Arriv'd in Triumph, from *Geryon* slain; ⎬
      Thrice liv'd the Gyant, and thrice liv'd in vain. ⎦

His Prize, the lowing Heards, *Alcides* drove
270   Near *Tyber*'s Bank, to graze the shady Grove.
Allur'd with Hope of Plunder, and intent
By Force to rob, by Fraud to circumvent;
The brutal *Cacus*, as by Chance they stray'd,
Four Oxen thence, and four fair Kine convey'd.
275   And, lest the printed Footsteps might be seen,
He drag'd 'em backwards to his rocky Den.
The Tracks averse, a lying Notice gave;
And led the Searcher backward from the Cave.
Mean time the Herdsman Heroe shifts his place:
280   To find fresh Pasture, and untrodden Grass.
The Beasts, who miss'd their Mates, fill'd all around
With Bellowings, and the Rocks restor'd the Sound.
One Heifar who had heard her Love complain,
Roar'd from the Cave; and made the Project vain.
285   *Alcides* found the Fraud: With Rage he shook,
And toss'd about his Head his knotted Oak.
Swift as the Winds, or *Scythian* Arrows flight,
He clomb, with eager haste, th' Aerial height.
Then first we saw the Monster mend his Pace:
290   Fear in his Eyes, and Paleness in his Face,
Confess'd the Gods approach: Trembling he springs,
As Terror had increas'd his Feet with Wings:
Nor stay'd for Stairs; but down the Depth he threw
His Body; on his Back the Door he drew.
295   The Door, a Rib of living Rock; with Pains
His Father hew'd it out, and bound with Iron Chains.
He broke the heavy Lincks; the Mountain clos'd;
And Bars and Leavers to his Foe oppos'd.
The Wretch had hardly made his Dungeon fast;
300   The fierce Avenger came with bounding haste:
Survey'd the Mouth of the forbidden hold;
And here and there his raging Eyes he rowl'd.
He gnash'd his Teeth; and thrice he compass'd round
With winged speed the Circuit of the Ground.
305   Thrice at the Cavern's Mouth he pull'd in vain,
And, panting, thrice desisted from his Pain.
A pointed flinty Rock, all bare, and black,
Grew gibbous from behind the Mountains Back:

Owls, Ravens, all ill Omens of the Night,
310   Here built their Nests, and hither wing'd their Flight.
The leaning Head hung threat'ning o're the Flood:
And nodded to the left: The Heroe stood
Averse, with planted Feet, and from the right,
Tugg'd at the solid Stone with all his might.
315   Thus heav'd, the fix'd Foundations of the Rock
Gave way: Heav'n echo'd at the ratling Shock.
Tumbling it choak'd the Flood: On either side
The Banks leap backward; and the Streams divide.
The Sky shrunk upward with unusual Dread:
320   And trembling *Tyber* div'd beneath his Bed.
The Court of *Cacus* stands reveal'd to sight;
The Cavern glares with new admitted Light.
So the pent Vapours with a rumbling Sound
Heave from below; and rend the hollow Ground:
325   A sounding Flaw succeeds: And from on high,
The Gods, with Hate beheld the neather Sky:
The Ghosts repine at violated Night;
And curse th' invading Sun; and sicken at the sight.
The graceless Monster caught in open Day,
330   Inclos'd, and in Despair to fly away;
Howls horrible from underneath, and fills
His hollow Palace, with unmanly Yells.
The Heroe stands above; and from afar
Plies him with Darts, and Stones, and distant War.
335   He, from his Nostrils, and huge Mouth, expires
Black Clouds of Smoke, amidst his Father's Fires.
Gath'ring, with each repeated Blast, the Night:
To make uncertain Aim, and erring Sight.
The wrathful God, then plunges from above,
340   And where in thickest Waves the Sparkles drove,
There lights; and wades thro' Fumes, and gropes his Way;
Half sing'd, half stifled, 'till he grasps his Prey.
The Monster, spewing fruitless Flames, he found;
He squeez'd his Throat, he writh'd his Neck around, }
345   And in a Knot his cripled Members bound.
Then, from their Sockets, tore his burning Eyes;
Rowld on a heap the breathless Robber lyes.

The Doors, unbarr'd, receive the rushing Day;
And thorough Lights disclose the ravish'd Prey.
350 The Bulls redeem'd, breathe open Air agen;
Next, by the Feet, they drag him from his Den.
The wond'ring Neighbourhood, with glad surprize,
Beheld his shagged Breast, his Gyant Size.
His Mouth that flames no more, and his extinguish'd
    Eyes.
355 From that auspicious Day, with Rites Divine,
We worship at the Hero's Holy Shrine.
Potitius first ordain'd these annual Vows,
As Priests, were added the *Pinarian* House:
Who rais'd this Altar in the Sacred Shade;
360 Where Honours, ever due, for ever shall be paid.
For these Deserts, and this high Virtue shown,
Ye warlike Youths, your Heads with Garlands crown.
Fill high the Goblets with a sparkling Flood:
And with deep Draughts invoke our common God.
365 This said, a double Wreath *Evander* twin'd:
And Poplars black and white his Temples bind.
Then Brims his ample Bowl: With like Design
The rest invoke the Gods, with sprinkled Wine.
Mean time the Sun descended from the Skies;
370 And the bright Evening-Star began to rise.
And now the Priests, *Potitius* at their Head,
In Skins of Beasts involv'd, the long Procession led:
Held high the flaming Tapers in their Hands;
As Custom had prescrib'd their holy Bands:
375 Then with a second Course the Tables load:
And with full Chargers offer to the God.
The *Salij* sing; and cense his Altars round
With *Saban* Smoke, their Heads with Poplar bound.
One Choir of old, another of the young;
380 To dance, and bear the Burthen of the Song.
The Lay records the Labours, and the Praise,
And all th' Immortal Acts of *Hercules*.
First, how the mighty Babe, when swath'd in Bands,
The Serpents strangled, with his Infant Hands.
385 Then, as in Years, and matchless Force he grew
Th' *Oechalian* Walls, and *Trojan* overthrew.

Besides a thousand Hazards they relate,
Procur'd by *Juno*'s, and *Euristheus*'s Hate.
Thy Hands, unconquer'd Heroe, cou'd subdue
390   The Cloud-born *Centaurs*, and the Monster Crew.
Nor thy resistless Arm the Bull withstood:
Nor He the roaring Terror of the Wood.
The triple Porter of the *Stygian* Seat,
With lolling Tongue, lay fawning at thy Feet:
395   And, seiz'd with Fear, forgot his mangled Meat.
Th' Infernal Waters trembled at thy Sight;
Thee, God, no face of Danger cou'd Affright;
Not huge *Typhœus*, nor th' unnumber'd Snake,
Increas'd with hissing Heads, in *Lerna*'s Lake.
400   Hail *Jove*'s undoubted Son! An added Grace
To Heav'n, and the great Author of thy Race.
Receive the grateful Off'rings, which we pay,
And smile propitious on thy solemn Day.
In Numbers, thus, they sung: Above the rest,
405   The Den, and Death of *Cacus* crown the Feast.
The Woods to hollow Vales convey the Sound;
The Vales to Hills, and Hills the Notes rebound.
The Rites perform'd, the chearful Train retire.
Betwixt young *Pallas*, and his aged Sire
410   The *Trojan* pass'd, the City to survey;
And pleasing Talk beguil'd the tedious Way.
The Stranger cast around his curious Eyes;
New Objects viewing still, with new Surprise.
With greedy Joys enquires of various Things;
415   And Acts and Monuments of Ancient Kings.
Then thus the Founder of the *Roman* Tow'rs:
These Woods were first the Seat of *Silvan* Pow'rs,
Of Nymphs, and Fauns, and salvage Men, who took
Their Birth from Trunks of Trees, and stubborn Oak.
420   Nor Laws they knew, nor Manners, nor the Care
Of lab'ring Oxen, or the shining Share:
Nor Arts of Gain, nor what they gain'd to spare.
Their Exercise the Chase: the running Flood
Supply'd their Thirst; the Trees supply'd their Food.
425   Then *Saturn* came, who fled the Pow'r of *Jove*,
Robb'd of his Realms, and banish'd from above.

The Men, dispers'd on Hills, to Towns he brought;
And Laws ordain'd, and Civil Customs taught:
And *Latium* call'd the Land where safe he lay,
430   From his Unduteous Son, and his Usurping Sway.
With his mild Empire, Peace and Plenty came:
And hence the Golden Times deriv'd their name.
A more degenerate, and discolour'd Age,
Succeeded this, with Avarice and Rage.
435   Th' *Ausonians*, then, and bold *Sicanians* came;
And *Saturn*'s Empire often chang'd the name.
Then Kings, Gygantick *Tybris*, and the rest,
With Arbitrary Sway the Land oppress'd.
For *Tybers* flood was *Albula* before:
440   Till, from the Tyrants Fate, his name it bore.
I last arriv'd, driv'n from my native home,
By Fortune's Pow'r, and Fate's resistless Doom.
Long toss'd on Seas I sought this happy Land:
Warn'd by my Mother Nymph, and call'd by Heav'ns
        Command.
445   Thus, walking on, he spoke: and shew'd the Gate,
Since call'd *Carmental* by the *Roman* State;
Where stood an Altar, Sacred to the Name
Of old *Carmenta*, the Prophetick Dame:
Who to her Son foretold th' *Ænean* Race,
450   Sublime in Fame, and *Rome*'s Imperial Place.
Then shews the Forest, which in after times,
Fierce *Romulus*, for perpetrated Crimes,
A Sacred Refuge made: with this, the Shrine
Where *Pan* below the Rock had Rites Divine.
455   Then tells of *Argus* death, his murder'd Guest,
Whose Grave, and Tomb, his Innocence attest.
Thence, to the steep *Tarpeian* Rock he leads;
Now Roof'd with Gold; then thatch'd with homely Reeds.
A Reverent fear (such Superstition reigns
460   Among the rude) ev'n then possess'd the Swains.
Some God they knew, what God they cou'd not tell,
Did there amidst the sacred horrour dwell.
Th' *Arcadians* thought him *Jove*; and said they saw
The mighty Thund'rer with Majestick awe;

465 Who shook his Shield, and dealt his Bolts around;
And scatter'd tempests on the teeming Ground.
Then saw two heaps of Ruins; once they stood
Two stately Towns, on either side the Flood.
Saturnia's and *Janicula*'s Remains:
470 And, either place, the Founder's Name retains.
Discoursing thus together, they resort
Where poor *Evander* kept his Country Court.
They view'd the ground of *Rome*'s litigious Hall;
Once Oxen low'd, where now the Lawyers bawl.
475 Then, stooping, through the Narrow Gate they press'd,
When thus the King bespoke his *Trojan* Guest.
Mean as it is, this Palace, and this Door,
Receiv'd *Alcides*, then a Conquerour.
Dare to be poor: accept our homely Food
480 Which feasted him; and emulate a God.
Then, underneath a lowly Roof, he led ⎫
The weary Prince; and laid him on a Bed: ⎬
The stuffing Leaves, with Hides of Bears o'respread. ⎭
　　　Now Night had shed her silver Dews around,
485 And with her sable Wings embrac'd the Ground,
When Love's fair Goddess, anxious for her Son,
(New Tumults rising, and new Wars begun)
Couch'd with her Husband, in his Golden Bed,
With these alluring Words invokes his aid.
490 And, that her pleasing Speech his Mind may move,
Inspires each accent with the Charms of Love.
While Cruel Fate conspir'd with *Grecian* Pow'rs,
To level with the Ground the *Trojan* Tow'rs;
I ask'd not Aid th' unhappy to restore:
495 Nor did the Succour of thy Skill implore.
Nor urg'd the Labours of my Lord in vain;
A sinking Empire longer to sustain.
Tho' much I ow'd to *Priam*'s House; and more
The Dangers of *Æneas* did deplore.
500 But now by *Jove*'s Command, and Fates Decree,
His Race is doom'd to reign in *Italy*;
With humble Suit I beg thy needful Art,
O still propitious Pow'r, that rules my Heart!

A Mother kneels a suppliant for her Son.
505   By *Thetis* and *Aurora* thou wert won
To forge impenetrable Shields; and grace,
With fated Arms, a less illustrious Race.
Behold, what haughty Nations are combin'd
Against the Relicks of the *Phrygian* Kind;
510   With Fire and Sword my People to destroy;
And conquer *Venus* twice, in conqu'ring *Troy*.
She said; and strait her Arms, of snowy hue,
About her unresolving Husband threw.
Her soft Embraces soon infuse Desire: ⎫
515   His Bones and Marrow sudden warmth inspire; ⎬
And all the Godhead feels the wonted Fire. ⎭
Not half so swift the ratling Thunder flies,
Or forky Lightnings flash along the Skies.
The Goddess, proud of her successful Wiles,
520   And conscious of her Form, in secret Smiles.
Then thus, the Pow'r, obnoxious to her Charms,
Panting, and half dissolving in her Arms:
Why seek you Reasons for a Cause so just;
Or your own Beauties, or my Love distrust?
525   Long since, had you requir'd my helpful Hand,
Th' Artificer and Art you might command,
To labour Arms for *Troy*: Nor *Jove*, nor Fate,
Confin'd their Empire to so short a Date.
And, if you now desire new Wars to wage,
530   My Skill I promise; and my Pains engage.
Whatever melting Metals can conspire,
Or breathing Bellows, or the forming Fire,
Is freely yours: Your anxious Fears remove:
And think no Task is difficult to Love.
535   Trembling he spoke; and eager of her Charms,
He snatch'd the willing Goddess to his Arms;
'Till in her Lap infus'd, he lay possess'd
Of full Desire, and sunk to pleasing Rest.
Now when the Night her middle race had rode;
540   And his first Slumber had refresh'd the God;
The time when early Housewifes leave the Bed;
When living Embers on the Hearth they spred;

Supply the Lamp, and call the Maids to rise,
With yawning Mouths, and with half open'd Eyes;
545   They ply the Distaff by the winking Light;
And to their daily Labour add the Night.
Thus frugally they earn their Childrens Bread:
And uncorrupted keep the Nuptial Bed.
Not less concern'd, nor at a later Hour,
550   Rose from his downy Couch the forging Pow'r.
      Sacred to *Vulcan*'s Name an Isle there lay,
Betwixt *Sicilia*'s Coasts and *Lipare*;
Rais'd high on smoaking Rocks, and deep below,
In hollow Caves the Fires of *Ætna* glow.
555   The *Cyclops* here their heavy Hammers deal;
Loud Strokes, and hissings of tormented Steel
Are heard around: The boyling Waters roar;
And smoaky Flames thro' fuming Tunnels soar.
Hether, the Father of the Fire, by Night,
560   Through the brown Air precipitates his Flight.
On their Eternal Anvils here he found
The Brethren beating, and the Blows go round:
A load of pointless Thunder now there lies
Before their Hands, to ripen for the Skies:
565   These Darts, for angry *Jove*, they dayly cast:
Consum'd on Mortals with prodigious waste.
Three Rays of writhen Rain, of Fire three more,
Of winged *Southern* Winds, and cloudy Store
As many parts, the dreadful Mixture frame:
570   And Fears are added, and avenging Flame.
Inferior Ministers, for *Mars* repair
His broken Axeltrees, and blunted War:
And send him forth agen, with furbish'd Arms,
To wake the lazy War, with Trumpets loud Alarms.
575   The rest refresh the scaly Snakes, that fold
The Shield of *Pallas*; and renew their Gold.
Full on the Crest the *Gorgon*'s Head they place,
With Eyes that rowl in Death, and with distorted Face.
      My Sons said *Vulcan*, set your Tasks aside,
580   Your Strength, and Master Skill, must now be try'd.
Arms, for a Heroe forge: Arms that require
Your Force, your Speed, and all your forming Fire.

He said: They set their former Work aside:
And their new Toils with eager haste divide.
585   A Flood of molten Silver, Brass, and Gold,
And deadly Steel, in the large Furnace rowl'd;
Of this, their artful Hands a Shield prepare;
Alone sufficient to sustain the War.
Sev'n Orbs within a spacious round they close;
590   One stirs the Fire, and one the Bellows blows.
The hissing Steel is in the Smithy drown'd;
The Grot with beaten Anvils groans around.
By turns their Arms advance, in equal time:
By turns their Hands descend, and Hammers chime.
595   They turn the glowing Mass, with crooked Tongs:
The fiery Work proceeds, with Rustick Songs.
While, at the *Lemnian* God's Command, they urge
Their Labours thus, and ply th' *Eolian* Forge:
The chearful Morn salutes *Evander*'s Eyes;
600   And Songs of chirping Birds invite to rise.
He leaves his lowly Bed; his Buskins meet
Above his Ancles; Sandals sheath his Feet:
He sets his trusty Sword upon his side;
And o're his Shoulder throws a Panther's Hide.
605   Two Menial Dogs before their Master press'd:
Thus clad, and guarded thus, he seeks his Kingly Guest.
Mindful of promis'd Aid, he mends his Pace:
But meets *Æneas* in the middle Space.
Young *Pallas* did his Father's Steps attend;
610   And true *Achates* waited on his Friend.
They joyn their Hands; a secret Seat they chuse;
Th' *Arcadian* first, their former Talk renews.
Undaunted Prince, I never can believe
The *Trojan* Empire lost, while you survive.
615   Command th' Assistance of a faithful Friend:
But feeble are the Succours I can send.
Our narrow Kingdom, here the *Tyber* bounds; ⎫
That other side the *Latian* State surrounds; ⎬
Insults our Walls, and wastes our fruitful Grounds. ⎭
620   But mighty Nations I prepare, to join
Their Arms with yours, and aid your just Design.

You come, as by your better Genius sent:
And Fortune seems to favour your intent.
Not far from hence there stands a Hilly Town,
625   Of ancient Building and of high renown;
Torn from the *Tuscans*, by the *Lydian* Race;
Who gave the Name of *Cære*, to the Place
Once *Agyllina* call'd: It flourish'd long
In Pride of Wealth; and warlike People strong.
630   'Till curs'd *Mezentius*, in a fatal Hour,
Assum'd the Crown, with Arbitrary Pow'r.
What Words can paint those execrable Times;
The Subjects Suff'rings, and the Tyrant's Crimes!
That Blood, those Murthers, O ye Gods replace
635   On his own Head, and on his impious Race!
The Living, and the Dead, at his Command
Were coupled, Face to Face, and Hand to Hand:
'Till choak'd with Stench, in loath'd Embraces ty'd,
The ling'ring Wretches pin'd away, and dy'd.
640   Thus plung'd in Ills, and meditating more,
The People's Patience try'd, no longer bore
The raging Monster: But with Arms beset
His House, and Vengeance and Destruction threat.
They fire his Palace: While the Flame ascends,
645   They force his Guards; and execute his Friends.
He cleaves the Crowd; and favour'd by the Night,
To *Turnus*'s friendly Court directs his flight.
By just Revenge the *Tuscans* set on Fire,
With Arms, their King to Punishment require:
650   Their num'rous Troops, now muster'd on the Strand,
My Counsel shall submit to your Command.
Their Navy swarms upon the Coasts: They cry
To hoist their Anchors; but the Gods deny.
An ancient Augur, skill'd in future Fate,
655   With these foreboding Words restrains their Hate.
Ye brave in Arms, ye *Lydian* Blood, the Flow'r
Of *Tuscan* Youth, and choice of all their Pow'r,
Whom just Revenge against *Mezentius* arms,
To seek your Tyrant's Death, by lawful Arms:
660   Know this; no Native of Our Land may lead
This pow'rful People: Seek a Foreign Head.

Aw'd with these Words, in Camps they still abide;
And wait with longing Looks their promis'd Guide.
Tarchon, the *Tuscan* Chief, to me has sent
665   Their Crown, and ev'ry Regal Ornament:
The People joyn their own with his Desire;
And All, my Conduct, as their King, require.
But the chill Blood that creeps within my Veins,
And Age, and listless Limbs unfit for Pains,
670   And a Soul conscious of its own Decay,
Have forc'd me to refuse Imperial Sway.
My *Pallas* were more fit to mount the Throne;
And shou'd, but he's a *Sabine* Mother's Son;
And half a Native: But in you combine
675   A Manly Vigour, and a Foreign Line.
Where Fate and smiling Fortune shew the Way,
Pursue the ready Path to Sov'raign Sway.
The Staff of my declining Days, my Son,
Shall make your good or ill Success his own.
680   In fighting Fields from you shall learn to dare:
And serve the hard Apprentiship of War.
Your matchless Courage, and your Conduct view;
And early shall begin t' admire and copy you.
Besides, two hundred Horse he shall command:
685   Tho' few, a warlike and well chosen Band.
These in my Name are listed: And my Son
As many more has added in his own.
Scarce had he said; *Achates* and his Guest,
With downcast Eyes their silent Grief exprest:
690   Who short of Succours; and in deep Despair,
Shook at the dismal Prospect of the War.
But his bright Mother, from a breaking Cloud,
To chear her Issue, thunder'd thrice aloud.
Thrice, forky Lightning flash'd along the Sky;
695   And *Tyrrhene* Trumpets thrice were heard on high.
Then, gazing up, repeated Peals they hear:
And, in a Heav'n serene, refulgent arms appear;
Red'ning the Skies, and glitt'ring all around,
The temper'd Metals clash; and yield a Silver sound.
700   The rest stood trembling, struck with awe divine,
Æneas only conscious to the Sign:

Presag'd th' Event; and joyful view'd, above,
Th' accomplish'd Promise of the Queen of Love.
Then, to th' *Arcadian* King: This Prodigy
705 (Dismiss your Fear) belongs alone to me.
Heav'n calls me to the War: Th' expected Sign
Is giv'n of promis'd Aid, and Arms Divine.
My Goddess-Mother; whose Indulgent Care,
Foresaw the Dangers of the growing War;
710 This Omen gave; when Bright *Vulcanian* Arms,
Fated from force of Steel by *Stygian* Charms,
Suspended, shone on high: She then foreshow'd
Approaching Fights, and Fields to float in Blood.
Turnus shall dearly pay for Faith forsworn:
715 And Corps, and Swords, and Shields, on *Tyber* born,
Shall choak his Flood: Now sound the loud Alarms;
And *Latian* Troops prepare your perjur'd Arms.

      He said; and rising from his homely Throne,
The Solemn Rites of *Hercules* begun:
720 And on his Altars wak'd the sleeping Fires:
Then chearful to his Household-Gods retires.
There offers chosen Sheep: Th' *Arcadian* King
And *Trojan* Youth the same Oblations bring.
Next of his Men, and Ships, he makes review,
725 Draws out the best, and ablest of the Crew.
Down with the falling Stream the Refuse run:
To raise with joyful News his drooping Son.
Steeds are prepar'd to mount the *Trojan* Band;
Who wait their Leader to the *Tyrrhene* Land.
730 A sprightly Courser, fairer than the rest,
The King himself presents his Royal Guest.
A Lyons Hide his Back and Limbs infold:
Precious with studded work, and Paws of Gold.
Fame through the little City spreads aloud
735 Th' intended March, amid the fearful Crowd:
The Matrons beat their Breasts; dissolve in Tears;
And Double their Devotion in their Fears.
The War at hand appears with more affright:
And rises ev'ry Moment to the sight.
740 Then, old *Evander*, with a close embrace,
Strain'd his departing Friend; and Tears o're-flow his Face:

Wou'd Heav'n, said he, my strength and youth recall,
Such as I was beneath *Preneste*'s Wall;
Then when I made the foremost Foes retire,
745   And set whole heaps of conquer'd Shields on Fire.
When *Herilus* in single Fight I slew;
Whom with three lives *Feronia* did endue:
And thrice I sent him to the *Stygian* Shore;
Till the last Ebbing Soul return'd no more:
750   Such, if I stood renew'd, not these Alarms,
Nor Death, shou'd rend me from my *Pallas* Arms:
Nor proud *Mezentius*, thus unpunish'd, boast
His Rapes and Murthers on the *Tuscan* Coast.
Ye Gods! and mighty *Jove*, in pity bring
755   Relief, and hear a Father, and a King.
If Fate and you, reserve these Eyes, to see
My Son return with Peace and Victory;
If the lov'd Boy shall bless his Father's sight;
If we shall meet again with more delight;
760   Then draw my Life in length, let me sustain,
In hopes of his Embrace, the worst of Pain.
But if your hard Decrees, which O! I dread,
Have doom'd to death his undeserving head;
This, O this very Moment, let me die;
765   While Hopes and Fears in equal ballance lye.
While yet Possest of all his Youthful Charms,
I strain him close within these Aged Arms:
Before that fatal news my Soul shall wound!
He said, and, swooning, sunk upon the ground;
770   His Servants bore him off: And softly laid
His languish'd Limbs upon his homely Bed.
     The Horsemen march; the Gates are open'd wide;
Æneas at their head, *Achates* by his side.
Next these the *Trojan* Leaders rode along:
775   Last, follows in the Reer, th' *Arcadian* Throng.
Young *Pallas* shone conspicuous o're the rest;
Guilded his Arms, Embroider'd was his Vest.
So, from the Seas, exerts his radiant head
The Star, by whom the Lights of Heav'n are led:
780   Shakes from his rosie Locks the perly Dews;
Dispels the darkness and the Day renews.

The trembling Wives, the Walls and Turrets crowd;
And follow, with their Eyes, the dusty Cloud:
Which Winds disperse by fits; and shew from far
785   The blaze of Arms, and Shields, and shining War.
The Troops, drawn up in beautiful Array,
O're heathy Plains pursue the ready way.
Repeated peals of showts are heard around: ⎫
The Neighing Coursers answer to the sound: ⎬
790   And shake with horny Hoofs the solid ground. ⎭
    A greenwood Shade, for long Religion known,
Stands by the Streams that wash the *Tuscan* Town:
Incompass'd round with gloomy Hills above,
Which add a holy horrour to the Grove.
795   The first Inhabitants, of *Grecian* Blood,
That sacred Forest to *Sylvanus* vow'd:
The Guardian of their Flocks, and Fields; and pay
Their due Devotions on his annual day.
Not far from hence, along the River's side,
800   In Tents secure, the *Tuscan* Troops abide;
By *Tarchon* led. Now, from a rising ground,
Æneas cast his wond'ring Eyes around;
And all the *Tyrrhene* Army had in sight,
Stretch'd on the spacious Plain from left to right.
805   Thether his warlike Train the *Trojan* led;
Refresh'd his Men, and weary'd Horses fed.
    Mean time the Mother Goddess, crown'd with Charms,
Breaks through the Clouds, and brings the fated Arms.
Within a winding Vale she finds her Son,
810   On the cool River's Banks, retir'd alone.
She shews her heav'nly Form, without disguise,
And gives her self to his desiring Eyes.
Behold, she said, perform'd, in ev'ry part
My promise made; and *Vulcan*'s labour'd Art.
815   Now seek, secure, the *Latian* Enemy;
And haughty *Turnus* to the Field defy.
She said: And having first her Son embrac'd;
The radiant Arms beneath an Oak she plac'd.
Proud of the Gift, he rowl'd his greedy sight
820   Around the Work, and gaz'd with vast delight.

He lifts, he turns, he poizes, and admires
The Crested Helm, that vomits radiant Fires:
His hands the fatal Sword, and Corslet hold:
One keen with temper'd Steel, one stiff with Gold.

825 Both ample, flaming both, and beamy bright:
So shines a Cloud, when edg'd with adverse Light.
He shakes the pointed Spear; and longs to try
The plated Cuishes, on his manly thigh.
But most admires the Shields Mysterious mould,

830 And *Roman* Triumphs rising on the Gold.
For those, emboss'd, the Heav'nly Smith had wrought,
(Not in the Rolls of future Fate untaught,)
The Wars in Order, and the Race Divine
Of Warriors, issuing from the *Julian* Line.

835 The Cave of *Mars* was dress'd with mossy Greens:
There, by the Wolf, were laid the Martial Twins.
Intrepid on her swelling Dugs they hung;
The foster Dam loll'd out her fawning Tongue:
They suck'd secure, while bending Back her Head,

840 She lick'd their tender Limbs; and form'd them as they
           fed.
Not far from thence new *Rome* appears, with Games
Projected for the Rape of *Sabine* Dames.
The Pit resounds with Shrieks: A War succeeds,
For breach of Public Faith, and unexample'd Deeds.

845 Here for Revenge the *Sabine* Troops contend:
The *Romans* there with Arms the Prey defend.
Weary'd with tedious War, at length they cease;
And both the Kings and Kingdoms plight the Peace.
The friendly Chiefs, before *Jove*'s Altar stand;

850 Both arm'd, with each a Charger in his Hand:
A fatted Sow, for Sacrifice is led;
With Imprecations on the perjur'd Head.
Near this, the Traytor *Metius*, stretch'd between
Four fiery Steeds, is dragg'd along the Green;

855 By *Tullus* doom: The Brambles drink his Blood;
And his torn Limbs are left, the Vulture's Food.
There, *Porsena* to *Rome* proud *Tarquin* brings;
And wou'd by Force restore the banish'd Kings.

One Tyrant, for his fellow Tyrant fights:
860   The *Roman* Youth assert their Native Rights.
Before the Town the *Tuscan* Army lies:
To win by Famine, or by Fraud surprise.
Their King, half threat'ning, half disdaining stood:
While *Cocles* broke the Bridge; and stem'd the Flood.
865   The Captive Maids there tempt the raging Tide:
Scap'd from their Chains, with *Clelia* for their Guide.
    High on a Rock Heroick *Manlius* stood;
To guard the Temple, and the Temple's God:
Then *Rome* was poor; and there you might behold
870   The Palace, thatch'd with Straw, now roof'd with Gold.
The Silver Goose before the shining Gate
There flew; and by her Cackle, sav'd the State.
She told the *Gauls* approach: Th' approaching *Gauls*,
Obscure in Night, ascend, and seize the Walls.
875   The Gold, dissembl'd well their yellow Hair:
And Golden Chains on their white Necks they wear.
Gold are their Vests: Long *Alpine* Spears they wield:
And their left Arm sustains a length of Shield.
Hard by, the leaping *Salian* Priests advance:
880   And naked thro' the Streets the mad *Luperci* dance:
In Caps of Wool. The Targets dropt from Heav'n:
Here modest Matrons in soft Litters driv'n,
To pay their Vows in solemn Pomp appear:
And odorous Gums in their chast Hands they bear.
885   Far hence remov'd, the *Stygian* Seats are seen:
Pains of the damn'd, and punish'd *Catiline*:
Hung on a Rock the Traytor; and around,
The Furies hissing from the neather Ground.
Apart from these, the happy Souls, he draws:
890   And *Cato*'s holy Ghost, dispensing Laws.
Betwixt the Quarters, flows a Golden Sea:
But foaming Surges, there, in Silver play.
The dancing Dolphins, with their Tails, divide
The glitt'ring Waves; and cut the precious Tide.
895   Amid the Main, two mighty Fleets engage
Their Brazen Beaks; oppos'd with equal Rage.
Actium, surveys the well disputed Prize:
Leucate's wat'ry Plain, with foamy Billows fries.

Young *Cesar*, on the Stern, in Armour bright;
900 Here leads the *Romans* and their Gods to fight:
His beamy Temples shoot their Flames afar;
And o're his Head is hung the *Julian* Star.
Agrippa seconds him, with prosp'rous Gales:
And, with propitious Gods, his Foes assails.
905 A Naval Crown, that binds his Manly Brows,
The happy Fortune of the Fight foreshows.
      Rang'd on the Line oppos'd, *Antonius* brings
Barbarian Aids, and Troops of *Eastern* Kings.
Th' *Arabians* near, and *Bactrians* from afar,
910 Of Tongues discordant, and a mingled War.
And, rich in gaudy Robes, amidst the Strife,
His ill Fate follows him; th' *Egyptian* Wife.
Moving they fight: With Oars, and forky Prows,
The Froth is gather'd; and the Water glows.
915 It seems, as if the *Cyclades* again
Were rooted up, and justled in the Main:
Or floating Mountains, floating Mountains meet:
Such is the fierce Encounter of the Fleet.
Fire-balls are thrown; and pointed Jav'lins fly:
920 The Fields of *Neptune* take a Purple Dye.
The Queen her self, amidst the loud Alarms,
With Cymbals toss'd her fainting Souldiers warms.
Fool as she was; who had not yet divin'd
Her cruel Fate; nor saw the Snakes behind.
925 Her Country Gods, the Monsters of the Sky,
Great *Neptune*, *Pallas*, and Love's Queen, defie.
The Dog *Anubis* barks, but barks in vain;
Nor longer dares oppose the Ætherial Train.
Mars, in the middle of the shining Shield
930 Is grav'd, and strides along the liquid Field.
The *Diræ* sowse from Heav'n, with swift Descent:
And Discord, dy'd in Blood, with Garments rent,
Divides the Preace: Her Steps, *Bellona* treads,
And shakes her Iron Rod above their Heads.
935 This seen, *Apollo*, from his *Actian* height,
Pours down his Arrows: At whose winged flight
The trembling *Indians*, and *Egyptians* yield:
And soft *Sabæans* quit the wat'ry Field.

The fatal Mistress hoists her silken Sails;
940 And, shrinking from the Fight, invokes the Gales.
Aghast she looks; and heaves her Breast, for Breath:
Panting, and pale with fear of future Death.
The God had figur'd her, as driv'n along,
By Winds and Waves; and scudding thro' the Throng.
945 Just opposite, sad *Nilus*, opens wide
His Arms, and ample Bosom, to the Tide.
And spreads his Mantle o're the winding Coast:
In which he wraps his Queen, and hides the flying Hoast.
The Victor, to the Gods his Thanks express'd:
950 And *Rome* triumphant, with his Presence bless'd.
Three hundred Temples in the Town he plac'd:
With Spoils and Altars ev'ry Temple grac'd.
Three shining Nights, and three succeeding Days,
The Fields resound with Shouts; the Streets with Praise:
955 The Domes with Songs, the Theatres with Plays.
All Altars flame: Before each Altar lies,
Drench'd in his Gore, the destin'd Sacrifice.
Great *Cæsar* sits sublime upon his Throne;
Before *Apollo*'s Porch of *Parian* Stone:
960 Accepts the Presents vow'd for Victory;
And hangs the Monumental Crowns on high.
Vast Crowds of Vanquish'd Nations march along:
Various in Arms, in Habit, and in Tongue.
Here, *Mulciber* assigns the proper Place
965 For *Carians*, and th' ungirt *Numidian* Race;
Then ranks the *Thracians* in the second Row;
With *Scythians*, expert in the Dart and Bow.
And here the tam'd *Euphrates* humbly glides;
And there the *Rhine* submits her swelling Tides.
970 And proud *Araxes*, whom no Bridge cou'd bind:
The *Danes* unconquer'd Offspring, march behind;
And *Morini*, the last of Human Kind.
These Figures, on the Shield divinely wrought,
By *Vulcan* labour'd, and by *Venus* brought,
975 With Joy and Wonder fill the Hero's thought.
Unknown the Names, he yet admires the Grace;
And bears aloft the Fame, and Fortune of his Race.

THE NINTH BOOK OF THE ÆNEIS

The Argument

Turnus *takes Advantage of* Æneas's *Absence, fires some of his Ships, (which are transform'd into Sea-Nymphs) and assaults his Camp. The* Trojans *reduc'd to the last Extremities, send* Nisus *and* Euryalus *to recall* Æneas; *which furnishes the Poet with that admirable Episode of their Friendship, Generosity; and the conclusion of their Adventures.*

While these Affairs in distant Places pass'd,
The various *Iris Juno* sends with haste,
To find bold *Turnus*, who, with anxious Thought,
The secret Shade of his great Grandsire sought.
5   Retir'd alone she found the daring Man;
And op'd her rosie Lips, and thus began.
What none of all the Gods cou'd grant thy Vows;
That, *Turnus*, this auspicious Day bestows.
Æneas, gone to seek th' *Arcadian* Prince,
10 Has left the *Trojan* Camp without defence;
And, short of Succours there; employs his Pains
In Parts remote to raise the *Tuscan* Swains:
Now snatch an Hour that favours thy Designs,
Unite thy Forces, and attack their Lines.
15 This said, on equal Wings she pois'd her Weight,
And form'd a radiant Rainbow in her flight.

    The *Daunian* Heroe lifts his Hands and Eyes;
And thus invokes the Goddess as she flies.
Iris, the Grace of Heav'n, what Pow'r Divine
20 Has sent thee down, thro' dusky Clouds to shine?
See they divide; immortal Day appears;
And glitt'ring Planets dancing in their Spheres!
With Joy, these happy Omens I obey;
And follow to the War, the God that leads the Way.

25   Thus having said, as by the Brook he stood,
He scoop'd the Water from the Crystal Flood;
Then with his Hands the drops to Heav'n he throws,
And loads the Pow'rs above with offer'd Vows.

    Now march the bold Confed'rates thro' the Plain;
30 Well hors'd, well clad, a rich and shining Train:
Messapus leads the Van; and in the Reer,
The Sons of *Tyrrheus* in bright Arms appear.

In the Main Battel, with his flaming Crest,
The mighty *Turnus* tow'rs above the rest:
35   Silent they move; majestically slow,
Like ebbing *Nile*, or *Ganges* in his flow.
The *Trojans* view the dusty Cloud from far;
And the dark Menace of the distant War.
Caicus from the Rampire saw it rise,
40   Blackning the Fields, and thickning thro' the Skies.
Then to his Fellows thus aloud he calls,
What rowling Clouds, my Friends, approach the Walls?
Arm, arm, and man the Works; prepare your Spears,
And pointed Darts; the *Latian* Hoast appears.
45   Thus warn'd, they shut their Gates; with Shouts ascend
The Bulwarks, and secure their Foes attend.
For their wise Gen'ral with foreseeing Care,
Had charg'd them not to tempt the doubtful War:
Nor, tho' provok'd, in open Fields advance;
50   But close within their Lines attend their chance.
Unwilling, yet they keep the strict Command;
And sourly wait in Arms the Hostile Band.
The fiery *Turnus* flew before the rest,
A Pye-ball'd Steed of *Thracian* Strain he press'd;
55   His Helm of massy Gold; and Crimson was his Crest.
With twenty Horse to second his Designs,
An unexpected Foe, he fac'd the Lines.
    Is there, he said, in Arms who bravely dare,
His Leader's Honour, and his Danger share?
60   Then, spurring on, his brandish'd Dart he threw,
In sign of War, applauding Shouts ensue.
    Amaz'd to find a dastard Race that Run
Behind the Rampires, and the Battel shun,
He rides around the Camp, with rowling Eyes,
65   And stops at ev'ry Post; and ev'ry Passage tries.
So roams the nightly Wolf about the Fold,
Wet with descending Show'rs, and stiff with cold;
He howls for Hunger, and he grins for Pain;
His gnashing Teeth are exercis'd in vain:
70   And impotent of Anger, finds no way
In his distended Paws to grasp the Prey.

The Mothers listen; but the bleating Lambs
Securely swig the Dug, beneath the Dams.
Thus ranges eager *Turnus* o're the Plain,
75 Sharp with Desire, and furious with Disdain:
Surveys each Passage with a piercing Sight;
To force his Foes in equal Field to fight.
Thus, while he gazes round, at length he spies
Where, fenc'd with strong Redoubts, their Navy lies;
80 Close underneath the Walls: The washing Tyde
Secures from all approach this weaker side.
He takes the wish'd Occasion; fills his Hand
With ready Fires, and shakes a flaming Brand:
Urg'd by his Presence, ev'ry Soul is warm'd,
85 And ev'ry Hand with kindled Firrs is arm'd.
From the fir'd Pines the scatt'ring Sparkles fly;
Fat Vapours mix'd with Flames involve the Sky.
What Pow'r, O Muses, cou'd avert the Flame
Which threaten'd, in the Fleet, the *Trojan* Name!
90 Tell: For the Fact thro' length of Time obscure,
Is hard to Faith; yet shall the Fame endure.
    'Tis said, that when the Chief prepar'd his flight,
And fell'd his Timber from Mount *Ida*'s height,
The Grandam Goddess then approach'd her Son,
95 And with a Mother's Majesty begun.
Grant me, she said, the sole Request I bring,
Since conquer'd Heav'n has own'd you for its King:
On *Ida*'s Brows, for Ages past, there stood,
With Firrs and Maples fill'd, a shady Wood:
100 And on the Summit rose a Sacred Grove,
Where I was worshipp'd with Religious Love;
Those Woods, that Holy Grove, my long delight,
I gave the *Trojan* Prince, to speed his flight.
Now fill'd with Fear, on their behalf I come;
105 Let neither Winds o'reset, nor Waves intomb
The floating Forests of the Sacred Pine;
But let it be their Safety to be mine.
Then thus reply'd her awful Son; who rowls
The radiant Stars, and Heav'n and Earth controuls;
110 How dare you, Mother, endless Date demand,
For Vessels moulded by a Mortal Hand?

What then is Fate? Shall bold *Æneas* ride
Of Safety certain, on th' uncertain Tide?
Yet what I can, I grant: When, wafted o're,
115   The Chief is landed on the *Latian* Shore,
Whatever Ships escape the raging Storms,
At my Command shall change their fading Forms
To Nymphs Divine: and plow the wat'ry Way,
Like *Dotis*, and the Daughters of the Sea.

120   To seal his sacred Vow, by *Styx* he swore,
The Lake of liquid Pitch, the dreery Shore;
And *Phlegethon*'s innavigable Flood,
And the black Regions of his Brother God:
He said; and shook the Skies with his Imperial Nod.

125   And now at length the number'd Hours were come,
Prefix'd by Fate's irrevocable Doom,
When the great Mother of the Gods was free
To save her Ships, and finish *Jove*'s Decree.
First, from the Quarter of the Morn, there sprung
130   A Light that sign'd the Heav'ns, and shot along:
Then from a Cloud, fring'd round with Golden Fires,
Were Timbrels heard, and *Berecynthian* Quires:
And last a Voice, with more than Mortal Sounds,
Both Hosts in Arms oppos'd, with equal Horrour wounds.

135   O *Trojan* Race, your needless Aid forbear;
And know my Ships are my peculiar Care.
With greater ease the bold *Rutulian* may,
With hissing Brands, attempt to burn the Sea,
Than sindge my sacred Pines. But you my Charge,
140   Loos'd from your crooked Anchors lanch at large,
Exalted each a Nymph: Forsake the Sand,
And swim the Seas, at *Cybele*'s Command.
No sooner had the Goddess ceas'd to speak,
When lo, th' obedient Ships, their Haulsers break;
145   And, strange to tell, like Dolphins in the Main,
They plunge their Prows, and dive, and spring again:
As many beauteous Maids the Billows sweep,
As rode before tall Vessels on the Deep.
The Foes, surpriz'd with Wonder, stood aghast,
150   *Messapus* curb'd his fiery Courser's haste;
Old *Tyber* roar'd; and raising up his Head,
Call'd back his Waters to their Oozy Bed.

Turnus alone, undaunted, bore the Shock;
And with these Words his trembling Troops bespoke.
155   These Monsters for the *Trojans* Fate are meant,
And are by *Jove* for black Presages sent.
He takes the Cowards last Relief away; ⎫
For fly they cannot; and, constrain'd to stay, ⎬
Must yield unsought, a base inglorious Prey. ⎭
160   The liquid half of all the Globe, is lost;
Heav'n shuts the Seas, and we secure the Coast.
Theirs is no more, than that small spot of Ground,
Which Myryads of our Martial Men surround.
Their Fates I fear not; or vain Oracles;
165   'Twas given to *Venus*, they shou'd cross the Seas:
And land secure upon the *Latian* Plains,
Their promis'd Hour is pass'd, and mine remains.
'Tis in the Fate of *Turnus*, to destroy
With Sword and Fire the faithless Race of *Troy*.
170   Shall such Affronts as these, alone inflame
The *Grecian* Brothers, and the *Grecian* Name?
My Cause and theirs is one; a fatal Strife,
And final Ruin, for a ravish'd Wife.
Was't not enough, that, punish'd for the Crime,
175   They fell; but will they fall a second Time?
One wou'd have thought they paid enough before,
To curse the costly Sex; and durst offend no more.
Can they securely trust their feeble Wall,
A slight Partition, a thin Interval,
180   Betwixt their Fate and them; when *Troy*, tho' built
By Hands Divine, yet perish'd by their Guilt?
Lend me, for once, my Friends, your valiant Hands,
To force from out their Lines these dastard Bands.
Less than a thousand Ships will end this War,
185   Nor *Vulcan* needs his fated Arms prepare.
Let all the *Tuscans*, all th' *Arcadians* join,
Nor these, nor those shall frustrate my Design.
Let them not fear the Treasons of the Night; ⎫
The robb'd *Palladium*, the pretended flight: ⎬
190   Our Onset shall be made in open Light. ⎭
No wooden Engine shall their Town betray,
Fires they shall have around, but Fires by Day.

No *Grecian* Babes before their Camp appear,
Whom *Hector*'s Arms detain'd, to the tenth tardy Year.
195   Now, since the Sun is rowling to the *West*,
Give we the silent Night to needful Rest:
Refresh your Bodies, and your Arms prepare,
The Morn shall end the small Remains of War.
　The Post of Honour to *Messapus* falls,
200   To keep the Nightly Guard; to watch the Walls;
To pitch the Fires at Distances around,
And close the *Trojans* in their scanty Ground.
Twice seven *Rutulian* Captains ready stand;
And twice seven hundred Horse these Chiefs command:
205   All clad in shining Arms the Works invest;
Each with a radiant Helm, and waving Crest.
Stretch'd at their length, they press the grassy Ground;
They laugh, they sing, the jolly Bowls go round:
With Lights, and chearful Fires renew the Day;
210   And pass the wakeful Night in Feasts and Play.
　The *Trojans*, from above, their Foes beheld;
And with arm'd Legions all the Rampires fill'd:
Seiz'd with Affright, their Gates they first explore,
Join Works to Works with Bridges; Tow'r to Tow'r:
215   Thus all things needful for Defence, abound;
Mnestheus, and brave *Seresthus* walk the round:
Commission'd by their Absent Prince, to share
The common Danger, and divide the Care.
The Souldiers draw their Lots; and as they fall,
220   By turns relieve each other on the Wall.
　Nigh where the Foes their utmost Guards advance,
To watch the Gate, was warlike *Nisus* chance.
His Father *Hyrtacus* of Noble Blood;
His Mother was a Hunt'ress of the Wood:
225   And sent him to the Wars; well cou'd he bear
His Lance in fight, and dart the flying Spear:
But better skill'd unerring Shafts to send:
Beside him stood *Euryalus* his Friend.
Euryalus, than whom the *Trojan* Hoast
230   No fairer Face, or sweeter Air could boast.
Scarce had the Down to shade his Cheeks begun;
One was their Care, and their Delight was one.

One Common hazard in the War they shar'd;
And now were both by choice upon the Guard.
235　　Then *Nisus*, thus: Or do the Gods inspire
This warmth, or make we Gods of our Desire?
A gen'rous ardour boils within my Breast,
Eager of Action, Enemy to Rest:
This urges me to fight, and fires my Mind,
240　To leave a memorable Name behind.
Thou see'st the Foe secure: how faintly shine
Their scatter'd Fires! the most in Sleep supine;
Along the ground, an easie Conquest lye;
The wakeful few, the fuming Flaggon ply:
245　All hush'd around. Now hear what I revolve;
A thought unripe; and scarcely yet resolve.
Our absent Prince both Camp and Council mourn;
By Message both wou'd hasten his return:
If they confer what I demand, on thee,
250　(For Fame is Recompence enough for me)
Methinks, beneath yon Hill, I have espy'd
A way that safely will my passage guide.
　　Euryalus stood list'ning while he spoke;
With love of Praise, and noble Envy struck;
255　Then to his ardent Friend expos'd his Mind: ⎫
All this alone, and leaving me behind,　　　⎬
Am I unworthy, *Nisus*, to be join'd?　　　⎭
Think'st thou I can my share of Glory yield,
Or send thee unassisted to the Field?
260　Not so my Father taught my Childhood Arms;
Born in a Siege, and bred among Alarms!
Nor is my Youth unworthy of my Friend,
Nor of the Heav'n-born Heroe I attend.
The thing call'd Life, with ease I can disclaim;
265　And think it oversold to purchase Fame.
　　Then *Nisus*, thus; alas! thy tender years
Wou'd minister new matter to my Fears:
So may the Gods, who view this friendly Strife,
Restore me to thy lov'd Embrace with life,
270　Condemn'd to pay my Vows (as sure I trust,)
This thy Request is Cruel and Unjust.

But if some Chance, as many Chances are,
And doubtful Hazards in the deeds of War;
If one shou'd reach my Head, there let it fall,
275 And spare thy Life; I wou'd not perish all.
Thy bloomy Youth deserves a longer date;
Live thou to mourn thy Love's unhappy Fate:
To bear my mangled Body from the Foe;
Or buy it back, and Fun'ral Rites bestow.
280 Or if hard Fortune shall those Dues deny,
Thou canst at least an empty Tomb supply.
O let not me the Widows Tears renew;
Nor let a Mother's Curse my Name pursue;
Thy Pious Parent, who, for love of thee,
285 Forsook the Coasts of Friendly *Sicily*,
Her Age, committing to the Seas and Wind,
When ev'ry weary Matron staid behind.
To this, *Euryalus*, you plead in vain,
And but protract the Cause you cannot gain:
290 No more delays, but haste. With that he wakes
The nodding Watch; each to his Office takes.
The Guard reliev'd, the gen'rous Couple went
To find the Council at the Royal Tent.
All Creatures else forgot their daily Care;
295 And Sleep, the common Gift of Nature, share:
Except the *Trojan* Peers, who wakeful sate
In nightly Council for th' indanger'd State.
They vote a Message to their absent Chief;
Shew their Distress; and beg a swift Relief.
300 Amid the Camp a silent Seat they chose,
Remote from Clamour, and secure from Foes.
On their left Arms their ample Shields they bear,
The right reclin'd upon the bending Spear.
Now *Nisus* and his Friend approach the Guard, ⎤
305 And beg Admission, eager to be heard: ⎬
Th' Affair important, not to be deferr'd. ⎦
Ascanius bids 'em be conducted in;
Ord'ring the more experienc'd to begin.
Then *Nisus* thus. Ye Fathers lend your Ears;
310 Nor judge our bold Attempt beyond our Years.
The Foe securely drench'd in Sleep and Wine,
Neglect their Watch; the Fires but thinly shine:

And where the Smoke, in cloudy Vapours flies,
Cov'ring the Plain, and curling to the Skies,
315 Betwixt two Paths, which at the Gate divide, ⎫
Close by the Sea, a Passage we have spy'd ⎬
Which will our way to great *Æneas* guide. ⎭
Expect each Hour to see him safe again,
Loaded with Spoils of Foes in Battel slain.
320 Snatch we the lucky Minute while we may:
Nor can we be mistaken in the way;
For hunting in the Vale, we both have seen
The rising Turrets, and the Stream between;
And know the winding Course, with ev'ry Ford.
325 He ceas'd: And old *Alethes* took the Word.

    Our Country Gods, in whom our Trust we place,
Will yet from Ruin save the *Trojan* Race;
While we behold such dauntless Worth appear
In dawning Youth; and Souls so void of Fear.
330 Then, into Tears of Joy the Father broke; ⎫
Each in his longing Arms by Turns he took: ⎬
Panted and paus'd; and thus again he spoke. ⎭
Ye brave young Men, what equal Gifts can we,
In recompence of such Desert, decree?
335 The greatest, sure, and best you can receive,
The Gods, and your own conscious Worth will give.
The rest our grateful Gen'ral will bestow;
And young *Ascanius* 'till his Manhood owe.

    And I, whose Welfare in my Father lies,
340 *Ascanius* adds, by the great Deities,
By my dear Country, by my household Gods,
By hoary *Vesta*'s Rites, and dark Abodes,
Adjure you both; (on you my Fortune stands,
That and my Faith I plight into your Hands:)
345 Make me but happy in his safe Return,
Whose wanted Presence I can only mourn;
Your common Gift shall two large Goblets be,
Of Silver, wrought with curious Imagery;
And high emboss'd, which, when old *Priam* reign'd,
350 My conqu'ring Sire at sack'd *Arisba* gain'd.
And more, two Tripods cast in antick Mould,
With two great Talents of the finest Gold:

Beside a costly Bowl, ingrav'd with Art,
Which *Dido* gave, when first she gave her Heart.
355   But if in conquer'd *Italy* we reign,
When Spoils by Lot the Victor shall obtain;
Thou saw'st the Courser by proud *Turnus* press'd,
That, *Nisus*, and his Arms, and nodding Crest,
And Shield, from Chance exempt, shall be thy Share; ⎫
360   Twelve lab'ring Slaves, twelve Handmaids young and ⎬
            fair,   ⎭
All clad in rich Attire, and train'd with Care.
And last, a *Latian* Field with fruitful Plains;
And a large Portion of the King's Domains.
But thou, whose Years are more to mine ally'd,
365   No Fate my vow'd Affection shall divide
From thee, Heroick Youth; be wholly mine:
Take full Possession; all my Soul is thine.
One Faith, one Fame, one Fate shall both attend;
My Life's Companion and my Bosom Friend.
370   My Peace shall be committed to thy Care,
And to thy Conduct, my Concerns in War.
        Then thus the young *Euryalus* reply'd;
Whatever Fortune, good or bad betide,
The same shall be my Age, as now my Youth;
375   No time shall find me wanting to my Truth.
This only from your Goodness let me gain;
(And this ungranted, all Rewards are vain)
Of *Priam*'s Royal Race my Mother came;
And sure the best that ever bore the Name:
380   Whom neither *Troy*, nor *Sicily* cou'd hold
From me departing, but o'respent, and old,
My Fate she follow'd; ignorant of this,
Whatever Danger, neither parting Kiss,
Nor pious Blessing taken, her I leave;
385   And, in this only Act of all my Life deceive.
By this right Hand, and conscious Night I swear,
My Soul so sad a farewel could not bear.
Be you her Comfort; fill my vacant place,
(Permit me to presume so great a Grace)
390   Support her Age, forsaken and distress'd,
That hope alone will fortifie my Breast

Against the worst of Fortunes, and of Fears.
He said: The mov'd Assistants melt in Tears.

   Then thus *Ascanius*, (wonder-struck to see
395 That Image of his filial Piety;)
So great Beginnings, in so green an Age,
Exact the Faith, which I again ingage.
Thy Mother all the Dues shall justly claim
Creusa had; and only want the Name.
400 Whate're Event thy bold Attempt shall have,
'Tis Merit to have born a Son so brave.
Now by my Head, a sacred Oath, I swear,
(My Father us'd it) what returning here
Crown'd with Success, I for thy self prepare,
405 That, if thou fail, shall thy lov'd Mother share.

   He said; and weeping while he spoke the Word,
From his broad Belt he drew a shining Sword,
Magnificent with Gold. *Lycaon* made,
And in an Iv'ry Scabbard sheath'd the Blade:
410 This was his Gift: Great *Mnestheus* gave his Friend
A Lyon's Hide, his Body to defend:
And good *Alethes* furnish'd him beside,
With his own trusty Helm, of Temper try'd.

   Thus arm'd they went. The Noble *Trojans* wait
415 Their issuing forth, and follow to the Gate.
With Prayers and Vows, above the rest appears
Ascanius, manly far beyond his Years.
And Messages committed to their Care,
Which all in winds were lost, and flitting Air.

420   The Trenches first they pass'd: Then took their Way
Where their proud Foes in pitch'd Pavilions lay;
To many fatal, e're themselves were slain:
They found the careless Hoast dispers'd upon the Plain.
Who gorg'd, and drunk with Wine, supinely snore;
425 Unharnass'd Chariots stand along the Shore:
Amidst the Wheels and Reins, the Goblet by,
A Medly of Debauch and War they lye.
Observing *Nisus* shew'd his Friend the sight;
Behold a Conquest gain'd without a Fight.
430 Occasion offers, and I stand prepar'd;
There lies our Way; be thou upon the Guard,

And look around; while I securely go,
And hew a Passage, thro' the sleeping Foe.
Softly he spoke; then striding, took his way,
435   With his drawn Sword, where haughty *Rhamnes* lay:
His Head rais'd high, on Tapestry beneath,
And heaving from his Breast, he drew his Breath:
A King and Prophet by King *Turnus* lov'd;
But Fate by Prescience cannot be remov'd.
440   Him, and his sleeping Slaves he slew. Then spies
Where *Rhemus*, with his rich Retinue lies:
His Armor-bearer first, and next he kills
His Charioteer, intrench'd betwixt the Wheels
And his lov'd Horses: Last invades their Lord;
445   Full on his Neck he drives the fatal Sword:
The gasping Head flies off; a Purple flood
Flows from the Trunk, that welters in the Blood:
Which by the spurning Heels, dispers'd around,
The Bed besprinkles, and bedews the Ground.
450   *Lamus* the bold, and *Lamyrus* the strong,
He slew; and then *Serranus* fair and young:
From Dice and Wine the Youth retir'd to Rest,
And puff'd the fumy God from out his Breast:
Ev'n then he dreamt of Drink and lucky Play;
455   More lucky had it lasted 'till the Day.
      The famish'd Lyon thus, with Hunger bold;
O'releaps the Fences of the Nightly Fold;
And tears the peaceful Flocks: With silent Awe
Trembling they lye, and pant beneath his Paw.
460   Nor with less Rage *Euryalus* employs
The wrathful sword, or fewer Foes destroys:
But on th' ignoble Crowd his Fury flew:
He *Fadus*, *Hebesus*, and *Rhœtus* slew.
Oppress'd with heavy Sleep the former fall,
465   But *Rhœtus* wakeful, and observing all:
Behind a spacious Jarr he slink'd for fear;
The fatal Iron found, and reach'd him there.
For as he rose, it pierc'd his naked side;
And reeking, thence return'd in Crimson dy'd.
470   The Wound pours out a Stream of Wine and Blood,
The Purple Soul comes floating in the flood.

Now where *Messapus* Quarter'd they arrive;
The Fires were fainting there, and just alive.
The Warriour-Horses ty'd in order fed;
475   *Nisus* observ'd the Discipline, and said,
Our eager thirst of Blood may both betray;
And see the scatter'd Streaks of dawning day,
Foe to Nocturnal Thefts: No more, my Friend,
Here let our glutted Execution end:
480   A Lane through slaughter'd Bodies we have made:
The bold *Euryalus*, tho' loath, obey'd.
Of Arms, and Arras, and of Plate they find
A precious load; but these they leave behind.
Yet fond of gaudy Spoils the Boy wou'd stay ⎫
485   To make the rich Caparison his prey,   ⎬
Which on the Steed of conquer'd *Rhamnes* lay. ⎭
Nor did his Eyes less longingly behold
The Girdle-Belt, with Nails of burnish'd Gold.
This Present *Cedicus* the Rich, bestow'd
490   On *Remulus*, when Friendship first they vow'd:
And absent, join'd in hospitable tyes;
He dying, to his Heir bequeath'd the Prize:
Till by the Conqu'ring *Ardean* Troops oppress'd
He fell; and they the Glorious Gift possess'd.
495   These Glitt'ring Spoils (now made the Victor's gain)
He to his body suits; but suits in vain.
Messapus Helm he finds among the rest,
And laces on, and wears the waving Crest.
Proud of their Conquest, prouder of their Prey,
500   They leave the Camp; and take the ready way.
But far they had not pass'd before they spy'd
Three hundred Horse with *Volscens* for their Guide.
The Queen a Legion to King *Turnus* sent, ⎫
But the swift Horse the slower Foot prevent; ⎬
505   And now advancing, sought the Leader's Tent. ⎭
They saw the Pair; for thro' the doubtful shade
His shineing Helm *Euryalus* betray'd,
On which the Moon with full reflexion play'd.
'Tis not for nought, cry'd *Volscens*, from the Crowd,
510   These Men go there; then rais'd his Voice aloud:

Stand, stand: why thus in Arms, and whither bent;
From whence, to whom, and on what Errand sent?
Silent they scud away, and haste their flight,
To Neighb'ring Woods, and trust themselves to night.
515   The speedy Horse all passages belay,
And spur their smoking Steeds to Cross their way;
And watch each Entrance of the winding Wood;
Black was the Forest, thick with Beech it stood:
Horrid with Fern, and intricate with Thorn,
520   Few Paths of Humane Feet or Tracks of Beasts were worn.
The darkness of the Shades, his heavy Prey,
And Fear, mis-led the Younger from his way.
But *Nisus* hit the Turns with happier haste,
And thoughtless of his Friend, the Forest pass'd:
525   And *Alban* Plains, from *Alba*'s Name so call'd,
Where King *Latinus* then his Oxen stall'd.
Till turning at the length, he stood his ground,
And miss'd his Friend, and cast his Eyes around;
Ah Wretch, he cry'd, where have I left behind
530   Th' unhappy Youth, where shall I hope to find?
Or what way take! again He ventures back:
And treads the Mazes of his former track.
He winds the Wood, and list'ning hears the noise
Of trampling Coursers, and the Riders voice.
535   The sound approach'd, and suddenly he viewed
The Foes inclosing, and his Friend pursu'd:
Forelay'd and taken, while he strove in vain,
The shelter of the friendly Shades to gain.
What shou'd he next attempt! what Arms employ,
540   What fruitless Force to free the Captive Boy?
Or desperate shou'd he rush and lose his Life,
With odds oppress'd, in such unequal strife?
Resolv'd at length, his pointed Spear he shook;
And casting on the Moon a mournful look,
545   Guardian of Groves, and Goddess of the Night;
Fair Queen, he said, direct my Dart aright:
If e're my Pious Father for my sake
Did grateful Off'rings on thy Altars make;
Or I increas'd them with my Silvan toils,
550   And hung thy Holy Roofs, with Savage Spoils;

Give me to scatter these. Then from his Ear
He pois'd, and aim'd, and lanch'd the trembling Spear.
The deadly Weapon, hissing from the Grove,
Impetuous on the back of *Sulmo* drove:
555   Pierc'd his thin Armour, drank his Vital Blood,
And in his Body left the broken Wood.
He staggers round, his Eyeballs rowl in Death,
And with short sobs he gasps away his Breath.
All stand amaz'd; a second Jav'lin flies,
560   With equal strength, and quivers through the Skies;
This through thy Temples, *Tagus*, forc'd the way,
And in the Brain-pan warmly bury'd lay.
Fierce *Volscens* foams with Rage, and gazing round,
Descry'd not him who gave the Fatal Wound:
565   Nor knew to fix Revenge: but thou, he cries,
Shalt pay for both, and at the Pris'ner flies,
With his drawn Sword. Then struck with deep Despair,
That cruel sight the Lover cou'd not bear:
But from his Covert rush'd in open view,
570   And sent his Voice before him as he flew.
Me, me, he cry'd, turn all your Swords alone
On me; the Fact confess'd, the Fault my own.
He neither cou'd nor durst, the guiltless Youth;
Ye Moon and Stars bear Witness to the Truth!
575   His only Crime, (if Friendship can offend)
Is too much Love, to his unhappy Friend.
Too late he speaks; the Sword, which Fury guides,
Driv'n with full Force, had pierc'd his tender Sides.
Down fell the beauteous Youth; the yawning Wound
580   Gush'd out a Purple Stream, and stain'd the Ground.
His snowy Neck reclines upon his Breast,
Like a fair Flow'r by the keen Share oppress'd:
Like a white Poppy sinking on the Plain,
Whose heavy Head is overcharg'd with Rain.
585   Despair, and Rage, and Vengeance justly vow'd,
Drove *Nisus* headlong on the hostile Crowd:
Volscens he seeks; on him alone he bends;
Born back, and bor'd, by his surrounding Friends,
Onward he press'd: and kept him still in sight;
590   Then whirl'd aloft his Sword, with all his might:

Th' unerring Steel descended while he spoke;
Pierc'd his wide Mouth, and thro' his Weazon broke:
Dying, he slew; and stagg'ring on the Plain,
With swimming Eyes he sought his Lover slain:
595 Then quiet on his bleeding Bosom fell;
Content in Death, to be reveng'd so well.
       O happy Friends! for if my Verse can give
Immortal Life, your Fame shall ever live:
Fix'd as the Capitol's Foundation lies;
600 And spread, where e're the *Roman* Eagle flies!
       The conqu'ring Party, first divide the Prey,
Then their slain Leader to the Camp convey.
With Wonder, as they went, the Troops were fill'd,
To see such Numbers whom so few had kill'd.
605 *Serranus, Rhamnes,* and the rest they found;   ⎫
Vast Crowds the dying and the dead surround: ⎬
And the yet reeking Blood o'reflows the Ground.   ⎭
All knew the Helmet which *Messapus* lost;
But mourn'd a Purchase, that so dear had cost.
610 Now rose the ruddy Morn from *Tithon*'s Bed;
And with the Dawns of Day, the Skies o'respread.
Nor long the Sun his daily Course withheld,
But added Colours to the World reveal'd.
When early *Turnus* wak'ning with the Light,
615 All clad in Armour calls his Troops to fight.
His Martial Men with fierce Harangues he fir'd;
And his own Ardor, in their Souls inspir'd.
This done, to give new Terror to his Foes,
The Heads of *Nisus*, and his Friend he shows,
620 Rais'd high on pointed Spears: A ghastly Sight;
Loud peals of Shouts ensue, and barbarous Delight.
       Mean time the *Trojans* run, where Danger calls,
They line their Trenches, and they man their Walls:
In Front extended to the left they stood:
625 Safe was the right surrounded by the Flood.
But casting from their Tow'rs a frightful view,
They saw the Faces, which too well they knew;
Tho' then disguis'd in Death, and smear'd all o're
With Filth obscene, and dropping putrid Gore.
630 Soon hasty Fame, thro' the sad City bears

The mournful Message to the Mother's Ears:
An icy Cold benums her Limbs: She shakes:
Her Cheeks the Blood, her Hand the Web forsakes.
She runs the Rampires round amidst the War,
635 Nor fears the flying Darts: She rends her Hair,
And fills with loud Laments the liquid Air.
Thus then, my lov'd *Euryalus* appears;
Thus looks the Prop of my declining Years!
Was't on this Face, my famish'd Eyes I fed,
640 Ah how unlike the living, is the dead!
And cou'dst thou leave me, cruel, thus alone,
Not one kind Kiss from a departing Son!
No look, no last adieu before he went,
In an ill-boding Hour to Slaughter sent!
645 Cold on the Ground, and pressing foreign Clay,
To *Latian* Dogs, and Fowls he lies a Prey!
Nor was I near to close his dying Eyes,
To wash his Wounds, to weep his Obsequies:
To call about his Corps his crying Friends,
650 Or spread the Mantle, (made for other ends,)
On his dear Body, which I wove with Care,
Nor did my daily Pains, or nightly labour spare.
Where shall I find his Corps, what Earth sustains
His Trunk dismember'd, and his cold Remains?
655 For this, alas, I left my needful Ease,
Expos'd my Life to Winds, and winter Seas!
If any pity touch *Rutulian* Hearts,
Here empty all your Quivers, all your Darts:
Or if they fail, thou *Jove* conclude my Woe,
660 And send me Thunder-struck to Shades below!
  Her Shrieks and Clamours, pierce the *Trojans* Ears,
Unman their Courage, and augment their Fears:
Nor young *Ascanius* cou'd the sight sustain,
Nor old *Ilioneus* his Tears restrain:
665 But *Actor* and *Idæus*, jointly sent,
To bear the madding Mother to her Tent.
And now the Trumpets terribly from far,
With rattling Clangor, rouze the sleepy War.
The Souldiers Shouts succeed the Brazen Sounds;
670 And Heav'n, from Pole to Pole, the Noise rebounds.

The *Volscians* bear their Shields upon their Head,
And rushing forward, form a moving Shed;
These fill the Ditch, those pull the Bulwarks down:
Some raise the Ladders, others scale the Town.
675 But where void Spaces on the Walls appear,
Or thin Defence, they pour their Forces there.
With Poles and missive Weapons, from afar,
The *Trojans* keep aloof the rising War.
Taught by their ten Years Siege defensive fight;
680 They rowl down Ribs of Rocks, an unresisted Weight:
To break the Penthouse with the pond'rous Blow;
Which yet the patient *Volscians* undergo.
But cou'd not bear th' unequal Combat long;
For where the *Trojans* find the thickest Throng,
685 The Ruin falls: Their shatter'd Shields give way,
And their crush'd Heads become an easie Prey.
They shrink for Fear, abated of their Rage,
Nor longer dare in a blind Fight engage.
Contented now to gaul them from below
690 With Darts and Slings, and with the distant Bow.
    Elsewhere *Mezentius*, terrible to view,
A blazing Pine within the Trenches threw.
But brave *Messapus*, *Neptune*'s warlike Son, ⎫
Broke down the Palisades, the Trenches Won, ⎬
695 And loud for Ladders calls, to scale the Town. ⎭
    Calliope begin: Ye sacred Nine,
Inspire your Poet in his high Design;
To sing what Slaughter manly *Turnus* made:
What Souls he sent below the *Stygian* Shade.
700 What Fame the Souldiers with their Captain share,
And the vast Circuit of the fatal War.
For you in singing Martial Facts excel;
You best remember; and alone can tell.
    There stood a Tow'r, amazing to the sight,
705 Built up of Beams; and of stupendous height;
Art, and the nature of the Place conspir'd,
To furnish all the Strength, that War requir'd.
To level this, the bold *Italians* join;
The wary *Trojans* obviate their design:
710 With weighty Stones o'rewhelm their Troops below,

Shoot through the Loopholes, and sharp Jav'lins throw.
Turnus, the Chief, toss'd from his thund'ring Hand,
Against the wooden Walls, a flaming Brand:
It stuck, the fiery Plague: The Winds were high;
715   The Planks were season'd, and the Timber dry.
Contagion caught the Posts: It spread along,
Scorch'd, and to distance drove the scatter'd Throng.
The *Trojans* fled; the Fire pursu'd amain,
Still gath'ring fast upon the trembling Train;
720   Till crowding to the Corners of the Wall,
Down the Defence, and the Defenders fall.
The mighty flaw makes Heav'n it self resound,
The Dead, and dying *Trojans* strew the Ground.
The Tow'r that follow'd on the fallen Crew,
725   Whelm'd o're their Heads, and bury'd whom it slew:
Some stuck upon the Darts themselves had sent;
All, the same equal Ruin underwent.

     Young *Lycus* and *Helenor* only scape;
Sav'd, how they know not, from the steepy Leap.
730   *Helenor*, elder of the two; by Birth,
On one side Royal, one a Son of Earth,
Whom to the *Lydian* King, *Lycimnia* bare, ⎫
And sent her boasted Bastard to the War: ⎬
(A Priviledge which none but Free-men share.) ⎭
735   Slight were his Arms, a Sword and Silver Shield,
No Marks of Honour charg'd its empty Field.
Light as he fell, so light the Youth arose,
And rising found himself amidst his Foes.
Nor flight was left, nor hopes to force his Way;
740   Embolden'd by Despair, he stood at Bay:
And like a Stag, whom all the Troop surrounds
Of eager Huntsmen, and invading Hounds;
Resolv'd on Death, he dissipates his Fears,
And bounds aloft, against the pointed Spears:
745   So dares the Youth, secure of Death; and throws
His dying Body, on his thickest Foes.

     But *Lycus*, swifter of his Feet, by far,
Runs, doubles, winds and turns, amidst the War:
Springs to the Walls, and leaves his Foes behind,
750   And snatches at the Beam he first can find.

Looks up, and leaps aloft at all the stretch,
In hopes the helping Hand of some kind Friend to reach.
But *Turnus* follow'd hard his hunted Prey,
(His Spear had almost reach'd him in the way,
755   Short of his Reins, and scarce a Span behind,)
Fool, said the Chief, tho' fleeter than the Wind,
Coud'st thou presume to scape, when I pursue?
He said, and downward by the Feet he drew
The trembling Dastard: at the Tug he falls,
760   Vast Ruins come along, rent from the smoking Walls.
Thus on some silver Swan, or tim'rous Hare,
Jove's Bird comes sowsing down, from upper Air;
Her crooked Tallons truss the fearful Prey:
Then out of sight she soars, and wings her way.
765   So seizes the grim Wolf the tender Lamb,
In vain lamented by the bleating Dam.
        Then rushing onward, with a barb'rous cry,
The Troops of *Turnus* to the Combat fly.
The Ditch with Faggots fill'd, the daring Foe
770   Toss'd Firebrands to the steepy Turrets throw.
        Ilioneus, as bold *Lucetius* came
To force the Gate, and feed the kindling Flame,
Rowl'd down the Fragment of a Rock so right;
It crush'd him double underneath the weight.
775   Two more young *Liger* and *Asylas* slew;
To bend the Bow young *Liger* better knew;
Asylas best the pointed Jav'lin threw.
Brave *Cæneus* laid *Ortygius* on the Plain,
The Victor *Cæneus* was by *Turnus* slain.
780   By the same Hand, *Clonius* and *Itys* fall,
Sagar, and *Ida*, standing on the Wall.
From *Capys* Arms his Fate *Privernus* found;
Hurt by *Themilla* first; but slight the Wound;
His Shield thrown by, to mitigate the smart,
785   He clap'd his Hand upon the wounded part:
The second Shaft came swift and unespy'd,
And pierc'd his Hand, and nail'd it to his side:
Transfix'd his breathing Lungs, and beating heart;
The Soul came issuing out, and hiss'd again'st the Dart.
790   The Son of *Arcens* shone amid the rest,
In glitt'ring Armour, and a Purple Vest.

Fair was his Face, his Eyes inspiring Love,
Bred by his Father in the *Martian* Grove;
Where the fat Altars of *Palicus* flame,
795 And sent in Arms to purchase early Fame.
Him, when he spy'd from far the *Thuscan* King,
Laid by the Lance, and took him to the Sling:
Thrice whirl'd the Thong around his head, and threw:
The heated Lead half melted as it flew:
800 It pierc'd his hollow Temples and his Brain;
The Youth came tumbling down, and spurn'd the Plain.
     Then young *Ascanius*, who before this day.
Was wont in Woods to shoot the savage Prey,
First bent in Martial Strife, the twanging Bow;
805 And exercis'd against a Humane Foe.
With this bereft *Numanus* of his life,
Who *Turnus* younger Sister took to Wife.
Proud of his Realm, and of his Royal Bride,
Vaunting before his Troops, and lengthen'd with a
          Stride,
810 In these Insulting terms, the *Trojans* he defy'd.
Twice Conquer'd Cowards, now your shame is shown,
Coop'd up a second time within your Town!
Who dare not issue forth in open Field,
But hold your Walls before you for a Shield:
815 Thus threat you War, thus our Alliance force!
What Gods what madness hether steer'd your Course!
You shall not find the Sons of *Atreus* here,
Nor need the Frauds of sly *Ulysses* fear.
Strong from the Cradle, of a sturdy Brood,
820 We bear our new-born Infants to the Flood;
There bath'd amid the Stream, our Boys we hold,
With Winter harden'd, and inur'd to Cold.
They wake before the Day to range the Wood,
Kill e're they eat, nor tast unconquer'd Food.
825 No Sports, but what belong to War they know,
To break the stubborn Colt, to bend the Bow.
Our youth, of Labour patient, earn their Bread;
Hardly they work, with frugal Diet fed.
From Ploughs and Harrows sent to seek Renown,
830 They fight in Fields, and storm the shaken Town.

No part of Life from Toils of War is free;
No change in Age, or diff'rence in Degree.
We plow, and till in Arms; our Oxen feel,
Instead of Goads, the Spur, and pointed Steel:
835   Th' inverted Lance makes Furrows in the Plain;
Ev'n time that changes all, yet changes us in vain:
The Body, not the Mind: Nor can controul
Th' immortal Vigour, or abate the Soul.
Our Helms defend the Young, disguise the Grey:
840   We live by Plunder, and delight in Prey.
Your Vests embroyder'd with rich Purple shine;
In Sloth you Glory, and in Dances join.
Your Vests have sweeping Sleeves: With female Pride,
Your Turbants underneath your Chins are ty'd.
845   Go, *Phrygians*, to your *Dindymus* agen;
Go, less than Women, in the Shapes of Men.
Go, mix'd with Eunuchs, in the Mother's Rites,
Where with unequal Sound the Flute invites.
Sing, dance, and howl by turns in *Ida*'s Shade;
850   Resign the War to Men, who know the Martial Trade.
    This foul Reproach, *Ascanius* cou'd not hear
With Patience, or a vow'd Revenge forbear.
At the full stretch of both his Hands, he drew,
And almost join'd the Horns of the tough Eugh.
855   But first, before the Throne of *Jove* he stood;
And thus with lifted Hands invok'd the God.
My first Attempt, great *Jupiter* succeed;
An annual Off'ring in thy Grove shall bleed:
A snow-white Steer, before thy Altar led,
860   Who like his Mother bears aloft his Head,
Buts with his threatning Brows, and bellowing stands,
And dares the Fight, and spurns the yellow Sands.
    Jove bow'd the Heav'ns, and lent a gracious Ear,
And thunder'd on the left, amidst the clear.
865   Sounded at once the Bow; and swiftly flies
The feather'd Death, and hisses thro' the Skies.
The Steel thro' both his Temples forc'd the way:
Extended on the Ground, *Numanus* lay.
Go now, vain Boaster, and true Valour scorn;
870   The *Phrygians* twice subdu'd, yet make this third Return.

Ascanius said no more: The *Trojans* shake
The Heav'ns with Shouting, and new Vigour take.
    Apollo then bestrode a Golden Cloud,
To view the feats of Arms, and fighting Crowd;
875 And thus the beardless Victor, he bespoke aloud.
Advance Illustrious Youth, increase in Fame,
And wide from East to West extend thy Name.
Offspring of Gods thy self; and *Rome* shall owe
To thee, a Race of Demigods below.
880 This is the Way to Heav'n: The Pow'rs Divine
From this beginning date the *Julian* Line.
To thee, to them, and their victorious Heirs,
The conquer'd War is due; and the vast World is theirs.
Troy is too narrow for thy Name. He said,
885 And plunging downward shot his radiant Head;
Dispell'd the breathing Air, that broke his Flight,
Shorn of his Beams, a Man to Mortal sight.
Old *Butes* Form he took, *Anchises* Squire,
Now left to rule *Ascanius*, by his Sire:
890 His wrinkled Visage, and his hoary Hairs,
His Meen, his Habit, and his Arms he wears;
And thus salutes the Boy, too forward for his Years.
Suffice it thee, thy Father's worthy Son,
The warlike Prize thou hast already won:
895 The God of Archers gives thy Youth a part
Of his own Praise; nor envies equal Art.
Now tempt the War no more. He said, and flew
Obscure in Air, and vanish'd from their view.
The *Trojans*, by his Arms, their Patron know;
900 And hear the twanging of his Heav'nly Bow.
Then duteous Force they use; and *Phœbus* Name,
To keep from Fight, the Youth too fond of Fame.
Undaunted they themselves no Danger shun:
From Wall to Wall, the Shouts and Clamours run.
905 They bend their Bows; they whirl their Slings around:
Heaps of spent Arrows fall; and strew the Ground;
And Helms, and Shields, and ratling Arms resound.
The Combate thickens, like the Storm that flies
From Westward, when the Show'ry Kids arise:

910   Or patt'ring Hail comes pouring on the Main,
When *Jupiter* descends in harden'd Rain.
Or bellowing Clouds burst with a stormy Sound,
And with an armed Winter strew the Ground.
    Pand'rus and *Bitias*, Thunder-bolts of War,
915   Whom *Hiera*, to bold *Alcanor* bare
On *Ida*'s Top, two Youths of Height and Size,
Like Firrs that on their Mother Mountain rise;
Presuming on their Force, the Gates unbar,
And of their own Accord invite the War.
920   With Fates averse, against their King's Command,
Arm'd on the right, and on the left they stand;
And flank the Passage: Shining Steel they wear,
And waving Crests, above their Heads appear.
Thus two tall Oaks, that *Padus* Banks adorn,
925   Lift up to Heav'n their leafy Heads unshorn;
And overpress'd with Nature's heavy load,
Dance to the whistling Winds, and at each other nod.
In flows a Tyde of *Latians*, when they see
The Gate set open, and the Passage free.
930   Bold *Quercens*, with rash *Tmarus* rushing on,
Equicolus, that in bright Armour shone,
And *Hæmon* first, but soon repuls'd they fly,
Or in the well-defended Pass they dye.
These with Success are fir'd, and those with Rage;
935   And each on equal Terms at length ingage.
Drawn from their Lines, and issuing on the Plain,
The *Trojans* hand to hand the Fight maintain.
    Fierce *Turnus* in another Quarter fought,
When suddenly th' unhop'd for News was brought;
940   The Foes had left the fastness of their Place,
Prevail'd in Fight, and had his Men in Chace.
He quits th' Attack, and, to prevent their Fate,
Runs, where the Gyant Brothers guard the Gate.
The first he met, *Antiphates* the brave,
945   But base begotten on a *Theban* Slave;
Sarpedon's Son he slew: The deadly Dart
Found Passage thro' his Breast, and pierc'd his Heart.
Fix'd in the Wound th' *Italian* Cornel stood;
Warm'd in his Lungs, and in his vital Blood.

950   *Aphidnus* next, and *Erymanthus* dies,
      And *Meropes*, and the Gygantick Size
      Of *Bitias*, threat'ning with his ardent Eyes.
      Not by the feeble Dart he fell oppress'd,
      A Dart were lost, within that roomy Breast;
955   But from a knotted Lance, large, heavy, strong;
      Which roar'd like Thunder as it whirl'd along:
      Not two Bull-hides th' impetuous Force withhold;
      Nor Coat of double Male, with Scales of Gold.
      Down sunk the Monster-Bulk, and press'd the Ground;
960   His Arms and clatt'ring Shield, on the vast Body sound.
      Not with less Ruin, than the *Bajan* Mole,
      (Rais'd on the Seas the Surges to controul,)
      At once comes tumbling down the rocky Wall,
      Prone to the Deep the Stones disjointed fall,
965   Of the vast Pile; the scatter'd Ocean flies;
      Black Sands, discolour'd Froth, and mingled Mud arise.
      The frighted Billows rowl, and seek the Shores:
      Then trembles *Prochyta*, then *Ischia* roars:
      Typhœus thrown beneath, by *Jove*'s Command,
970   Astonish'd at the Flaw, that shakes the Land,
      Soon shifts his weary Side, and scarce awake,
      With Wonder feels the weight press lighter on his Back.
         The Warrior God the *Latian* Troops inspir'd;
      New strung their Sinews, and their Courage fir'd:
975   But chills the *Trojan* Hearts with cold Affright;
      Then black Despair precipitates their Flight.
         When *Pandarus* beheld his Brother kill'd,
      The Town with Fear, and wild Confusion fill'd,
      He turns the Hindges of the Heavy Gate
980   With both his Hands; and adds his Shoulders to the weight.
      Some happier Friends, within the Walls inclos'd;
      The rest shut out, to certain Death expos'd:
      Fool as he was, and frantick in his Care,
      T' admit young *Turnus*, and include the War.
985   He thrust amid the Crowd, securely bold;
      Like a fierce Tyger pent amid the Fold.
      Too late his blazing Buckler they descry;
      And sparkling Fires that shot from either Eye:

His mighty Members, and his ample Breast,
990   His ratt'ling Armour, and his Crimson Crest.
        Far from that hated Face the *Trojans* fly;
All but the Fool who sought his Destiny.
Mad *Pandarus* steps forth, with Vengeance vow'd
For *Bitias*'s Death, and threatens thus aloud.
995   These are not *Ardea*'s Walls, nor this the Town
Amata proffers with *Lavinia*'s Crown:
'Tis hostile Earth you tread; of hope bereft,
No means of safe Return by flight are left.
To whom with Count'nance calm, and Soul sedate,
1000   Thus *Turnus*: Then begin; and try thy Fate:
My Message to the Ghost of *Priam* bear,
Tell him a new *Achilles* sent thee there.
        A Lance of tough ground-Ash the *Trojan* threw,
Rough in the Rind, and knotted as it grew,
1005   With his full force he whirl'd it first around;
But the soft yielding Air receiv'd the wound:
Imperial *Juno* turn'd the Course before;
And fix'd the wand'ring Weapon in the door.
        But hope not thou, said *Turnus*, when I strike,
1010   To shun thy Fate, our Force is not alike:
Nor thy Steel temper'd by the *Lemnian* God:
Then rising, on his utmost stretch he stood:
And aim'd from high: the full descending blow
Cleaves the broad Front, and beardless Cheeks in two:
1015   Down sinks the Giant with a thund'ring sound, ⎫
His pond'rous Limbs oppress the trembling ground; ⎬
Blood, Brains, and Foam, gush from the gaping Wound. ⎭
Scalp, Face, and Shoulders, the keen Steel divides;
And the shar'd Visage hangs on equal sides.
1020   The *Trojans* fly from their approaching Fate:
And had the Victor then secur'd the Gate,
And, to his Troops without, unclos'd the Barrs;
One lucky Day had ended all his Wars.
But boiling Youth, and blind Desire of Blood,
1025   Push'd on his Fury, to pursue the Crowd:
Hamstring'd behind unhappy *Gyges* dy'd;
Then *Phalaris* is added to his side:

The pointed Jav'lins from the dead he drew,
And their Friends Arms against their Fellows threw.
1030 Strong *Halys* stands in vain; weak *Phlegys* flies;
Saturnia, still at hand, new Force and Fire supplies.
Then *Halius*, *Prytanis*, *Alcander* fall;
(Ingag'd against the Foes who scal'd the Wall:)
But whom they fear'd without, they found within:
1035 At last, tho' late, by *Linceus* he was seen.
He calls new Succours, and assaults the Prince,
But weak his Force, and vain is their Defence.
Turn'd to the right, his Sword the Heroe drew;
And at one blow the bold Aggressor slew.
1040 He joints the Neck: And with a stroke so strong
The Helm flies off; and bears the Head along.
Next him, the Huntsman *Amycus* he kill'd,
In Darts, invenom'd, and in Poyson skill'd.
Then *Clytius* fell beneath his fatal Spear,
1045 And *Creteus*, whom the Muses held so dear:
He fought with Courage, and he sung the fight:
Arms were his buis'ness, Verses his delight.
     The *Trojan* Chiefs behold, with Rage and Grief,
Their slaughter'd Friends, and hasten their Relief.
1050 Bold *Mnestheus* rallies first the broken Train,
Whom brave *Seresthus*, and his Troop sustain.
To save the living, and revenge the dead;
Against one Warriour's Arms all *Troy* they led.
O, void of Sense and Courage, *Mnestheus* cry'd,
1055 Where can you hope your Coward Heads to hide?
Ah, where beyond these Rampires can you run!
One Man, and in your Camp inclos'd, you shun!
Shall then a single Sword such Slaughter boast,
And pass unpunish'd from a Num'rous Hoast?
1060 Forsaking Honour, and renouncing Fame,
Your Gods, your Country, and your King you shame.
     This just Reproach their Vertue does excite,
They stand, they joyn, they thicken to the Fight.
     Now *Turnus* doubts, and yet disdains to yield;
1065 But with slow paces measures back the Field.
And Inches to the Walls, where *Tyber*'s Tide,
Washing the Camp, defends the weaker side.

The more he loses, they advance the more;
And tread in ev'ry Step he trod before.
1070 They shout, they bear him back, and whom by Might
They cannot Conquer, they oppress with Weight.

As compass'd with a Wood of Spears around,
The Lordly Lyon, still maintains his Ground;
Grins horrible, retires, and turns again;
1075 Threats his distended Paws, and shakes his Mane;
He loses while in vain he presses on,
Nor will his Courage let him dare to run:
So *Turnus* fares; and unresolv'd of flight,
Moves tardy back, and just recedes from fight.
1080 Yet twice, inrag'd, the Combat he renews;
Twice breaks, and twice his broken Foes pursues:
But now they swarm; and with fresh Troops supply'd,
Come rowling on, and rush from ev'ry side.
Nor *Juno*, who sustain'd his Arms before,
1085 Dares with new strength suffice th' exhausted store.
For *Jove*, with sour Commands, sent *Iris* down,
To force th' Invader from the frighted Town.

With Labour spent, no longer can he wield
The heavy Fauchion, or sustain the Shield:
1090 O'rewhelmed with Darts, which from afar they fling,
The Weapons round his hollow Temples ring:
His golden Helm gives way: with stony blows
Batter'd, and flat, and beaten to his Brows.
His Crest is rash'd away; his ample Shield
1095 Is falsify'd, and round with Jav'lins fill'd.

The Foe now faint, the *Trojans* overwhelm:
And *Mnestheus* lays hard load upon his Helm.
Sick sweat succeeds, he drops at ev'ry pore,
With driving Dust his Cheeks are pasted o're.
1100 Shorter and shorter ev'ry Gasp he takes,
And vain Efforts, and hurtless Blows he makes.
Arm'd as he was, at length, he leap'd from high;
Plung'd in the Flood, and made the Waters fly.
The yellow God, the welcome Burthen bore,
1105 And wip'd the Sweat, and wash'd away the Gore:
Then gently wafts him to the farther Coast;
And sends him safe to chear his anxious Hoast.

THE TENTH BOOK OF THE ÆNEIS

The Argument

Jupiter *calling a Council of the Gods, forbids them to engage in either Party. At* Æneas's *return there is a bloody Battel:* Turnus *killing* Pallas; Æneas, Lausus *and* Mezentius. Mezentius *is describ'd as an Atheist;* Lausus *as a pious and virtuous Youth: The different Actions and Death of these two, are the Subject of a Noble Episode.*

THE TENTH BOOK OF THE ÆNEIS

The Argument

The Gates of Heav'n unfold; *Jove* summons all
The Gods to Council, in the Common Hall.
Sublimely seated, he surveys from far
The Fields, the Camp, the Fortune of the War;
5   And all th' inferior World: From first to last
The Sov'raign Senate in Degrees are plac'd.
     Then thus th' Almighty Sire began. Ye Gods,
Natives, or Denizons, of blest Abodes;
From whence these Murmurs, and this change of Mind,
10 This backward Fate from what was first design'd?
Why this protracted War? When my Commands
Pronounc'd a Peace, and gave the *Latian* Lands.
What Fear or Hope on either part divides
Our Heav'ns, and arms our Pow'rs on diff'rent sides?
15 A lawful Time of War at length will come,
(Nor need your haste anticipate the Doom,)
When *Carthage* shall contend the World with *Rome*:
Shall force the rigid Rocks, and *Alpine* Chains;
And like a Flood come pouring on the Plains.
20 Then is your time for Faction and Debate,
For partial Favour, and permitted Hate.
Let now your immature Dissention cease;
Sit quiet, and compose your Souls to Peace.
     Thus *Jupiter* in few unfolds the Charge:
25 But lovely *Venus* thus replies at large.
O Pow'r immense, Eternal Energy!
(For to what else Protection can we fly,)
Seest thou the proud *Rutulians*, how they dare
In Fields, unpunish'd, and insult my Care?
30 How lofty *Turnus* vaunts amidst his Train,
In shining Arms, triumphant on the Plain?
Ev'n in their Lines and Trenches they contend;
And scarce their Walls the *Trojan* Troops defend:

The Town is fill'd with Slaughter, and o'refloats,
35   With a red Deluge, their increasing Moats.
Æneas ignorant, and far from thence,
Has left a Camp expos'd, without Defence.
This endless outrage shall they still sustain?
Shall *Troy* renew'd be forc'd, and fir'd again?
40   A second Siege my banish'd Issue fears,
And a new *Diomede* in Arms appears.
One more audacious Mortal will be found;
And I thy Daughter wait another Wound.
Yet, if with Fates averse, without thy Leave,
45   The *Latian* Lands my Progeny receive;
Bear they the Pains of violated Law,
And thy Protection from their Aid withdraw.
But if the Gods their sure Success fortel,
If those of Heav'n consent with those of Hell,
50   To promise *Italy*; who dare debate
The Pow'r of *Jove*, or fix another Fate?
What shou'd I tell of Tempests on the Main,
Of *Eolus* usurping *Neptune*'s Reign?
Of *Iris* sent; with *Bachanalian* Heat,
55   T' inspire the Matrons, and destroy the Fleet.
Now *Juno* to the *Stygian* Sky descends,
Sollicites Hell for Aid, and arms the Fiends.
That new Example wanted yet above:
An Act that well became the Wife of *Jove*.
60   *Alecto*, rais'd by her, with Rage inflames
The peaceful Bosoms of the *Latian* Dames.
Imperial Sway no more exalts my Mind:
(Such hopes I had indeed, while Heav'n was kind)
Now let my happier Foes possess my place,
65   Whom *Jove* prefers before the *Trojan* Race; }
And conquer they, whom you with Conquest grace. }
Since you can spare, from all your wide Command,
No spot of Earth, no hospitable Land,
Which may my wand'ring Fugitives receive;
70   (Since haughty *Juno* will not give you leave)
Then, Father, (if I still may use that Name)
By ruin'd *Troy*, yet smoking from the Flame,

I beg you let *Ascanius*, by my Care,
Be freed from Danger, and dismiss'd the War:
75 Inglorious let him live, without a Crown; ⎫
The Father may be cast on Coasts unknown, ⎬
Strugling with Fate; but let me save the Son. ⎭
Mine is *Cythera*, mine the *Cyprian* Tow'rs;
In those Recesses, and those sacred Bow'rs,
80 Obscurely let him rest; his Right resign
To promis'd Empire, and his *Julian* Line.
Then *Carthage* may th' *Ausonian* Towns destroy,
Nor fear the Race of a rejected Boy.
What profits it my Son, to scape the Fire,
85 Arm'd with his Gods, and loaded with his Sire;
To pass the Perils of the Seas and Wind,
Evade the *Greeks*, and leave the War behind;
To reach th' *Italian* Shores: If after all,
Our second *Pergamus* is doom'd to fall?
90 Much better had he curb'd his high Desires,
And hover'd o're his ill extinguish'd Fires.
To *Simois* Banks the Fugitives restore,
And give them back to War, and all the Woes before.
    Deep indignation swell'd *Saturnia*'s Heart:
95 And must I own, she said, my secret Smart?
What with more decence were in silence kept,
And but for this unjust Reproach had slept?
Did God, or Man, your Fav'rite Son advise,
With War unhop'd the *Latians* to surprise?
100 By Fate you boast, and by the Gods Decree,
He left his Native Land for *Italy*:
Confess the Truth; by mad *Cassandra*, more
Than Heav'n inspir'd, he sought a foreign Shore!
Did I perswade to trust his second *Troy*,
105 To the raw Conduct of a beardless Boy?
With Walls unfinish'd, which himself forsakes,
And thro' the Waves a wand'ring Voyage takes?
When have I urg'd him meanly to demand
The *Tuscan* Aid, and arm a quiet Land?
110 Did I or *Iris* give this mad Advice,
Or made the Fool himself the fatal Choice?

You think it hard, the *Latians* shou'd destroy
With Swords your *Trojans*, and with Fires your *Troy*:
Hard and unjust indeed, for Men to draw
115   Their Native Air, nor take a foreign Law:
That *Turnus* is permitted still to live,
To whom his Birth a God and Goddess give:
But yet 'tis just and lawful for your Line,
To drive their Fields, and Force with Fraud to join.
120   Realms, not your own, among your Clans divide,
And from the Bridegroom tear the promis'd Bride:
Petition, while you publick Arms prepare;
Pretend a Peace, and yet provoke a War.
'Twas giv'n to you, your darling Son to shrowd, ⎫
125   To draw the Dastard from the fighting Crowd; ⎬
And for a Man obtend an empty Cloud. ⎭
From flaming Fleets you turn'd the Fire away,
And chang'd the Ships to Daughters of the Sea.
But 'tis my Crime, the Queen of Heav'n offends,
130   If she presume to save her suff'ring Friends.
Your Son, not knowing what his Foes decree,
You say is absent: Absent let him be.
Yours is *Cythera*, yours the *Cyprian* Tow'rs,
The soft Recesses, and the Sacred Bow'rs.
135   Why do you then these needless Arms prepare,
And thus provoke a People prone to War?
Did I with Fire the *Trojan* Town deface,
Or hinder from return your exil'd Race?
Was I the Cause of Mischief or the Man,
140   Whose lawless Lust the fatal War began?
Think on whose Faith th' Adult'rous Youth rely'd;
Who promis'd, who procur'd the *Spartan* Bride?
When all th' united States of *Greece* combin'd,
To purge the World of the perfidious Kind;
145   Then was your time to fear the *Trojan* Fate:
Your Quarrels and Complaints are now too late.
    Thus *Juno*. Murmers rise, with mix'd Applause;
Just as they favour, or dislike the Cause:
So Winds, when yet unfledg'd in Woods they lie,
150   In whispers first their tender Voices try:

Then issue on the Main with bellowing rage,
And Storms to trembling Mariners presage.
  Then thus to both reply'd th' Imperial God,
Who shakes Heav'ns Axels with his awful Nod.
155 (When he begins, the silent Senate stand
With Rev'rence, list'ning to the dread Command:
The Clouds dispel; the Winds their Breath restrain;
And the hush'd Waves lie flatted on the Main.)
  Cœlestials! Your attentive Ears incline;
160 Since, said the God, the *Trojans* must not join ⎞
In wish'd Alliance with the *Latian* Line,   ⎠
Since endless jarrings, and immortal Hate, ⎞
Tend but to discompose our happy State;   ⎬
The War henceforward be resign'd to Fate.   ⎠
165 Each to his proper Fortune stand or fall,
Equal and unconcern'd I look on all.
Rutulians, *Trojans*, are the same to me;
And both shall draw the Lots their Fates decree.
Let these assault; if Fortune be their Friend;
170 And if she favours those, let those defend:
The Fates will find their way. The Thunderer said;
And shook the sacred Honours of his Head;
Attesting *Styx*, th' Inviolable Flood,   ⎞
And the black Regions of his Brother God   ⎬
175 Trembled the Poles of Heav'n; and Earth confess'd the ⎠
        Nod.
This end the Sessions had: The Senate rise,
And to his Palace wait their Sov'raign thro' the Skies.
  Mean time, intent upon their Siege, the Foes
Within their Walls the *Trojan* Hoast inclose:
180 They wound, they kill, they watch at ev'ry Gate:
Renew the Fires, and urge their happy Fate.
  Th' *Ænean* wish in vain their wanted Chief,
Hopeless of flight, more hopeless of Relief:
Thin on the Tow'rs they stand; and ev'n those few,
185 A feeble, fainting, and dejected Crew:
Yet in the face of Danger some there stood:
The two bold Brothers of *Sarpedon*'s Blood,
Asius, and *Acmon*: both th' *Assaraci*;
Young *Hæmon*, and tho' young, resolv'd to dye.

190   With these were *Clarus* and *Thymetes* join'd;
       Tibris and *Castor*, both of *Lycian* Kind.
       From *Acmon*'s Hands a rowling Stone there came,
       So large, it half deserv'd a Mountain's Name:
       Strong sinew'd was the Youth, and big of Bone, ⎫
195   His Brother *Mnestheus* cou'd not more have done: ⎬
       Or the great Father of th' intrepid Son. ⎭
       Some Firebrands throw, some flights of Arrows send;
       And some with Darts, and some with Stones defend.
           Amid the Press appears the beauteous Boy,
200   The Care of *Venus*, and the Hope of *Troy*.
       His lovely Face unarm'd, his Head was bare,
       In ringlets o're his Shoulders hung his Hair.
       His forehead circled with a Diadem;
       Distinguish'd from the Crow'd he shines a Gem,
205   Enchas'd in Gold, or Polish'd Iv'ry set,
       Amidst the meaner foil of sable Jett.
           Nor *Ismarus* was wanting to the War,
       Directing Ointed Arrows from afar;
       And Death with Poyson arm'd: In *Lydia* born,
210   Where plenteous Harvests the fat Fields adorn:
       Where proud *Pactolus* floats the fruitful Lands,
       And leaves a rich manure of Golden Sands.
       There *Capys*, Author of the *Capuan* Name: ⎫
       And there was *Mnestheus* too increas'd in Fame: ⎬
215   Since *Turnus* from the Camp He cast with shame. ⎭
           Thus Mortal War was wag'd on either side,
       Mean time the Heroe cuts the Nightly Tyde.
       For, anxious, from *Evander* when he went,
       He sought the *Tyrrhene* Camp, and *Tarchon*'s Tent;
220   Expos'd the Cause of coming to the Chief;
       His Name, and Country told, and ask'd Relief:
       Propos'd the Terms; his own small strength declar'd,
       What Vengeance proud *Mezentius* had prepar'd:
       What *Turnus*, bold and violent, design'd;
225   Then shew'd the slipp'ry state of Humane-kind,
       And fickle Fortune; warn'd him to beware:
       And to his wholsom Counsel added Pray'r.
       Tarchon, without delay, the Treaty signs;
       And to the *Trojan* Troops the *Tuscan* joins.

230   They soon set sail; nor now the Fates withstand;
        Their Forces trusted with a Foreign Hand.
        Æneas leads; upon his Stern appear
        Two Lyons carv'd, which rising *Ida* bear: }
        Ida, to wand'ring *Trojans* ever dear.
235   Under their grateful Shade *Æneas* sate,
        Revolving Wars Events, and various Fate.
        His left young *Pallas* kept, fix'd to his side,
        And oft of Winds enquir'd, and of the Tyde:
        Oft of the Stars, and of their wat'ry Way;
240   And what he suffer'd both by Land and Sea.
            Now sacred Sisters open all your Spring,
        The *Tuscan* Leaders, and their Army sing;
        Which follow'd great *Æneas* to the War:
        Their Arms, their Numbers, and their Names declare.
245   A thousand Youths brave *Massicus* obey,
        Born in the *Tyger*, thro' the foaming Sea;
        From *Asium* brought, and *Cosa*, by his Care;
        For Arms, light Quivers, Bows, and Shafts they bear.
        Fierce *Abas* next, his Men bright Armour wore;
250   His Stern, *Apollo*'s Golden Statue bore.
        Six hundred *Populonea* sent along,
        All skill'd in Martial Exercise, and strong.
        Three hundred more for Battel *Ilva* joins,
        An Isle renown'd for Steel, and unexhausted Mines.
255   *Asylas* on his Prow the third appears,
        Who Heav'n interprets, and the wand'ring Stars:
        From offer'd Entrails Prodigies expounds,
        And Peals of Thunder, with presaging Sounds.
        A thousand Spears in warlike Order stand,
260   Sent by the *Pisans* under his Command.
            Fair *Astur* follows in the wat'ry Field,
        Proud of his manag'd Horse, and painted Shield.
        Gravisca noisom from the neighb'ring Fen,
        And his own *Cære* sent three hundred Men:
265   With those which *Minio*'s Fields, and *Pyrgi* gave;
        All bred in Arms, unanimous and brave.
            Thou Muse the Name of *Cyniras* renew,
        And brave *Cupavo* follow'd but by few:

Whose Helm confess'd the Lineage of the Man,
270 And bore, with Wings display'd, a silver Swan.
Love was the fault of his fam'd Ancestry,
Whose Forms, and Fortunes in his Ensigns fly.
For *Cycnus* lov'd unhappy *Phaeton,*
And sung his Loss in Poplar Groves, alone;
275 Beneath the Sister shades to sooth his Grief;
Heav'n heard his Song, and hasten'd his Relief:
And chang'd to snowy Plumes his hoary Hair,
And wing'd his Flight, to chant aloft in Air.
His Son *Cupavo* brush'd the briny Flood;
280 Upon his Stern a brawny *Centaur* stood,
Who heav'd a Rock, and threat'ning still to throw,
With lifted Hands, alarm'd the Seas below:
They seem'd to fear the formidable Sight,
And rowl'd their Billows on, to speed his Flight.
285   *Ocnus* was next, who led his Native Train,
Of hardy Warriors, thro' the wat'ry Plain.
The Son of *Manto,* by the *Tuscan* Stream,
From whence the *Mantuan* Town derives the Name.
An ancient City, but of mix'd Descent,
290 Three sev'ral Tribes compose the Government:
Four Towns are under each; but all obey
The *Mantuan* Laws, and own the *Tuscan* Sway.
    Hate to *Mezentius,* arm'd five hundred more,
Whom *Mincius* from his Sire *Benacus* bore;
295 (*Mincius* with Wreaths of Reeds his forehead cover'd
        o're.)
These grave *Auletes* leads. A hundred sweep,
With stretching Oars at once the glassy deep:
Him, and his Martial Train, the *Triton* bears,
High on his Poop the Sea-green God appears:
300 Frowning he seems his crooked Shell to sound,
And at the Blast the Billows dance around.
A hairy Man above the Waste he shows,
A *Porpoise* Tail beneath his Belly grows;
And ends a Fish: His Breast the Waves divides,
305 And Froth and Foam augment the murm'ring Tides.
    Full thirty Ships transport the chosen Train,
For *Troy*'s Relief, and scour the briny Main.

Now was the World forsaken by the Sun,
And *Phœbe* half her nightly Race had run.
310 The careful Chief, who never clos'd his Eyes,
Himself the Rudder holds, the Sails supplies.
A Choir of *Nereids* meet him on the Flood,
Once his own Gallies, hewn from *Ida*'s Wood:
But now as many Nymphs the Sea they sweep,
315 As rode before tall Vessels on the Deep.
They know him from afar; and, in a Ring,
Inclose the Ship that bore the *Trojan* King.
Cymodoce, whose Voice excell'd the rest,
Above the Waves advanc'd her snowy Breast,
320 Her right Hand stops the Stern, her left divides
The curling Ocean, and corrects the Tides:
She spoke for all the Choir; and thus began,
With pleasing Words to warn th' unknowing Man.
Sleeps our lov'd Lord? O Goddess-born! awake,
325 Spread ev'ry Sail, pursue your wat'ry Track;
And haste your Course. Your Navy once were we,
From *Ida*'s Height descending to the Sea:
'Till *Turnus*, as at Anchor fix'd we stood,
Presum'd to violate our holy Wood.
330 Then loos'd from Shore we fled his Fires prophane; ⎫
(Unwillingly we broke our Master's Chain)   ⎬
And since have sought you thro' the *Tuscan* Main. ⎭
The mighty Mother chang'd our Forms to these,
And gave us Life Immortal in the Seas.
335 But young *Ascanius*, in his Camp distress'd,
By your insulting Foes is hardly press'd.
Th' *Arcadian* Horsemen, and *Etrurian* Hoast
Advance in order on the *Latian* Coast:
To cut their way the *Daunian* Chief designs,
340 Before their Troops can reach the *Trojan* Lines.
Thou, when the rosie Morn restores the Light,
First arm thy Souldiers for th' ensuing Fight:
Thy self the fated Sword of *Vulcan* wield,
And bear aloft th' impenetrable Shield.
345 To Morrow's Sun, unless my Skill be vain,
Shall see huge heaps of Foes in Battel slain.

Parting, she spoke; and with Immortal Force,
Push'd on the Vessel in her wat'ry Course:
(For well she knew the Way) impell'd behind,
350   The Ship flew forward, and outstrip'd the Wind.
The rest make up: Unknowing of the cause
The Chief admires their Speed, and happy Omens draws.
    Then thus he pray'd, and fix'd on Heav'n his Eyes;
Hear thou, great Mother of the Deities!
355   With Turrets crown'd, (on *Ida*'s holy Hill,
Fierce Tygers, rein'd and curb'd, obey thy Will.)
Firm thy own Omens, lead us on to fight,
And let thy *Phrygians* conquer in thy right.
    He said no more. And now renewing Day
360   Had chas'd the Shadows of the Night away.
He charg'd the Souldiers with preventing Care,
Their Flags to follow, and their Arms prepare;   ⎫
Warn'd of th' ensuing Fight, and bad 'em hope the War. ⎬
    Now, from his lofty Poop, he view'd below   ⎭
365   His Camp incompass'd, and th' inclosing Foe.
His blazing Shield imbrac'd, he held on high;
The Camp receive the sign, and with loud Shouts reply.
Hope arms their Courage: From their Tow'rs they throw
Their Darts with double Force, and drive the Foe.
370   Thus, at the signal giv'n, the Cranes arise
Before the stormy South, and blacken all the Skies.
    King *Turnus* wonder'd at the Fight renew'd;
'Till, looking back, the *Trojan* Fleet he view'd:
The Seas with swelling Canvass cover'd o're;
375   And the swift Ships descending on the Shore.
The *Latians* saw from far, with dazl'd Eyes,
The radiant Crest that seem'd in Flames to rise,
And dart diffusive Fires around the Field;
And the keen glitt'ring of the Golden Shield.
380   Thus threatning Comets, when by Night they rise,
Shoot sanguine Streams, and sadden all the Skies:
So *Sirius*, flashing forth sinister Lights,
Pale humane kind with Plagues, and with dry Famine frights.
Yet *Turnus*, with undaunted Mind is bent
385   To man the Shores, and hinder their Descent:

And thus awakes the Courage of his Friends.
What you so long have wish'd, kind Fortune sends:
In ardent Arms to meet th' invading Foe:
You find, and find him at Advantage now.
390 Yours is the Day, you need but only dare:
Your Swords will make you Masters of the War.
Your Sires, your Sons, your Houses, and your Lands,
And dearest Wifes, are all within your Hands.
Be mindful of the Race from whence you came;
395 And emulate in Arms your Fathers Fame.
Now take the Time, while stagg'ring yet they stand
With Feet unfirm; and prepossess the Strand:
Fortune befriends the bold. Nor more he said,
But ballanc'd whom to leave, and whom to lead:
400 Then these elects, the Landing to prevent;
And those he leaves to keep the City pent.
    Mean time the *Trojan* sends his Troops ashore:
Some are by Boats expos'd, by Bridges more.
With lab'ring Oars they bear along the Strand,
405 Where the Tide languishes, and leap a-land.
Tarchon observes the Coast with careful Eyes,
And where no Foord he finds, no Water fryes,
Nor Billows with unequal Murmurs roar;
But smoothly slide along, and swell the Shoar;
410 That Course he steer'd, and thus he gave command,
Here ply your Oars, and at all hazard land:
Force on the Vessel that her Keel may wound
This hated Soil, and furrow hostile Ground.
Let me securely land, I ask no more,
415 Then sink my Ships, or shatter on the Shore.
    This fiery Speech inflames his fearful Friends,
They tug at ev'ry Oar; and ev'ry Stretcher bends:
They run their Ships aground, the Vessels knock,
(Thus forc'd ashore) and tremble with the shock.
420 *Tarchon*'s alone was lost, that stranded stood,
Stuck on a Bank, and beaten by the Flood.
She breaks her Back, the loosen'd Sides give way,
And plunge the *Tuscan* Souldiers in the Sea.
Their broken Oars, and floating Planks withstand ⎤
425 Their Passage, while they labour to the Land;   ⎬
And ebbing Tides bear back upon th' uncertain Sand. ⎦

Now *Turnus* leads his Troops, without delay,
Advancing to the Margin of the Sea.
The Trumpets sound: *Æneas* first assail'd
430 The Clowns new rais'd and raw; and soon prevail'd.
Great *Theron* fell, an Omen of the Fight:
Great *Theron* large of Limbs, of Gyant height.
He first in open Field defy'd the Prince,
But Armour scal'd with Gold was no Defence
435 Against the fated Sword, which open'd wide
His plated Shield, and pierc'd his naked side.
    Next, *Lycas* fell; who, not like others born,
Was from his wretched Mother rip'd and torn:
Sacred, O *Phœbus*! from his Birth to thee,
440 For his beginning Life from biting Steel was free.
Not far from him was *Gyas* laid along,
Of monst'rous Bulk; with *Cisseus* fierce and strong:
Vain Bulk and Strength; for when the Chief assail'd,
Nor Valour, nor *Herculean* Arms avail'd;
445 Nor their fam'd Father, wont in War to go
With great *Alcides*, while he toil'd below.
The noisie *Pharos* next receiv'd his Death,
Æneas writh'd his Dart, and stopp'd his bawling Breath.
Then wretched *Cydon* had receiv'd his Doom,
450 Who courted *Clytius* in his beardless Bloom,
And sought with lust obscene polluted Joys:
The *Trojan* Sword had cur'd his love of Boys,
Had not his sev'n bold Brethren stop'd the Course
Of the fierce Champion, with united Force.
455 Sev'n Darts were thrown at once, and some rebound
From his bright Shield, some on his Helmet sound:
The rest had reach'd him, but his Mother's Care
Prevented those, and turn'd aside in Air.
    The Prince then call'd *Achates*, to supply
460 The Spears, that knew the way to Victory.
Those fatal Weapons, which inur'd to Blood,
In *Grecian* Bodies under *Ilium* stood:
Not one of those my Hand shall toss in vain
Against our Foes, on this contended Plain.
465 He said: Then seiz'd a mighty Spear, and threw;
Which, wing'd with Fate, thro' *Mæon*'s Buckler flew:

Pierc'd all the brazen Plates, and reach'd his Heart:
He stagger'd with intolerable Smart.
Alcanor saw; and reach'd, but reach'd in vain,
470   His helping Hand, his Brother to sustain.
A second Spear, which kept the former Course,
From the same Hand, and sent with equal Force,
His right Arm pierc'd, and holding on, bereft
His use of both, and pinion'd down his left.
475   Then *Numitor*, from his dead Brother drew
Th' ill-omend Spear, and at the *Trojan* threw:
Preventing Fate directs the Lance awry,
Which glancing, only mark'd *Achates* Thigh.

      In Pride of Youth the *Sabine Clausus* came,
480   And from afar, at *Driops* took his Aim.
The Spear flew hissing thro' the middle Space,
And pierc'd his Throat, directed at his Face:
It stop'd at once the Passage of his Wind,
And the free Soul to flitting Air resign'd:
485   His Forehead was the first that struck the Ground;
Life-blood, and Life rush'd mingl'd thro' the Wound.
He slew three Brothers of the *Borean* Race,   ⎫
And three, whom *Ismarus*, their Native Place,   ⎬
Had sent to War, but all the Sons of *Thrace*.   ⎭
490   *Halesus* next, the bold *Aurunci* leads;
The Son of *Neptune* to his Aid succeeds,
Conspicuous on his Horse: On either Hand
These fight to keep, and those to win the Land.
With mutual Blood th' *Ausonian* Soil is dy'd,
495   While on its Borders each their Claim decide.
      As wint'ry Winds contending in the Sky,
With equal force of Lungs their Titles try,
They rage, they roar; the doubtful rack of Heav'n
Stands without Motion, and the Tyde undriv'n:
500   Each bent to conquer, neither side to yield;
They long suspend the Fortune of the Field.
Both Armies thus perform what Courage can;
Foot set to Foot, and mingled Man to Man.
      But in another part, th' *Arcadian* Horse,
505   With ill Success ingage the *Latin* Force.

For where th' impetuous Torrent rushing down,
Huge craggy Stones, and rooted Trees had thrown:
They left their Coursers, and unus'd to Fight
On Foot, were scatter'd in a shameful flight.
510   *Pallas*, who with Disdain and Grief, had view'd
His Foes pursuing, and his Friends pursu'd;
Us'd Threatnings mix'd with Pray'rs, his last Ressource;
With these to move their Mind, with those to fire their
          Force.
Which way, Companions! Whether wou'd you run?
515   By you your selves, and mighty Battels won;
By my great Sire, by his establish'd Name,
And early promise of my Future Fame;
By my Youth emulous of equal Right,
To share his Honours, shun ignoble Flight.
520   Trust not your Feet, your Hands must hew your way
Thro' yon black Body, and that thick Array:
'Tis thro' that forward Path that we must come:
There lies our Way, and that our Passage home.
Nor Pow'rs above, nor Destinies below,
525   Oppress our Arms; with equal Strength we go; }
With Mortal Hands to meet a Mortal Foe.
See on what Foot we stand: A scanty Shore;
The Sea behind, our Enemies before:
No Passage left, unless we swim the Main;
530   Or forcing these, the *Trojan* Trenches gain.
This said, he strode with eager haste along,
And bore amidst the thickest of the Throng.
Lagus, the first he met, with Fate to Foe,
Had heav'd a Stone of mighty weight to throw:
535   Stooping, the Spear descended on his Chine,
Just where the Bone distinguish'd either Loin:
It stuck so fast, so deeply bury'd lay,
That scarce the Victor forc'd the Steel away.
          Hisbon came on, but while he mov'd too slow
540   To wish'd Revenge, the Prince prevents his Blow:
For warding his at once, at once he press'd;
And plung'd the fatal Weapon in his Breast.
Then leud *Anchemolus* he laid in Dust,
Who stain'd his Stepdam's Bed with impious Lust.

545 And after him the *Daucian* Twins were slain,
     Laris and *Thimbrus*, on the *Latian* Plain:
     So wond'rous like in Feature, Shape, and Size,
     As caus'd an Error in their Parents Eyes.
     Grateful Mistake! but soon the Sword decides
550 The nice Distinction, and their Fate divides.
     For *Thimbrus* Head was lop'd: and *Laris* Hand
     Dismember'd, sought its Owner on the Strand:
     The trembling Fingers yet the Fauchion strain,
     And threaten still th' intended Stroke in vain.

555   Now, to renew the Charge, th' *Arcadians* came: ⎫
     Sight of such Acts, and sense of honest Shame, ⎬
     And Grief, with Anger mix'd, their Minds inflame. ⎭
     Then, with a casual Blow was *Rhæteus* slain,
     Who chanc'd, as *Pallas* threw, to cross the Plain:
560 The flying Spear was after *Ilus* sent,
     But *Rhæteus* happen'd on a Death unmeant:
     From *Teuthras*, and from *Tyres* while he fled,
     The Lance, athwart his Body, laid him dead:
     Rowl'd from his Chariot with a Mortal Wound,
565 And intercepted Fate, he spurn'd the Ground.
         As, when in Summer, welcome Winds arise,
     The watchful Shepherd to the Forest flies,
     And fires the midmost Plants; Contagion spreads,
     And catching Flames infect the neighb'ring Heads;
570 Around the Forest flies the furious Blast, ⎫
     And all the leafie Nation sinks at last; ⎬
     And *Vulcan* rides in Triumph o're the Wast; ⎭
     The Pastor pleas'd with his dire Victory,
     Beholds the satiate Flames in Sheets ascend the Sky:
575 So *Pallas*'s Troops their scatter'd Strength unite;
     And pouring on their Foes, their Prince delight.
         Halesus came, fierce with desire of Blood,
     (But first collected in his Arms he stood)
     Advancing then, he ply'd the Spear so well,
580 *Ladon*, *Demodocus*, and *Pheres* fell:
     Around his Head he toss'd his glitt'ring Brand,
     And from *Strimonius* hew'd his better Hand,
     Held up to guard his Throat: Then hurl'd a Stone
     At *Thoas* ample Front, and pierc'd the Bone:

585   It struck beneath the space of either Eye,
       And Blood, and mingled Brains, together fly.
       Deep skill'd in future Fates, *Halesus* Sire,
       Did with the Youth to lonely Groves retire:
       But when the Father's Mortal Race was run,
590   Dire Destiny laid hold upon the Son,
       And haul'd him to the War: to find beneath
       Th' *Evandrian* Spear, a memorable Death.
           Pallas th' Encounter seeks, but e're he throws,
       To *Tuscan Tyber* thus address'd his Vows:
595   O sacred Stream direct my flying Dart;
       And give to pass the proud *Halesus* Heart:
       His Arms and Spoils thy holy Oak shall bear:
       Pleas'd with the Bribe, the God receiv'd his Pray'r.
       For while his Shield protects a Friend distress'd,
600   The Dart came driving on, and pierc'd his Breast.
           But *Lausus*, no small portion of the War,
       Permits not Panick Fear to reign too far,
       Caus'd by the Death of so renown'd a Knight;
       But by his own Example chears the Fight.
605   Fierce *Abas* first he slew, *Abas*, the stay
       Of *Trojan* Hopes, and hind'rance of the Day.
       The *Phrygian* Troops escap'd the *Greeks* in vain,
       They, and their mix'd Allies, now load the Plain.
           To the rude shock of War both Armies came,
610   Their Leaders equal, and their Strength the same.
       The Rear so press'd the Front, they cou'd not wield
       Their angry Weapons, to dispute the Field.
       Here *Pallas* urges on, and *Lausus* there,
       Of equal Youth and Beauty both appear,   ⎫
615   But both by Fate forbid to breath their Native Air. ⎬
       Their Congress in the Field great *Jove* withstands, ⎭
       Both doom'd to fall, but fall by greater Hands.
           Mean time *Juturna* warns the *Daunian* Chief
       Of *Lausus* Danger, urging swift Relief.
620   With his driv'n Chariot he divides the Crowd,
       And making to his Friends, thus calls aloud:
       Let none presume his needless Aid to join;
       Retire, and clear the Field, the Fight is mine:

To this right Hand is *Pallas* only due:
625   Oh were his Father here my just Revenge to view!
From the forbidden Space his Men retir'd;
Pallas, their Awe, and his stern Words admir'd:
Survey'd him o're and o're with wond'ring sight,
Struck with his haughty Meen, and tow'ring Height.
630   Then to the King; your empty Vaunts forbear:
Success I hope, and Fate I cannot fear.
Alive or dead, I shall deserve a Name:
Jove is impartial, and to both the same.
He said, and to the void advanc'd his Pace;
635   Pale Horror sate on each *Arcadian* Face.
Then *Turnus*, from his Chariot leaping light,
Address'd himself on Foot to single Fight.
And, as a Lyon, when he spies from far
A Bull, that seems to meditate the War;
640   Bending his Neck, and spurning back the Sand,
Runs roaring downward from his hilly Stand:
Imagine eager *Turnus* not more slow,
To rush from high on his unequal Foe.
      Young *Pallas*, when he saw the Chief advance
645   Within due distance of his flying Lance;
Prepares to charge him first: Resolv'd to try
If Fortune wou'd his want of Force supply.
And thus to Heav'n and *Hercules* address'd.
Alcides, once on Earth *Evander*'s Guest,
650   His Son adjures you by those Holy Rites,
That hospitable Board, those Genial Nights;
Assist my great Attempt to gain this Prize,
And let proud *Turnus* view, with dying Eyes,
His ravish'd Spoils. 'Twas heard, the vain Request;
655   *Alcides* mourn'd: And stifled Sighs within his Breast.
Then *Jove*, to sooth his Sorrow, thus began:
Short bounds of Life are set to Mortal Man,   ⎫
'Tis Vertues work alone to stretch the narrow Span. ⎬
So many Sons of Gods in bloody Fight,   ⎭
660   Around the Walls of *Troy*, have lost the Light:
My own *Sarpedon* fell beneath his Foe,
Nor I, his mighty Sire, cou'd ward the Blow.

Ev'n *Turnus* shortly shall resign his Breath;
And stands already on the Verge of Death.
665 This said, the God permits the fatal Fight,
But from the *Latian* Fields averts his sight.
   Now with full Force his Spear young *Pallas* threw;
And having thrown, his shining Fauchion drew:
The Steel just graz'd along the Shoulder Joint,
670 And mark'd it slightly with the glancing Point.
Fierce *Turnus* first to nearer distance drew,
And poiz'd his pointed Spear before he threw:
Then, as the winged Weapon whiz'd along;
See now, said he, whose Arm is better strung.
675 The Spear kept on the fatal Course, unstay'd
By Plates of Ir'n, which o're the Shield were laid:
Thro' folded Brass, and tough Bull-hides it pass'd,
His Corslet pierc'd, and reach'd his Heart at last.
In vain the Youth tugs at the broken Wood,
680 The Soul comes issuing with the vital Blood:
He falls; his Arms upon his Body sound;
And with his bloody Teeth he bites the Ground.
   Turnus bestrode the Corps: *Arcadians* hear,
Said he; my Message to your Master bear:
685 Such as the Sire deserv'd, the Son I send:
It costs him dear to be the *Phrygians* Friend.
The lifeless Body, tell him, I bestow
Unask'd, to rest his wand'ring Ghost below.
He said, and trampled down with all the Force
690 Of his left Foot, and spurn'd the wretched Corse:
Then snatch'd the shining Belt, with Gold inlaid;
The Belt *Eurytion*'s artful Hands had made:
Where fifty fatal Brides, express'd to sight, ⎫
All, in the compass of one mournful Night, ⎬
695 Depriv'd their Bridegrooms of returning Light. ⎭
   In an ill Hour insulting *Turnus* tore
Those Golden Spoils, and in a worse he wore.
O Mortals! blind in Fate, who never know
To bear high Fortune, or endure the low!
700 The Time shall come, when *Turnus*, but in vain,
Shall wish untouch'd the Trophies of the slain:

Shall wish the fatal Belt were far away;
And curse the dire Remembrance of the Day.
     The sad *Arcadians* from th' unhappy Field,
705 Bear back the breathless Body on a Shield.
O Grace and Grief of War! at once restor'd
With Praises to thy Sire, at once deplor'd.
One Day first sent thee to the fighting Field,
Beheld whole heaps of Foes in Battel kill'd;
710 One Day beheld thee dead, and born upon thy Shield.
This dismal News, not from uncertain Fame,
But sad Spectators, to the Heroe came:
His Friends upon the brink of Ruin stand,
Unless reliev'd by his victorious Hand.
715 He whirls his Sword around, without delay,
And hews through adverse Foes an ample Way;
To find fierce *Turnus*, of his Conquest proud:
Evander, *Pallas*, all that Friendship ow'd
To large Deserts, are present to his Eyes;
720 His plighted Hand, and hospitable Ties.
     Four Sons of *Sulmo*, four whom *Ufens* bred,
He took in fight, and living Victims led,
To please the Ghost of *Pallas*; and expire
In Sacrifice, before his Fun'ral Fire.
725 At *Magus* next he threw: He stoop'd below
The flying Spear, and shun'd the promis'd Blow.
Then creeping, clasp'd the Hero's Knees, and pray'd:
By young *Iulus*, by thy Father's Shade,
O spare my Life, and send me back to see
730 My longing Sire, and tender Progeny.
A lofty House I have, and Wealth untold,
In Silver Ingots, and in Bars of Gold:
All these, and Sums besides, which see no Day,
The Ransom of this one poor Life shall pay.
735 If I survive, will *Troy* the less prevail?
A single Soul's too light to turn the Scale.
He said. The Heroe sternly thus reply'd:
Thy Barrs, and Ingots, and the Sums beside,
Leave for thy Childrens Lot. Thy *Turnus* broke
740 All Rules of War, by one relentless Stroke

When *Pallas* fell: So deems, nor deems alone,
My Father's Shadow, but my living Son.
Thus having said, of kind Remorse bereft,
He seiz'd his Helm, and drag'd him with his left:
745 Then with his right Hand, while his Neck he wreath'd,
Up to the hilts his shining Fauchion sheath'd.
   Apollo's Priest, *Emonides*, was near,
His holy Fillets on his Front appear;
Glitt'ring in Arms he shone amidst the Crowd;
750 Much of his God, more of his Purple proud:
Him the fierce *Trojan* follow'd thro' the Field;
The holy Coward fell: and forc'd to yield,
The Prince stood o're the Priest; and, at one Blow,
Sent him an Off'ring to the Shades below.
755 His Arms *Seresthus* on his Shoulders bears,
Design'd a Trophee to the God of Wars.
   Vulcanian Cæculus renews the Fight;
And *Umbro* born upon the Mountains Height.
The Champion chears his Troops t' encounter those:
760 And seeks Revenge himself on other Foes.
At *Anxur*'s Shield he drove, and at the Blow,
Both Shield and Arm to Ground together go.
Anxur had boasted much of magick Charms,
And thought he wore impenetrable Arms;
765 So made by mutter'd Spells: And from the Spheres,
Had Life secur'd, in vain, for length of Years.
Then *Tarquitus* the Field in Triumph trod;
A Nymph his Mother, and his Sire a God.
Exulting in bright Arms he braves the Prince;
770 With his protended Lance he makes defence:
Bears back his feeble Foe; then pressing on,
Arrests his better Hand, and drags him down.
Stands o're the prostrate Wretch, and as he lay,
Vain Tales inventing, and prepar'd to pray:
775 Mows off his Head, the Trunk a Moment stood,
Then sunk, and rowl'd along the Sand in Blood.
   The vengeful Victor thus upbraids the slain;
Lye there, proud Man, unpity'd on the Plain:
Lye there, inglorious, and without a Tomb,
780 Far from thy Mother, and thy Native Home:

Expos'd to savage Beasts, and Birds of Prey;
Or thrown for Food to Monsters of the Sea.
    On *Lycas* and *Antæus* next he ran,
Two Chiefs of *Turnus*, and who led his Van.
785 They fled for Fear; with these he chas'd along,
Camers the yellow Lock'd, and *Numa* strong,
Both great in Arms, and both were fair, and young:
Camers, was Son to *Volscens* lately slain;
In Wealth surpassing all the *Latian* Train,
790 And in *Amycla* fix'd his silent, easie Reign.
    And as *Ægeon*, when with Heav'n he strove,
Stood opposite in Arms to mighty *Jove*;
Mov'd all his hundred Hands, provok'd the War,
Defy'd the forky Lightning from afar:
795 At fifty Mouths his flaming Breath expires,
And Flash for Flash returns, and Fires for Fires:
In his right Hand as many Swords he wields,
And takes the Thunder on as many Shields:
With Strength like his the *Trojan* Heroe stood,
800 And soon the Fields with falling Corps were strowd,
When once his Fauchion found the Taste of Blood.
    With Fury scarce to be conceiv'd, he flew
Against *Niphæus*, whom four Coursers drew.
They, when they see the fiery Chief advance,
805 And pushing at their Chests his pointed Lance;
Wheel'd with so swift a Motion, mad with Fear,
They threw their Master headlong from the Chair:
They stare, they start, nor stop their Course before
They bear the bounding Chariot to the Shore.
810   Now *Lucagus*, and *Liger* scour the Plains,
With two white Steeds, but *Liger* holds the Reins,
And *Lucagus* the lofty Seat maintains.
Bold Brethren both, the former wav'd in Air
His flaming Sword; *Æneas* couch'd his Spear,
815 Unus'd to Threats, and more unus'd to Fear.
Then *Liger* thus. Thy Confidence is vain
To scape from hence, as from the *Trojan* Plain:
Nor these the Steeds which *Diomede* bestrode,
Nor this the Chariot where *Achilles* rode:

820   Nor *Venus*'s Veil is here, nor *Neptune*'s Shield:
       Thy fatal Hour is come; and this the Field.
       Thus *Liger* vainly vaunts: The *Trojan* Peer
       Return'd his answer with his flying Spear.
       As *Lucagus* to lash his Horses bends,
825   Prone to the Wheels, and his left Foot protends:
       Prepar'd for Fight, the fatal Dart arrives,
       And thro' the borders of his Buckler drives.
       Pass'd through; and pierc'd his Groin, the deadly Wound,
       Cast from his Chariot, rowl'd him on the Ground.
830   Whom thus the Chief upbraids with scornful spight:
       Blame not the slowness of your Steeds in flight;
       Vain Shadows did not force their swift Retreat:
       But you your self forsake your empty Seat.
       He said, and seiz'd at once the loosen'd Rein,
835   (For *Liger* lay already on the Plain,
       By the same Shock) then, stretching out his Hands,
       The Recreant thus his wretched Life demands.
       Now by thy self, O more than Mortal Man!
       By her and him from whom thy Breath began,
840   Who form'd thee thus Divine, I beg thee spare
       This forfeit Life, and hear thy Suppliant's Pray'r.
       Thus much he spoke, and more he wou'd have said,
       But the stern Heroe turn'd aside his Head,
       And cut him short. I hear another Man,
845   You talk'd not thus before the Fight began;
       Now take your turn: And, as a Brother shou'd,
       Attend your Brother to the *Stygian* Flood:
       Then thro' his Breast his fatal Sword he sent,
       And the Soul issu'd at the gaping Vent.
850   As Storms the Skies, and Torrents tear the Ground,
       Thus rag'd the Prince, and scatter'd Deaths around:
       At length *Ascanius*, and the *Trojan* Train,
       Broke from the Camp, so long besieg'd in vain.
       Mean time the King of Gods and Mortal Man,
855   Held Conference with his Queen, and thus began:
       My Sister Goddess, and well pleasing Wife,
       Still think you *Venus*'s Aid supports the Strife;
       Sustains her *Trojans*: Or themselves alone,
       With inborn Valour force their Fortune on?

860   How fierce in Fight, with Courage undecay'd;
       Judge if such Warriors want immortal Aid.
       To whom the Goddess, with the charming Eyes,
       Soft in her Tone submissively replies.
       Why, O my Sov'raign Lord, whose Frown I fear,
865   And cannot, unconcern'd, your Anger bear;
       Why urge you thus my Grief? When if I still,
       (As once I was) were Mistress of your Will:
       From your Almighty Pow'r, your pleasing Wife
       Might gain the Grace of lengthning *Turnus*'s Life:
870   Securely snatch him from the fatal Fight,
       And give him to his aged Father's sight.
       Now let him perish, since you hold it good,
       And glut the *Trojans* with his pious Blood.
       Yet from our Lineage he derives his Name,
875   And in the fourth degree, from God *Pilumnus* came:
       Yet he devoutly pays you Rites Divine,
       And offers daily Incense at your Shrine.
           Then shortly thus the Sov'raign God reply'd;
       Since in my Pow'r and Goodness you confide;
880   If for a little Space, a lengthen'd Span,
       You beg Reprieve for this expiring Man:
       I grant you leave to take your *Turnus* hence,
       From Instant Fate, and can so far dispense.
       But if some secret Meaning lies beneath,
885   To save the short-liv'd Youth from destin'd Death:
       Or if a farther Thought you entertain,
       To change the Fates; you feed your hopes in vain.
           To whom the Goddess thus, with weeping Eyes,
       And what if that Request your Tongue denies,
890   Your Heart shou'd grant; and not a short Reprieve,
       But length of certain Life to *Turnus* give.
       Now speedy Death attends the guiltless Youth,
       If my presaging Soul divines with Truth.
       Which, O! I wish might err thro' causeless Fears,
895   And you, (for you have Pow'r) prolong his Years.
           Thus having said, involv'd in Clouds, she flies,
       And drives a Storm before her thro' the Skies.
       Swift she descends, alighting on the Plain,
       Where the fierce Foes a dubious Fight maintain.

900 Of Air condens'd, a Spectre soon she made,
     And what *Æneas* was, such seem'd the Shade.
     Adorn'd with *Dardan* Arms, the Phantom bore
     His Head aloft, a Plumy Crest he wore:
     This Hand appear'd a shining Sword to wield,
905 And that sustain'd an imitated Shield:
     With manly Meen He stalk'd along the Ground;
     Nor wanted Voice bely'd, nor vaunting Sound.
     (Thus haunting Ghosts appear to waking Sight,
     Or dreadful Visions in our Dreams by Night.)
910 The Spectre seems the *Daunian* Chief to dare,
     And flourishes his empty Sword in Air:
     At this advancing *Turnus* hurl'd his Spear;
     The Phantom wheel'd, and seem'd to fly for Fear.
     Deluded *Turnus* thought the *Trojan* fled,
915 And with vain hopes his haughty Fancy fed.
     Whether, O Coward, (thus he calls aloud,
     Nor found he spoke to Wind, and chas'd a Cloud;)
     Why thus forsake your Bride? Receive from me
     The fated Land you sought so long by Sea.
920 He said, and brandishing at once his Blade,
     With eager Pace pursu'd the flying Shade.
     By chance a Ship was fasten'd to the Shore,
     Which from old *Clusium* King *Osinius* bore:
     The Plank was ready laid for safe ascent;   ⎫
925 For shelter there the trembling Shadow bent: ⎬
     And skip'd, and sculk'd, and under Hatches went. ⎭
     Exulting *Turnus*, with regardless haste,
     Ascends the Plank, and to the Gally pass'd:
     Scarce had he reach'd the Prow, *Saturnia*'s Hand
930 The Haulsers cuts, and shoots the Ship from Land.
     With Wind in Poop, the Vessel plows the Sea,
     And measures back with speed her former Way.
     Mean time *Æneas* seeks his absent Foe,
     And sends his slaughter'd Troops to Shades below.
935   The guileful Phantom now forsook the shrowd,
     And flew sublime, and vanish'd in a Cloud.
     Too late young *Turnus* the Delusion found,
     Far on the Sea, still making from the Ground.

Then thankless for a Life redeem'd by Shame;
940 With Sense of Honour stung, and forfeit Fame:
Fearful besides of what in Fight had pass'd,
His Hands, and hagger'd Eyes to Heav'n he cast.
O *Jove*! he cry'd, for what offence have I
Deserv'd to bear this endless Infamy:
945 Whence am I forc'd, and whether am I born,
How, and with what Reproach shall I return?
Shall ever I behold the *Latian* Plain,
Or see *Laurentum*'s lofty Tow'rs again?
What will they say of their deserting Chief?
950 The War was mine, I fly from their Relief:
I led to Slaughter, and in Slaughter leave;
And ev'n from hence their dying Groans receive.
Here over-match'd in Fight, in heaps they lye,
There scatter'd o're the Fields ignobly fly.
955 Gape wide, O Earth! and draw me down alive, ⎫
Or, oh ye pitying Winds, a Wretch relieve; ⎬
On Sands or Shelves the splitting Vessel drive: ⎭
Or set me Shipwrack'd on some desart Shore,
Where no *Rutulian* Eyes may see me more;
960 Unknown to Friends, or Foes, or conscious Fame,
Lest she should follow, and my flight proclaim.
⠀⠀⠀Thus *Turnus* rav'd, and various Fates revolv'd,
The Choice was doubtful, but the Death resolv'd.
And now the Sword, and now the Sea took place:
965 That to revenge, and this to purge Disgrace.
Sometimes he thought to swim the stormy Main,
By stretch of Arms the distant Shore to gain:
Thrice he the Sword assay'd, and thrice the Flood;
But *Juno* mov'd with Pity both withstood:
970 And thrice repress'd his Rage: strong Gales supply'd,
And push'd the Vessel o're the swelling Tide.
At length she lands him on his Native Shores,
And to his Father's longing Arms restores.
⠀⠀⠀Mean time, by *Jove*'s Impulse, *Mezentius* arm'd:
975 Succeeding *Turnus* with his ardor warm'd
His fainting Friends, reproach'd their shameful flight,
Repell'd the Victors, and renew'd the Fight.

Against their King the *Tuscan* Troops conspire,
Such is their Hate, and such their fierce desire
980   Of wish'd Revenge: On him, and him alone,
All Hands employ'd, and all their Darts are thrown.
He, like a solid Rock by Seas inclos'd,
To raging Winds and roaring Waves oppos'd;
From his proud Summit looking down, disdains
985   Their empty Menace, and unmov'd remains.
      Beneath his Feet fell haughty *Hebrus* dead,
Then *Latagus*; and *Palmus* as he fled:
At *Latagus* a weighty Stone he flung,
His Face was flatted, and his Helmet rung.
990   But *Palmus* from behind receives his Wound,
Hamstring'd he falls, and grovels on the Ground:
His Crest and Armor from his Body torn,
Thy Shoulders, *Lausus*, and thy Head adorn.
Evas and *Mymas*, both of *Troy*, he slew,
995   *Mymas* his Birth from fair *Theano* drew:
Born on that fatal Night, when, big with Fire,
The Queen produc'd young *Paris* to his Sire.
But *Paris* in the *Phrygian* Fields was slain,
Unthinking *Mymas* on the *Latian* Plain.
1000   And as a savage Boar on Mountains bred,
With forest Mast, and fatning Marshes fed;
When once he sees himself in Toils inclos'd,
By Huntsmen and their eager Hounds oppos'd:
He whets his Tusks, and turns, and dares the War:
1005   Th' Invaders dart their Jav'lins from afar;
All keep aloof, and safely shout around,
But none presumes to give a nearer Wound.
He frets and froths, erects his bristled Hide,
And shakes a Grove of Lances from his Side:
1010   Not otherwise the Troops, with Hate inspir'd,
And just Revenge, against the Tyrant fir'd;
Their Darts with Clamour at a distance drive:
And only keep the languish'd War alive.
      From *Coritus*, came *Acron* to the Fight,
1015   Who left his Spouse betroath'd, and unconsummate Night.
Mezentius sees him thro' the Squadrons ride,
Proud of the Purple Favours of his Bride.

Then, as a hungry Lyon, who beholds
A Gamesom Goat, who frisks about the Folds;
1020 Or beamy Stag that grazes on the Plain:
He runs, he roars, he shakes his rising Mane;
He grins, and opens wide his greedy Jaws,
The Prey lyes panting underneath his Paws:
He fills his famish'd Maw, his Mouth runs o're
1025 With unchew'd Morsels, while he churns the Gore:
So proud *Mezentius* rushes on his Foes,
And first unhappy *Acron* overthrows:
Stretch'd at his length, he spurns the swarthy Ground,
The Lance besmear'd with Blood, lies broken in the wound.
1030   Then with Disdain the haughty Victor view'd
Orodes flying, nor the Wretch pursu'd:
Nor thought the Dastard's Back deserv'd a Wound;
But running gain'd th' Advantage of the Ground.
Then turning short, he met him Face to Face,
1035 To give his Victory the better grace.
Orodes falls, in equal Fight oppress'd:
Mezentius fix'd his Foot upon his Breast,
And rested Lance: And thus aloud he cries,
Lo here the Champion of my Rebels lies.
1040 The Fields around with *Io Pæan* ring,
And peals of Shouts applaud the conqu'ring King.
At this the vanquish'd, with his dying Breath,
Thus faintly spoke, and prophesy'd in Death:
Nor thou, proud Man, unpunish'd shalt remain;
1045 Like Death attends thee on this fatal Plain.
Then, sourly smiling, thus the King reply'd,
For what belongs to me let *Jove* provide:
But dye thou first, whatever Chance ensue:
He said, and from the Wound the Weapon drew:
1050 A hov'ring Mist came swimming o're his sight,
And seal'd his Eyes in everlasting Night.
     By *Cædicus, Alcathous* was slain,
Sacrator laid *Hydaspes* on the Plain:
Orses the strong to greater Strength must yield;
1055 He, with *Parthenius*, were by *Rapo* kill'd.
Then brave *Messapus Ericetes* slew,
Who from *Lycaon*'s Blood his Lineage drew.

But from his headstrong Horse his Fate he found, ⎫
Who threw his Master as he made a bound,   ⎬
1060   The Chief alighting, stuck him to the Ground. ⎭
Then *Clonius* hand to hand, on Foot assails,
The *Trojan* sinks, and *Neptune*'s Son prevails.
      Agis the *Lycian* stepping forth with Pride,
To single Fight the boldest Foe defy'd.
1065   Whom *Tuscan Valerus* by Force o'recame,
And not bely'd his mighty Father's Fame.
Salius to Death the great *Antronius* sent,
But the same Fate the Victor underwent:
Slain by *Nealces* Hand, well skill'd to throw
1070   The flying Dart, and draw the far-deceiving Bow.
      Thus equal Deaths are dealt with equal Chance;
By turns they quit their Ground, by turns advance:
Victors, and vanquish'd, in the various Field,
Nor wholly overcome, nor wholly yield.
1075   The Gods from Heav'n survey the fatal Strife,
And mourn the Miseries of Human Life.
Above the rest two Goddesses appear
Concern'd for each: Here *Venus*, *Juno* there:
Amidst the Crowd Infernal *Atè* shakes
1080   Her Scourge aloft, and Crest of hissing Snakes.
      Once more the proud *Mezentius*, with Disdain,
Brandish'd his Spear, and rush'd into the Plain:
Where tow'ring in the midmost Ranks he stood,
Like tall *Orion* stalking o're the Flood:
1085   When with his brawny Breast he cuts the Waves,
His Shoulders scarce the topmost Billow laves.
Or like a Mountain Ash, whose Roots are spread,
Deep fix'd in Earth, in Clouds he hides his Head.
      The *Trojan* Prince beheld him from afar,
1090   And dauntless undertook the doubtful War.
Collected in his Strength, and like a Rock,
Poiz'd on his Base, *Mezentius* stood the Shock.
He stood, and measuring first with careful Eyes,
The space his spear cou'd reach, aloud he cries:
1095   My strong right Hand, and Sword, assist my Stroke;
(Those only Gods *Mezentius* will invoke)

His Armour from the *Trojan* Pyrate torn,
By my triumphant *Lausus* shall be worn.
He said, and with his utmost force he threw
1100   The massy Spear, which, hissing as it flew,
Reach'd the Cœlestial Shield that stop'd the course;
But glancing thence, the yet unbroken Force
Took a new bent obliquely, and betwixt
The Side and Bowels fam'd *Anthores* fix'd.
1105   *Anthores* had from *Argos* travell'd far,
Alcides Friend, and Brother of the War:
'Till tir'd with Toils, fair *Italy* he chose,
And in *Evander*'s Palace sought Repose:
Now falling by another's Wound, his Eyes
1110   He casts to Heav'n, on *Argos* thinks, and dyes.
        The pious *Trojan* then his Jav'lin sent,
The Shield gave way: Thro' treble Plates it went
Of solid Brass, of Linnen trebly rowl'd,
And three Bull-hides which round the Buckler rowl'd.
1115   All these it pass'd, resistless in the Course,
Transpierc'd his Thigh, and spent its dying Force.
The gaping Wound gush'd out a Crimson Flood;
The *Trojan*, glad with sight of hostile Blood,
His Fauchion drew, to closer Fight address'd,
1120   And with new Force his fainting Foe oppress'd.
        His Father's Peril *Lausus* view'd with Grief,
He sigh'd, he wept, he ran to his Relief.
And here, Heroick Youth, 'tis here I must
To thy immortal Memory be just;
1125   And sing an Act so noble and so new,
Posterity will scarce believe 'tis true.
Pain'd with his Wound, and useless for the Fight,
The Father sought to save himself by Flight:
Incumber'd, slow he drag'd the Spear along,
1130   Which pierc'd his thigh, and in his Buckler hung.
The pious Youth, resolv'd on Death, below
The lifted Sword, springs forth to face the Foe; ⎫
Protects his Parent, and prevents the Blow.   ⎬
Shouts of Applause ran ringing thro' the Field, ⎭
1135   To see the Son the vanquish'd Father shield:

All fir'd with gen'rous Indignation strive;
And with a storm of Darts, to distance drive
The *Trojan* Chief; who held at Bay from far,
On his *Vulcanian* Orb sustain'd the War.

1140   As when thick Hail comes ratling in the Wind,
The Plowman, Passenger, and lab'ring Hind,
For shelter to the neighb'ring Covert fly;
Or hous'd, or safe in hollow Caverns lye:
But that o'reblown, when Heav'n above 'em smiles,

1145   Return to Travel, and renew their Toils:
Æneas thus o'rewhelmed on ev'ry side,
The storm of Darts, undaunted, did abide;
And thus to *Lausus* loud with friendly threatning cry'd.
Why wilt thou rush to certain Death, and Rage

1150   In rash Attempts, beyond thy tender Age:
Betray'd by pious Love? Nor thus forborn
The Youth desists, but with insulting Scorn
Provokes the ling'ring Prince: Whose Patience tyr'd,
Gave Place, and all his Breast with Fury fir'd.

1155   For now the Fates prepar'd their sharpen'd Sheers;
And lifted high the flaming Sword appears:
Which full descending, with a frightful sway,
Thro' Shield and Corslet forc'd th' impetuous Way,
And bury'd deep in his fair Bosom lay.

1160   The purple Streams thro' the thin Armour strove,
And drench'd th' imbroider'd Coat his Mother wove:
And Life at length forsook his heaving Heart,
Loath from so sweet a Mansion to depart.

But when, with Blood, and Paleness all o'respread,

1165   The pious Prince beheld young *Lausus* dead;
He griev'd, he wept, the sight an Image brought
Of his own filial Love; a sadly pleasing Thought.
Then stretch'd his Hand to hold him up, and said,
Poor hapless Youth! what Praises can be paid

1170   To love so great, to such transcendent Store
Of early Worth, and sure Presage of more?
Accept what e're *Æneas* can afford,
Untouch'd thy Arms, untaken be thy Sword:
And all that pleas'd thee living still remain

1175   Inviolate, and sacred to the slain.

Thy Body on thy Parents I bestow,
To rest thy Soul, at least if Shadows know,
Or have a sense of human Things below.
There to thy fellow Ghosts with Glory tell,
1180 'Twas by the great *Æneas* hand I fell.
With this his distant Friends he beckons near,
Provokes their Duty, and prevents their Fear:
Himself assists to lift him from the Ground,
With clotted Locks, and Blood that well'd from out the
        Wound.

1185   Mean time his Father, now no Father, stood,
And wash'd his Wounds by *Tyber*'s yellow Flood:
Oppress'd with Anguish, panting, and o'respent,
His fainting Limbs against an Oak he leant.
A Bough his Brazen Helmet did sustain,
1190 His heavier Arms lay scatter'd on the Plain.
A chosen Train of Youth around him stand,
His drooping Head was rested on his hand:
His grisly Beard his pensive Bosom sought,
And all on *Lausus* ran his restless thought.
1195 Careful, concern'd his Danger to prevent,
He much enquir'd, and many a Message sent
To warn him from the Field: Alas! in vain,
Behold his mournful Followers bear him slain:
O're his broad Shield still gush'd the yawning Wound,
1200 And drew a bloody Trail along the Ground.
    Far off he heard their Cries, far off divin'd
The dire Event, with a foreboding Mind.
With Dust he sprinkled first his hoary Head,
Then both his lifted hands to Heav'n he spread;
1205 Last, the dear Corps embracing, thus he said.
What Joys, alas! cou'd this frail Being give,
That I have been so covetous to live?
To see my Son, and such a Son, resign
His Life a Ransom for preserving mine?
1210 And am I then preserv'd, and art thou lost?
How much too dear has that Redemption cost!
'Tis now my bitter Banishment I feel;
This is a Wound too deep for time to heal.

My Guilt thy growing Virtues did defame;
1215   My Blackness blotted thy unblemish'd Name.
       Chas'd from a Throne, abandon'd, and exil'd
       For foul Misdeeds, were Punishments too mild;
       I ow'd my People these, and from their hate,
       With less Resentment cou'd have born my Fate.
1220   And yet I live, and yet sustain the sight
       Of hated Men, and of more hated Light:
       But will not long. With that he rais'd from Ground
       His fainting Limbs, that stagger'd with his Wound.
       Yet with a Mind resolv'd, and unappal'd
1225   With Pains or Perils, for his Courser call'd:
       Well mouth'd, well manag'd, whom himself did dress, ⎫
       With daily Care, and mounted with Success;   ⎬
       His Aid in Arms, his Ornament in Peace.   ⎭
          Soothing his Courage with a gentle Stroke,
1230   The Steed seem'd sensible, while thus he spoke.
       O *Rhæbus* we have liv'd too long for me,
       (If Life and Long were Terms that cou'd agree)
       This Day thou either shalt bring back the Head,
       And bloody Trophees of the *Trojan* dead:
1235   This Day thou either shalt revenge my Woe
       For murther'd *Lausus*, on his cruel Foe;
       Or if inexorable Fate deny
       Our Conquest, with thy conquer'd Master dye:
       For after such a Lord, I rest secure,
1240   Thou wilt no foreign Reins, or *Trojan* Load endure.
       He said: And straight th' officious Courser kneels
       To take his wonted Weight. His Hands he fills
       With pointed Jav'lins: On his Head he lac'd
       His glitt'ring Helm, which terribly was grac'd
1245   With Waving Horse–hair, nodding from afar;
       Then spurr'd his thund'ring Steed amidst the War.
       Love, Anguish, Wrath, and Grief, to Madness wrought,
       Despair, and secret Shame, and conscious thought
       Of inborn Worth, his lab'ring Soul oppress'd,
1250   Rowl'd in his Eyes, and rag'd within his Breast.
       Then loud he call'd *Æneas* thrice by Name,
       The loud repeated Voice to glad *Æneas* came.

Great *Jove*, he said, and the far-shooting God,
Inspire thy Mind to make thy Challenge good.
1255   He spoke no more, but hasten'd, void of Fear,
And threaten'd with his long protended Spear.
      To whom *Mezentius* thus. Thy Vaunts are vain,
My *Lausus* lies extended on the Plain:
He's lost! thy Conquest is already won,
1260   The wretched Sire is murther'd in the Son.
Nor Fate I fear, but all the Gods defy,
Forbear thy Threats, my Bus'ness is to dye; }
But first receive this parting Legacy.
He said: And straight a whirling Dart he sent:
1265   Another after, and another went.
Round in a spacious Ring he rides the Field,
And vainly plies th' impenetrable Shield:
Thrice rode he round, and thrice *Æneas* wheel'd.
Turn'd as he turn'd; the Golden Orb withstood
1270   The Strokes, and bore about an Iron Wood.
Impatient of Delay, and weary grown,
Still to defend, and to defend alone:
To wrench the Darts which in his Buckler light,
Urg'd, and o're-labour'd in unequal Fight:
1275   At length resolv'd, he throws with all his Force,
Full at the Temples of the Warrior Horse.
Just where the Stroke was aim'd, th' unerring Spear
Made way, and stood transfix'd thro' either Ear.
Seiz'd with unwonted Pain, surpriz'd with Fright,
1280   The wounded Steed curvets; and, rais'd upright,
Lights on his Feet before: His Hoofs behind
Spring up in Air aloft, and lash the Wind.
Down comes the Rider headlong from his height,
His Horse came after with unweildy weight:
1285   And flound'ring forward, pitching on his Head,
His Lord's incumber'd Shoulder overlaid.
      From either Hoast the mingl'd Shouts, and Cries,
Of *Trojans* and *Rutulians* rend the Skies.
Æneas hast'ning, wav'd his fatal Sword
1290   High o're his head, with this reproachful Word.
Now, where are now thy Vaunts, the fierce Disdain
Of proud *Mezentius*, and the lofty Strain?

Strugling, and wildly staring on the Skies,
With scarce recover'd Sight, he thus replies.
1295 Why these insulting Words, this waste of Breath,
To Souls undaunted, and secure of Death?
'Tis no Dishonour for the Brave to dye,
Nor came I here with hope of Victory:
Nor ask I Life, nor fought with that design,
1300 As I had us'd my Fortune, use thou thine.
My dying Son contracted no such Band;
The Gift is hateful from his Murd'rer's hand.
For this, this only Favour let me sue,
(If Pity can to conquer'd Foes be due)
1305 Refuse it not: But let my Body have,
The last Retreat of Human Kind, a Grave.
Too well I know th' insulting People's Hate;
Protect me from their Vengeance after Fate:
This Refuge for my poor Remains provide, ⎫
1310 And lay my much lov'd *Lausus* by my side: ⎬
He said, and to the Sword his Throat apply'd. ⎭
The Crimson Stream distain'd his Arms around,
And the disdainful Soul came rushing thro' the Wound.

THE ELEVENTH BOOK OF THE ÆNEIS

The Argument

Æneas *erects a Trophy of the Spoils of* Mezentius; *grants a Truce for burying the dead; and sends home the Body of* Pallas *with great Solemnity.* Latinus *calls a Council to propose offers of Peace to* Æneas, *which occasions great Animosity betwixt* Turnus *and* Drances: *In the mean time there is a sharp Engagement of the Horse; wherein* Camilla *signalizes her self; is kill'd: And the* Latine *Troops are entirely defeated.*

Scarce had the rosie Morning rais'd her Head
Above the Waves, and left her wat'ry Bed;
The Pious Chief, whom double Cares attend
For his unbury'd Souldiers, and his Friend:
5   Yet first to Heav'n perform'd a Victor's Vows;
He bar'd an ancient Oak of all her Boughs:
Then on a rising Ground the Trunk he plac'd;
Which with the Spoils of his dead Foe he grac'd.
The Coat of Arms by proud *Mezentius* worn,
10 Now on a naked Snag in Triumph born,
Was hung on high; and glitter'd from afar:
A Trophy sacred to the God of War.
Above his Arms, fix'd on the leafless Wood,
Appear'd his Plumy Crest, besmeard with Blood;
15 His brazen Buckler on the left was seen;
Trunchions of shiver'd Lances hung between:
And on the right was plac'd his Corslet, bor'd;
And to the Neck was ty'd his unavailing Sword.
A Crowd of Chiefs inclose the Godlike Man:
20 Who thus, conspicuous in the midst, began.
     Our Toils, my Friends, are crown'd with sure Success:
The greater Part perform'd, atchieve the less.
Now follow chearful to the trembling Town;
Press but an Entrance, and presume it won.
25 Fear is no more: For fierce *Mezentius* lies,
As the first Fruits of War, a Sacrifice.
Turnus shall fall extended on the Plain;
And in this Omen is already slain.
Prepar'd in Arms pursue your happy Chance;
30 That none unwarn'd may plead his Ignorance:
And I, at Heav'n's appointed Hour, may find
Your warlike Ensigns waving in the Wind.

Mean time the Rites and Fun'ral Pomps prepare,
Due to your dead Companions of the War:
35 The last Respect the living can bestow,
To shield their Shadows from Contempt below.
That conquer'd Earth be theirs for which they fought;
And which for us with their own blood they bought.
But first the Corps of our unhappy Friend,
40 To the sad City of *Evander* send:
Who not inglorious in his Ages bloom
Was hurry'd hence by too severe a Doom.

Thus, weeping while he spoke, he took his Way,
Where, new in Death, lamented *Pallas* lay:
45 *Acætes* watch'd the Corps; whose Youth deserv'd
The Father's Trust, and now the Son he serv'd
With equal Faith, but less auspicious Care:
Th' Attendants of the slain, his Sorrow share.
A Troop of *Trojans* mix'd with these appear,
50 And mourning Matrons with dishevell'd Hair.
Soon as the Prince appears, they raise a Cry;
All beat their Breasts, and Echoes rend the Sky.
They rear his drooping Forehead from the Ground;
But when *Æneas* view'd the grisly Wound
55 Which *Pallas* in his Manly Bosom bore,
And the fair Flesh distain'd with Purple Gore:
First, melting into Tears, the pious Man
Deplor'd so sad a sight, then thus began.

Unhappy Youth! When Fortune gave the rest
60 Of my full Wishes, she refus'd the best!
She came; but brought not thee along; to bless
My longing Eyes, and share in my Success:
She grudg'd thy safe Return the Triumphs due
To prosp'rous Valour, in the publick View.
65 Not thus I promis'd, when thy Father lent
Thy needless Succour with a sad Consent;
Embrac'd me parting for th' *Etrurian* Land,
And sent me to possess a large Command.
He warn'd, and from his own Experience told,
70 Our Foes were warlike, disciplin'd, and bold:
And now perhaps, in hopes of thy return,
Rich Odours on his loaded Altars burn;

While we, with vain officious Pomp, prepare
To send him back his Portion of the War;
75 A bloody breathless Body: which can owe
No farther Debt, but to the Pow'rs below.
The wretched Father, e're his Race is run,
Shall view the Fun'ral Honours of his Son.
These are my Triumphs of the *Latian* War;
80 Fruits of my plighted Faith, and boasted Care.
And yet, unhappy Sire, thou shalt not see
A Son, whose Death disgrac'd his Ancestry:
Thou shalt not blush, old Man, however griev'd:
Thy *Pallas* no dishonest Wound receiv'd.
85 He dy'd no Death to make thee wish, too late,
Thou hadst not liv'd to see his shameful Fate:
But what a Champion has th' *Ausonian* Coast,
And what a Friend hast thou, *Ascanius*, lost!
     Thus having mourn'd, he gave the Word around,
90 To raise the breathless Body from the Ground;
And chose a thousand Horse, the flow'r of all
His warlike Troops, to wait the Funeral:
To bear him back, and share *Evander*'s Grief;
(A well becoming, but a weak Relief.)
95 Of Oaken Twigs they twist an easie Bier;
Then on their Shoulders the sad Burden rear.
The Body on this Rural Herse is born,
Strewd Leaves and Funeral Greens the Bier adorn.
All pale he lies, and looks a lovely Flow'r,
100 New cropt by Virgin Hands, to dress the Bow'r;
Unfaded yet, but yet unfed below,
No more to Mother Earth or the green Stem shall owe.
Then two fair Vests, of wond'rous Work and Cost,
Of Purple woven, and with Gold emboss'd,
105 For Ornament the *Trojan* Heroe brought,
Which with her Hands *Sidonian Dido* wrought.
One Vest array'd the Corps, and one they spread
O're his clos'd Eyes, and wrap'd around his Head:
That when the yellow Hair in Flame shou'd fall,
110 The catching Fire might burn the Golden Caul.
Besides, the Spoils of Foes in Battel slain,
When he descended on the *Latian* Plain:

Arms, Trappings, Horses, by the Herse are led
In long Array, (th' Atchievments of the Dead.)
115   Then, pinion'd with their hands behind, appear
Th' unhappy Captives, marching in the Rear:
Appointed Off'rings in the Victor's Name,
To sprinkle with their Blood, the Fun'ral Flame.
Inferior Trophees by the Chiefs are born;
120   Gantlets and Helms, their loaded hands adorn:
And fair Inscriptions fix'd, and Titles read,
Of *Latian* Leaders conquer'd by the Dead.
      Acætes on his Pupil's Corps attends,
With feeble Steps; supported by his Friends:
125   Pausing at every Pace; in Sorrow drown'd,
Betwixt their Arms he sinks upon the Ground.
Where grov'ling, while he lies in deep Despair,
He beats his Breast, and rends his hoary Hair.
The Champion's Chariot next is seen to rowl,
130   Besmear'd with hostile blood, and honourably foul.
To close the Pomp, *Æthon*, the Steed of State,
Is led, the Fun'rals of his Lord to wait.
Stripp'd of his Trappings, with a sullen Pace
He walks, and the big Tears run rowling down his Face.
135   The Lance of *Pallas*, and the Crimson Crest,
Are born behind; the Victor seiz'd the rest.
The March begins: The Trumpets hoarsly sound,
The Pikes and Lances trail along the Ground.
Thus while the *Trojan* and *Arcadian* Horse,
140   To *Pallantean* Tow'rs direct their Course,
In long Procession rank'd; the pious Chief
Stop'd in the Rear, and gave a vent to Grief.
The publick Care, he said, which War attends
Diverts our present Woes, at least suspends:
145   Peace with the *Manes* of great *Pallas* dwell;
Hail holy Relicks, and a last farewel!
He said no more, but inly though he mourn'd,
Restrain'd his Tears, and to the Camp return'd.
      Now Suppliants, from *Laurentum* sent, demand
150   A Truce, with Olive Branches in their hand.
Obtest his Clemency, and from the Plain
Beg leave to draw the Bodies of their slain.

They plead, that none those common Rites deny
To conquer'd Foes, that in fair Battel dye.
155 All cause of Hate was ended in their Death;
Nor cou'd he War with Bodies void of Breath.
A King, they hop'd, wou'd hear a King's Request:
Whose Son he once was call'd, and once his Guest.
    Their Suit, which was too just to be deny'd,
160 The Heroe grants, and farther thus reply'd:
O *Latian* Princes, how severe a Fate
In causeless Quarrels has involv'd your State!
And arm'd against an unoffending Man,
Who sought your Friendship e're the War began!
165 You beg a Truce, which I wou'd gladly give,
Not only for the slain, but those who live.
I came not hether but by Heav'n's Command,
And sent by Fate to share the *Latian* Land.
Nor wage I Wars unjust; your King deny'd
170 My proffer'd Friendship, and my promis'd Bride.
Left me for *Turnus*; *Turnus* then should try
His Cause in Arms, to Conquer or to dye.
My Right and his are in dispute: The slain
Fell without fault, our Quarrel to maintain.
175 In equal Arms let us alone contend;
And let him vanquish, whom his Fates befriend.
This is the way, so tell him, to possess
The Royal Virgin, and restore the Peace.
Bear this my Message back; with ample leave
180 That your slain Friends may Fun'ral Rights receive.
    Thus having said, th' Embassadors amaz'd,
Stood mute a while, and on each other gaz'd:
Drances, their Chief, who harbour'd in his Breast
Long hate to *Turnus*, as his Foe profess'd,
185 Broke silence first, and to the Godlike Man,
With graceful action bowing, thus began.
    Auspicious Prince, in Arms a mighty Name,
But yet whose Actions far transcend your Fame;
Wou'd I your Justice or your Force express,
190 Thought can but equal; and all Words are less:
Your Answer we shall thankfully relate,
And Favours granted to the *Latian* State:

If wish'd Success our Labour shall attend,
Think Peace concluded, and the King your Friend:
195 Let *Turnus* leave the Realm to your Command;
And seek Alliance in some other Land:
Build you the City which your Fates assign;
We shall be proud in the great Work to join.
    Thus *Drances*; and his Words so well perswade
200 The rest impower'd, that soon a Truce is made.
Twelve days the term allow'd: And during those,
Latians and *Trojans*, now no longer Foes,
Mix'd in the Woods, for Fun'ral Piles prepare,
To fell the Timber, and forget the War.
205 Loud Axes thro' the groaning Groves resound:
Oak, Mountain Ash, and Poplar, spread the Ground:
Firrs fall from high: and some the Trunks receive,
In Loaden Wains, with Wedges some they cleave.
And now the Fatal News, by Fame is blown
210 Thro' the short Circuit of th' *Arcadian* Town,
Of *Pallas* slain: By Fame, which just before
His Triumphs on distended Pinions bore.
Rushing from out the Gate, the People stand,
Each with a Fun'ral Flambeau in his hand:
215 Wildly they stare, distracted with amaze:
The Fields are lighten'd with a fiery blaze,
That cast a sullen Splendor on their Friends,
(The marching Troop which their dead Prince attends.)
Both Parties meet: They raise a doleful Cry: ⎫
220 The Matrons from the Walls with shrieks reply; ⎬
And their mix'd mourning rends the vaulted Sky. ⎭
The Town is fill'd with Tumult and with Tears;
Till the loud Clamours reach *Evander*'s Ears:
Forgetful of his State, he runs along,
225 With a disorder'd pace, and cleaves the Throng:
Falls on the Corps, and groaning there he lies,
With silent Grief that speaks but at his Eyes:
Short Sighs and Sobs succeed; 'till Sorrow breaks
A passage, and at once he weeps and speaks.
230   O *Pallas*! thou hast fail'd thy plighted Word!
To fight with Caution, not to tempt the Sword:

I warn'd thee, but in vain; for well I knew
What Perils youthful Ardour wou'd pursue:
That boiling Blood wou'd carry thee too far;
235   Young as thou wert in Dangers, raw to War!
O curst Essay of Arms, disast'rous Doom,
Prelude of bloody Fields, and Fights to come!
Hard Elements of unauspicious War,
Vain Vows to Heav'n, and unavailing Care!
240   Thrice happy thou, dear Partner of my Bed,
Whose holy Soul the Stroke of Fortune fled:
Præscious of Ills, and leaving me behind,
To drink the dregs of Life by Fate assign'd.
Beyond the Goal of Nature I have gon;
245   My *Pallas* late set out, but reach'd too soon.
If, for my League against th' *Ausonian* State,
Amidst their Weapons I had found my Fate,
(Deserv'd from them,) then I had been return'd
A breathless Victor, and my Son had mourn'd.
250   Yet will I not my *Trojan* Friend upbraid,
Nor grudge th' Alliance I so gladly made.
'Twas not his Fault my *Pallas* fell so young,
But my own Crime for having liv'd too long.
Yet, since the Gods had destin'd him to dye,
255   At least he led the way to Victory:
First for his Friends he won the fatal Shore, ⎫
And sent whole Herds of slaughter'd Foes before: ⎬
A Death too great, too glorious to deplore. ⎭
Nor will I add new Honours to thy Grave;
260   Content with those the *Trojan* Heroe gave.
That Funeral Pomp thy *Phrygian* Friends design'd;
In which the *Tuscan* Chiefs, and Army join'd:
Great Spoils, and Trophees gain'd by thee, they bear:
Then let thy own Atchievments be thy share.
265   Even thou, O *Turnus*, hadst a Trophy stood,
Whose mighty Trunk had better grac'd the Wood,
If *Pallas* had arriv'd, with equal length
Of Years, to match thy Bulk with equal Strength.
But why, unhappy Man, dost thou detain
270   These Troops, to view the Tears thou shedst in vain!

Go, Friends, this Message to your Lord relate;
Tell him, that if I bear my bitter Fate,
And after *Pallas* Death, live ling'ring on,
'Tis to behold his Vengeance for my Son.
275 I stay for *Turnus*; whose devoted Head
Is owing to the living and the dead:
My Son and I expect it from his Hand;
'Tis all that he can give, or we demand.
Joy is no more: But I would gladly go,
280 To greet my *Pallas* with such News below.
     The Morn had now dispell'd the Shades of Night;
Restoring Toils, when she restor'd the Light:
The *Trojan* King, and *Tuscan* Chief, command
To raise the Piles, along the winding Strand:
285 Their Friends convey the dead to Fun'ral Fires; ⎫
Black smould'ring Smoke from the green Wood expires; ⎬
The Light of Heav'n is choak'd, and the new Day retires. ⎭
Then thrice around the kindled Piles they go:
(For ancient Custom had ordain'd it so)
290 Thrice Horse and Foot about the Fires are led,
And thrice with loud Laments they hail the dead.
Tears trickling down their Breasts bedew the Ground;
And Drums and Trumpets mix their mournful Sound.
Amid the Blaze, their pious Brethren throw
295 The Spoils, in Battel taken from the Foe:
Helms, Bitts emboss'd, and Swords of shining Steel,
One casts a Target, one a Chariot Wheel:
Some to their Fellows their own Arms restore;
The Fauchions which in luckless Fight they bore:
300 Their Bucklers pierc'd, their Darts bestow'd in vain,
And shiver'd Lances gather'd from the Plain.
Whole Herds of offer'd Bulls about the Fire,
And bristled Boars, and wooly Sheep expire.
Around the Piles a careful Troop attends,
305 To watch the wasting Flames, and weep their burning
          Friends.
Ling'ring along the Shore, 'till dewy Night,
New decks the Face of Heaven with starry Light.
     The conquer'd *Latians*, with like Pious Care,
Piles without number for their Dead prepare;

310   Part, in the Places where they fell, are laid;
      And part are to the neighb'ring Fields convey'd.
      The Corps of Kings, and Captains of Renown,
      Born off in State, are bury'd in the Town:
      The rest, unhonour'd, and without a Name,
315   Are cast a common heap to feed the Flame.
      Trojans and *Latians* vie with like desires:⎫
      To make the Field of Battel shine with Fires:⎬
      And the promiscuous Blaze to Heav'n aspires.⎭
           Now had the Morning thrice renew'd the Light,
320   And thrice dispell'd the Shadows of the Night;
      When those who round the wasted Fires remain,
      Perform the last sad Office to the slain:
      They rake the yet warm Ashes, from below;
      These, and the Bones unburn'd, in Earth bestow:
325   These Relicks with their Country Rites they grace,
      And raise a mount of Turf to mark the place.
           But in the Palace of the King, appears
      A Scene more solemn, and a Pomp of Tears.
      Maids, Matrons, Widows, mix their common Moans:
330   Orphans their Sires, and Sires lament their Sons.
      All in that Universal Sorrow share,
      And curse the Cause of this unhappy War.
      A broken League, a Bride unjustly sought,
      A Crown usurp'd, which with their Blood is bought!
335   These are the Crimes, with which they load the Name
      Of *Turnus*, and on him alone exclaim.
      Let him, who lords it o're th' *Ausonian* Land,
      Engage the *Trojan* Heroe hand to hand:
      His is the Gain, our Lot is but to serve;
340   'Tis just, the sway he seeks, he shoud deserve.
      This *Drances* aggravates; and adds, with spight,
      His Foe expects, and dares him to the Fight.
      Nor *Turnus* wants a Party to support
      His Cause and Credit, in the *Latian* Court.
345   His former Acts secure his present Fame;
      And the Queen shades him with her mighty Name.
           While thus their factious Minds with fury burn;
      The Legats from th' *Ætolian* Prince return:

Sad News they bring, that after all the Cost,
350   And Care employ'd their Embassy is lost:
That *Diomede* refus'd his Aid in War;
Unmov'd with Presents, and as deaf to Pray'r.
Some new Alliance must elsewhere be sought;
Or Peace with *Troy* on hard Conditions bought.

355   *Latinus*, sunk in Sorrow, finds too late,
A Foreign Son is pointed out by Fate:
And till *Æneas* shall *Lavinia* wed,
The wrath of Heav'n is hov'ring o're his Head.
The Gods, he saw, espous'd the juster side,
360   When late their Titles in the Field were try'd: ⎫
Witness the fresh Laments, and Fun'ral Tears undry'd. ⎬
                                                      ⎭

        Thus, full of anxious Thought, he summons all
The *Latian* Senate to the Council Hall:
The Princes come, commanded by their Head,
365   And crowd the Paths that to the Palace lead.
Supream in Pow'r, and reverenc'd for his Years,
He takes the Throne, and in the midst appears:
Majestically sad, he sits in State,
And bids his Envoys their Success relate.

370   When *Venulus* began, the murmuring Sound
Was hush'd, and sacred Silence reign'd around.
We have, said he, perform'd your high Command;
And pass'd with Peril a long Tract of Land:
We reach'd the Place desir'd, with Wonder fill'd,
375   The *Grecian* Tents, and rising Tow'rs beheld.
Great *Diomede* has compass'd round with Walls
The City, which *Argyripa* he calls;
From his own *Argos* nam'd: We touch'd, with Joy,
The Royal Hand that raz'd unhappy *Troy*.

380   When introduc'd, our Presents first we bring,
Then crave an instant Audience from the King:
His Leave obtain'd, our Native Soil we name;
And tell th' important Cause for which we came.
Attentively he heard us, while we spoke;
385   Then, with soft Accents, and a pleasing Look,
Made this return. *Ausonian* Race, of old
Renown'd for Peace, and for an Age of Gold,

What Madness has your alter'd Minds possess'd,
To change for War hereditary Rest?
390 Sollicit Arms unknown, and tempt the Sword,
(A needless Ill your Ancestors abhorr'd?)
We; (for my self I speak, and all the Name
Of *Grecians*, who to *Troy*'s Destruction came;)
Omitting those who were in Battel slain,
395 Or born by rowling *Simois* to the Main:
Not one but suffer'd, and too dearly bought
The Prize of Honour which in Arms he sought.
Some doom'd to Death, and some in Exile driv'n,
Out-casts, abandon'd by the Care of Heav'n:
400 So worn, so wretched, so despis'd a Crew,
As ev'n old *Priam* might with Pity view.
Witness the Vessels by *Minerva* toss'd
In Storms, the vengeful *Capharæan* Coast;
Th' *Eubœan* Rocks! The Prince, whose Brother led
405 Our Armies to revenge his injur'd Bed,
In *Egypt* lost; *Ulysses*, with his Men,
Have seen *Charybdis*, and the *Cyclops* Den:
Why shou'd I name *Idomeneus*, in vain
Restor'd to Scepters, and expell'd again? }
410 Or young *Achilles* by his Rival slain?
Ev'n he, the King of Men, the foremost Name
Of all the *Greeks*, and most renown'd by Fame,
The proud Revenger of another's Wife,
Yet by his own Adult'ress lost his Life:
415 Fell at his Threshold, and the Spoils of *Troy*,
The foul Polluters of his Bed enjoy.
The Gods have envy'd me the sweets of Life,
My much lov'd Country, and my more lov'd Wife:
Banish'd from both, I mourn; while in the Sky
420 Transform'd to Birds, my lost Companions fly:
Hov'ring about the Coasts they make their Moan;
And cuff the Cliffs with Pinions not their own.
What squalid Spectres, in the dead of Night,
Break my short Sleep, and skim before my sight!
425 I might have promis'd to my self those Harms,
Mad as I was, when I with Mortal Arms

Presum'd against Immortal Pow'rs to move;
And violate with Wounds the Queen of Love.
Such Arms, this Hand shall never more employ;
430   No Hate remains with me to ruin'd *Troy*.
I war not with its Dust; nor am I glad
To think of past Events, or good or bad.
Your Presents I return: What e're you bring
To buy my Friendship, send the *Trojan* King.
435   We met in fight, I know him to my Cost;
With what a whirling force his Lance he toss'd:
Heav'ns what a spring was in his Arm, to throw:
How high he held his Shield, and rose at ev'ry blow!
Had *Troy* produc'd two more, his Match in Might,
440   They would have chang'd the Fortune of the Fight:
Th' Invasion of the *Greeks* had been return'd:
Our Empire wasted, and our Cities burn'd.
The long Defence the *Trojan* People made,
The War protracted, and the Siege delay'd,
445   Were due to *Hector*'s and this Heroe's hand:
Both brave alike, and equal in Command;
Æneas not inferior in the Field,
In pious reverence to the Gods, excell'd.
Make peace, ye *Latians*, and avoid with Care
450   Th' impending Dangers of a fatal War.
He said no more; but with this cold Excuse,
Refus'd th' Alliance, and advis'd a Truce.
    Thus *Venulus* concluded his Report.
A Jarring Murmur fill'd the factious Court:
455   As when a Torrent rowls with rapid force,
And dashes o're the Stones that stop the Course;
The Flood, constrain'd within a scanty space,
Roars horrible along th' uneasie race:
White foam in gath'ring Eddies floats around:
460   The rocky Shores rebellow to the sound.
    The Murmur ceas'd: Then from his lofty Throne
The King invok'd the Gods, and thus begun.
I wish, ye *Latins*, what we now debate
Had been resolv'd before it was too late:
465   Much better had it been for you and me,
Unforc'd by this our last Necessity,

To have been earlier wise; than now to call
A Council, when the Foe surrounds the Wall.
O Citizens! we wage unequal War,
470   With men, not only Heav'n's peculiar Care,
But Heav'n's own Race: Unconquer'd in the Field,
Or Conquer'd, yet unknowing how to yield.
What Hopes you had in *Diomede*, lay down:
Our Hopes must center on our selves alone.
475   Yet those how feeble, and, indeed, how vain,
You see too well; nor need my Words explain.
Vanquish'd without ressource; laid flat by Fate,
Factions within, a Foe without the Gate;
Not but I grant, that all perform'd their parts,
480   With manly Force, and with undaunted Hearts:
With our united Strength the War we wag'd;
With equal Numbers, equal Arms engag'd:
You see th' Event – Now hear what I propose,
To save our Friends, and satisfie our Foes:
485   A Tract of Land the *Latins* have possess'd
Along the *Tyber*, stretching to the West,
Which now *Rutulians* and *Auruncans* till:
And their mix'd Cattle graze the fruitful Hill;
Those Mountains fill'd with Firs, that lower Land,
490   If you consent, the *Trojan* shall Command.
Call'd into part of what is ours; and there,
On terms agreed, the common Country share.
There let 'em build, and settle if they please;
Unless they chuse once more to cross the Seas,
495   In search of Seats remote from *Italy*;
And from unwelcome Inmates set us free.
Then twice ten Gallies let us build with Speed,
Or twice as many more, if more they need;
Materials are at hand: A well-grown Wood
500   Runs equal with the Margin of the Flood:
Let them the Number, and the Form assign;
The Care and Cost of all the Stores be mine.
To treat the Peace, a hundred Senators
Shall be commission'd hence with ample Pow'rs;
505   With Olive crown'd: The Presents they shall bear,
A Purple Robe, a Royal Iv'ry Chair;
And all the marks of Sway that *Latian* Monarchs wear;

And Sums of Gold. Among your selves debate
This great Affair, and save the sinking State.
510   Then *Drances* took the word; who grudg'd, long since,
The rising Glories of the *Daunian* Prince.
Factious and rich, bold at the Council Board, ⎫
But cautious in the Field, he shun'd the Sword; ⎬
A closs Caballer, and Tongue-valiant Lord. ⎭
515   Noble his Mother was, and near the Throne,
But what his Father's Parentage, unknown.
He rose, and took th' Advantage of the Times,
To load young *Turnus* with invidious Crimes.
Such Truths, O King, said he, your Words contain,
520   As strike the Sence, and all Replies are vain.
Nor are your Loyal Subjects now to seek
What common Needs require; but fear to speak.
Let him give leave of Speech, that haughty Man,
Whose Pride this unauspicious War began:
525   For whose Ambition (let me dare to say,
Fear set apart, though Death is in my Way)
The Plains of *Latium* run with Blood around;
So many Valiant Heroes bite the Ground:
Dejected Grief in ev'ry Face appears;
530   A Town in Mourning, and a Land in Tears.
While he th' undoubted Author of our Harms,
The Man who menaces the Gods with Arms,
Yet, after all his Boasts, forsook the Fight,
And sought his safety in ignoble Flight.
535   Now, best of Kings, since you propose to send
Such bounteous Presents to your *Trojan* Friend;
Add yet a greater at our joint Request,
One which he values more than all the rest;
Give him the fair *Lavinia* for his Bride: ⎫
540   With that Alliance let the League be ty'd: ⎬
And for the bleeding Land a lasting Peace provide. ⎭
Let Insolence no longer awe the Throne,
But with a Father's Right bestow your own.
For this Maligner of the general Good,
545   If still we fear his Force, he must be woo'd:
His haughty Godhead we with Pray'rs implore,
Your Scepter to release, and our just Rights restore.

O cursed Cause of all our Ills, must we
Wage Wars unjust, and fall in Fight for thee!
550 What right hast thou to rule the *Latian* State,
And send us out to meet our certain Fate?
'Tis a destructive War; from *Turnus* Hand
Our Peace and publick safety we demand.
Let the fair Bride to the brave Chief remain;
555 If not, the Peace without the Pledge is vain.
Turnus, I know you think me not your Friend,
Nor will I much with your Belief contend:
I beg your Greatness not to give the Law
In other Realms, but, beaten, to withdraw.
560 Pity your own, or pity our Estate;
Nor twist our Fortunes with your sinking Fate.
Your Interest is the War shou'd never cease;
But we have felt enough, to wish the Peace:
A Land exhausted to the last remains,
565 Depopulated Towns, and driven Plains.
Yet, if desire of Fame, and thirst of Pow'r,
A Beauteous Princess, with a Crown in Dow'r,
So fire your Mind, in Arms assert your Right;
And meet your Foe, who dares you to the Fight.
570 Mankind, it seems, is made for you alone;
We, but the Slaves who mount you to the Throne:
A base ignoble Crowd, without a Name,
Unwept, unworthy of the Fun'ral Flame:
By Duty bound to forfeit each his Life,
575 That *Turnus* may possess a Royal Wife.
Permit not, Mighty Man, so mean a Crew
Shou'd share such Triumphs; and detain from you }
The Post of Honour, your undoubted Due:
Rather alone your matchless Force employ;
580 To merit, what alone you must enjoy.
    These Words, so full of Malice, mix'd with Art,
Inflam'd with Rage the youthful Hero's Heart.
Then groaning from the bottom of his Breast,
He heav'd for Wind, and thus his Wrath express'd.
585 You, *Drances*, never want a Stream of Words,
Then, when the Publick Need requires our Swords.

First in the Council-hall to steer the State;
And ever foremost in a Tongue debate.
While our strong Walls secure us from the Foe,
590   E're yet with Blood our Ditches overflow:
But let the potent Orator declaim,
And with the brand of Coward blot my Name;
Free leave is giv'n him, when his fatal Hand
Has cover'd with more Corps the sanguine Strand; }
595   And high as mine his tow'ring Trophies stand.
If any Doubt remains who dares the most,
Let us decide it at the *Trojans* cost:
And issue both abrest, where Honour calls;
Foes are not far to seek without the Walls.
600   Unless his noisie Tongue can only fight;
And Feet were giv'n him but to speed his Flight.
I beaten from the Field? I forc'd away?
Who, but so known a Dastard, dares to say?
Had he but ev'n beheld the Fight, his Eyes
605   Had witness'd for me what his Tongue denies:
What heaps of *Trojans* by this Hand were slain,
And how the bloody *Tyber* swell'd the Main.
All saw, but he, th' *Arcadian* Troops retire,
In scatter'd Squadrons, and their Prince expire.
610   The Gyant Brothers, in their Camp have found,
I was not forc'd with ease to quit my Ground.
Not such the *Trojans* try'd me, when inclos'd,
I singly their united Arms oppos'd:
First forc'd an Entrance through their thick Array;
615   Then, glutted with their Slaughter, freed my Way.
'Tis a destructive War? So let it be,
But to the *Phrygian* Pirate, and to thee.
Mean time proceed to fill the People's Ears
With false Reports, their Minds with panick Fears:
620   Extol the Strength of a twice conquer'd Race,
Our Foes encourage, and our Friends debase.
Believe thy Fables, and the *Trojan* Town
Triumphant stands, the *Grecians* are o'rethrown:
Suppliant at *Hector*'s Feet *Achilles* lyes;
625   And *Diomede* from fierce *Æneas* flies.

Say rapid *Aufidus* with awful Dread
Runs backward from the Sea, and hides his Head,
When the Great *Trojan* on his Bank appears:
For that's as true as thy dissembl'd Fears
630 Of my Revenge: Dismiss that Vanity,
Thou, *Drances*, art below a Death from me.
Let that vile Soul in that vile Body rest;
The Lodging is well worthy of the Guest.
　　Now, Royal Father, to the present state
635 Of our Affairs, and of this high Debate;
If in your Arms thus early you diffide,
And think your Fortune is already try'd;
If one Defeat has brought us down so low;
As never more in Fields to meet the Foe;
640 Then I conclude for Peace: 'Tis time to treat,
And lye like Vassals at the Victor's Feet.
But oh, if any ancient Blood remains,
One drop of all our Father's in our Veins;
That Man would I prefer before the rest,
645 Who dar'd his Death with an undaunted Breast;
Who comely fell, by no dishonest Wound,
To shun that sight; and dying gnaw'd the Ground.
But if we still have fresh Recruits in store,
If our Confederates can afford us more;
650 If the contended Field we bravely fought;
And not a bloodless Victory was bought:
Their Losses equall'd ours, and for their slain,
With equal Fires they fill'd the shining Plain;
Why thus unforc'd shou'd we so tamely yield;
655 And e're the Trumpet sounds, resign the Field?
Good unexpected, Evils unforeseen,
Appear by Turns, as Fortune shifts the Scene:
Some, rais'd aloft, come tumbling down amain;
Then fall so hard, they bound and rise again.
660 If *Diomede* refuse his Aid to lend,
The great *Messapus* yet remains our Friend:
Tolumnius, who foretels Events, is ours;
Th' *Italian* Chiefs, and Princes, joyn their Pow'rs:
Nor least in Number, nor in Name the last,
665 Your own brave Subjects have your Cause embrac'd.

Above the rest, the *Volscian Amazon*
Contains an Army in her self alone:
And heads a Squadron, terrible to sight,
With glitt'ring Shields, in Brazen Armour bright.
670 Yet if the Foe a single Fight demand,
And I alone the Publick Peace withstand;
If you consent, he shall not be refus'd,
Nor find a Hand to Victory unus'd.
This new *Achilles*, let him take the Field,
675 With fated Armour, and *Vulcanian* Shield;
For you, my Royal Father, and my Fame,
I, *Turnus*, not the least of all my Name,
Devote my Soul. He calls me hand to hand,
And I alone will answer his Demand.
680 *Drances* shall rest secure, and neither share
The Danger, nor divide the Prize of War.
    While they debate; nor these nor those will yield;
Æneas draws his Forces to the Field:
And moves his Camp. The Scouts, with flying Speed
685 Return, and thro' the frighted City spread
Th' unpleasing News, the *Trojans* are descry'd,
In Battel marching by the River side;
And bending to the Town. They take th' Allarm,
Some tremble, some are bold, all in Confusion arm.
690 Th' impetuous Youth press forward to the Field;
They clash the Sword, and clatter on the Shield:
The fearful Matrons raise a screaming Cry; ⎫
Old feeble Men with fainter Groans reply: ⎬
A jarring Sound results, and mingles in the Sky. ⎭
695 Like that of Swans remurm'ring to the Floods;
Or Birds of diff'ring kinds in hollow Woods.
Turnus th' occasion takes, and cries aloud,
Talk on, ye quaint Haranguers of the Crowd:
Declaim in praise of Peace, when Danger calls;
700 And the fierce Foes in Arms approach the Walls.
He said, and turning short, with speedy Pace,
Casts back a scornful Glance, and quits the Place.
    Thou, *Volusus*, the *Volscian* Troops command
To mount; and lead thy self our *Ardean* Band.

705   *Messapus*, and *Catillus*, post your Force
      Along the Fields, to charge the *Trojan* Horse.
      Some guard the Passes, others man the Wall;
      Drawn up in Arms, the rest attend my Call.
         They swarm from ev'ry Quarter of the Town;
710   And with disorder'd haste the Rampires crown.
      Good old *Latinus*, when he saw, too late,
      The gath'ring Storm, just breaking on the State,
      Dismiss'd the Council, 'till a fitter time.
      And own'd his easie Temper as his Crime:
715   Who, forc'd against his reason, had comply'd
      To break the Treaty for the promis'd Bride.
         Some help to sink new Trenches, others aid
      To ram the Stones, or raise the Palisade.
      Hoarse Trumpets sound th' Alarm: Around the Walls
720   Runs a distracted Crew, whom their last Labour calls.
      A sad Procession in the Streets is seen,
      Of Matrons that attend the Mother Queen:
      High in her Chair she sits, and at her side,
      With downcast Eyes appears the fatal Bride.
725   They mount the Cliff, where *Pallas*'s Temple stands;
      Pray'rs in their Mouths, and Presents in their Hands:
      With Censers, first they fume the sacred Shrine;
      Then in this common Supplication joyn.
      O Patroness of Arms, unspotted Maid,
730   Propitious hear, and lend thy *Latins* Aid:
      Break short the Pirat's Lance; pronounce his Fate,
      And lay the *Phrygian* low before the Gate.
      Now *Turnus* arms for Fight: His Back and Breast
      Well temper'd Steel, and scaly Brass invest:
735   The Cuishes, which his brawny Thighs infold,
      Are mingled Metal damask'd o're with Gold.
      His faithful Fauchion sits upon his side;
      Nor Casque, nor Crest, his manly Features hide:
      But bare to view, amid surrounding Friends,
740   With Godlike Grace, he from the Tow'r descends.
      Exulting in his Strength, he seems to dare
      His absent Rival, and to promise War.
         Freed from his Keepers, thus with broken Reins,
      The wanton Courser prances o're the Plains:

745   Or in the Pride of Youth o'releaps the Mounds;
     And snuffs the Females in forbidden Grounds.
     Or seeks his wat'ring in the well known Flood,
     To quench his Thirst, and cool his fiery Blood:
     He swims luxuriant, in the liquid Plain,
750   And o're his Shoulder flows his waving Mane:
     He neighs, he snorts, he bears his Head on high;
     Before his ample Chest the frothy Waters fly.
       Soon as the Prince appears without the Gate,
     The *Volcians*, with their Virgin Leader, wait
755   His Last Commands. Then with a graceful Meen,
     Lights from her lofty Steed, the Warrior Queen:
     Her Squadron imitates, and each descends;
     Whose common Sute *Camilla* thus commends.
       If Sence of Honour, if a Soul secure
760   Of inborn Worth, that can all Tests endure,
     Can promise ought; or on it self rely,
     Greatly to dare, to conquer or to dye:
     Then, I alone, sustain'd by these, will meet
     The *Tyrrhene* Troops, and promise their Defeat.
765   Ours be the Danger, ours the sole Renown;
     You, Gen'ral, stay behind, and guard the Town.
       Turnus a while stood mute, with glad Surprize,
     And on the fierce Virago fix'd his Eyes:
     Then thus return'd: O Grace of *Italy*,
770   With what becoming Thanks can I reply!
     Not only Words lye lab'ring in my Breast;
     But Thought it self is by thy Praise opprest.
     Yet rob me not of all, but let me join
     My Toils, my Hazard, and my Fame, with thine.
775   The *Trojan*, (not in Stratagem unskill'd,)
     Sends his light Horse before to scour the Field:
     Himself, through steep Ascents, and thorny Brakes,
     A larger Compass to the City takes.
     This news my Scouts confirm: And I prepare
780   To foil his Cunning, and his Force to dare.
     With chosen Foot his Passage to forelay;
     And place an Ambush in the winding way.
     Thou, with thy *Volscians*, face the *Tuscan* Horse:
     The brave *Messapus* shall thy Troops inforce;

785   With those of *Tibur*; and the *Latian* Band:
      Subjected all to thy Supream Command.
         This said, he warns *Messapus* to the War:
      Then ev'ry Chief exhorts, with equal Care.
      All thus encourag'd, his own Troops he joins,
790   And hastes to prosecute his deep Designs.
         Inclos'd with Hills, a winding Valley lies,
      By Nature form'd for Fraud, and fitted for Surprize:
      A narrow Track, by Human Steps untrode,
      Leads, thro' perplexing Thorns, to this obscure abode.
795   High o're the Vale a steepy Mountain stands;
      Whence the surveying Sight the neather Ground
            commands.
      The top is level: an offensive Seat
      Of War; and from the War a safe Retreat.
      For, on the right, and left, is room to press
800   The Foes at hand, or from afar distress:
      To drive 'em headlong downward; and to pour
      On their descending backs, a stony show'r.
      Thither Young *Turnus* took the well known way;
      Possess'd the Pass, and in blind Ambush lay.
805   Mean time, *Latonian Phœbe* from the Skies,
      Beheld th' approaching War with hateful Eies.
      And call'd the light-foot *Opis* to her aid,
      Her most belov'd, and ever trusty Maid.
      Then with a sigh began: *Camilla* goes
810   To meet her Death, amidst her Fatal Foes.
      The Nymph I lov'd of all my Mortal Train;
      Invested with *Diana*'s Arms, in vain.
      Nor is my kindness for the Virgin, new,
      'Twas born with Her, and with her Years it grew:
815   Her Father *Metabus*, when forc'd away
      From old *Privernum*, for Tyrannick sway;
      Snatch'd up, and sav'd from his prevailing Foes,
      This tender Babe, Companion of his Woes.
      Casmilla was her Mother; but he drown'd,
820   One hissing Letter in a softer sound,
      And call'd *Camilla*. Thro the Woods, he flies;
      Wrap'd in his Robe the Royal Infant lies.

His Foes in sight, he mends his weary pace;
With shouts and clamours they pursue the Chace.

825 The Banks of *Amasene* at length he gains;
The raging Flood his farther flight restrains:
Rais'd o're the Borders with unusual Rains.
Prepar'd to Plunge into the Stream, He fears:
Not for himself, but for the Charge he bears.

830 Anxious he stops a while; and thinks in haste;
Then, desp'rate in Distress, resolves at last.
A knotty Lance of well–boil'd Oak he bore;
The middle part with Cork he cover'd o're:
He clos'd the Child within the hollow Space;

835 With Twigs of bending Osier bound the Case.
Then pois'd the Spear, heavy with Human Weight;
And thus invok'd my Favour for the Freight.
Accept, great Goddess of the Woods, he said,
Sent by her Sire, this dedicated Maid:

840 Thro' Air she flies a Suppliant to thy Shrine;
And the first Weapons that she knows, are thine.
He said; and with full Force the Spear he threw:
Above the sounding Waves *Camilla* flew.
Then, press'd by Foes, he stemm'd the stormy Tyde;

845 And gain'd, by stress of Arms, the farther Side.
His fasten'd Spear he pull'd from out the Ground;
And, Victor of his Vows, his Infant Nymph unbound.
Nor after that, in Towns which Walls inclose,
Wou'd trust his hunted Life amidst his Foes.

850 But rough, in open Air he chose to lye:
Earth was his Couch, his Cov'ring was the Sky.
On Hills unshorn, or in a desart Den,
He shunn'd the dire Society of Men.
A Shepherd's solitary Life he led:

855 His Daughter with the Milk of Mares he fed;
The Dugs of Bears, and ev'ry Salvage Beast,
He drew, and thro' her Lips the Liquor press'd.
The little *Amazon* cou'd scarcely go,
He loads her with a Quiver and a Bow:

860 And, that she might her stagg'ring Steps command,
He with a slender Jav'lin fills her Hand:

Her flowing Hair no golden Fillet bound;
Nor swept her trayling Robe the dusty Ground.
Instead of these, a Tyger's Hide o'respread
865 Her Back and Shoulders, fasten'd to her Head.
The flying Dart she first attempts to fling;
And round her tender Temples toss'd the Sling:
Then, as her Strength with Years increas'd, began }
To pierce aloft in Air the soaring Swan: }
870 And from the Clouds to fetch the Heron and the Crane. }
The *Tuscan* Matrons with each other vy'd,
To bless their Rival Sons with such a Bride:
But she disdains their Love; to share with me
The Silvan Shades, and vow'd Virginity.
875 And oh! I wish, contented with my Cares
Of Salvage Spoils, she had not sought the Wars:
Then had she been of my Cœlestial Train;
And shun'd the Fate that dooms her to be slain.
But, since opposing Heav'n's Decree, she goes
880 To find her Death among forbidden Foes;
Haste with these Arms, and take thy steepy flight,
Where, with the Gods averse, the *Latins* fight:
This Bow to thee, this Quiver, I bequeath,
This chosen Arrow to revenge her Death:
885 By what e're Hand *Camilla* shall be slain, }
Or of the *Trojan*, or *Italian* Train, }
Let him not pass unpunish'd from the Plain. }
Then, in a hollow Cloud, my self will Aid,
To bear the breathless Body of my Maid:
890 Unspoil'd shall be her Arms, and unprophan'd }
Her holy Limbs with any Human Hand: }
And in a Marble Tomb laid in her Native Land. }
    She said: The faithful Nymph descends from high }
With rapid flight, and cuts the sounding Sky; }
895 Black Clouds and stormy Winds around her Body fly. }
    By this, the *Trojan* and the *Tuscan* Horse,
Drawn up in Squadrons, with united Force,
Approach the Walls; the sprightly Coursers bound;
Press forward on their Bitts, and shift their Ground:
900 Shields, Arms, and Spears, flash horribly from far;
And the Fields glitter with a waving War.

Oppos'd to these, come on with furious force,
Messapus, *Coras*, and the *Latian* Horse;
These in the Body plac'd; on either hand
905 Sustain'd, and clos'd by fair *Camilla's* Band.
Advancing in a Line, they couch their Spears;
And less and less the middle Space appears.
Thick Smoke obscures the Field: And scarce are seen
The neighing Coursers, and the shouting Men.
910 In distance of their Darts they stop their Course;
Then Man to Man they rush, and Horse to Horse.
The face of Heav'n their flying Jav'lins hide;
And Deaths unseen are dealt on either side.
Tyrrhenus, and *Aconteus*, void of Fear,
915 By metled Coursers born in full Carreer,
Meet first oppos'd: and, with a mighty Shock,
Their Horses Heads against each other knock.
Far from his Steed is fierce *Aconteus* cast; ⎫
As with an Engin's force, or Lightning's blast: ⎬
920 He rowls along in Blood, and breaths his last. ⎭
The *Latin* Squadrons take a sudden fright;
And sling their Shields behind, to save their Backs in flight.
Spurring at Speed to their own Walls they drew;
Close in the rear the *Tuscan* Troops pursue:
925 And urge their flight. *Asylas* leads the Chase;
'Till seiz'd with Shame they wheel about and face:
Receive their Foes, and raise a threat'ning Cry:
The *Tuscans* take their turn to fear and fly.
    So swelling Surges, with a thund'ring Roar,
930 Driv'n on each others Backs, insult the Shoar;
Bound o're the Rocks, incroach upon the Land;
And far upon the Beach eject the Sand.
Then backward with a Swing, they take their Way;
Repuls'd from upper Ground, and seek their Mother Sea:
935 With equal hurry quit th' invaded Shore;
And swallow back the Sand, and Stones they spew'd before.
Twice were the *Tuscans* Masters of the Field,
Twice by the *Latins*, in their turn repell'd.
Asham'd at length, to the third charge they ran,
940 Both Hoasts resolv'd, and mingled Man to Man:

Now dying Groans are heard, the Fields are strow'd
With falling Bodies, and are drunk with Blood:
Arms, Horses, Men, on heaps together lye:
Confus'd the Fight, and more confus'd the Cry.
945 *Orsilochus*, who durst not press too near
Strong *Remulus*, at distance drove his Spear;
And stuck the Steel beneath his Horses Ear:
The fiery Steed, impatient of the Wound,
Curvets, and springing upward with a Bound,
950 His helpless Lord cast backward on the Ground.
Catillus pierc'd *Iolas* first; then drew
His reeking Lance, and at *Herminius* threw:
The mighty Champion of the *Tuscan* Crew,
His Neck and Throat unarm'd, his Head was bare,
955 But shaded with a length of yellow Hair:
Secure, he fought, expos'd on ev'ry part,
A spacious mark for Swords, and for the flying Dart:
Across the Shoulders came the feather'd Wound;
Transfix'd, he fell, and doubled to the Ground.
960   The Sands with streaming Blood are sanguine dy'd;
And Death with Honour, sought on either side.
    Resistless through the War, *Camilla* rode;
In Danger unappall'd, and pleas'd with Blood.
One side was bare for her exerted Breast;
965 One Shoulder with her painted Quiver press'd.
Now from afar her Fatal Jav'lins play;
Now with her Axe's edge she hews her Way:
Diana's Arms upon her Shoulder sound;
And when, too closely press'd, she quits the Ground;
970 From her bent Bow she sends a backward Wound.
Her Maids, in Martial Pomp, on either side
Larina, *Tulla*, fierce *Tarpeia* ride;
Italians all: in Peace, their Queen's delight:
In War the bold Companions of the Fight.
975   So march'd the *Thracian Amazons* of old,
When *Thermodon* with bloody Billows rowl'd:
Such Troops as these in shining Arms were seen;
When *Theseus* met in Fight their Maiden Queen.
Such to the Field *Penthisilea* led,
980 From the fierce Virgin when the *Grecians* fled:

With such, return'd Triumphant from the War;
Her maids with Cries attend the lofty Carr:
They clash with manly force their Moony Shields;
With Female Showts resound the *Phrygian* Fields.

985　　Who formost, and who last, Heroick Maid
On the cold Earth were by thy Courage laid?
Thy Spear, of Mountain Ash, *Eumenius* first,
With fury driv'n, from side to side transpierc'd:
A purple Stream came spowting from the Wound;
990　Bath'd in his Blood he lies, and bites the Ground.
Lyris and *Pagasus* at once she slew;
The former, as the slacken'd Reins he drew,
Of his faint steed: the latter, as he stretch'd
His Arm to prop his Friend, the Jav'lin reach'd.
995　By the same Weapon, sent from the same Hand,
Both fall together, and both spurn the Sand.
Amastrus next is added to the slain:
The rest in Rout she follows o're the Plain.
Tereus, Harpalicus, Demophöon,
1000　And *Chromys,* at full Speed her Fury shun.
Of all her deadly Darts, not one she lost;
Each was attended with a *Trojan* Ghost.
Young *Ornithus* bestrode a Hunter Steed,
Swift for the Chase, and of *Apulian* Breed:
1005　Him, from afar, she spy'd in Arms unknown;
O're his broad Back an Oxes hide was thrown:
His Helm a Wolf, whose gaping Jaws were spread,
A cov'ring for his Cheeks, and grinn'd around his Head.
He clench'd within his Hand an Iron Prong;
1010　And tow'rd above the rest, conspicuous in the Throng.
Him soon she singled from the flying Train,
And slew with ease: Then thus insults the slain.
Vain Hunter didst thou think thro' Woods to chase
The Savage Herd, a vile and trembling Race:
1015　Here cease thy Vaunts, and own my Victory;
A Woman-Warrior was too strong for thee.
Yet if the Ghosts demand the Conqu'ror's Name,
Confessing great *Camilla,* save thy Shame.
Then *Butes,* and *Orsilochus,* she slew:
1020　The bulkiest Bodies of the *Trojan* Crew.

But *Butes* Breast to Breast: the Spear descends
Above the Gorget, where his Helmet ends;
And o're the Shield which his left Side defends.
Orsilochus and she, their Coursers ply;
1025 He seems to follow, and she seems to fly.
But in a narrower Ring she makes the Race;
And then he flies, and she pursues the Chase.
Gath'ring at length on her deluded Foe,
She swings her Axe, and rises to the Blow:
1030 Full on the Helm behind, with such a sway
The Weapon falls, the riven Steel gives way:
He groans, he roars, he sues in vain for Grace;
Brains, mingled with his Blood, besmear his Face.
Astonish'd *Aunus* just arrives by Chance,
1035 To see his Fall, nor farther dares advance:
But fixing on the horrid Maid his Eye,
He stares, and shakes, and finds it vain to fly.
Yet like a true *Ligurian*, born to cheat,
(At least while Fortune favour'd his Deceit)
1040 Cries out aloud, what Courage have you shown,
Who trust your Coursers Strength, and not your own?
Forego the vantage of your Horse, alight,
And then on equal Terms begin the Fight:
It shall be seen, weak Woman, what you can,
1045 When Foot to Foot, you combat with a Man.
He said: She glows with Anger and Disdain,
Dismounts with speed to dare him on the Plain;
And leaves her Horse at large among her Train.
With her drawn Sword defies him to the Field;
1050 And marching, lifts aloft her maiden Shield:
The Youth, who thought his Cunning did succeed,
Reins round his Horse, and urges all his Speed,
Adds the remembrance of the Spur, and hides
The goring Rowels in his bleeding Sides.
1055 Vain Fool, and Coward, cries the lofty Maid,
Caught in the Train, which thou thy self hast laid!
On others practise thy *Ligurian* Arts;
Thin Stratagems, and Tricks of little Hearts
Are lost on me. Nor shalt thou safe retire,
1060 With vaunting Lyes to thy fallacious Sire.

At this, so fast her flying Feet she sped,
That soon she strain'd beyond his Horse's Head:
Then turning short, at once she seiz'd the Rein,
And laid the Boaster grov'ling on the Plain.
1065 Not with more ease the Falcon from above,
Trusses, in middle Air, the trembling Dove:
Then Plumes the Prey, in her strong Pounces bound;
The Feathers foul with Blood come tumbling to the ground.
    Now mighty *Jove*, from his superior height,
1070 With his broad Eye surveys th' unequal Fight.
He fires the Breast of *Tarchon* with Disdain;
And sends him to redeem th' abandon'd Plain.
Betwixt the broken Ranks the *Tuscan* rides,
And these encourages, and those he chides:
1075 Recalls each Leader, by his Name, from flight;
Renews their Ardour; and restores the Fight.
What Panick Fear has seiz'd your Souls, O shame,
O Brand perpetual of th' *Etrurian* Name;
Cowards incurable, a Woman's Hand
1080 Drives, breaks, and scatters your ignoble Band!
Now cast away the Sword, and quit the Shield:
What use of Weapons which you dare not wield?
Not thus you fly your Female Foes, by Night,
Nor shun the Feast, when the full Bowls invite:
1085 When to fat Off'rings the glad *Augur* calls;
And the shrill Horn-pipe sounds to *Bacchanals*.
These are your study'd Cares; your lewd Delight:
Swift to debauch; but slow to Manly Fight.
    Thus having said, he spurs amid the Foes;
1090 Not managing the Life he meant to lose.
The first he found he seiz'd, with headlong haste,
In his strong Gripe; and clasp'd around the Waste:
'Twas *Venulus*; whom from his Horse he tore,
And (laid athwart his own,) in Triumph bore.
1095 Loud Shouts ensue: The *Latins* turn their Eyes,
And view th' unusual sight with vast Surprize.
The fiery *Tarchon*, flying o're the Plains,
Press'd in his Arms the pond'rous Prey sustains:
Then, with his shorten'd Spear, explores around
1100 His jointed Arms, to fix a deadly Wound.

Nor less the Captive struggles for his Life;
He writhes his Body to prolong the Strife:
And, fencing for his naked Throat, exerts
His utmost Vigour, and the point averts.
1105   So stoops the yellow Eagle from on high,
And bears a speckled Serpent thro' the Sky;
Fast'ning his crooked Tallons on the Prey:
The Pris'ner hisses thro' the liquid Way,
Resists the Royal Hawk, and tho' opprest,
1110   She fights in Volumes, and erects her Crest:
Turn'd to her Foe, she stiffens ev'ry Scale;
And shoots her forky Tongue, and whisks her threat'ning
        Tail.
Against the Victour all Defence is weak;
Th' imperial Bird still plies her with his Beak:
1115   He tears her Bowels, and her Breast he gores;
Then claps his Pinions, and securely soars.
    Thus, thro' the midst of circling Enemies,
Strong *Tarchon* snatch'd and bore away his Prize:
The *Tyrrhene* Troops, that shrunk before, now press
1120   The *Latins*, and presume the like Success.
    Then, *Aruns* doom'd to Death, his Arts assay'd
To murther, unespy'd, the *Volscian* Maid,
This way, and that his winding Course he bends;
And wheresoe're she turns, her Steps attends.
1125   When she retires victorious from the Chase,
He wheels about with Care, and shifts his place:
When rushing on, she seeks her Foes in Fight,
He keeps aloof, but keeps her still in sight:
He threats, and trembles, trying ev'ry Way
1130   Unseen to kill, and safely to betray.
    Chloreus, the Priest of *Cybelè*, from far,
Glitt'ring in *Phrygian* Arms amidst the War,
Was by the Virgin view'd: The Steed he press'd
Was proud with Trappings; and his brawny Chest
1135   With Scales of guilded Brass was cover'd o're:
A Robe of *Tyrian* Dye the Rider wore.
With deadly Wounds he gaul'd the distant Foe;
Gnossian his Shafts, and *Lycian* was his Bow:

A Golden Helm his Front, and head surrounds;
1140   A guilded Quiver from his Shoulder sounds.
         Gold, weav'd with Linen, on his Thighs he wore: ⎫
         With Flowers of Needlework distinguish'd o're: ⎬
         With Golden Buckles bound, and gather'd up before. ⎭
         Him, the fierce Maid beheld with ardent Eyes;
1145   Fond and Ambitious of so Rich a Prize:
         Or that the Temple might his Trophees hold,
         Or else to shine her self in *Trojan* Gold:
         Blind in her haste, she chases him alone,
         And seeks his Life, regardless of her own.
1150   This lucky Moment the slye Traytor chose: ⎫
         Then, starting from his Ambush up he rose, ⎬
         And threw, but first to Heav'n address'd his Vows. ⎭
         O Patron of *Soractes* high Abodes,
         Phœbus the Ruling Pow'r among the Gods;
1155   Whom first we serve, whole Woods of unctuous Pine
         Are fell'd for thee, and to thy Glory shine;
         By thee protected, with our naked Soles,
         Thro' Flames unsing'd we march, and tread the kindled
              Coals:
         Give me, propitious Pow'r, to wash away
1160   The Stains of this dishonourable Day:
         Nor Spoils, nor Triumph, from the Fact I claim;
         But with my future Actions trust my Fame.
         Let me, by stealth; this Female Plague o'recome;
         And from the Field, return inglorious home.
1165   *Apollo* heard, and granting half his Pray'r,
         Shuffled in Winds the rest, and toss'd in empty Air.
         He gives the Death desir'd; his safe return,
         By Southern Tempests to the Seas is born.
            Now, when the Jav'lin whiz'd along the Skies,
1170   Both Armies on *Camilla* turn'd their Eyes,
         Directed by the Sound: Of either Host,
         Th' unhappy Virgin, tho' concern'd the most,
         Was only deaf; so greedy was she bent
         On Golden Spoils, and on her Prey intent:
1175   Till in her Pap the winged Weapon stood
         Infix'd; and deeply drunk the purple Blood.

Her sad Attendants hasten to sustain
Their dying Lady drooping on the Plain.
Far from their sight the trembling *Aruns* flies,
1180 With beating Heart, and Fear confus'd with Joys;
Nor dares he farther to pursue his Blow;
Or ev'n to bear the sight of his expiring Foe.

As when the Wolf has torn a Bullocks Hide,
At unawares, or ranch'd a Shepherd's Side:
1185 Conscious of his audacious deed, he flies,
And claps his quiv'ring Tail between his Thighs:
So, speeding once, the Wretch no more attends;
But spurring forward herds among his Friends.
She wrench'd the Jav'lin with her dying Hands;
1190 But wedg'd within her Breast the Weapon stands:
The Wood she draws, the steely Point remains,
She staggers in her Seat, with agonizing Pains:
A gath'ring Mist o'reclouds her chearful Eyes;
And from her Cheeks the rosie Colour flies.

1195 Then, turns to her, whom, of her Female Train,
She trusted most, and thus she speaks with Pain.
Acca, 'tis past! He swims before my sight;
Inexorable Death; and claims his right.
Bear my last Words to *Turnus*, fly with speed,
1200 And bid him timely to my Charge succeed:
Repel the *Trojans*, and the Town relieve:
Farewel; and in this Kiss my parting breath receive.
She said; and sliding, sunk upon the Plain;
Dying, her open'd Hand forsakes the Rein;
1205 Short, and more short, she pants: by slow degrees
Her Mind the Passage from her Body frees.
She drops her Sword, she nods her plumy Crest;
Her drooping Head declining on her Breast:
In the last sigh her strugling Soul expires;
1210 And murm'ring with Disdain, to *Stygian* Sounds retires.

A Shout, that struck the Golden Stars, ensu'd:
Despair and Rage, the languish'd Fight renew'd.
The *Trojan* Troops, and *Tuscans* in a Line,
Advance to charge; the mix'd *Arcadians* join.
1215 But *Cynthia*'s Maid, high seated, from afar
Surveys the Field, and fortune of the War:

Unmov'd a while, 'till prostrate on the Plain,
Welt'ring in Blood, she sees *Camilla* slain;
And round her Corps, of Friends and Foes a fighting
    Train.

1220 Then, from the bottom of her Breast, she drew
A mournful Sigh, and these sad Words ensue:
Too dear a Fine, ah much lamented Maid,
For warring with the *Trojans*, thou hast paid!
Nor ought avail'd, in this unhappy Strife,

1225 *Diana*'s sacred Arms, to save thy Life.
Yet unreveng'd thy Goddess will not leave
Her Vot'rys Death, nor with vain Sorrow grieve.
Branded the Wretch, and be his Name abhorr'd;
But after Ages shall thy Praise record.

1230 Th' inglorious Coward soon shall press the Plain;
Thus vows thy Queen, and thus the Fates ordain.
    High o're the Field, there stood a hilly Mound;
Sacred the Place, and spread with Oaks around;
Where, in a Marble Tomb, *Dercennus* lay,

1235 A King that once in *Latium* bore the Sway.
The beauteous *Opis* thither bent her flight,
To mark the Traytor *Aruns*, from the height.
Him, in refulgent Arms she soon espy'd,
Swoln with success, and loudly thus she cry'd.

1240 Thy backward steps, vain Boaster, are too late;
Turn, like a Man at length, and meet thy Fate.
Charg'd with my Message to *Camilla* go;
And say I sent thee to the Shades below;
An Honour undeserv'd from *Cynthia*'s Bow.

1245   She said: and from her Quiver chose with speed
The winged Shaft, predestin'd for the Deed:
Then, to the stubborn Eugh her strength apply'd;
Till the far distant Horns approach'd on either side.
The Bow-string touch'd her Breast, so strong she drew;

1250 Whizzing in Air the fatal Arrow flew.
At once the twanging Bow, and sounding Dart
The Traytor heard, and felt the point within his heart.
Him, beating with his heels, in pangs of death,
His flying Friends to foreign Fields bequeath.

1255   The Conqu'ring Damsel, with expanded Wings,
       The welcome Message to her Mistress brings.
           Their Leader lost, the *Volscians* quit the Field;
       And, unsustain'd, the Chiefs of *Turnus* yield.
       The frighted Souldiers, when their Captains fly,
1260   More on their speed than on their Strength rely.
       Confus'd in flight, they bear each other down:
       And spur their Horses headlong to the Town.
       Driv'n by their Foes, and to their Fears resign'd,
       Not once they turn; but take their Wounds behind.
1265   These drop the Shield, and those the Lance forego;
       Or on their Shoulders bear the slacken'd Bow.
       The Hoofs of Horses with a ratling sound,
       Beat short, and thick, and shake the rotten ground.
       Black clouds of dust, come rowling in the Sky,
1270   And o're the darken'd Walls, and Rampires fly.
       The trembling Matrons, from their lofty Stands,
       Rend Heaven with Female Shrieks; and wring their Hands.
       All pressing on, Pursuers and pursu'd,
       Are crush'd in Crowds, a mingled Multitude.
1275   Some happy few escape: the Throng too late
       Rush on for Entrance, till they choak the Gate.
       Ev'n in the sight of home, the wretched Sire
       Looks on, and sees his helpless Son expire.
       Then, in a fright, the folding Gates they close:
1280   But leave their Friends excluded with their Foes.
       The vanquish'd cry; the Victors loudly shout;
       Tis Terror all within; and Slaughter all without.
       Blind in their Fear, they bounce against the wall,
       Or to the Moats pursu'd, precipitate their fall.
1285   The *Latian* Virgins, valiant with despair,
       Arm'd on the Tow'rs the Common Danger share:
       So much of Zeal their Country's Cause inspir'd;
       So much *Camilla*'s great Example fir'd.
       Poles, sharpen'd in the flames, from high they throw;
1290   With imitated Darts to gaul the Foe.
       Their Lives, for Godlike freedom they bequeath;
       And crow'd each other to be first in death.
       Mean time, to *Turnus*, ambush'd in the shade,
       With heavy tydings, came th' Unhappy Maid.

1295   The *Volscians* overthrown, *Camilla* kill'd,
       The Foes entirely Masters of the Field,
       Like a resistless Flood, come rowling on:
       The cry goes off the Plain, and thickens to the Town.
           Inflam'd with Rage, (for so the Furies fire
1300   The *Daunian*'s Breast, and so the Fates require,)
       He leaves the hilly Pass, the Woods in vain
       Possess'd, and downward issues on the Plain:
       Scarce was he gone, when to the Streights, now freed
       From secret Foes, the *Trojan* Troops succeed.
1305   Thro' the black Forrest, and the ferny Brake,
       Unknowingly secure, their Way they take.
       From the rough Mountains to the Plain descend;
       And there, in Order drawn, their Line extend.
       Both Armies, now, in open Fields are seen:
1310   Nor far the distance of the Space between.
       Both to the City bend: *Æneas* sees,
       Thro' smoking Fields, his hast'ning Enemies.
       And *Turnus* views the *Trojans* in Array,
       And hears th' approaching Horses proudly neigh.
1315   Soon had their Hoasts in bloody Battel join'd;
       But westward to the Sea the Sun declin'd.
       Intrench'd before the Town, both Armies lye:
       While Night with sable Wings involves the Sky.

THE TWELFTH BOOK OF THE ÆNEIS

The Argument

Turnus *challenges* Æneas *to a single Combat: Articles are agreed on, but broken by the* Rutuli, *who wound* Æneas: *He is miraculously cur'd by* Venus, *forces* Turnus *to a Duel, and concludes the Poem with his Death.*

When *Turnus* saw the *Latins* leave the Field;
Their Armies broken, and their Courage quell'd;
Himself become the Mark of publick Spight,
His Honour question'd for the promis'd Fight:
5   The more he was with Vulgar hate oppress'd;
The more his Fury boil'd within his Breast:
He rowz'd his Vigour for the last Debate;
And rais'd his haughty Soul, to meet his Fate.
     As when the Swains the *Lybian* Lion chase,
10 He makes a sour Retreat, nor mends his Pace;
But if the pointed Jav'lin pierce his Side,
The Lordly Beast returns with double Pride:
He wrenches out the Steel, he roars for Pain;
His sides he lashes, and erects his Mane.
15 So *Turnus* fares; his Eye-balls flash with Fire,
Through his wide Nostrils Clouds of Smoke expire.
     Trembling with Rage, around the Court he ran;
At length approach'd the King, and thus began.
No more excuses or Delays: I stand
20 In Arms prepar'd to Combat, hand to hand,
This base Deserter of his Native Land.
The *Trojan*, by his Word, is bound to take
The same Conditions which himself did make.
Renew the Truce, the solemn Rites prepare;
25 And to my single Virtue trust the War.
The *Latians* unconcern'd shall see the Fight;
This Arm unaided shall assert your Right:
Then, if my prostrate Body press the Plain,
To him the Crown, and beauteous Bride remain.
30   To whom the King sedately thus reply'd;
Brave Youth, the more your Valour has been try'd,
The more becomes it us, with due Respect
To weigh the chance of War, which you neglect.

You want not Wealth, or a successive Throne,
35   Or Cities, which your Arms have made your own;
My Towns and Treasures are at your Command;
And stor'd with blooming Beauties is my Land:
Laurentum more than one *Lavinia* sees,
Unmarry'd, fair, of Noble Families.
40   Now let me speak; and you with Patience hear,
Things which perhaps may grate a Lover's Ear:
But sound Advice, proceeding from a heart,
Sincerely yours, and free from fraudful Art.
    The Gods, by Signs, have manifestly shown,
45   No Prince, *Italian* born, should heir my Throne:
Oft have our Augurs, in Prediction skill'd,
And oft our Priests a Foreign Son reveal'd.
Yet, won by Worth, that cannot be withstood,
Brib'd by my Kindness to my kindred Blood,
50   Urg'd by my Wife, who wou'd not be deny'd;
I promis'd my *Lavinia* for your Bride:
Her from her plighted Lord by force I took;
All tyes of Treaties, and of Honour broke:
On your Account I wag'd an impious War,
55   With what Success 'tis needless to declare;
I, and my Subjects feel; and you have had your Share.
Twice vanquish'd, while in bloody Fields we strive,
Scarce in our Walls, we keep our Hopes alive:
The rowling Flood runs warm with human Gore;
60   The Bones of *Latians* glance the neighb'ring Shore:
Why put I not an end to this Debate,
Still unresolv'd, and still a Slave to Fate?
If *Turnus*'s Death a lasting Peace can give,
Why shou'd I not procure it, whilst you live.
65   Shou'd I to doubtful Arms your Youth betray,
What wou'd my Kinsmen, the *Rutulians*, say?
And shou'd you fall in Fight, (which Heav'n defend)
How curse the Cause, which hasten'd to his end,
The Daughter's Lover, and the Father's Friend?
70   Weigh in your Mind, the various Chance of War,
Pity your Parent's Age; and ease his Care.
    Such balmy Words he pour'd, but all in vain;
The proffer'd Med'cine but provok'd the Pain.

The wrathful Youth disdaining the Relief,
75 With intermitting Sobs, thus vents his Grief.
The care, O best of Fathers, which you take
For my Concerns, at my Desire, forsake.
Permit me not to languish out my Days;
But make the best exchange of Life for Praise.
80 This Arm, this Lance, can well dispute the Prize;
And the Blood follows, where the Weapon flies:
His Goddess Mother is not near, to shroud
The flying Coward, with an empty Cloud.

But now the Queen, who fear'd for *Turnus* Life,
85 And loath'd the hard Conditions of the Strife,
Held him by Force; and, dying in his Death,
In these sad Accents gave her Sorrow breath.
O *Turnus* I adjure thee by these Tears;
And what-e're price *Amata*'s Honour bears
90 Within thy Breast, since thou art all my hope,
My sickly Mind's repose, my sinking Age's prop;
Since on the safety of thy Life alone,
Depends *Latinus*, and the *Latian* Throne:
Refuse me not this one, this only Pray'r;
95 To wave the Combat, and pursue the War.
Whatever chance attends this fatal Strife,
Think it includes in thine *Amata*'s Life.
I cannot live a Slave; or see my Throne
Usurp'd by Strangers, or a *Trojan* Son.
100 At this, a Flood of Tears *Lavinia* shed;   ⎫
A crimson Blush her beauteous Face o'respread;   ⎬
Varying her Cheeks by Turns, with white and red. ⎭
The driving Colours, never at a stay,
Run here and there; and flush, and fade away.
105 Delightful change! Thus *Indian* Iv'ry shows,   ⎫
Which with the bord'ring Paint of Purple glows;   ⎬
Or Lillies damask'd by the neighb'ring Rose.   ⎭
The Lover gaz'd, and burning with desire,
The more he look'd, the more he fed the Fire:
110 Revenge, and jealous Rage, and secret Spight;
Rowl in his Breast, and rowze him to the Fight.
Then fixing on the Queen his ardent Eyes,
Firm to his first intent, he thus replies.

O Mother, do not by your Tears prepare
115 Such boding Omens, and prejudge the War.
Resolv'd on Fight, I am no longer free
To shun my Death, if Heav'n my Death decree.
      Then turning to the Herald, thus pursues;
Go, greet the *Trojan* with ungrateful News,
120 Denounce from me, that when to Morrows Light
Shall guild the Heav'ns, he need not urge the Fight:
The *Trojan* and *Rutulian* Troops, no more
Shall dye, with mutual Blood, the *Latian* Shore:
Our single Swords the Quarrel shall decide,
125 And to the Victor be the beauteous Bride.
      He said, and striding on, with speedy Pace,
He sought his Coursers of the *Thracian* Race.
At his Approach, they toss their Heads on high;
And proudly neighing, promise Victory.
130 The Sires of these *Orythia* sent from far,
To grace *Pilumnus*, when he went to War.
The drifts of *Thracian* Snows were scarce so white,
Nor Northern Winds in fleetness match'd their Flight.
Officious Grooms stand ready by his Side;
135 And some with Combs their flowing Manes divide,
And others stroke their Chests, and gently sooth their
      Pride.
      He sheath'd his Limbs in Arms; a temper'd Mass
Of golden Metal those, and Mountain Brass.
Then to his Head his glitt'ring Helm he ty'd;
140 And girt his faithful Fauchion to his side.
In his *Ætnean* Forge, the God of Fire
That Fauchion labour'd for the Hero's Sire:
Immortal Keenness on the Blade bestow'd,
And plung'd it hissing in the *Stygian* Flood.
145 Prop'd on a Pillar, which the Ceiling bore,
Was plac'd the Lance *Auruncan Actor* wore;
Which with such Force he brandish'd in his Hand,
The tough Ash trembled like an Osyer Wand.
Then cry'd, O pond'rous Spoil of *Actor* slain,
150 And never yet by *Turnus* toss'd in vain,
Fail not this Day thy wonted Force: But go,
Sent by this Hand to pierce the *Trojan* Foe:

Give me to tear his Corslet from his Breast,
And from that Eunuch Head, to rend the Crest:
155 Drag'd in the Dust, his frizled Hair to soil;
Hot from the vexing Ir'n, and smear'd with fragrant Oyl.
     Thus while he raves, from his wide Nostrils flies
A fiery Stream, and Sparkles from his Eyes.
So fares the Bull in his lov'd Female's sight;
160 Proudly he bellows, and preludes the fight:
He tries his goring Horns against a Tree;
And meditates his absent Enemy:
He pushes at the Winds, he digs the Strand
With his black Hoofs, and spurns the yellow Sand.

165   Nor less the *Trojan*, in his *Lemnian* Arms,
To future Fight his Manly Courage warms:
He whets his Fury, and with Joy prepares,
To terminate at once the ling'ring Wars.
To chear his Chiefs, and tender Son, relates
170 What Heav'n had promis'd, and expounds the Fates.
Then to the *Latian* King he sends, to cease
The Rage of Arms, and ratifie the Peace.

     The Morn ensuing from the Mountain's height,
Had scarcely spread the Skies with rosie Light;
175 Th' Etherial Coursers bounding from the Sea,
From out their flaming Nostrils breath'd the Day:
When now the *Trojan* and *Rutulian* Guard,
In friendly Labour join'd, the List prepar'd.
Beneath the Walls, they measure out the Space;
180 Then sacred Altars rear, on sods of Grass;
Where, with Religious Rites, their common Gods they
          place.
In purest white, the Priests their Heads attire,
And living Waters bear, and holy Fire:
And o're their Linnen Hoods, and shaded Hair,
185 Long twisted Wreaths of sacred Vervain wear.
     In Order issuing from the Town, appears
The *Latin* Legion, arm'd with pointed Spears;
And from the Fields, advancing on a Line,
The *Trojan* and the *Tuscan* Forces join:
190 Their various Arms afford a pleasing Sight;
A peaceful Train they seem, in Peace prepar'd for Fight.

Betwixt the Ranks the proud Commanders ride,
Glitt'ring with Gold, and Vests in Purple dy'd.
Here *Mnestheus* Author of the *Memmian* Line,
195   And there *Messapus* born of Seed Divine.
The Sign is giv'n, and round the listed Space,
Each Man in order fills his proper Place.
Reclining on their ample Shields, they stand;
And fix their pointed Lances in the Sand.
200   Now, studious of the sight, a num'rous Throng
Of either Sex promiscuous, old and young,
Swarm from the Town: By those who rest behind,
The Gates and Walls, and Houses tops are lin'd.
    Mean time the Queen of Heav'n beheld the sight,
205   With Eyes unpleas'd, from Mount *Albano*'s height:
(Since call'd *Albano*, by succeeding Fame,
But then an empty Hill, without a Name.)
She thence survey'd the Field, the *Trojan* Pow'rs,
The *Latian* Squadrons, and *Laurentine* Tow'rs.
210   Then thus the Goddess of the Skies bespake,
With Sighs and Tears, the Goddess of the Lake;
King *Turnus* Sister, once a lovely Maid,
E're to the Lust of lawless *Jove* betray'd,
Compress'd by Force, but by the grateful God,
215   Now made the *Nais* of the neighb'ring Flood.
    O Nymph, the Pride of living Lakes, said she,
O most renown'd, and most belov'd by me,
Long hast thou known, nor need I to record
The wanton sallies of my wand'ring Lord:
220   Of ev'ry *Latian* fair, whom *Jove* mis-led,
To mount by Stealth my violated Bed,
To thee alone I grudg'd not his Embrace;
But gave a part of Heav'n, and an unenvy'd Place.
Now learn from me, thy near approaching Grief,
225   Nor think my Wishes want to thy Relief.
While fortune favour'd, nor Heav'n's King deny'd,
To lend my Succour to the *Latian* side,
I sav'd thy Brother, and the sinking State:
But now he struggles with unequal Fate;
230   And goes with Gods averse, o'rematch'd in Might,
To meet inevitable Death in Fight:
Nor must I break the Truce, nor can sustain the sight.

Thou, if thou dar'st, thy present Aid supply;
It well becomes a Sister's Care to try.
235   At this the lovely Nymph, with Grief oppress'd,
Thrice tore her Hair, and beat her comely Breast.
To whom *Saturnia* thus; thy Tears are late;
Haste, snatch him, if he can be snatch'd from Fate:
New Tumults kindle, violate the Truce;
240 Who knows what changeful Fortune may produce?
'Tis not a Crime t' attempt what I decree,
Or if it were, discharge the Crime on me.
She said, and, sailing on the winged Wind,
Left the sad Nymph suspended in her Mind.
245   And now in Pomp the peaceful Kings appear:
Four Steeds the Chariot of *Latinus* bear:
Twelve golden Beams around his Temples play,
To mark his Lineage from the God of Day.
Two snowy Coursers *Turnus*'s Chariot yoke,
250 And in his Hand two Massy Spears he shook:
Then issu'd from the Camp, in Arms Divine,
Æneas, Author of the *Roman* Line:
And by his side *Ascanius* took his Place,
The second Hope of *Rome*'s Immortal Race.
255 Adorn'd in white, a rev'rend Priest appears;
And Off'rings to the flaming Altars bears;
A Porker, and a Lamb, that never suffer'd Shears.
Then, to the rising Sun he turns his Eyes,
And strews the Beasts, design'd for Sacrifice,
260 With Salt, and Meal: With like officious Care
He marks their Foreheads, and he clips their Hair.
Betwixt their Horns the Purple Wine he sheds,
With the same gen'rous Juice the Flame he feeds.
Æneas then unsheath'd his shining Sword,
265 And thus with pious Pray'rs the Gods ador'd.
   All-seeing Sun, and thou *Ausonian* Soil,
For which I have sustain'd so long a Toil,
Thou King of Heav'n, and thou the Queen of Air,
(Propitious now, and reconcil'd by Pray'r,)
270 Thou God of War, whose unresisted Sway
The Labours and Events of Arms obey;
Ye living Fountains, and ye running Floods,
All Pow'rs of Ocean, all Etherial Gods,

Hear, and bear Record: if I fall in Field,
275 Or Recreant in the Fight, to *Turnus* yield,
My *Trojans* shall encrease *Evander*'s Town;
Ascanius shall renounce th' *Ausonian* Crown:
All Claims, all Questions of Debate shall cease;
Nor he, nor they, with Force infringe the Peace.
280 But if my juster Arms prevail in Fight,
As sure they shall, if I divine aright,
My *Trojans* shall not o're th' *Italians* Reign;
Both equal, both unconquer'd shall remain:
Join'd in their Laws, their Lands, and their Abodes;
285 I ask but Altars for my weary Gods:
The Care of those Religious Rites be mine;
The Crown to King *Latinus* I resign:
His be the Sov'raign Sway. Nor will I share
His Pow'r in Peace, or his Command in War.
290 For me, my Friends another Town shall frame,
And bless the rising Tow'rs, with fair *Lavinia*'s Name.
    Thus he. Then with erected Eyes and Hands,
The *Latian* King before his Altar stands.
By the same Heav'n, said he, and Earth, and Main,
295 And all the Pow'rs, that all the three contain;
By Hell below, and by that upper God,
Whose Thunder signs the Peace, who seals it with his Nod;
So let *Latona*'s double Offspring hear,
And double fronted *Janus*, what I swear;
300 I touch the sacred Altars, touch the Flames,
And all those Pow'rs attest, and all their Names:
Whatever Chance befall on either Side,
No term of time this Union shall divide:
No Force, no Fortune, shall my Vows unbind,
305 Or shake the stedfast Tenour of my Mind:
Not tho' the circling Seas shou'd break their Bound,
O'reflow the Shores, or sap the solid Ground;
Not tho' the Lamps of Heav'n their Spheres forsake,
Hurl'd down, and hissing in the neather Lake:
310 Ev'n as this Royal Scepter, (for he bore
A Scepter in his Hand) shall never more
Shoot out in Branches, or renew the Birth;
(An Orphan now, cut from the Mother Earth

By the keen Axe, dishonour'd of its Hair,
315 And cas'd in Brass, for *Latian* Kings to bear.)
    When thus in publick view the Peace was ty'd,
With solemn Vows, and sworn on either side,
All dues perform'd which holy Rites require;
The Victim Beasts are slain before the Fire:
320 The trembling Entrails from their Bodies torn,
And to the fatten'd Flames in Chargers born.
    Already the *Rutulians* deem their Man
O'rematch'd in Arms, before the Fight began.
First rising Fears are whisper'd thro' the Crowd;
325 Then, gath'ring sound, they murmur more aloud.
Now side to side, they measure with their Eyes
The Champions bulk, their Sinews, and their Sise:
The nearer they approach, the more is known
Th' apparent Disadvantage of their own.
330 *Turnus* himself, appears in publick sight,
Conscious of Fate, desponding of the Fight.
Slowly he moves; and at his Altar stands
With Eyes dejected, and with trembling hands:
And while he mutters undistinguish'd Pray'rs,
335 A livid deadness in his Cheeks appears.
    With anxious Pleasure when *Juturna* view'd
Th' increasing Fright of the mad Multitude,
When their short Sighs, and thickning Sobs she heard,
And found their ready Minds for Change prepar'd;
340 Dissembling her immortal Form, she took
Camertus Meen, his Habit, and his Look;
A Chief of ancient Blood: in Arms well known
Was his great Sire, and he, his greater Son.
His Shape assum'd, amid the Ranks she ran,
345 And humouring their first Motions, thus began.
    For shame, *Rutulians*, can you bear the sight,
Of one expos'd for all, in single Fight?
Can we, before the Face of Heav'n, confess
Our Courage colder, or our Numbers less?
350 View all the *Trojan* Hoast, th' *Arcadian* Band,
And *Tuscan* Army; count 'em as they stand,
Undaunted to the Battel, if we goe,
Scarce ev'ry second Man will share a Foe.

Turnus, 'tis true, in this unequal Strife
355 Shall lose, with Honour, his devoted Life:
Or change it rather for immortal Fame,
Succeeding to the Gods, from whence he came:
But you, a servile, and inglorious Band,
For Foreign Lords shall sow your Native Land:
360 Those fruitful Fields, your fighting Fathers gain'd,
Which have so long their lazy Sons sustain'd.

     With Words like these, she carry'd her Design;
A rising Murmur runs along the Line.
Then ev'n the City Troops, and *Latians*, tir'd
365 With tedious War, seem with new Souls inspir'd:
Their Champion's Fate with Pity they lament;
And of the League, so lately sworn, repent.

     Nor fails the Goddess to foment the Rage
With lying Wonders, and a false Presage:
370 But adds a Sign, which, present to their Eyes,
Inspires new Courage, and a glad Surprize.
For, sudden, in the fiery Tracts above,
Appears in Pomp th' Imperial Bird of *Jove*:
A plump of Fowl he spies, that swim the Lakes;
375 And o're their Heads his sounding Pinions shakes.
Then stooping on the fairest of the Train,
In his strong Tallons truss'd a silver Swan.
Th' *Italians* wonder at th' unusual sight;
But while he lags, and labours in his flight,
380 Behold the Dastard Fowl return anew;
And with united force the Foe pursue:
Clam'rous around the Royal Hawk they fly;
And thick'ning in a Cloud, o'reshade the Sky.
They cuff, they scratch, they cross his airy Course;
385 Nor can th' incumber'd Bird sustain their Force:
But vex'd, not vanquish'd, drops the pond'rous Prey;
And, lighten'd of his Burthen, wings his Way.

     Th' *Ausonian* Bands with Shouts salute the sight:
Eager of Action, and demand the Fight.
390 Then King *Tolumnius*, vers'd in Augurs Arts,
Cries out, and thus his boasted Skill imparts.
At length 'tis granted, what I long desir'd;
This, this is what my frequent Vows requir'd.

Ye Gods, I take your Omen, and obey:
395   Advance, my Friends, and charge, I lead the Way.
These are the Foreign Foes, whose impious Band,
Like that rapacious Bird, infest our Land:
But soon, like him, they shall be forc'd to Sea
By Strength united, and forego the Prey:
400   Your timely Succour to your Country bring;
Haste to the Rescue; and redeem your King.
    He said: and pressing onward, thro' the Crew,
Poiz'd in his lifted Arm, his Lance he threw.
The winged Weapon, whistling in the Wind,
405   Came driving on; nor miss'd the Mark design'd.
At once the Cornel rattled in the Skies;
At once tumultuous Shouts, and Clamours rise.
Nine Brothers in a goodly Band there stood,
Born of *Arcadian* mix'd with *Tuscan* Blood:
410   *Gylippus* Sons: The fatal Jav'lin flew,
Aim'd at the midmost of the friendly Crew.
A Passage thro' the jointed Arms it found,   ⎫
Just where the Belt was to the Body bound;   ⎬
And struck the gentle Youth, extended on the Ground. ⎭
415   Then fir'd with pious Rage, the gen'rous Train
Run madly forward, to revenge the slain.
And some with eager haste their Jav'lins throw;
And some, with Sword in hand, assault the Foe.
    The wish'd Insult the *Latine* Troops embrace;
420   And meet their Ardour in the middle Space.
The *Trojans*, *Tuscans*, and *Arcadian* Line,
With equal Courage obviate their Design.
Peace leaves the violated Fields; and Hate
Both Armies urges to their mutual Fate.
425   With impious Haste their Altars are o'return'd,
The Sacrifice half broil'd, and half unburn'd.
Thick Storms of Steel from either Army fly,
And Clouds of clashing Darts obscure the Sky:
Brands from the Fire, are missive Weapons made;
430   With Chargers, Bowls, and all the Priestly Trade.
Latinus frighted, hastens from the Fray,
And bears his unreguarded Gods away.

These on their Horses vault, those yoke the Car;
The rest with Swords on high, run headlong to the War.
435   *Messapus*, eager to confound the Peace,
Spurr'd his hot Courser thro' the fighting Preace,
At King *Aulestes*; by his Purple known
A *Tuscan* Prince, and by his Regal Crown:
And with a Shock encount'ring, bore him down.
440   Backward he fell; and as his Fate design'd,
The Ruins of an Altar were behind:
There pitching on his Shoulders, and his Head,
Amid the scatt'ring Fires he lay supinely spread.
The beamy Spear, descending from above,
445   His Cuirass pierc'd, and through his Body drove.
Then, with a scornful Smile, the Victor cries;
The Gods have found a fitter Sacrifice.
Greedy of Spoils, th' *Italians* strip the dead
Of his rich Armour; and uncrown his Head.
450   Priest *Chorinæus* arm'd his better Hand,
From his own Altar, with a blazing Brand:
And, as *Ebusus* with a thund'ring Pace
Advanc'd to Battel, dash'd it on his Face:
His bristly Beard shines out with sudden Fires,
455   The crackling Crop a noisom scent expires.
Following the blow, he seiz'd his curling Crown
With his left Hand; his other cast him down.
The prostrate Body with his Knees he press'd;
And plung'd his holy Ponyard in his Breast.
460   While *Podalirius*, with his Sword, pursu'd
The Shepherd *Alsus* thro' the flying Crowd,
Swiftly he turns; and aims a deadly Blow,
Full on the Front of his unwary Foe.
The broad Axe enters, with a crashing Sound,
465   And cleaves the Chin, with one continu'd Wound:
Warm Blood, and mingled Brains, besmear his Arms
            around.
An Iron Sleep his stupid Eyes oppress'd,
And seal'd their heavy Lids in endless rest.
But good *Æneas* rush'd amid the Bands,
470   Bare was his Head, and naked were his Hands,

In sign of Truce: Then thus he cries aloud,
What sudden Rage, what new Desire of Blood
Inflames your alter'd Minds? O *Trojans* cease
From impious Arms, nor violate the Peace.
475   By Human Sanctions, and by Laws Divine,
The terms are all agreed, the War is mine.
Dismiss your Fears, and let the Fight ensue;
This Hand alone shall right the Gods and you:
Our injur'd Altars, and their broken Vow,
480   To this avenging Sword the faithless *Turnus* owe.
   Thus while he spoke, unmindful of Defence,
A winged Arrow struck the Pious Prince.
But whether from some Humane Hand it came,
Or Hostile God, is left unknown by Fame:
485   No Human Hand, or Hostile God was found,
To boast the Triumph of so base a Wound.
   When *Turnus* saw the *Trojan* quit the Plain,
His Chiefs dismay'd, his Troops a fainting Train:
Th' unhop'd Event his heighten'd Soul inspires,
490   At once his Arms and Coursers he requires.
Then, with a leap, his lofty Chariot gains,
And with a ready hand assumes the Reins.
He drives impetuous, and where e're he goes,
He leaves behind a Lane of slaughter'd Foes.
495   These his Lance reaches, over those he rowls
His rapid Car, and chrushes out their Souls:
In vain the vanquish'd fly; the Victor sends
The dead Mens Weapons at their living Friends.
   Thus on the Banks of *Hebrus* freezing Flood
500   The God of Battel's in his angry Mood,
Clashing his Sword against his brazen Shield,
Lets loose the Reins, and scours along the Field:
Before the Wind his fiery Coursers fly,
Groans the sad Earth, resounds the ratling Sky.
505   Wrath, Terror, Treason, Tumult, and Despair, ⎫
Dire Faces, and deform'd, surround the Car; ⎬
Friends of the God, and Followers of the War. ⎭
   With Fury not unlike, nor less Disdain,
Exulting *Turnus* flies along the Plain:

510 His smoking Horses, at their utmost Speed,
He lashes on; and urges o're the dead.
Their Fetlocks run with Blood; and when they bound,
The Gore, and gath'ring Dust, are dash'd around.
Thamyris and *Pholus*, Masters of the War,
515 He kill'd at hand, but *Sthelenus* afar:
From far the Sons of *Imbracus* he slew,
Glaucus, and *Lades*, of the *Lycian* Crew:
Both taught to fight on Foot, in Battel join'd;
Or mount the Courser that outstrips the Wind.

520   Mean time *Eumedes*, vaunting in the Field,
New fir'd the *Trojans*, and their Foes repell'd.
This Son of *Dolon* bore his Grandsire's Name;
But emulated more his Father's Fame.
His guileful Father, sent a nightly Spy,
525 The *Grecian* Camp and Order to descry:
Hard Enterprise, and well he might require
Achilles Carr, and Horses for his hire:
But, met upon the Scout, th' *Etolian* Prince
In Death bestow'd a Juster Recompence.

530   Fierce *Turnus* view'd the *Trojan* from afar;
And lanch'd his Jav'lin from his lofty Carr:
Then lightly leaping down pursu'd the Blow,
And, pressing with his Foot, his prostrate Foe,
Wrench'd from his feeble hold the shining Sword;
535 And plung'd it in the Bosom of its Lord.
Possess, said he, the fruit of all thy Pains,
And measure, at thy length, our *Latian* Plains.
Thus are my Foes rewarded by my hand,
Thus may they build their Town, and thus enjoy the Land.

540   Then *Dares*, *Butes*, *Sybaris* he slew,
Whom o're his Neck his flound'ring Courser threw.
As when loud *Boreas* with his blust'ring Train,
Stoops from above, incumbent on the Main;
Where e're he flies, he drives the Rack before;
545 And rowls the Billows on th' *Ægean* Shore:
So where resistless *Turnus* takes his Course,
The scatter'd Squadrons bend before his force:
His Crest of Horses Hair is blown behind,
By adverse Air; and rustles in the Wind.

550   This, haughty *Phegeus* saw with high Disdain,
       And as the Chariot rowl'd along the Plain,
       Light from the Ground he leapt, and seiz'd the Rein.
       Thus hung in Air, he still retain'd his hold;
       The Coursers frighted, and their Course control'd.
555   The Lance of *Turnus* reach'd him as he hung,
       And pierc'd his plated Arms; but pass'd along,
       And only raz'd the Skin: he turn'd, and held
       Against his threatning Foe his ample Shield:
       Then call'd for Aid: but while he cry'd in vain,
560   The Chariot bore him backward on the Plain.
       He lies revers'd; the Victor King descends,
       And strikes so justly where his Helmet ends,
       He lops the Head. The *Latian* Fields are drunk
       With streams that issue from the bleeding Trunk.
565   While he triumphs, and while the *Trojans* yield,
       The wounded Prince is forc'd to leave the Field:
       Strong *Mnestheus*, and *Achates* often try'd,
       And young *Ascanius*, weeping by his side,
       Conduct him to his Tent: Scarce can he rear
570   His Limbs from Earth, supported on his Spear.
       Resolv'd in Mind, regardless of the Smart,
       He tugs with both his Hands, and breaks the Dart.
       The Steel remains. No readier way he found
       To draw the Weapon, than t' inlarge the Wound.
575   Eager of Fight, impatient of delay,
       He begs; and his unwilling Friends obey.
          Iäpis was at hand to prove his Art,
       Whose blooming Youth so fir'd *Apollo*'s Heart,
       That for his Love he proffer'd to bestow
580   His tuneful Harp, and his unerring Bow.
       The pious Youth, more studious how to save
       His aged Sire, now sinking to the Grave,
       Preferr'd the pow'r of Plants, and silent Praise
       Of healing Arts, before *Phœbeian* Bays.
585   Prop'd on his Lance the pensive Heroe stood,
       And heard, and saw unmov'd, the mourning Crowd.
       The fam'd Physician tucks his Robes around,
       With ready Hands, and hastens to the Wound.

With gentle Touches he performs his part,
590   This way and that, solliciting the Dart,
And excercises all his Heav'nly Art.
All softning Simples, known of Sov'raign Use,
He presses out, and pours their noble Juice;
These first infus'd, to lenifie the Pain,
595   He tugs with Pincers, but he tugs in vain.
Then, to the Patron of his Art he pray'd;
The Patron of his Art refus'd his Aid.
    Mean time the War approaches to the Tents;
Th' Allarm grows hotter, and the Noise augments:
600   The driving Dust proclaims the Danger near,
And first their Friends, and then their Foes appear;
Their Friends retreat, their Foes pursue the Rear.
The Camp is fill'd with Terror and Affright,
The hissing Shafts within the Trench alight:
605   An undistinguish'd Noise ascends the Sky;
The Shouts of those who kill, and Groans of those who dye.
    But now the Goddess Mother, mov'd with Grief,
And pierc'd with Pity, hastens her Relief.
A branch of healing *Dittany* she brought;
610   Which in the *Cretan* Fields with Care she sought:
Rough is the Stem, which wooly Leafs surround;
The Leafs with Flow'rs, the Flow'rs with Purple crown'd:
Well known to wounded Goats; a sure Relief
To draw the pointed Steel, and ease the Grief.
615   This *Venus* brings, in Clouds involv'd; and brews
Th' extracted Liquor with *Ambrosian* Dews,
And od'rous *Panacee*: Unseen she stands,
Temp'ring the mixture with her Heav'nly Hands:
And pours it in a Bowl, already crown'd
620   With Juice of medc'nal herbs prepar'd to bathe the Wound.
The Leech, unknowing of superior Art,
Which aids the Cure, with this foments the part;
And in a Moment ceas'd the raging smart.
Stanch'd is the Blood, and in the bottom stands:
625   The Steel, but scarcely touch'd with tender Hands,
Moves up, and follows of its own Accord;
And Health and Vigour are at once restor'd.

Iäpis first perceiv'd the closing Wound;
And first the footsteps of a God he found.

630   Arms, Arms, he cries, the Sword and Shield prepare,
And send the willing Chief, renew'd to War.
This is no Mortal Work, no cure of mine,
Nor Art's effect, but done by Hands Divine:
Some God our General to the Battel sends;

635   Some God preserves his Life for greater Ends.

The Heroe arms in haste: His hands infold
His Thighs with Cuisses of refulgent Gold:
Inflam'd to fight, and rushing to the Field,
That Hand sustaining the Cœlestial Shield,

640   This gripes the Lance; and with such Vigour shakes,
That to the rest the beamy Weapon quakes.
Then, with a close Embrace he strain'd his Son;
And kissing thro' his Helmet, thus begun.
My Son, from my Example learn the War, ⎫

645   In Camps to suffer, and in Fields to dare: ⎬
But happier Chance than mine attend thy Care. ⎭
This Day my hand thy tender Age shall shield,
And crown with Honours of the conquer'd Field:
Thou, when thy riper Years shall send thee forth,

650   To toils of War, be mindful of my Worth:
Assert thy birthright; and in Arms be known,
For *Hector*'s Nephew, and *Æneas*'s Son.

He said, and, striding, issu'd on the Plain;
Anteus, and *Mnestheus*, and a num'rous Train

655   Attend his Steps: The rest their Weapons take,
And crowding to the Field, the Camp forsake.
A cloud of blinding Dust is rais'd around;
Labours beneath their Feet the trembling ground.

Now *Turnus*, posted on a Hill, from far

660   Beheld the progress of the moving War:
With him the *Latins* view'd the cover'd Plains;
And the chill Blood ran backward in their Veins.
Juturna saw th' advancing Troops appear;
And heard the hostile Sound, and fled for Fear.

665   *Æneas* leads; and draws a sweeping Train,
Clos'd in their Ranks, and pouring on the Plain.

As when a Whirlwind rushing to the Shore,
From the mid Ocean, drives the Waves before:
The painful Hind, with heavy Heart foresees,
670 The flatted Fields, and slaughter of the Trees;
With like impetuous Rage the Prince appears,
Before his doubled Front; nor less Destruction bears.
And now both Armies shock, in open Field;
Osyris is by strong *Thymbræus* kill'd.
675 *Archetius*, *Ufens*, *Epulon*, are slain;
(All fam'd in Arms, and of the *Latian* Train;)
By *Gyas*, *Mnestheus*, and *Achates* Hand:
The fatal Augur falls, by whose command
The Truce was broken, and whose Lance embru'd
680 With *Trojan* Blood, th' unhappy Fight renew'd,
Loud Shouts and Clamours rend the liquid Sky;
And o're the Field the frighted *Latins* fly.
The Prince disdains the Dastards to pursue,
Nor moves to meet in Arms the fighting few:
685 *Turnus* alone, amid the dusky Plain,
He seeks, and to the Combat calls in vain.
Juturna heard, and seiz'd with Mortal Fear,
Forc'd from the Beam her Brother's Charioteer;
Assumes his Shape, his Armour, and his Meen;
690 And like *Metiscus*, in his Seat is seen.
    As the black Swallow near the Palace plies;
O're empty Courts, and under Arches flies;
Now hawks aloft, now skims along the Flood,
To furnish her loquacious Nest with Food:
695 So drives the rapid Goddess o're the Plains;
The smoaking Horses run with loosen'd Reins.
She steers a various Course among the Foes;
Now here, now there, her conqu'ring Brother shows:
Now with a straight, now with a wheeling flight,
700 She turns, and bends, but shuns the single Fight.
Æneas, fir'd with Fury, breaks the Crowd,
And seeks his Foe, and calls by name aloud:
He runs within a narrower Ring, and tries
To stop the Chariot, but the Chariot flies.
705 If he but gain a glimps, *Juturna* fears,
And far away the *Daunian* Heroe bears.

What shou'd he do! nor Arts nor Arms avail;
And various Cares in vain his Mind assail.
The great *Messapus* thund'ring thro' the Field,
710   In his left hand two pointed Jav'lins held;
Encountring on the Prince, one Dart he drew,
And with unerring aim, and utmost Vigour threw.
Æneas saw it come, and stooping low
Beneath his Buckler, shunn'd the threatning blow.
715   The Weapon hiss'd above his Head, and tore
The waving Plume, which on his Helm he wore.
Forc'd by this hostile Act, and fir'd with spight,
That flying *Turnus* still declin'd the Fight;
The Prince, whose Piety had long repell'd
720   His inborn ardour, now invades the Field:
Invokes the Pow'rs of violated Peace,
Their Rites, and injur'd Altars to redress:
Then, to his Rage abandoning the Rein,
With Blood and slaughter'd Bodies fills the Plain.
725   What God can tell, what Numbers can display
The various Labours of that fatal Day!
What Chiefs, and Champions fell on either side,
In Combat slain, or by what Deaths they dy'd?
Whom *Turnus*, whom the *Trojan* Heroe kill'd:
730   Who shar'd the Fame, and fortune of the Field?
Jove, cou'dst thou view, and not avert thy sight,
Two jarring Nations join'd in cruel fight,
Whom Leagues of lasting Love so shortly shall unite!
Æneas first *Rutulian Sucro* found,
735   Whose Valour made the *Trojans* quit their Ground:
Betwixt his Ribs the Jav'lin drove so just,
It reach'd his Heart, nor needs a second Thrust.
Now *Turnus*, at two blows, two Brethren slew;
First from his Horse fierce *Amycus* he threw;
740   Then leaping on the Ground, on Foot assail'd
Diores, and in equal Fight prevail'd.
Their lifeless Trunks he leaves upon the place;
Their Heads distilling Gore, his Chariot grace.
Three cold on Earth the *Trojan* Heroe threw;
745   Whom without respite at one Charge he slew:
Cethegus, *Tanais*, *Tagus*, fell oppress'd,
And sad *Onythes*, added to the rest;

Of *Theban* Blood, whom *Peridia* bore.
  Turnus, two Brothers from the *Lycian* Shore,
750 And from *Apollo*'s Fane to Battel sent,
O'rethrew, nor *Phœbus* cou'd their Fate prevent.
Peaceful *Menœtes* after these he kill'd,
Who long had shunn'd the Dangers of the Field:
On *Lerna*'s Lake a silent Life he led,
755 And with his Nets and Angle earn'd his Bread.
Nor pompous Cares, nor Palaces he knew,
But wisely from th' infectious World withdrew.
Poor was his House; his Father's painful Hand
Discharg'd his Rent, and plough'd another's Land.
760   As Flames among the lofty Woods are thrown,
On diff'rent sides, and both by Winds are blown,
The Laurels crackle in the sputt'ring Fire;
The frighted Silvans from their Shades retire:
Or as two neighb'ring Torrents fall from high,
765 Rapid they run; the foamy Waters fry:
They rowl to Sea with unresisted Force,
And down the Rocks precipitate their Course:
Not with less rage the Rival Heroes take
Their diff'rent Ways; nor less Destruction make.
770 With Spears afar, with Swords at hand they strike;
And zeal of Slaughter fires their Souls alike.
Like them, their dauntless Men maintain the Field,
And Hearts are pierc'd unknowing how to yield:
They blow for blow return, and wound for wound;
775 And heaps of Bodies raise the level Ground.
  Murranus, boasting of his Blood, that springs
From a long Royal Race of *Latian* Kings,
Is by the *Trojan* from his Chariot thrown,
Crush'd with the Weight of an unweildy Stone:
780 Betwixt the Wheels he fell; the Wheels that bore
His living Load, his dying Body tore.
His starting Steeds, to shun the glitt'ring Sword,
Paw down his trampled Limbs, forgetful of their Lord.
  Fierce *Hillus* threaten'd high; and face to face
785 Affronted *Turnus* in the middle space:
The Prince encounter'd him in full Carreer,
And at his Temples aim'd the deadly Spear:

So fatally the flying Weapon sped,
That thro' his Brazen Helm it pierc'd his Head.
790 Nor *Cisseus* cou'dst thou scape from *Turnus* hand,
In vain the strongest of th' *Arcadian* Band:
Nor to *Cupentus* cou'd his Gods afford,
Availing Aid against th' *Ænean* Sword:
Which to his naked Heart pursu'd the Course:
795 Nor could his plated Shield sustain the Force.
    Iölas fell, whom not the *Grecian* Pow'rs,
Nor great Subvertor of the *Trojan* Tow'rs,
Were doom'd to kill, while Heaven prolong'd his Date:
But who can pass the Bounds prefix'd by Fate?
800 In high *Lyrnessus*, and in *Troy*, he held
Two Palaces, and was from each expell'd:
Of all the mighty Man, the last Remains
A little spot of Foreign Earth contains.
    And now both Hosts their broken Troops unite,
805 In equal Ranks, and mix in mortal Fight,
Seresthus, and undaunted *Mnestheus* join
The *Trojan*, *Tuscan*, and *Arcadian* Line:
Sea-born *Messapus*, with *Atinas*, heads
The *Latin* Squadrons, and to Battel leads.
810 They strike, they push, they throng the scanty space;
Resolv'd on Death, impatient of Disgrace;
And where one falls, another fills his Place.
    The *Cyprian* Goddess now inspires her Son
To leave th' unfinish'd Fight, and storm the Town.
815 For while he rowls his Eyes around the Plain,
In quest of *Turnus*, whom he seeks in vain,
He views th' unguarded City from afar,
In careless quiet, and secure of War:
Occasion offers, and excites his Mind,
820 To dare beyond the Task he first design'd.
Resolv'd, he calls his Chiefs: they leave the Fight;
Attended thus, he takes a neighb'ring Height:
The crowding Troops about their Gen'ral stand,
All under Arms, and wait his high Command.
825 Then thus the lofty Prince: Hear and obey,
Ye *Trojan* Bands, without the least delay.

Jove is with us, and what I have decreed
Requires our utmost Vigour, and our Speed.
Your instant Arms against the Town prepare;
830   The source of Mischief, and the Seat of War.
This Day the *Latian* Tow'rs, that mate the Sky,
Shall level with the Plain in Ashes lye:
The People shall be Slaves; unless in time
They kneel for Pardon, and repent their Crime.
835   Twice have our Foes been vanquish'd on the Plain;
Then shall I wait till *Turnus* will be slain?
Your Force against the perjur'd City bend:
There it began, and there the War shall end.
The Peace profan'd our rightful Arms requires:
840   Cleanse the polluted Place with purging Fires.

He finish'd; and one Soul inspiring all,
Form'd in a Wedge, the Foot approach the Wall.
Without the Town, an unprovided Train
Of gaping, gazing Citizens are slain.
845   Some Firebrands, others scaling Ladders bear;
And those they toss aloft, and these they rear:
The Flames now lanch'd, the feather'd Arrows fly,
And Clouds of missive Arms obscure the Sky.
Advancing to the Front the Heroe stands,
850   And stretching out to Heav'n his Pious Hands;
Attests the Gods, asserts his Innocence,
Upbraids with breach of Faith th' *Ausonian* Prince:
Declares the Royal Honour doubly stain'd.
And twice the Rites of holy Peace profan'd.
855   Dissenting Clamours in the Town arise;
Each will be heard, and all at once advise.
One part for Peace, and one for War contends:
Some wou'd exclude their Foes, and some admit their
        Friends.
The helpless King is hurry'd in the Throng;
860   And what e're Tide prevails, is born along.
Thus when the Swain, within a hollow Rock,
Invades the Bees with suffocating Smoke,
They run around, or labour on their Wings,
Disus'd to flight; and shoot their sleepy Stings:
865   To shun the bitter Fumes in vain they try;
Black Vapours, issuing from the Vent, involve the Sky.

But Fate, and envious Fortune, now prepare
To plunge the *Latins* in the last despair.
The Queen, who saw the Foes invade the Town;
870 And Brands on tops of burning Houses thrown:
Cast round her Eyes, distracted with her Fear;
No Troops of *Turnus* in the Field appear.
Once more she stares abroad, but still in vain:
And then concludes the Royal Youth is slain.
875 Mad with her Anguish, impotent to bear
The mighty Grief, she loaths the vital Air.
She calls her self the Cause of all this Ill,
And owns the dire Effects of her ungovern'd Will:
She raves against the Gods, she beats her Breast,
880 She tears with both her hands her Purple Vest.
Then round a Beam a running Noose she ty'd;
And, fasten'd by the Neck, obscenely dy'd.
  Soon as the fatal News by Fame was blown,
And to her Dames, and to her Daughter known;
885 The sad *Lavinia* rends her yellow Hair,
And rosie Cheeks; the rest her Sorrow share:
With Shrieks the Palace rings, and Madness of Despair.
The spreading Rumor fills the Public Place;
Confusion, Fear, Distraction, and Disgrace,
890 And silent shame, are seen in ev'ry Face.
Latinus tears his Garments as he goes,
Both for his publick, and his private Woes:
With Filth his venerable Beard besmears,
And sordid Dust deforms his Silver Hairs.
895 And much he blames the softness of his Mind,
Obnoxious to the Charms of Womankind,
And soon seduc'd to change, what he so well design'd:
To break the solemn League so long desir'd,
Nor finish what his Fates, and those of *Troy* requir'd.
900 Now *Turnus* rowls aloof o're empty Plains,
And here and there some stragling Foes he gleans.
His flying Coursers please him less and less,
Asham'd of easie Fight, and cheap Success.
Thus half contented, anxious in his Mind,
905 The distant Cries come driving in the Wind:
Shouts from the Walls, but Shouts in Murmurs drown'd;
A jarring mixture, and a boding sound.

Alas, said he, what mean these dismal Cries,
What doleful Clamours from the Town arise?
910 Confus'd he stops, and backward pulls the Reins:
She, who the Driver's Office now sustains,
Replies; Neglect, my Lord, these new Alarms;
Here fight, and urge the Fortune of your Arms:
There want not others to defend the Wall:
915 If by your Rival's Hand th' *Italians* fall,
So shall your fatal Sword his Friends oppress,
In Honour equal, equal in Success.

　　To this, the Prince; O Sister, (for I knew
The Peace infring'd, proceeded first from you,)
920 I knew you, when you mingled first in Fight,
And now in vain you wou'd deceive my Sight:
Why, Goddess, this unprofitable Care?
Who sent you down from Heav'n, involv'd in Air,
Your share of Mortal Sorrows to sustain,
925 And see your Brother bleeding on the Plain?
For, to what Pow'r can *Turnus* have recourse,
Or how resist his Fates prevailing force!
These Eyes beheld *Murranus* bite the Ground,
Mighty the Man, and mighty was the Wound.
930 I heard my dearest Friend, with dying Breath,
My Name invoking to revenge his Death:
Brave *Ufens* fell with Honour on the Place;
To shun the shameful sight of my disgrace.
On Earth supine, a Manly Corps he lies;
935 His Vest and Armour are the Victor's Prize.
Then, shall I see *Laurentum* in a flame,
Which only wanted to compleat my shame?
How will the *Latins* hoot their Champion's flight;
How *Drances* will insult, and point them to the sight!
940 Is Death so hard to bear? Ye Gods below,
(Since those above so small Compassion show,)
Receive a Soul unsully'd yet with shame,
Which not belies my great Forefather's Name.

　　He said: And while he spoke, with flying speed,
945 Came *Sages* urging on his foamy Steed;
Fix'd on his wounded Face a Shaft he bore,
And seeking *Turnus* sent his Voice before:

Turnus, on you, on you alone depends
Our last Relief; compassionate your Friends.
950 Like Lightning, fierce *Æneas*, rowling on,
With Arms invests, with Flames invades the Town:
The Brands are toss'd on high; the Winds conspire
To drive along the Deluge of the Fire:
All Eyes are fix'd on you; your Foes rejoice;
955 Ev'n the King staggers, and suspends his Choice:
Doubts to deliver, or defend the Town;
Whom to reject, or whom to call his Son.
The Queen, on whom your utmost hopes were plac'd,
Her self suborning Death, has breath'd her last.
960 'Tis true, *Messapus*, fearless of his Fate,
With fierce *Atinas* Aid, defends the Gate:
On ev'ry side surrounded by the Foe;
The more they kill, the greater Numbers grow;
An Iron Harvest mounts, and still remains to mow.
965 You, far aloof from your forsaken Bands,
Your rowling Chariot drive o're empty Sands.
    Stupid he sate, his Eyes on earth declin'd,
And various Cares revolving in his Mind:
Rage boiling from the bottom of his Breast,
970 And Sorrow mix'd with Shame, his Soul oppress'd:
And conscious Worth lay lab'ring in his Thought;
And Love by Jealousie to Madness wrought.
By slow degrees his Reason drove away
The Mists of Passion, and resum'd her Sway.
975 Then, rising on his Car, he turn'd his Look;
And saw the Town involv'd in Fire and Smoke.
A wooden Tow'r with Flames already blaz'd,
Which his own Hands on Beams and Rafters rais'd:
And Bridges laid above to join the Space;
980 And Wheels below to rowl from place to place.
Sister, the Fates have vanquish'd: Let us go
The way which Heav'n and my hard Fortune show.
The Fight is fix'd: Nor shall the branded Name
Of a base Coward blot your Brother's Fame.
985 Death is my choice; but suffer me to try
My Force, and vent my Rage before I dye.

He said, and leaping down without delay,
Thro' Crowds of scatter'd Foes he free'd his way.
Striding he pass'd, impetuous as the Wind,
990 And left the grieving Goddess far behind.
As when a Fragment, from a Mountain torn
By raging Tempests, or by Torrents born,
Or sapp'd by time, or loosen'd from the Roots,
Prone thro' the Void the Rocky Ruine shoots,
995 Rowling from Crag to Crag, from Steep to Steep;
Down sink, at once the Shepherds and their Sheep,
Involv'd alike, they rush to neather Ground,
Stun'd with the *shock* they fall, and stun'd from *Earth*
        rebound:
So *Turnus*, hasting headlong to the Town,
1000 Should'ring and shoving, bore the Squadrons down.
Still pressing onward, to the Walls he drew,
Where Shafts, and Spears, and Darts promiscuous flew;
And sanguine Streams the slipp'ry Ground embrew.
First stretching out his Arm, in sign of Peace,
1005 He cries aloud, to make the Combat cease:
Rutulians hold, and *Latin* Troops retire;
The Fight is mine, and me the Gods require.
'Tis just that I shou'd vindicate alone
The broken Truce, or for the Breach atone.
1010 This Day shall free from Wars th' *Ausonian* State;
Or finish my Misfortunes in my Fate.
    Both Armies from their bloody Work desist:
And bearing backward, form a spacious List.
The *Trojan* Heroe who receiv'd from Fame
1015 The welcome Sound, and heard the Champion's Name,
Soon leaves the taken Works, and mounted Walls,
Greedy of War, where greater Glory calls.
He springs to Fight, exulting in his Force;
His jointed Armour rattles in the Course.
1020 Like *Eryx*, or like *Athos*, great he shows,
Or Father *Apennine*, when white with Snows,
His Head Divine, obscure in Clouds he hides:
And shakes the sounding Forest on his sides.
    The Nations over-aw'd, surcease the Fight,
1025 Immoveable their Bodies, fix'd their sight:

Ev'n Death stands still; nor from above they throw
Their Darts, nor drive their batt'ring Rams below.
In silent Order either Army stands;
And drop their Swords, unknowing, from their Hands.
1030   Th' *Ausonian* King beholds, with wond'ring sight,
Two mighty Champions match'd in single Fight:
Born under Climes remote; and brought by Fate,
With Swords to try their Titles to the State.
    Now in clos'd Field, each other from afar
1035   They view; and rushing on, begin the War.
They launch their Spears, then hand to hand they meet;
The trembling Soil resounds beneath their Feet:
Their Bucklers clash; thick blows descend from high,
And flakes of Fire from their hard Helmets fly.
1040   Courage conspires with Chance; and both ingage
With equal Fortune yet, and mutual Rage.
    As when two Bulls for their fair Female fight,
In *Sila*'s Shades, or on *Taburnus* height;
With Horns adverse they meet: the Keeper flies:
1045   Mute stands the Herd, the Heifars rowl their Eyes;
And wait th' Event; which Victor they shall bear,
And who shall be the Lord, to rule the lusty Year:
With rage of Love the jealous Rivals burn,
And Push for Push, and Wound for Wound return:
1050   Their Dewlaps gor'd, their sides are lav'd in Blood;
Loud Cries and roaring Sounds rebellow thro' the Wood:
Such was the Combat in the listed Ground;
So clash their swords and so their Shields resound.
    Jove sets the Beam; in either Scale he lays
1055   The Champions Fate, and each exactly weighs.
On this side Life, and lucky Chance ascends:
Loaded with Death, that other Scale descends.
Rais'd on the Stretch, young *Turnus* aims a blow,
Full on the Helm of his unguarded Foe:
1060   Shrill Shouts and Clamours ring on either side;
As Hopes and Fears their panting Hearts divide.
But all in pieces flies the Traytor Sword,
And, in the middle Stroke, deserts his Lord.
Now 'tis but Death, or Flight: disarm'd he flies,
1065   When in his Hand, an unknown Hilt he spies.

Fame says that *Turnus*, when his Steeds he join'd,
Hurrying to War, disorder'd in his Mind,
Snatch'd the first Weapon, which his haste cou'd find.
'Twas not the fated Sword his Father bore;
1070 But that his Charioteer *Metiscus* wore.
This, while the *Trojans* fled, the Toughness held;
But vain against the great *Vulcanian* Shield,
The mortal-temper'd Steel deceiv'd his Hand:
The shiver'd fragments shone amid the Sand.
1075 Surpriz'd with fear, he fled along the Field;
And now forthright, and now in Orbits wheel'd.
For here the *Trojan* Troops the List surround;
And there the Pass is clos'd with Pools and marshy Ground.
Æneas hastens, tho' with heavier Pace,
1080 His Wound, so newly knit, retards the Chase:
And oft his trembling Knees their Aid refuse,
Yet pressing foot by foot his Foe pursues.
Thus, when a fearful Stag is clos'd around
With Crimson Toils, or in a River found;
1085 High on the Bank the deep-mouth'd Hound appears;
Still opening, following still, where e're he steers:
The persecuted Creature, to, and fro,
Turns here and there to scape his *Umbrian* Foe:
Steep is th' Ascent, and if he gains the Land,
1090 The Purple Death is pitch'd along the Strand:
His eager Foe determin'd to the Chace,
Stretch'd at his length gains Ground at ev'ry Pace:
Now to his beamy Head he makes his way,
And now he holds, or thinks he holds his Prey:
1095 Just at the pinch the Stag springs out with fear,
He bites the Wind, and fills his sounding Jaws with Air.
The Rocks, the Lakes, the Meadows ring with Cries;
The mortal Tumult mounts, and thunders in the Skies.
Thus flies the *Daunian* Prince: and, flying, blames
1100 His tardy Troops; and calling by their Names,
Demands his trusty Sword. The *Trojan* threats
The Realm with Ruin, and their ancient Seats
To lay in Ashes, if they dare supply
With Arms or Aid, his vanquish'd Enemy:

1105　Thus menacing, he still pursues the Course,
　　　With Vigour, tho' diminish'd of his Force.
　　　Ten times, already, round the listed place,
　　　One Chief had fled, and t' other giv'n the Chace:
　　　No trivial Prize is play'd; for on the Life
1110　Or Death of *Turnus*, now depends the Strife.
　　　　Within the space, an Olive Tree had stood,
　　　A sacred Shade, a venerable Wood,
　　　For Vows to *Faunus* paid, the *Latins* Guardian God.
　　　Here hung the Vests, and Tablets were ingrav'd,
1115　Of sinking Mariners from Shipwrack sav'd.
　　　With heedless Hands the *Trojans* fell'd the Tree,
　　　To make the Ground inclos'd for Combat free.
　　　Deep in the Root, whether by Fate, or Chance,
　　　Or erring haste, the *Trojan* drove his Lance:
1120　Then stoop'd, and tug'd with Force immense to free
　　　Th' incumber'd Spear, from the tenacious Tree:
　　　That whom his fainting Limbs pursu'd in vain,
　　　His flying Weapon might from far attain.
　　　　Confus'd with Fear, bereft of Human Aid,
1125　Then *Turnus* to the Gods, and first to *Faunus* pray'd.
　　　O *Faunus* pity, and thou Mother Earth,
　　　Where I thy foster Son receiv'd my Birth,
　　　Hold fast the Steel; if my Religious Hand
　　　Your Plant has honour'd, which your Foes profan'd;
1130　Propitious hear my pious Pray'r! He said,
　　　Nor with successless Vows invok'd their Aid.
　　　Th' incumbent Heroe wrench'd, and pull'd, and strain'd;
　　　But still the stubborn Earth the Steel detain'd.
　　　Juturna took her time; and while in vain
1135　He strove, assum'd *Metiscus* Form again:
　　　And, in that imitated Shape, restor'd
　　　To the despairing Prince, his *Daunian* Sword.
　　　The Queen of Love, who, with Disdain and Grief,
　　　Saw the bold Nymph afford this prompt Relief;
1140　T' assert her Off-spring, with a greater Deed,
　　　From the rough Root the ling'ring Weapon freed.
　　　　Once more erect, the Rival Chiefs advance;
　　　One trusts the Sword, and one the pointed Lance:
　　　And both resolv'd alike, to try their fatal Chance.

1145   Mean time Imperial *Jove* to *Juno* spoke,
       Who from a shining Cloud beheld the shock;
       What new Arrest, O Queen of Heav'n, is sent
       To stop the Fates now lab'ring in th' Event.
       What farther hopes are left thee to pursue?   ⎫
1150   Divine *Æneas*, (and thou know'st it too,)   ⎬
       Fore-doom'd to these Cœlestial Seats is due,   ⎭
       What more Attempts for *Turnus* can be made,
       That thus thou ling'rest in this lonely Shade!
       Is it becoming of the due Respect,
1155   And awful Honour of a God Elect,
       A Wound unworthy of our State to feel;
       Patient of Human Hands, and earthly Steel?
       Or seems it Just, the Sister shou'd restore,   ⎫
       A second Sword, when one was lost before;   ⎬
1160   And arm a conquer'd Wretch, against his Conqueror? ⎭
       For what without thy knowledge and avow,
       Nay more, thy Dictate, durst *Juturna* do?
       At last, in deference to my Love, forbear
       To lodge within thy Soul this anxious Care:
1165   Reclin'd upon my Breast, thy Grief unload;
       Who shou'd relieve the Goddess, but the God?
       Now, all things to their utmost Issue tend;
       Push'd by the Fates to their appointed End:
       While leave was giv'n thee, and a lawful Hour
1170   For Vengeance, Wrath, and unresisted Pow'r:
       Toss'd on the Seas thou cou'd'st thy Foes distress,
       And driv'n ashore, with Hostile Arms oppress:
       Deform the Royal House; and from the side
       Of the Just Bridegroom, tear the plighted Bride:
1175   Now cease at my Command. The Thund'rer said:
       And with dejected Eyes this Answer *Juno* made.
          Because your dread Decree too well I knew;
       From *Turnus*, and from Earth unwilling I withdrew.
       Else shou'd you not behold me here alone,
1180   Involv'd in empty Clouds my Friends bemoan:
       But girt with vengeful Flames, in open sight,
       Engag'd against my Foes in Mortal Fight.
       'Tis true *Juturna* mingled in the Strife
       By my Command, to save her Brother's Life;

1185   At least to try: But by the *Stygian* Lake,
       (The most religious Oath the Gods can take,)
       With this restriction, not to bend the Bow,
       Or toss the Spear, or trembling Dart to throw.
       And now resign'd to your Superior Might,
1190   And tir'd with fruitless Toils, I loath the Fight.
       This let me beg, (and this no Fates withstand)
       Both for my self, and for your Fathers Land,
       That when the Nuptial Bed shall bind the Peace;
       (Which I, since you ordain, consent to bless,)
1195   The Laws of either Nation be the same;
       But let the *Latins* still retain their Name:
       Speak the same Language which they spoke before;
       Wear the same Habits which their Grandsires wore:
       Call them not *Trojans*: Perish the Renown,
1200   And Name of *Troy*, with that detested Town.
       Latium be *Latium* still; let *Alba* reign,
       And *Rome*'s immortal Majesty remain.
         Then thus the Founder of Mankind replies:
       (Unruffled was his Front, serene his Eyes,)
1205   Can *Saturn*'s Issue, and Heav'n's other Heir,
       Such endless Anger in her Bosom bear?
       Be Mistress, and your full Desires obtain:
       But quench the Choler you foment in vain.
       From ancient Blood th' *Ausonian* People sprung,
1210   Shall keep their name, their Habit, and their Tongue.
       The *Trojans* to their Customs shall be ty'd,
       I will, my self, their common Rites provide;
       The Natives shall command, the Foreigners subside.
       All shall be *Latium*; *Troy* without a Name:
1215   And her lost Sons forget from whence they came.
       From Blood so mix'd, a pious Race shall flow,
       Equal to Gods, excelling all below.
       No Nation more Respect to you shall pay,
       Or greater Off'rings on your Altars lay.
1220   *Juno* consents, well pleas'd that her Desires
       Had found Success, and from the Cloud retires.
         The Peace thus made, the Thund'rer next prepares
       To force the wat'ry Goddess from the Wars.

Deep in the dismal Regions, void of Light,
1225 Three Daughters at a Birth were born to Night:
These their brown Mother, brooding on her Care,
Indu'd with windy Wings to flit in Air:
With Serpents girt alike; and crown'd with hissing Hair.
In Heav'n the *Diræ* call'd, and still at hand,
1230 Before the Throne of angry *Jove* they stand.
His Ministers of Wrath; and ready still
The Minds of Mortal Men with Fears to fill:
When e're the moody Sire, to wreak his Hate
On Realms, or Towns deserving of their Fate,
1235 Hurls down Diseases, Death, and deadly Care,
And terrifies the guilty World with War.
One Sister Plague of these from Heav'n he sent,
To fright *Juturna* with a dire Portent.
The Pest comes whirling down: by far more slow
1240 Springs the swift Arrow from the *Parthian* Bow,
Or *Cydon* Eugh; when traversing the Skies,
And drench'd in pois'nous Juice, the sure Destruction flies.
With such a sudden, and unseen a flight,
Shot thro' the Clouds the Daughter of the Night.
1245 Soon as the Field inclos'd she had in view,
And from afar her destin'd Quarry knew:
Contracted, to the boding Bird she turns,
Which haunts the ruin'd Piles, and hallow'd Urns;
And beats about the Tombs with nightly Wings;
1250 Where Songs obscene on Sepulchres she sings.
Thus lessen'd in her Form, with frightful Cries,
The Fury round unhappy *Turnus* flies,
Flaps on his Shield, and flutters o're his Eyes.
      A lazy Chilness crept along his Blood,
1255 Choak'd was his Voice, his Hair with Horror stood.
Juturna from afar beheld her fly,
And knew th' ill Omen, by her screaming Cry,
And stridour of her Wings. Amaz'd with Fear,
Her beauteous Breast she beat, and rent her flowing Hair.
1260 Ah me, she cries, in this unequal Strife,
What can thy Sister more to save thy Life!
Weak as I am, can I, alas, contend
In Arms, with that inexorable Fiend!

Now, now, I quit the Field! forbear to fright
1265   My tender Soul, ye baleful Birds of Night!
The lashing of your Wings I know too well:
The sounding Flight, and Fun'ral Screams of Hell!
These are the Gifts you bring from haughty *Jove*,
The worthy Recompence of ravish'd Love!
1270   Did he for this exempt my Life from Fate?
O hard Conditions of Immortal State!
Tho' born to Death, not priviledg'd to dye,
But forc'd to bear impos'd Eternity!
Take back your envious Bribes, and let me go
1275   Companion to my Brother's Ghost below!
The Joys are vanish'd: Nothing now remains,
Of Life Immortal, but Immortal Pains.
What Earth will open her devouring Womb,
To rest a weary Goddess in the Tomb!
1280   She drew a length of Sighs; nor more she said;
But in her Azure Mantle wrap'd her Head:
Then plung'd into her Stream, with deep Despair,
And her last Sobs came bubling up in Air.

    Now stern *Æneas* waves his weighty Spear
1285   Against his Foe, and thus upbraids his Fear,
What farther Subterfuge can *Turnus* find;
What empty Hopes are harbour'd in his Mind?
'Tis not thy Swiftness can secure thy Flight:
Not with their Feet, but Hands, the Valiant fight.
1290   Vary thy Shape in thousand Forms, and dare
What Skill and Courage can attempt in War:
Wish for the Wings of Winds, to mount the Sky;
Or hid, within the hollow Earth to lye.
The Champion shook his Head; and made this short
      reply.
1295   No threats of thine, my manly Mind can move:
'Tis Hostile Heav'n I dread, and Partial *Jove*.
He said no more: but with a Sigh, repress'd
The mighty Sorrow, in his swelling Breast.
Then, as he rowl'd his troubled Eyes around,
1300   An Antique Stone he saw: the Common Bound
Of Neighb'ring Fields; and Barrier of the Ground:
So vast, that Twelve strong Men of modern Days,
Th' enormous weight from Earth cou'd hardly raise.

He heav'd it at a Lift: and poiz'd on high,
1305 Ran stagg'ring on, against his Enemy.
But so disorder'd, that he scarcely knew
His Way: or what unwieldy weight he threw.
His knocking Knees are bent beneath the Load:
And shiv'ring Cold congeals his vital Blood.
1310 The Stone drops from his Arms: and falling short,
For want of Vigour, mocks his vain Effort.
And as, when heavy Sleep has clos'd the sight,
The sickly Fancy labours in the Night:
We seem to run; and, destitute of Force,
1315 Our sinking Limbs forsake us in the Course:
In vain we heave for Breath; in vain we cry:
The Nerves unbrac'd, their usual Strength deny;
And, on the Tongue the falt'ring Accents dye:
So *Turnus* far'd: what ever means he try'd,
1320 All force of Arms, and points of Art employ'd,
The Fury flew athwart; and made th' Endeavour void.

A thousand various Thoughts his Soul confound:
He star'd about; nor Aid nor Issue found:
His own Men stop the Pass; and his own Walls surround.
1325 Once more he pauses; and looks out again:
And seeks the Goddess Charioteer in vain.
Trembling he views the Thund'ring Chief advance:
And brandishing aloft the deadly Lance:
Amaz'd he cow'rs beneath his conqu'ring Foe,
1330 Forgets to ward; and waits the coming Blow.
Astonish'd while he stands, and fix'd with Fear,
Aim'd at his Shield he sees th' impending Spear.

The Heroe measur'd first, with narrow view,
The destin'd Mark: And rising as he threw,
1335 With its full swing the fatal Weapon flew.
Not with less Rage the rattling Thunder falls;
Or Stones from batt'ring Engins break the Walls:
Swift as a Whirlwind, from an Arm so strong,
The Lance drove on; and bore the Death along.
1340 Nought cou'd his sev'n-fold Shield the Prince avail,
Nor ought beneath his Arms the Coat of Mail;
It pierc'd thro' all; and with a grizly Wound,
Transfix'd his Thigh, and doubled him to ground.

With Groans the *Latins* rend the vaulted Sky:
1345　Woods, Hills, and Valleys, to the Voice reply.
　　　Now low on Earth the lofty Chief is laid;
　　With Eyes cast upward, and with Arms display'd;
　　And Recreant thus to the proud Victor pray'd.
　　I know my Death deserv'd, nor hope to live:
1350　Use what the Gods, and thy good Fortune give.
　　　Yet think; oh think, if Mercy may be shown,
　　(Thou hadst a Father once; and hast a Son:)
　　Pity my Sire, now sinking to the Grave;
　　And for *Anchises* sake, old *Daunus* save!
1355　Or, if thy vow'd Revenge pursue my Death;
　　Give to my Friends my Body void of Breath!
　　The *Latian* Chiefs have seen me beg my Life;
　　Thine is the Conquest, thine the Royal Wife:
　　Against a yielded Man, 'tis mean ignoble Strife.
1360　　In deep Suspence the *Trojan* seem'd to stand;
　　And just prepar'd to strike repress'd his Hand.
　　He rowl'd his Eyes, and ev'ry Moment felt
　　His manly Soul with more Compassion melt.
　　When, casting down a casual Glance, he spy'd
1365　The Golden Belt that glitter'd on his side:
　　The fatal Spoils which haughty *Turnus* tore
　　From dying *Pallas*, and in Triumph wore.
　　Then rowz'd anew to Wrath, he loudly cries,
　　(Flames, while he spoke, came flashing from his Eyes:)
1370　Traytor, dost thou, dost thou to Grace pretend,
　　Clad, as thou art, in Trophees of my Friend?
　　To his sad Soul a grateful Off'ring go;
　　'Tis *Pallas*, *Pallas* gives this deadly Blow.
　　He rais'd his Arm aloft; and at the Word,
1375　Deep in his Bosom drove the shining Sword.
　　The streaming Blood distain'd his Arms around:
　　And the disdainful Soul came rushing thro' the Wound.

FINIS

EMENDATIONS

Each entry lists an emendation with, following the slash, what in the copy-text has been emended. Nearly all the emendations are from the corrected state of the first-edition text. Two emendations, preceded by an *E*, are from the 'Errata' list accompanying that text. Emendations supplied by the present editor, in addition to those made silently according to the principles explained in the section of the Preface headed 'The Text', are preceded by an asterisk.

Those principles exclude from the list some emendations which are supported by the corrected state of the first edition but do not require such support because the expression in the copy-text is clearly incorrect and there seems no alternative to the emendation adopted (for example, 'Sicilian' replacing the copy-text's 'Cicilian' at 1.774). Those principles also exclude from the list some emendations not supported by that edition, prominently emendations rectifying intersubstitution of the ligatures *æ* and *œ* which might confuse the reader (for example, 'Phœnix' replacing the copy-text's 'Phænix' at 2.1036).

A zero indicates absent, ambiguous, or illegible punctuation.

1.134	./,
1.326	;/o
1.428	Fleet/Feet
*1.686	;/o
1.1064	Tropick/Topick
2.210	adjur'd/abjur'd
*2.457	Iph'tus/Iph'itas [the 1697 corrected text has 'Iph'itus' (the apostrophe was evidently meant to replace the *i*, to preserve the metre here as is not necessary at 2.591)]
2.660	Yield/Yeilds
2.763	[footnote] Denham/Derhan
2.836	,/;
2.883	What,/What
*3.103	ashore,/ashore
3.290	invited/invitest
3.411	you/your

3.482	;/;)
3.564	on a/on
3.577	./,
3.728	Cloud/Clouds
3.767	were/wear
4.107	declines,/declines.
4.360	God/Gods
4.373	seek/seeks
4.556	her/here
4.585	./,
4.732	./,
4.780	;/?
4.791	pity, Sister,/pity,
5.181	./o
5.382	and the/and
5.464	may/my
5.617	,/.
5.652	Archers/Arches
5.707	give/gave
5.733	./,
5.1090	lye/lay
5.1102	;/.
6.19	,/.
*6.63	Art/Art.
6.419	Freights/Frights
6.435	wond'ring/wand'ring
6.443	which/with
6.519	calm'd/claim'd
6.528	./,
6.574	,/o
6.579	./o
6.615	:)/:
6.635	more/more.
6.696	And,/And
6.717	tell/till
6.733	Lo/Let
6.828	and/an
6.847	Statutes/Statues
6.892	the Chair/their Chair
*6.892	maintain/maintain.
6.948	Embraces/Embrace

7.24	they/the
7.165	destin'd/distin'd
7.169	Trenchers/Trenches
7.179	blest/best
7.224	Troop/Troops
7.257	a long/along
7.262	Then/The
7.288	ascended/ascend
7.302	Tempest, from/Tempest,
7.307	bounded/bound
7.334	./,
7.360	All/And
7.421	Storms/Storm's
7.430	prevail not,/prevail,
7.456	Sister-Furies/Sister-Fruits
7.540	ways,/.
7.554	shrieks/shrikes
7.716	as was/as
7.723	./,
7.734	,/.
7.797	Proclaims/Proclaim
7.802	lead/leads
7.872	Tybur/Tyber
7.912	Son/Sun
7.931	Tyburs/Tybers
7.1042	sighs/sights
7.1047	Altars/Altar
8.45	of the/of
8.101	Stores/Stories
8.148	singly/signally
8.189	your/you
8.259	This Hold,/This, Hold
8.268	the/in
8.344	around,/around.
8.349	thorough/through
8.352	wond'ring/wand'ring
8.384	with his/with
8.446	Carmental/Carmetal
8.512	said/sad
8.524	or/of
8.558	Flames/Flame

8.593	By/But
8.644	Flame/Fame
8.664	Tarchon/Trochon
8.828	plated/plaited
9.587	he/be
10.363	./:
E 10.497	,/.
E 10.735	will/shall
10.770	:/.
11.245	set/sate
11.509	State./State,
11.1004	:/o
12.174	scarcely/scarely
12.222	Embrace/Embace
12.671	like/less
12.769	;/o
*12.1175	[paragraph indentation transferred to 12.1177]
12.1242	./o

GLOSSARY

As the Preface explains in its concluding section, this glossary is selective, concentrating on the literal sense of names and other expressions important to the narrative in Dryden's poem but not adequately comprehensible from nearby or earlier contexts there.

Chiefly the reader should keep in mind that explanations of expressions other than names are only of such senses as are not now usual, and do not rule out the possibility that one or more current senses may apply instead, or also, in any given instance in Dryden's text. Where an explanation is preceded by a citation, by Book and line number, of one or more specific instances in the text, the explanation applies only to that or those instances. If an entry includes several distinct senses of an expression, as much as is practicable they are numbered in descending order according to their relative frequency in the text.

Some entries provide etymological information, in brackets and marked by a wedge pointing from the original expression to the later one. The entry for 'Alba' exemplifies this practice and also illustrates how any adjectival form of a noun, if the text employs both, parenthetically follows the noun.

Entries for multiple-word expressions are alphabetized by the first word in each which is crucial to comprehension of that expression as it occurs in the poem. Usually this word is a name, a common noun, or a pronoun, and the word may be a possessive. (The expression 'his Sister's Court' is entered as 'Sister's Court', because in context it is clear who 'his' refers to; but 'his Temple' is entered just as given in the text because it is the reference of 'his' which is not clear in the context.) If the expression includes a name, the entry is alphabetized by that name; if more than one name, by the first to appear. If there are no outright names, then the same principles apply to common nouns or pronouns. (Epithets such as 'God of Day' are entered as in the text, but the text's 'Son of Neptune' is entered as 'Neptune, Son of'.) A name in adjectival form is regarded as a name, and a word which may be a common noun is regarded as a noun even when functioning as an adjective. (Hence the entries for 'Egyptian Wife' and 'Five Cities' have those headings.)

If the sense of an expression hinges especially on a pronoun for which the reference is not readily evident (for example, a 'he'), there is an entry for that pronoun alone, and the entry heading cites, by Book and line number, the instance of the pronoun in the text to which the entry applies.

A single entry sometimes collects explanations of several expressions which the text presents together in a given passage or set of passages, regarding a particular person, or people, or place (for example, 'Hercules', 'Marrubians', 'Capitol'). If the text presents a distinct series of places, that series is entered under the name given first in it ('Præneste') or under any collective expression introducing the series ('Five Cities').

There is an entry for a geographical name only if the name calls for more information than the maps provide, or if the maps do not include the name, or if the maps' Latin spelling of the name differs substantially from the spelling in the text.

Some Roman names are given in English form if that has become standard (for example, 'Mark Antony'). The first name (the *praenomen*) in the threefold name which came to be conventional for a male Roman citizen was regularly represented by an initial, as are these in this glossary: C[aius or Gaius], L[ucius], M[arcus], P[ublius]. (The second name, the *nomen*, identified his *gens*, or clan, and the third name, the *cognomen*, might identify his family within that *gens*. An additional name, an *agnomen*, might signalize some particular accomplishment, as P. Cornelius Scipio acquired the fourth name 'Africanus' to commemorate his military success in Africa. Roman women typically went by a twofold name; that of Livia Drusilla derives from, respectively, the *gens* and family of her birth.)

Major dates related to Virgil's poem, all B.C. and some only traditional, are as follows. (They suggest the facts of increased Roman domination of first Italy and then the other directly Mediterranean lands, and more, and of the increased internal dissension which transformed oligarchic republican Rome into an autocracy.)

753	Rome founded, as a kingdom
509	Rome becomes a republic
396	Rome's conquest of Veii, a nearby Etruscan city
390	the Gauls briefly capture Rome
264–241, 218–201	First and Second Punic (or Carthaginian) Wars
149–146	Third Punic War; destruction of Carthage
48	Julius Caesar defeats Pompey at Pharsala
31	the Battle of Actium gives Octavian, soon named Augustus, control of Rome

Most citations by Book and line numbers are of Dryden's poem. The other Book-and-line citations are identified as referring to Virgil's text. Italicized Latin expressions attributed to Virgil are quoted, hence they are sometimes not given in the nominative or other form in which a Latin dictionary enters them.

Because Dryden translates in a manner decidedly not servile, the glossary's references to Virgil are only for comparison, not prescription; and because the present edition seeks to balance concern for both Dryden's poem and Virgil's, the citations of Virgil's text here refer to a modern edition which is widely available and which combines the Latin text with an English translation.

Dryden evidently relied most on the second edition, published in Paris in 1682 and republished afterwards in London and elsewhere, of *P. Virgilii Maronis Opera*, edited by Carolus Ruaeus (Charles de la Rue). This and other editions available to Dryden differ, mostly in quite small ways, from modern editions. All parts of Virgil's text referred to in the glossary of the present edition have been compared with the corresponding parts of Ruaeus' version in the second, Paris edition and, except as noted within this glossary or in some minor, inconsequential matters of spelling, punctuation, and the like, have been found to be the same there.

The annotation of Dryden's text in, particularly, the California Edition (cited above in the section on Further Reading) includes selective products of extensive comparison with Ruaeus' edition and other editions and translations preceding Dryden's. The interpretative commentaries in the editions Dryden used are of considerable value in elucidating subtle aspects of his poem. For an example of such elucidation from the California Edition, see the entry 'Hecat' below.

The glossary's references to notes by Dryden cite his 'Notes and Observations', from the copy-text *Works*. The quoted material may readily be located elsewhere because Dryden arranged this annotation by Book and line numbers.

The glossary is much indebted to the *Oxford English Dictionary* (*OED*). All my citations of it are identical in the two editions, and quotations from it employ these abbreviations: *a.* for adjective; *sb.* for substantive (noun); *v.* for verb. Other sources cited are each identified by an italicized capital letter:

A   *The Aeneid*, in H. Rushton Fairclough, *Virgil* (*Loeb Classical Library*), rev. ed., 2 vols. (1935; reprinted Cambridge, Mass. and London: Harvard University Press, 1994).

J   Samuel Johnson, *A Dictionary of the English Language*, 4th ed., 2 vols. (1773; reprinted Beirut: Librairie du Liban, 1978).

L   Charleton T. Lewis and Charles Short, *A New Latin Dictionary* (New York: Harper & Brothers; Oxford: Clarendon Press, 1880).

As a few glossary entries suggest, Dryden's *Æneis* was a major supplier of the illustrative quotations in both Johnson's *Dictionary* and the *OED*.

The glossary has references also to the epics of Homer, the *Argonautica* of Apollonius Rhodius, and Livy's *Ab Urbe Condita*. These are available in the Loeb Classical Library and also (though not all of Livy's very long but incompletely preserved book) in translation in the Penguin Classics series.

Acarnanian: relating to Acarnania, a region of the Greek mainland facing the island of Ithaca

Achilles, young: Pyrrhus, Achilles' son; regarding 'his Rival', see *Orestes* and 3.428–30

Actian height: alluding to the temple of Apollo at Actium, a temple which Augustus restored after his victory there

adjur'd 2.210: the textual emendation preferring 'adjur'd' to 'abjur'd' is subtle; Sinon's declaration is clearer in *A*, that on the whole he both implores assistance from (adjures) divinities and renounces (abjures) loyalty to the Greeks

Adrastus: see *Seven against Thebes*

Æacian Spoils: Achillean (*A*); Dryden's reference is by way of Achilles' grandfather Aeacus, the 'Spoils' being Achilles' armour, which his friend Patroclus wore and which Hector, after slaying Patroclus, put on (*Iliad* 16–17)

Ægeon: same as *Briareus*

Æsculapian: alluding to Apollo's son Aesculapius, god of medicine

æther (ethereal, etherial): ether, literally the special, airy and luminous atmosphere of high, celestial altitudes

Ætna: the volcanic mountain about a third of the way down and some twelve miles inland from Sicily's eastern shore

Ætolian Prince: Diomede, from Aetolia, a region of Greece east of Acarnania. See also *Calydon*

Africk, Affrick (Affrican): Africa, i.e. Libya, the site and later the domain of Carthage; still later a Roman province, east of Mauritania and west of Cyrenaica (and beyond that, Egypt). (Other than in this entry, this glossary's references to Africa are to the continent)

Agrippa: M. Vipsanius Agrippa, Augustus' close associate, given a special crown for his signal contribution to the naval victory at Actium. See also *Cæsar*

Ajax: see *Pallas* 1

Alba [< *alba*, Latin for 'white'], Alba-longa (Alban): (1) the city of Alba Longa in Latium to be built by Ascanius and to produce the 'Alban Fathers' (1.9; *A*: *patres* > patricians) including Romulus, founder of Rome (1.364–77); (2) 6.1035, pertaining to the original Latian inhabitants of the site of Alba, on the slopes of Mount Albano

Albano, Mount: see *Alba* 2

Alcides: Hercules, as grandson of Alceus

all, the God: compare 1.1010

Alœan Twins: Otus and Ephialtes (stepsons of Aloeus), who in their attack on Jove attempted to dismantle the sky (*A*) and piled Mount Pelion on Mount Ossa

Alpheus: a river in Greece flowing in the direction of Sicily and mythologically personified as surfacing there so as to unite with the nymph Arethusa, who had been metamorphosed into a spring on the island of Ortygia, the older part of Syracuse

amain: vigorously

Amasene: the river Amasenus

amaze: bewilderment; regarding whether 'a maze' is simply a typographical error for 'amaze', see *OED*, 'maze', *sb.*, 3

ambrosial, ambrosian: referring to ambrosia, (1) a curative herb; the 'Dews' of 12.616 are liquids from it (*A*: *sucos*); (2) more generally, referring to the food of the gods

Amician: Amycian (see *Eryx* 2)

Ammon: Egyptian god who came to be identified with Jove

Amycla: Amyclae, a town in southern Latium

Androgeos: see *Theseus*

another: 6.1147, L. Mummius; in 146, the year Carthage fell and Macedonia became the first Roman province, Mummius destroyed Corinth; 6.1150, L. Aemilius Paullus, who some years earlier had defeated Perseus, king of Macedonia and reputed descendant of Achilles

Antenor: Trojan immigrant first to Illyria, site of the river Timavus, then to an Italian settlement he founded as Padua. At Troy, Antenor had urged that Helen be returned to the Greeks, and had lost several sons in combat (*Iliad* 7, etc.)

antick: possibly 'antic' (fantastically ornamented) rather than 'antique'

Antonius: Mark Antony

Anubis: jackal-headed Egyptian god associated with death

anvils 6.858: walls made in the Cyclops' forges (*A*)

Apennine: the Apennines, Italy's most prominent mountain range – as such, 'Father'

Apollo's Porch: that of his temple where the records of his oracles were kept, in accordance with Aeneas' pledge (6.110–15). Augustus had built this temple, on the Palatine Hill (see *Palanteum*). 'Parian Stone' would be marble from the Greek island of Paros (*A*, describing the temple entrance, compares it to snow)

ardent 2.645: though paralleling the instance in 2.277, here (where *A* has *arduus*, 'steep') a questionable translation. At least physically, the more ardent the less reflective

Arethusa: see *Alpheus*

Argos (Argive, Argolick): (1) capital of the Greek region Argolis; (2) Greece itself

Arunci: Aurunci (see *Auruncans*)

Asia (Asian): (1) a Roman province embracing most of Asia Minor and including Mysia, Lydia, Caria, and Phrygia; (2) 7.968, a town and the land surrounding it, in Lydia

Asium: Clusium (*A*), in Etruria, as also were Cosa[e] and Populon[i]a, Gravisca[e] and the other towns referred to at 10.247–65 including Cære, for which see 8.624–31

Assaracus: see *Dardanus*

assert: (1) 'To maintain; to defend either by words or actions' (*J*); (2) 'To claim; to vindicate a title to' (*J*)

assistants: others present

associate: 'To adopt as a friend upon equal terms' (*J*, citing 1.844)

Astyanax: the dead son, in *Iliad* 6 famously frightened by his father's helmet, of Andromache and Hector

Atè: Ate, Greek female divinity personifying destructive madness (*A* refers instead to the Fury Tisiphone, who *saevit*, 'rages')

Atlas: son of a Titan, responsible for holding aloft the sky, and identifiable with a mountain or group of them in northern Africa towards the Atlantic

atone, attone: (1) appease or gain reconciliation with someone, in some cases by making amends for behaviour resented by that person; (2) to suffer harm so as to prevent harm to another

Atreus: see *Brother-Kings*

attest: 'To call to witness' (*J*, citing 6.443–4)

Aufidus: a river in Apulia

augur: a practitioner of augury, the interpretation of omens – i.e. of what the omens augur (predict or otherwise signify) including any auspices, which specifically were divinations from the behaviour of birds as at 1.543ff.

Aurora: the dawn-goddess (see also *Memnon*)

Auruncans, Aurunci (Auruncan): the people of the town of Aurunca, in Campania

Ausonia (Ausonian): the territory, as indicated at 8.435, of one of the peoples first to settle in Latium; see also *Latium 2*

auspice: see *augur*

author: progenitor

Automedon: charioteer of Achilles

Aventine: one of Rome's seven hills

Avernus (Avernian): a word said to derive from the equivalent in Greek of 'without birds' (*L*), as explained at 6.341–7

avert 2.196: turn yourselves away
avow: sanction, support
axe, axes 6.1119, 7.236: see *Brutus*

Bactrians: from Bactra (*A*), a city east of the Caspian Sea
baffl'd: defeated
Bajan: at Baiae
Barcæan: from the Libyan town of Barce; 'Barcæan' applies also to the
    family of Hannibal, descended from Barcas
bars 7.253: of gates (*A*)
battalia: battle formation ('embodi'd': massed)
battel: 'The main body of an army' (*OED*, 'battle', *sb.*, 9)
bays: see *Phœbeian Bays*
beams: see *beamy*
beamy: (1) radiant; (2) tree-like in form or bulk (*A: arboreis*, describing
    the horns of the stags in Dryden's 1.260). Old English 'beam', for
    tree, survives in the names of some trees ('hornbeam') and the
    'beam' of a stag horn is the trunk-like base which branches or
    radiates into the antlers (*OED*, 'beam', *sb.*^{1}, esp. 12, and 'beamy',
    1–3)
bed: cushion
belay: 'To block up' (*J*)
belies: disguises (*OED*, 'belie', *v.*^{2}, 4.b)
Bellona: Roman goddess of war
Berecynthian: relating to Cybele because she was worshipped on Bere-
    cynthius, a mountain in Phrygia
better: with reference to a person's hand or side: the right; hence the
    'worse' is the left
big: pregnant
bore: pierce; at 9.588 the text may include this sense, though the primary
    sense would seem to be 'turned away' (from *proturbant* in *A* 9.441),
    since *A* almost immediately describes the dead Nisus as 'pierced'
    (*confossus, A* 9.445)
Boreas (Borean): the north wind
born: borne
Briareus: also called Ægeon and described at 10.791–8
Brides, fatal: the fifty daughters, of Danaüs ruler of Argos, who (as
    described at 10.693–5) retaliated on his brother Aegyptus' fifty
    sons, who had forced those daughters into marriage
brood: see *race* 2
Brother-Kings: Agamemnon, king of Mycenae and leader of the Greeks
    against Troy, and Menelaus, king of Sparta, sons of Atreus
Brothers, Kingly: same as *Brother-Kings*

Brutus: L. Junius Brutus had vengeance on the last king of Rome, Tarquin the Proud, for Tarquin's tyranny and for the rape of Lucretia by Tarquin's son. Brutus with Lucretia's husband led a rebellion which drove the Tarquins into exile and established the Republic and the consulship in place of a king. The *fasces*, rods bound about an axe and carried by lictors, symbolized the public authority of the kings as 'renew[ed]' by Brutus (6.1119), i.e. as transferred to the consuls. As one of the first consuls Brutus had his sons executed for seeking to restore the monarchy of Tarquin. See also *Cato*

buckler: shield; Minerva's 'snaky' buckler is described in detail at 8.575–8

Butes: see *Eryx* 2

buxom: plump, blithe, indulgent, and possibly amorous

Byrsa: the citadel of Carthage, its name suggesting 'bull's hide' in Greek and hence connected with the Phoenician settlers' purchase, from the Libyans, of as much land as might be bounded by such a hide – much, because the settlers cut the hide into threads

caballer: this word, in Dryden's time, very strongly suggested manipulation of government by a small ('clos[e]' or secretive) group. Not only had political parties still to achieve any reputability; five of Charles II's ministers, the initials of whose names spelled 'cabal', were unforgettable for successfully promoting an alliance with Catholic France against Protestant Holland (*OED*, 'cabal', *sb.*¹, 6)

Cæneus: a hero exalted in *Iliad* 1 who, born female, had been transformed into a man by Neptune and, according to *Argonautica* 1, was slain by Centaurs

Cæsar, Cesar: Octavian or C. Julius Caesar Octavianus, i.e. Augustus, the honorific name which the Senate accorded him in 27 B.C. In 29, after his victories over Mark Antony and Cleopatra, at Actium and subsequently in Egypt, he celebrated a triple triumph (*A*) – a major public celebration of those victories together with his earlier, successful military campaign in Illyria. (Dryden's reference to Caesar at 6.1078 appears to be a reference to Julius Caesar, but *A* in the equivalent passage refers to him only indirectly, as Augustus' divine parent)

Cajeta: Caieta

Calliope: see *Muses*

Calydon: town in Aetolia, Greece. Its king, Oeneus, enlisted the aid of Jason and Theseus among other heroes, and of the virgin huntress Atalanta, to hunt that boar, finally killed by Oeneus' son Meleager. Oeneus' daughter Deianira unintentionally contributed to the death of Hercules by giving him Nessus' shirt. Oeneus' son Tydeus, his successor as king, was the father of Diomede

Camarine: Camarina, a town protected by a marsh. An oracle warned the townspeople not to drain it, was unheeded, and invasion ensued

Camertus: Camers (*A*)

Camillus: M. Furius Camillus, 4th-century dictator who conquered Veii and liberated Rome from the Gauls, and whose other exploits included victories over the Aequi and Volsci[ans]

Campania: with the 'Massick Soil' of Mount Massicus near its northern border, the coastal region below Latium with peoples including the Sidicini and towns including Abella, Batulum, and Cales

Cape, lofty: now Capo Miseno, south of Baiae

Capharæan Coast: see *Pallas*

Capitol: (1) the Capitoline Hill – site of Rome's citadel and in time dominated by the great Temple of Jupiter Capitolinus, its roof and other features resplendently gilded. The hill also held a thatched 'House of Romulus', the 'Palace' (*A*: *regia*) of 8.870, like that on the Palatine (see *Palanteum*). M. Manlius acquired the name 'Capitolinus' because, alerted by the noisy unrest of geese to the fact that the Gauls, having captured the rest of Rome, were attacking the Capitol, he was instrumental in defending it; (2) that temple in particular

Capri: *Capreae* in Latin, 'Teleboan' because settled by the Telaboae, a people from Acarnania

Capuan Name: that of the town of Capua

care: 'The object of care, of caution, or of love' (*J*)

Carmenta: more plainly than at 8.444–50, *A* identifies her as Evander's mother

Carrhae: see *Parthian*

casque: helmet

Cassandra: daughter of Hecuba and Priam; the 'God[']s decree' (2.324) was Apollo's, that her accurate prophecies would not be believed

Catiline: L. Sergius Catilina, opposed and overcome by Cicero for conspiracy despite some support from Julius Caesar

Cato: one of two renowned statesmen both named M. Porcius Cato – (1) 'the Elder' or 'the Censor', who defended austere, traditional Roman morals against the Scipios, among others, and promoted the destruction of Carthage; (2) 'the Younger' or 'of Utica', great-grandson of the former (and political opponent of Julius Caesar) who at Utica in Africa took his own life after the defeat of Pompey.

In a note to 6.115[6], Dryden insists that Virgil therein means the former Cato and thus, because no waster of words, must refer to the latter at 8.890. The note generally affirms Dryden's opinion that Virgil 'was of Republican Principles', proceeding to the remark that Virgil's praise of L. Junius Brutus at 6.1118–29 makes no more than a comparatively minor concession: that Brutus was 'only an unhappy Man, for being forc'd to ... severe Action' against his children, 'who conspir'd to restore Tyranny'. (Regarding Dryden's 'unhappy', see *happier*)

caul: 'a netted cap or head-dress, often richly ornamented' (*OED*, *sb.*[1], 1)

Centaurs: a race of composite creatures, traditionally with a human body down to the waist and a horse's four-legged body beneath; inhabitants of Thessaly. Centaurs are 'Cloud-born' because, when Ixion sought to make love to Juno, Jove fashioned an image of her from a cloud, and from Ixion's union with it the Centaurs were born. Mars caused the Centaurs to fight the Lapiths when he was not invited to the nuptials of the Lapiths' king Pirithous and Hippodamia, daughter of Adrastus. (Where Dryden refers to this battle, 7.422, doing so as if it were a Centaurian 'mutual' or civil war, *A* mentions the Lapiths but not the Centaurs and provides no precedent for Dryden's 'mutual'. But Ixion, who fathered the Centaurs, was a Lapith; and Hippodamia's name means 'horse-tamer', as reflected by the English 'hippodame' [*OED*]; and some distinctions may fade where remote, alien nations are concerned; see *Thrace*)

Ceres['] sacred Priest: Polyboetes (*A*)

certain 8.89: unquestionable (*A* here refers to Tiber's *domus*, 'home', as *magna*, 'great')

Cesar: same as *Cæsar*

chance: lot, fortune; see *happier*

Chaon: a son of Priam

Chaos: see *fate* 2

chaplet: garland adorning the head

charger: platter

Charibdis: Charybdis, one of two monsters (Scylla the other, both described at 3.527–46) on, respectively, the Sicilian and the Italian sides of the sea-passage between them (the Strait of Messina), a route dared by Ulysses (*Odyssey* 12) and Jason (*Argonautica* 4) but avoided by Aeneas, who instead seeks to circumnavigate Sicily

chine: 'The part of the back, in which the spine or backbone is found' (*J*)

Chymæra: Chimæra, a lion-headed monster with goat's body and snake's tail

Circe[']s Hills [or] Shores: those by the promontory and town of Circeii

circuits 1.370: years

circumvent: deceive

cirque: circle

Cisseus: see *Thrace*

city 3.359: Actium

Claudian Race: when the Republic was but a few years old and at war

with the Sabines, the Sabine Attius Clausus and his followers
became citizens of Rome and he acquired the name Appius Claudius
(Livy 2.16). For two important bearers of the Claudian name, see
Marcellus

Clelia: Cloelia; see *Porsena*

closet: private chamber

clown (clownish): peasant or churl

Cluentius: a *gens* (*A* apostrophizes a representative member, hence
Dryden's 'his')

Cocles: see *Porsena*

confess: (1) acknowledge; (2) manifest

conscious: (1) having an especially intense, felt, personal and even poss-
ibly private or secretly shared knowledge and awareness of some-
thing; being particularly alive to its truth, reality, consequence (even
guilt), or value, as when Aeneas refers to his own 'self-conscious
Worth' (8.174; *A* has only *virtus*, 'worth'); (2) figuratively, of in-
animate objects or beasts, personifying them as witnesses, perhaps
as sympathetically so, even as guiltily implicated

conspire: unite or cooperate

consul: one of the two annually chosen presiding executives of the Roman
Republic

Coritum, Coritus: Corythus (*A*), an Etrurian town

cornel: (1) the cornel-tree or cornelian cherry-tree; (2) the fruit or wood
of such a tree; (3) a weapon made of that wood

corps, corse: corpse; 'corps' may also be plural

corslet: armour for the trunk of the body

Cossus: Aulus Cornelius Cossus, who slew the king of the Veians

cost: expense in time and work

couch: to level a spear for attack

cou'd 2.777: could, might be able to do. But given that this 'cou'd' of
Dryden's and the clause including it have no equivalent in *A*, and
that what Deiphobus reports later concerning Helen's behaviour
(Dryden's 6.685–712), the word may here display its etymological
relation to 'know', as in 'couth' and 'coud', the latter sometimes
spelled 'cou'd' (*OED*, 'can', *v.*¹, headnote and A.2). Dryden's word
may therefore represent an imaginative effort to transform the dis-
crepancy between the two episodes in *A* into an irony, by emphasiz-
ing the dramatic possibilities of Aeneas' response to the sight of
Helen. If Aeneas is ignorant of what Helen knows, then his thoughts
about what she 'dreads' (2.780–81) are only conjectures

crest: a plume or distinctive ornament, or both, atop a helmet

Cretan, Cretin: Cretan, of or from Crete

Cretan Queen: Pasiphaë

croslet: same as *corslet*

cuirass: armour covering the chest and back

cuishes, cuisses: thigh-armour

Cumæan, Cuman: relating to the town of Cumae

curious: painstaking, elaborate

Cybel, Cybele, Cybelè: Cybele, a Phrygian goddess incorporated into Roman religion as *Magna Mater*, the 'Great Mother', regarded as the wife of Saturn and hence as the mother or grandmother of the subsequent generations of deities. She wears a crown representing what *A* refers to as her affection for towered cities. (The accent on the final *e* in 11.1131 emphasizes that the name has three syllables, indicating that earlier in the line, to maintain the metre, 'Chloreus' must have only two)

Cyclops (Cyclopean): one or more of a race of one-eyed giants in Sicily; the story of the blinding of Polypheme (Polyphemus) is essentially as given in *Odyssey* 9

Cycnus: a Ligurian (*cycnus* or *cygnus* is Latin for 'swan')

Cydon: from Cydonia, a town in Crete whose archers produced effects which *A* calls 'incurable'

Cylennius: Mercury (8.182–3) or Hermes (his Greek name in its English spelling, which Dryden sometimes employs); 'all his Wings' (1.413), where *A* has the phrase which Dryden at 6.24 translates as 'steerage of his Wings', may include those of his 'Rod' or 'Wand' (1.415, 4.355), the caduceus, as well as those of his feet (4.350–51)

cymarr: cymar, 'A robe or loose light garment for women; *esp.* an undergarment, a chemise' (*OED* 1, adding 'Used somewhat vaguely in poetry and fiction' and citing 4.196)

Cymothoe: a Nereid

Cynthia, Cynthus: see *Delos*

Cyprian: see *Paphian Queen*

Cythæra: Cythera, Greek island sacred to Venus

Danae: made pregnant with the mythical Perseus (great-grandfather of Hercules and slayer of the Gorgon Medusa) by a shower of gold, i.e. Jove in that form; see also *Inachus*

Dardan, Dardanian, Darden [< Dardanus]: Trojan

Dardanus: with his brother Iasius (Jasius), a founder of Troy. They were the sons of Jove and Electra, her parents being Atlas and Pleione. Dardanus married the Cretan Teucer's daughter, and their grandson was Tros (> 'Troy', 'Trojan'). Two sons of Tros, Ilus (> 'Ilium') and Assaracus, were respectively kings of Troy and Phrygia; a third son was Ganymede. Ilus' son and royal successor Laomedon was Priam's father, and Assaracus' grandson was

Anchises. (This is relatively standard legendary information, some of it delivered more fully in *Iliad* 20, in Aeneas' speech to Achilles before their combat. Neither Dryden nor Virgil is as explicit as Homer about the relations of lineage involved. The crucial passages in Dryden are 3.148–50, 225 and 6.666–70, 884; also 8.178)

darkling: as darkness falls (*A*: in the depth of night)

dart: (1) a comparatively small spear; (2) an arrow

Daughter of the Sun: see *God of Day* 2

Daunian [< Daunus]: see *Goddess-born*

Day, the: Phoebus as the 'God of Day'

debate: a contest or a fight, or to engage in one or the other

Decij, the two devoted: Decii, members of the *gens* Decius who, each in a different, difficult battle of the 4th–3rd centuries, ritually 'devoted' himself, i.e. vowed to incur, voluntarily, death from the enemy so as to procure divinely assisted victory. Each was faithful to his vow. The 'two', though, is in Livy 9.17; *A* gives no number; and the fact deserves mention because there were reputedly three such Decii: father, son, and grandson, each named P. Decius Mus. Livy's surviving text describes the deeds of the first two, and records that Rome won both battles. The third battle, at Asculum, Rome lost, but the enemy was Pyrrhus of Epirus (see *Fabritius*) and his victory was of the 'Pyrrhic', too costly kind named after him. (Dryden's 'Errata' in the first edition replaces 'three' with 'two' in this reference to the Decii)

Dedalus: Daedalus; see *Theseus*

degree: rank

Deiopeia: Deiopea (Dryden's odd, quasi-Greek spelling, besides conceivably producing a pair of diphthongs which a reader *might* rhyme with the vowel-sound of 'thine' here [1.110], suits the metre by possibly reducing the name from five to four syllables)

Deiphobus: Helen's Trojan husband, succeeding his brother Paris

Delos (Delian): Aegean island sacred to Apollo. He and Diana were born there on Mount Cynthus (4.204–10); hence Diana is 'Cynthia'

Delphian Oracle: the priestly interpreter of the priestess Pythia, in the foremost temple of Apollo, at Delphi in mainland Greece. She prophesied while seated on a golden tripod (*tripos*, a three-legged chair). Because Aeneas is not said to have been to Delphi, his reference is to *an* oracle of Apollo (*A* here refers to such oracles in Asia Minor)

delude: 'To disappoint; to frustrate' (*J*)

Denham [in footnote to 2.763]: the 'line' in question is from John Denham's 'The Destruction of Troy', a translation published in 1656 of part of *Aeneid* 2

denounce: proclaim ominously

deplore: lament

desart, desert: deserted; 4.837, by the Trojans themselves (*A*: *deseruere*)

devices: insignia

devote, devoted, devotion: (1) relating to a vow of dedication to accomplishment of a particular purpose (thus Camilla's 'vow'd Virginity' makes her Diana's 'vot[a]ry' [11.874, 1227]; (2) being doomed to death, in some cases on account of such a vow. See also *Decij* and *Gabin Gown*

dews 3.743: moisture from the splashing sea-foam (*A*)

Diana's, three: referring to Diana as 'presider over child-birth . . . , the chase, and nocturnal incantations (on this account her statues were three-formed and set up in the trivia', that is, a place 'where three roads meet' [*L*])

diffide: 'To distrust; to have no confidence in' (*J*)

Dindymus: mountain in Asia Minor associated with worship of Cybele

Diomede: Diomedes, Prince of Aetolia in Greece and one of the ablest warriors who besieged Troy. His exploits notably included the wounding of Aeneas – and of Venus when (as contemptuously recalled at 10.820) she rescued Aeneas by screening him with her veil (*Iliad* 5); also a foray with Ulysses in which Diomede surprised and slew the Trojan scout Dolon and from which Diomede and Ulysses returned astride the fine white horses they had taken from Rhesus (*Iliad* 10)

Dionæan Venus: referring to Venus as daughter of Dione, by 'Father' Jove (10.71), rather than as born from the sea (5.1046) near Cythera

Diræ: see *fury* 2

dishonest: dishonoured or dishonourable

distain: stain

dodder'd: decayed

Dodona (Dodonean): the sacred Epirian site where such vessels were employed in oracular ceremonies

Dolon: see *Diomede*

Doris: see *Nereids*

Dotis: see *Nereids*

doubted: paused as if hesitant

doubtful: (1) unpredictable in outcome, as explained at 4.865; (2) undependable

Driads: Dryads, nymphs 'of the Woods' as explained in 3.46

driven: see 1.745 (cited by *OED*, 'drive', *v.*, 4)

Drusian: pertaining to the Drusus family of the *gens* Livius with notable members including M. Livius Drusus, a tribune who effectively opposed the reforms of C. Sempronius Gracchus, and by adoption

Livia Drusilla, the fourth wife of Augustus and the mother of his stepson, Tiberius (who would succeed him as Emperor)

Earth 4.241, 7.186: Tellus (*A*); see *Titan*

Egerian: relating to the nymph Egeria, who was the wife of Numa Pompilius and whose sacred groves included one at Aricia, a town possibly personified at 7.1045

Egyptian Wife: Cleopatra, the 'Queen' of 8.921 and 'fatal Mistress' of 8.939. In *A* her 'Cymbals' are a sistrum, an instrument employed in worship of the horned goddess Isis – i.e. one of the Egyptian 'Country Gods' and 'Monsters' of 8.925. (By 28 B.C. Isis, together with another Egyptian divinity Serapis, had attracted enough Italian adherence for Augustus to outlaw their rites in Rome.) The 'Snakes behind' Cleopatra (8.924) cannot but suggest others, including the asps of her suicide. Dryden had dramatized that event in *All for Love*, a re-working of Shakespeare's *Antony and Cleopatra*

Electra: see *Dardanus*; 'her' in 1.41 refers to Juno

elephant: 'Ivory; the teeth of elephants' (*J*)

Elis: a coastal region of Greece, west of Arcadia

Elisa, Eliza: Dido

empty 1.652: *inani*, a mere (*A*)

Enceladus: a Giant (see *Titan*)

Eneas: Aeneas

Enos: Aeneadae

ensign: same as *standard*

Eolus (Eolian): same as *Æolus*

Epirian Continent: Epirus and inland from it, i.e. Greece

equal: (1) fair, equitable, just, disinterested; (2) 1.475, identical

Equicolæ: the Aequi, a people residing south of the Sabines who resisted the expansion of Rome; see *Camillus*

Erato: see *Muses*

Erebus: see *fate* 2

err: 'To wander' (*J*) or stray

error: 'Roving excursion; irregular course' (*J*)

Erymanthus: a mountain range in Arcadia; see *Hercules*

Eryphile: see *Seven against Thebes*

Eryx: (1) a mountain in Sicily, also a town there; (2) their namesake, the son of Butes and Venus. Butes' father Bebryx (or Amycus), king of Bebrycia in Asia Minor and renowned for boxing with the caestus (gauntlet), is killed therewith in *Argonautica* 2. See also *Pandarus*

Etna: same as *Ætna*

Etolian Prince: same as *Ætolian Prince*

Etruria (Etrurian): see *Tyrrhene*

Eubœan Rocks: see *Pallas*

Eurota's: the river Eurotas, site of ancient Sparta

eugh: yew

Eurus: the east wind

Evadne: see *Seven against Thebes*

event: outcome

Evoe: *euhoe* (*A*), an exclamation of Bacchanalian excitement

exerted: the equivalent in *A* (*exserta*) is expressed by the 'bare' earlier in this line, so Dryden's 'exerted' may refer to muscular effort put forth in shooting arrows, etc.; if 'exerted' means 'projecting' (*OED* 1), Dryden's line may also reflect the Amazons' reputed removal of one breast to facilitate archery

expect: await

expire: breathe forth

Fabij: Fabii, members of the *gens* Fabius, the 'greatest' having been Quintus Fabius Maximus Verrucosus, called *Cunctator* or 'delayer' for his evasive military strategy against Hannibal in the Second Punic War

Fabritius: Fabricius, a *gens*. One 3rd-century member, the consul C. Fabricius Luscinus – famously unbribable and fair-minded though not wealthy – had a major part in securing Italy from Greek power as exercised by the Pyrrhus who was a king of Epirus and reputedly of Achilles' line

falchion, fauchion: sword

Faliscans: from the town Aequi Falisci, in Etruria, as was another town mentioned in 7.959–62, Fescennia, together with Lake Ciminus and a grove sacred to Feronia

falsify'd: In a note to 9.1095, Dryden explains, 'I use the word falsifie . . . to mean that the Shield of *Turnus* was not of Proof against the Spears and Javlins of the *Trojans*; which had pierc'd it through and through (as we say) in many places,' and adds, 'The words which accompany this new one [which Dryden acknowledges adapting from an Italian word of the poet Ariosto] make my meaning plain . . .'

fane: temple

fate: either, though the point of demarcation is not always clear, (1) a grammatically singular abstract force, often personified, which produces the individual and collective destinies of everything else; in a note to 10.662 Dryden defends the idea 'that Fate was superiour to the Gods; and that *Jove* could neither defer no[r] alter its Decrees', but Dryden also finds Virgil less 'a Fatalist' than Homer on the grounds that Virgil makes room for 'Fortune' whereas

398   GLOSSARY

Homer does not; or (2) a Fate (*Parca*), any of three 'Sisters' (the
Parcae) who respectively spun, measured, and cut (i.e. terminated)
the thread of every mortal's life. In that note to 10.662 Dryden
also enlists a passage from Ovid's *Metamorphoses* to argue that Jove
'is only Library-Keeper . . . to the Fates, [whose] Decrees . . . the
inferiour Gods were not permitted to read without his leave', and
Dryden employs the genealogy of divinities in Hesiod's *Theogony*
to derive the Fates from '*Chaos, Night,* and *Erebus* . . . the most
Antient of the Deities, [who instituted] those fundamental laws by
which [Jove] was afterwards to govern'. (Erebus broadly personifies
the region of Hades; an alternative genealogy for the Hesperides
derives them from Erebus and Night [see *Hercules*].) At 4.1000–
1001 Dryden refers to the 'Sisters' where *A* has singular 'fate'
(*fato*). Dryden seems to combine the Fates' part in determining
the span of Dido's life with Proserpina's part, of accepting a tribu-
tary lock permitting entrance into Hades.
fated: secure, protected
Fate to Foe, with: by fate to be Pallas' opponent (*A*)
Father, fam'd: Melampus (*A*). (*Argonautica* 1 happens to mention him
    just before listing Hercules among the Argonauts, and *Odyssey* 15
    describes Melampus as having, like Hercules, successfully com-
    pleted a period of imposed labour)
Father of the Gods: Jove
feeds 7.548: lets [her hair] grow long (*A*)
fencing for: defending
Feretrian Jove: Jove's title as dedicatee, at a special ancient temple on
    the Capitol, of the *opima spolia* or 'spoils of honour', the armour
    stripped from an enemy general when slain in battle directly by
    his Roman counterpart. M. Claudius Marcellus, the consul, was
    only the third to accomplish this feat, after Romulus and Cossus.
    Augustus had this temple rebuilt
Feronia: Italian earth-goddess
field: surface of a shield
fillet: headband (usually plural) worn by priests, sacrificial victims, etc.
fire 10.996: explained somewhat at 7.445–8, alluding to Hecuba (whom
    A identifies in both instances) as bringing forth a torch-like 'Brand'
    when she gave birth to Paris
firm: confirm
Five Cities: including Atina, the originally Sabine towns of Antemnae
    and Crustumeri, and Tibur
fix: affix, apply, establish, or direct
fix'd: 1.338, put away; 7.753, definitely begun
flaggon: flagon, a wine-pitcher

flatter: to raise unfounded hopes in another or oneself

flaw: 'A tumult; a tempestuous uproar' (*J*)

flood: (1) a river; (2) whether singular or plural, the sea or another substantial body of water

flying: fleeing

fond: 'To show fondness for; caress, fondle' (*OED*, *v.*, 4, citing 1.962)

foredoom'd: already destined or ordained

forelay: stealthily take prior control of

former 9.464: the passage in *A* may be taken to indicate that the men named in Dryden's preceding line, including Rhoetus, are asleep; then excepts Rhoetus, as does Dryden (unless Dryden's spelling the name 'Rhaetus' in that preceding line represents an attempt to resolve a contradiction)

Friend, greater: Hercules (*A*)

front: (1) forehead; (2) face

fun'rals, funerals: 2.373, of Hector's associates (*A*); 2.491, bodies of the slain (*A*)

fury: (1) consuming passion, usually of rage, sometimes personified (*A*: *furia, furor*); (2) one of the three Furies (*A*: *Dirae, Furiae*), 'dire' goddesses described in detail at 12.1224–36 and including Alecto and Tisiphone; (3) 3.329, 'Fury's' (plural), the Harpies. In his note on 12.1224–5 Dryden says: 'They were call'd Furies in Hell, on Earth Harpies, and in Heaven *Diræ*. . . .' The note identifies Celaeno with Alecto, 'chief of the Furies'

Gabian: of Gabii (see *Præneste*)

Gabin Gown: a short *trabea* (*A*), a garment signifying high rank. Dryden's note to 4.944–7 refers to Dido's way of arranging her gown at 4.752 as 'putting her self into the *Habitus Gabinus* ['Gabine attire'], which was the girding her self round with one sleeve of her Vest'. The reference is to the *cinctus Gabinus*, a manner of wearing the toga with part of it passed back over the left shoulder and then brought forward, under the right arm, to the breast – a priestly, ceremonial practice of marked solemnity. Dryden refers to Livy's descriptions of the Decii, who, like Dido, by conforming to this style and a certain ritual style of speech, displayed their 'devoting themselves to *Death*'; but, Dryden points out, the Decii were devoted to 'the destruction of the Enemy', which Dryden calls 'a better Cause' than Dido's 'Vengeance'. See also *devote* and, under *Præneste*, 'Gabii'

Ganimed, Ganymed: Ganymede, a Trojan youth whose beauty drew Jove to abduct him; see *Dardanus*

Garamantis: a nymph of the Garamantes (*A*), an African people

gave 6.760: gave [to me] 'rule' [of]; i.e. placed me in charge of

gen'rous: of noble origin; regarding wine, *OED* 5

genius: soul or spirit, especially a local deity (e.g., 'Genius of the Place', 7.185)

Geryon: see *Hercules*

Getulia (Getulian): Gaetulia, the north-African region inhabited by the Gaetuli

gibbous: hump-backed

give: expose

giv'n: to be preserved

glance: strike against in passing

Glaucus: prominent in the Trojan War for reasons including his loyalty to his commander, Sarpedon (*Iliad* 16, etc.)

glimps 12.705: a glimpse of Turnus (*A*)

Gnosian: Gnossian, of or from Crete (< Knossos, in Latin *Cnossus*, *Gnossus*, etc., its capital)

god 7.516: Faunus (7.70); see *gods* 3

God and Goddess: see *Goddess-born*

Goddess-born: as applied to Turnus, referring to his mother Venilia, identified in *A* 10.76 (but nowhere in Dryden's poem). There too Virgil names Pilumnus as Turnus's grandfather or ancestor; Dryden's equivalent reference (10.117) is to 'a God' instead, and at 9.4, where *A* names Pilumnus, Dryden refers perhaps equivocally to Turnus's 'great Grandsire'. Dryden's way of translating *A* 10.619 at his 10.875 supports the sense 'great-grandfather'. Pilumnus, an indigenous Italian god (*L*), was not Turnus's father, who is Daunus (hence 'Daunian' in epithets for Turnus)

Goddess Mother, Goddess-Mother: Venus, as mother of Aeneas, but, at 2.1071, as mother-in-law of Creusa (*A*: Venus' *nurus*, daughter-in-law)

Goddess of the Night: the daughter of Latona (*A*), i.e. Diana

God, far-shooting: Apollo

God of Arms: Mars

God of Battel's: Mars

God of Day: (1) 4.78, Apollo (*A*: Phoebus); (2) 12.248, Sol (*A*), an Italian god identifiable with Helios, son of the Titan Hyperion and father of Circe (7.13). The reference suggests (contrary to 7.260–63) that Circe had consummated her love for Picus

gods: (1) major Greek deities given the Latin names and to some extent the characteristics of indigenous Italian deities – primarily the ruling Olympian gods Jove (or Jupiter) and his sister and wife Juno, their other siblings including Ceres, Neptune, and Pluto, and some additional relatives, Jove's daughter Minerva and others, as well as lesser deities (e.g., the nymph Thetis); (2) the particularly Italian set of deities protecting a given family's household, land ('country'), and hearth (deities broadly distinguishable as, respectively: the Penates, one or more Lares, and the goddess Vesta, who came to be identified with the Olympian goddess Hestia); (3) these domestic deities (or representations or representatives of them) as protectors of a people or city – notably the statues of such deities which Aeneas rescues from both his dwelling in Troy and the city itself (e.g., 1.7, 523; 2.389–96); (4) other distinctly Italian deities such as Janus and Faunus (the father of Latinus and an oracular, tutelary god of farmers and shepherds); (5) deities distinctly originating in foreign places other than Italy or Greece, as did Cybele. See also *Titan*

God's Command 7.154: Jupiter's direction (*A*)

Gorgon (Gorgonean): Medusa or either of her sisters; they each had snakes for hair and a face which turned beholders to stone. At 7.476, 'Smear'd ... with black Gorgonean Blood', the equivalent in *A* is 'infected ... with Gorgonian venom', befitting the Fury's Gorgon-like appearance (7.456–8)

Gracchi: especially the brothers Tiberius Sempronius Gracchus and C. Sempronius Gracchus, tribunes who successively, in the two decades after the Third Punic War, opposed the Senate in order to effect reforms benefiting the non-aristocratic classes and were killed, as were those reforms

graff: graft

Grandam Goddess: Cybele (*A*: Berecynthia), as grandmother of the offspring of Jove and of his siblings

grateful: pleasing

Grecian Babes: Greek youth (*A*: *pube*)

Grecian Brothers: same as *Brother-Kings*

Grecian's, proud: referring to Achilles, slain by Paris (*A*), the 'only Mortal part' being Achilles' heel

guilty 5.307: 'bound to the performance of (a vow) = L[atin] *reus voti*' (*OED* 4); here *A* has this Latin phrase (see also *devote*)

Hall, litigious: the Roman Forum (*A*), referring to what would be Rome's central public area; the reference in Dryden is evidently to the Senate building which would be there, and 'litigious' may have the general meaning 'disputatious'

Hands Divine 2.316, 9.181: see *Laomedon*

happier, happy: 'Having [better or] good "hap" or fortune' (*OED*, 'happy', 2) – and thus, regarding what happens or perhaps shall, not hapless or unhappy (see *fate* 1)

haulser: hawser, a ship's towing or mooring rope

he: 2.318, the horse, perhaps because the gender of Latin *equus*, 'horse', is masculine (see also *struck*); 9.591, Volscens (*A*)

Head, perjur'd: as signified by the sacrificial smiting of the animal (described in Livy, 1.24 and elsewhere), that of anyone who breaks the treaty

Heav'n, Entitl'd to your: to whom Jove promised the celestial court (*A*) – apparently an expression of expected protection from Jove and perhaps of the deification of Aeneas and some of his progeny to occur after death, as well as of (the line goes on to indicate) the Trojans' entitlement to practise the ceremonies of worship sanctioned by Jove

Hebrus: a river in Thrace

Hecat: Hecate, a goddess of Hades who presides over supernatural spells, 'threefold' because associated with Diana and the trivia (see *Diana's, three*). As a note to 4.740 in the California Edition points out, Dryden's reference to a 'hundred Names' is apparently based on an identification of Hecate's name with the Greek word for 'hundred' (as in 'hecatomb'), an identification asserted by the early commentator Servius and cited by Ruaeus

Helen's lovely Daughter: Hermione (*A*)

Helenus: a son of Priam renowned for augury; in *Iliad* 5 he gives advice to Hector and Aeneas, including the recommendation that the Trojan women go in procession to beseech aid from Pallas, as they do in *Iliad* 6

Helicon: see *Muses*

Hell: Dryden's usual word for the region of Pluto and the dead, a region to which Dryden also applies the adjective 'infernal' (< *infernus*, Latin for 'lower', 'nether', or 'subterranean') as well as (also following Virgil's example) other words including adjectival names such as 'Stygian' – but not the Greek name 'Hades', regularly employed in this glossary

Hercules: Greek hero sometimes said to be from Thebes, son of Jove by Alcmena. Resentful Juno sent the serpents to kill Hercules and later afflicted him in other ways. He performed his Twelve Labours in service to Eurystheus, king of Mycenae. These included: slaying the lion of Nemea ('the roaring Terror of the Wood', 8.392) and the Hydra of Lake Lerna, a serpent whose multiple heads 'increas'd' in the sense that they sprouted anew when cut off (8.399); catching the 'brazen-footed' Ceryneian deer (6.1094), also the boar of Erymanthus and a bull of Crete; raiding the Amazons to acquire Hippolyte's girdle; and both killing Geryon (a king in Spain, with a triple body) and carrying off his cattle; capturing Cerberus, 'the triple Porter' (8.393); and, after killing their guardian dragon, removing

golden apples from the 'Hesperian Temple' (4.700; the temple of
the Hesperides [*A*], i.e. daughters of Hesperus). Dryden's account
at 8.381–401 of some of these and other Herculean deeds is only
loosely connected with the equivalent passage in *A*, which names
two Centaurs slain, Hylaeus and Pholus, and refers expansively to
plural Cretan monsters, whereas Dryden's 'Monster Crew' may
well contract the references so as to include only those monsters
mentioned in the lines that follow. Virgil's highly allusive passage
does not account for Hercules' destroying the 'Walls' of both
Oechalia and, more importantly, Troy, or explain his relation to
Typhœus. The site of Oechalia may be the island of Euboea off the
mainland of eastern Greece, and the attack on Troy was evidently in
retribution for one of Laomedon's broken promises (see *Laomedon*,
especially regarding walls); Hercules went uncompensated for res-
cuing Laomedon's daughter Hesione from a sea-serpent. Hercules
assisted his father against Typhœus, and was also one of the Argo-
nauts seeking the Golden Fleece under the command of Jason.
Hercules finally sought death for relief from a shirt which burned
his flesh (a shirt from the Centaur Nessus, who had tried to rape
Hercules' wife Deianira and whom Hercules had slain). Philoctetes
helped Hercules prepare his death-pyre; in return, Hercules gave
his poisoned arrows to Philoctetes, and with them Philoctetes slew
Paris at Troy. Hercules, dying, became a god, prominently wor-
shipped in Rome. See also *Pinarian House* and *Theseus*

Herilus: *A* explicitly identifies his mother as Feronia

Hermus: a river in Lydia

Hesperia (Hesperian) [< *hesperius*, western]: pertaining to a land in the
west, especially Italy from the viewpoint of Greece or Troy, but
also to what is still farther west, such as the 'Hesperian Temple',
for which see *Hercules*

him 6.884: Dardanus (*A*)

hind: 'A peasant' (*J*)

Hippolitus: Hippolytus; see *Theseus*

Hircanian: Hyrcanian

his Temple: that of Janus; in *A* the 'Gates' of 7.840 are those of War
(*Belli*) rather than directly of Mars

hit: hit on, discover

honours: ornaments signifying the special station or other distinction
belonging to someone or something; e.g., such 'holy Honours' as
the fillets of a priest

horns 4.321: projections or corners

horror (horrid): with other *horr*- words (and 'abhor'), having a range of
senses beyond those of repugnance and even fearful loathing. The

further senses derive from several related Latin words, for 'bristling', 'bristled', 'shuddering' or 'trembling', 'shaggy', etc. (*OED*, 'Horre' and following entries)

humane: human

Hydra: the Hydra of 6.400 *A* identifies as that of Lerna, which *L* says had seven heads (see *Hercules*); regarding the Hydra of 6.778, *A* specifies only that it has fifty mouths

Hymen: god of marriage, figuratively marriage itself

Hyrcanian: pertaining to Hyrcania, a country east of the Caspian Sea

Icarus: fell to his death when flying on wings made by Daedalus

Ida (Idæan, Idean): a mountain near Troy; the warrior Ida (9.781) is Idas in *A*

Idalia (Idalian): see *Paphian Queen*

Ideus: Idaeus, in *Iliad* 7 a Trojan herald to the Greeks who voices opinions like Antenor's and in *Iliad* 24 serves as the chariot-driver taking Priam to buy Hector's body from Achilles

Idomeneus: fought on the Greek side at Troy; later, he was driven from Crete after the discovery that a vow he had made, to secure his safe return there, required the sacrificial death of his son

ignoble: 'Mean of birth . . . ; not of illustrious race' (*J*)

Ilium (Ilian): Troy (5.986, as in *A*, evidently distinguishes between only the two names of the city)

Ilus: see *Dardanus* and *Iulus*

Inachus: king of Argos, god of the river Inachus in Argolis, and father of Io; *A* couples his name with that of Acrisius, a later king of Argos and the father of Danae

India (Indian): see *Memnon*

indigested: disorderly

inferior: of lesser rank

infernal: see *Hell*

inspire: breathe in

insult: 'leaping upon' (*J*)

inter'st: influence

invest: surround militarily

involve: enfold, enclose, and obscure

Io: (1) as an exclamation, 'Look'; (2) as a name, referring to a maiden who, when Jove desired her and Juno became jealous, was transformed into a heifer and guarded by Argus. Io at last took refuge in Egypt. See also *Inachus*

Ionian Deep [or] Main: the Ionian Sea, the part of the Mediterranean Sea between Greece and Sicily south of the Adriatic Sea

Io Pæan: a shout derived from a Greek hymn to Apollo, of triumph or of thanksgiving for victory

Iris: goddess personifying the rainbow

irremeable: 'Admitting no return' (*J*)

Ischia: the island, in Latin *Imarine*

Ismarus: a river in Thrace

issue: (1) outcome, result; (2) offspring; (3) in the plural, furious military consequences (see *Janus*); (4) means of escape

it 1.814: apparently referring to a 'way' of escaping or dispelling the cloud, by consideration of the reassuring circumstances which Achates goes on to describe

Ithacus: Ulysses, as king of Ithaca

Iulus: with regard to Ascanius' acquiring this name (1.364–5), in *A* Jove adds that Ascanius was called 'Ilus' while the Trojan kingdom endured, and foretells a 300-year reign in Alba by the people of Hector. (Regarding 'Ilus', see *Dardanus*.) Jove also foretells that Caesar shall be of Trojan descent, and explains that his name 'Julius' derives from that of Iulus – Dryden's 1.390. (The references are to Augustus and to his name 'Julius', signifying membership in the Julian *gens*, acquired when he was adopted by Julius Caesar.) Ascanius is '*Hector*'s Nephew' (12.652) because Creusa was a daughter of Hecuba and Priam

Ixion: son of Phlegyas; see *Centaurs*

Janicula: Janiculum (*A*), a fortress built by Janus on the hill named Janiculum

Janus: an Italian deity, patron especially of beginnings. He had two faces, the additional one at the back of his head, and his temple in the Roman Forum had two doors, kept open when Rome was at war, kept closed in peacetime, and to be closed when Augustus has established universal peace

Jasius: Iasius (see *Dardanus*)

Jove, Bird of: the eagle

Julian, Julius, Julus: see *Iulus*

Julian Star: the star of Augustus' father (*A*), a comet seen just after the death of Julius Caesar

Juturna: elder sister of Turnus (9.807, 12.212)

ken, in: within view

Kids: *Haedi* (*A*), a double star in the constellation Auriga

kind: see *race*

King of Men: Agamemnon (see *Orestes*)

Labicans: the people of the Latian town of Labicum

lab'ring: labouring, struggling to be relieved or rid of

Læda's: Leda's, referring to Leda, the mother of Castor, Clytemnestra, and Pollux, as well as Helen (Jove was the father of all these)

Laodamia: followed her husband, slain when attacking Troy, to Hades; she was Sarpedon's mother

Laomedon: a king of Troy (see *Dardanus*), notoriously untrustworthy. Laomedon refused to pay Neptune and Apollo for services including Neptune's building the walls of Troy, as Neptune complains in *Iliad* 21

Latian, Latin, Latine: see *Latium*

Latium (Latian, Latin, Latine): (1) historically, the area south of the Tiber to Circei; (2) synonymous with 'Ausonia' and similarly extendable to include more or less all of Italy

Latona (Latonian): mother of Apollo and Diana

Lawrel's God: Apollo; see *Phœbeian Bays*

lean: famished in appearance (*A*)

leave to 5.559: dismiss (*A*: *solve*)

Lemnian: pertaining to the Aegean island of Lemnos, sacred to Vulcan; he fell to it after having opposed Jove, who responded by hurling him from the heavens (an event described in *Iliad* 1)

lenifie: lenify, soften or palliate

Lerna's (Lernæan): pertaining to a wetland near Argos (see *Hercules*)

Libian, Libyan: pertaining to Libya; see *Africk*

lictors: see *Brutus*

Ligurian: from or related to the northern Italian region of Liguria

liquid: 'Of . . . the air: clear, transparent, bright' (*OED* A.2)

list, lists (listed): an area listed (i.e. bordered in some manner) as the site of combat or of an athletic contest

loads 3.626: loads him (Iulus)

lock: a dangerously confined space close to jutting rocks (*A*)

Love: Cupid or, in the plural, beings like him (e.g., putti)

lunar: see *moony*

Luperci: youths cavorting in the Lupercalia, an annual fertility festival (see *Pan*)

Lycas: he had been surgically delivered unharmed from his dead mother's womb (*A*)

Lycian: (1) pertaining to a country in south-western Asia Minor; (2) Lycian Lotts 4.544: oracles (*A*: *sortes*) there, of Apollo

Lycimnia: a slave (*A*)

Lydia (Lydian): see *Phrygian*

Mæotian Lake: a northern bay of the Black Sea

Maid, loving: Ariadne (see *Theseus*)

make up: make haste to catch up

Malæan Flood: the sea off the Greek promontory of Malea

managing: carefully conserving

man'd: manned (compare 'unman', 9.662)

Manes: (1) the spirit of a dead person – a 'Ghost; shade', or, more diffusely, 'that which remains of [a human being] after death' (*J*); (2) several such spirits; (3) 6.1006, their respective 'Penances'

Manlius: (1) M. Manlius Capitolinus; see *Capitol* 1; (2) Titus Manlius Imperiosus Torquatus, a distinguished 4th-century soldier and consul who had his son executed for disobeying military orders

Mantuan Town: Mantua, on the river Mincius near Andes, Virgil's birthplace

marbles: *saxo*, a stone (*A*)

Marcellus: (1) M. Claudius Marcellus, consul whose exploits included capturing Syracuse in the Second Punic War (see also *Feretrian Jove*); (2) the youth of the same name who was Augustus' nephew, adopted son, and heir apparent, but predeceased him. (The importance of this Marcellus in Dryden's elegy 'To the Memory of Mr Oldham' should not go unmentioned.) In a note on 6.122 Dryden rejects as too literal the translation 'Thou shalt *Marcellus* be' for *A*'s 'Tu Marcellus eris', especially because the requisite 1,000-year term (stipulated at 6.1013) for 'Transmigration of [the earlier Marcellus's] Soul' could not have been completed by the time the later Marcellus was born

Marrubians: the Marsi, a people whose capital was Marrubium and whose territory included Lake Fucina and the 'Angitian Woods' (7.1040–41) sacred to Angitia, sister of Circe

Martial, Martian: pertaining to Mars

Martial Twins: Romulus and Remus, as sons of Mars

Martian Field: the Campus Martius (Field of Mars), an open area and military and political assembly place just outside Rome

Massick Soil: see *Campania*

Massylian: pertaining to a North African people, the Massyli

Matrons, modest: the women of Rome accorded the privilege of driving in litters or certain kinds of carriages, in recognition of their sacrificing their gold ornaments to help pay for the gift which Camillus insisted was owed to Apollo after the conquest of Veii

maze, a: see *amaze*

Medon: a Trojan mentioned in *Iliad* 17

Meleager's Race: Parthenopaeus (*A*), Meleager's son and one of the 'Seven against Thebes' (see *Calydon*; also *race* 2 for usage)

Memmian: pertaining to the *gens* Memmius

Memnon: a king of the Ethiopians, mentioned in *Odyssey* 11. He was the son of Priam's brother Tithon[us] and Aurora, and was armed by Vulcan. 'Indian' as referring to Memnon's troops, together with other references to India, pertains broadly to an area east of the river Indus

mend: (1) augment; (2) 'add fuel to' (*OED* 5.d)

Metius: Metius Fufetius, Alban general whose treachery led to his harsh execution by Tullus Hostilius (of 6.1109) and the destruction of Alba

Mincius: see *Mantuan Town*

Minerva's Temple: at the tip of the peninsula south of Tarentum and across the Gulf of Tarentum from Lacinium

minister: offer, provide

Mistress, fatal: see *Egyptian Wife*

mitre: at Dryden's one instance of this word, *A* does not have the Latin equivalent, *mitra*, but does have it in the plural where Dryden has 'Turbants', turbans (9.844)

monsters: extraordinary events

monuments: memorials, reminders

moony: 'Lunar' (1.691), shaped like a half-moon

Moorish Race: the Mauri, from Mauritania in Africa or simply Africa

Mother of the Gods: Cybele

Mother's Rites: those of Cybele

motions: impulses

Mulciber: Vulcan

Musæus: early Greek poet

Muses: the nine goddesses of particular arts and sciences who dwelt on Mount Helicon in Greece and who include Calliope, for epic poetry, and Erato, for love poetry

Mycenae: the city ruled by Agamemnon

myrtle: a shrub of the Mediterranean area

Nais: a Naiad or fresh-water nymph

nation: see *race*

Nation of the Gown: of the toga (*A*), possibly implying the Roman legacy of law and order

Nations, Vanquish'd: including those from Caria in Asia Minor, Numidia in North Africa, and Scythia (see *Thrace*). Like other rivers named here, the Araxes, in eastern Asia Minor, represents one or more peoples bordering it. The Morini were a people of north-west (Belgic) Gaul and were 'last' as so extremely remote (*A*) from Rome. Dryden substitutes Danes for *A*'s Scythian Dahae

native: natural

nephew: 'grandson' or 'descendant, however distant' (*J*)

Neptune, Son of: Messapus (*A*)

Neptune's Bars: holy doorpost (*A*) – evidently that of a temple of Neptune

Neptune's Shield: alluding to his 'spread[ing] a Cloud' (5.1060) to save Aeneas from Achilles, in *Iliad* 20; regarding 'Venus's Veil', see *Diomede*

Nereids: the fifty sea-nymphs, including Dotis (Doto in *A*), of whom Doris and Nereus (sea-deities of Titanian descent) were the mother and father

Nereus: see *Nereids*

Neritos: apparently an island rather than the mountain of that name on Ithaca

Night: see *fate* 2

Nilus: the river Nile

Nisus: (1) the 'Vows' (9.270) of the Trojan of this name have no equivalent in *A* but may have that in his 'Sacred Bonds of Amity' (5.435); (2) Nysa, a city on the mountain in India where Bacchus was born

Numicus (Numician): a spring with a pool and one or more rivulets, in Latium

Numidian: referring to the people of Numidia in north-west Africa, who sided with Rome in the Punic Wars but later became subject to Rome after allying themselves with Pompey against Julius Caesar

Nursia, Nursians: Nursia is *Nersae* in *A* (*Nursæ* in Ruaeus' text), a town of the Aequi and not to be confused with the town of the Nursians (see *Sabine*)

nymph: in either case typically a virgin: (1) a lesser goddess or demigoddess, of the sea, a fountain, or some other prominent object in nature (e.g., a Nereid, though a line such as 5.1081 with its reference to 'Nymphs and Nereids' may be taken to indicate both that there is some distinction between them and that Dryden does not directly attach much importance to it); (2) a young woman

obnoxious: (1) submissive; (2) vulnerable

obscene: repulsive

obscure: (1) scarcely visible; (2) invisible

obtend: spread forth; in her reference to the 'Cloud' here, Juno confuses Venus' effort to rescue Aeneas with Apollo's completion of that rescue, after Diomede had wounded Venus (*Iliad* 5)

obtest: plead for

officious: 'Dutiful' (*OED* 2)

ointed: anointed, 'smear'd with ... O[i]l' (12.156) or a comparable substance

Orestes: killed his mother, Clytemnestra (together with her lover Aegisthus), for her part in the murder of his father, Agamemnon, and was therefore pursued by the Furies

Orion: huge mythological hunter who became a constellation

Orpheus: the 'Thracian Bard' who would have won the release of his dead wife, Eurydice, from Hades, had he not broken the promise he had made as the price of her release by turning to look at her as the couple departed

Orythia: Orithya, Athenian princess, mother of the 'winged Warriors'

outrageous: 'violent; furious' (J)

Pactolus: a river in Lydia

Padus: the river Po

pair 6.1134: Julius Caesar and his son-in-law Pompey

Palanteum (Pallantean): Pallanteum – according to Livy (1.5) the name also of Evander's native town in Arcadia and the etymological source of 'Palatine', the name of one of Rome's seven hills and the word from which 'palace' is derived. The Palatine held Augustus' mansion; also, a preserved thatched hut called the 'House of Romulus'. Evander's modest 'Palace' (8.477) may be thought to resemble the latter as well as the Regia, the house of 'the Roman King' Numa Pompilius near the boundary of the Roman Forum

Palicus: A refers to the Palici, twin sons of Jove worshipped in Sicily

Palladium: the statue of Minerva referred to in 2.216–50

Pallas: (1) Minerva, who – as Juno complains at 1.60–69 – had punished not only the 'one offending Foe' Ajax Oileus (named in A) but also many of the Greeks because he had abused Cassandra (2.543–51), wrecking their ships at Caphareus on the island of Euboea as they sought to return from Troy; (2) 'nobler' (7.1097) as goddess of war rather than goddess of woollen-work

Pan: his 'Shrine' was Lupercal, a grotto in Rome sacred to Lupercus (Pan was worshipped at Lycaeus, a mountain in Arcadia)

panacee: panacea; herb curing all ailments

Pandarus: at the instigation of Minerva, he broke a truce during the Trojan War by wounding Menelaus with an arrow, and was killed by Diomede (Iliad 4–5); Eurytion's invoking Pandarus as his 'Brother God' (5.680, but not in A) parallels Dares' relation to his 'Brother ['The God'] Eryx' (5.521, 548)

Panopea: a sea-nymph

Paphian Queen, Paphos: Venus, the queen, as especially honoured at the latter, a city of Cyprus (see 1.575–81), as she was at Idalia, another city there

Parent of the Gods: Cybele

Parian: see Apollo's Porch

Paris 1.38–9: referring to his giving judgment ('Doom') that Venus was more beautiful than Juno or Minerva; regarding the equity of the judgment, see Juno's complaint at 12.141–2

Parthian: relating to the people of Parthia, south-east of the Caspian Sea and famous for the tactics of their mounted archers. Having established an empire extending as far west as the Euphrates, the Parthians successfully resisted Roman domination, most notably with a victory – hence capturing the Roman 'Eagles' (*A*: *signa*, standards) – at Carrhae in Mesopotamia (53 B.C.). See also *Thrace*

Pasiphae: Pasiphaë; see *Theseus*

pastor: shepherd (Latin *pastor*, in *A*)

Pelides: Achilles, as son of Peleus

Pentheus: king of Thebes, slain by women including his mother for opposing worship of Bacchus

Penthisilea: Penthesilea, an Amazon queen who, according to sources other than Homer, fought against the Greeks at Troy

Pergamus: Troy and particularly its citadel, Pergama; the town which Aeneas founds in Crete is Pergamae

Perithous: Pirithous, son of Ixion (see *Centaurs* and *Theseus*)

Phædra: see *Theseus*

Pheneus: a town in Arcadia

Philoctetes: see *Hercules*

Phlegias: Phlegyas, Ixion's father, who burned Apollo's temple at Delphi

Phœbe: Diana, particularly as goddess of the moon

Phœbeian Bays: the laureate wreath of honour, especially as accorded to a poet, woven from the leafy twigs of the bay-tree (also called the bay-laurel), a tree, like poetry, sacred to Apollo

Phœbus (Phœbeian): Apollo, particularly as god of the sun, of light, and of poetry

Phœnix: Achilles' childhood guardian, who sought unsuccessfully to reconcile him to Agamemnon (*Iliad* 9)

Phorcus: a sea-god, a son of Neptune and father of the Gorgons

Phosphor: Phosphorus, the morning-star

Phrygian: (1) Trojan, from Troy's location in Asia Minor, site of the very ancient country of Phrygia. The name 'Phrygian', especially because of unrestrained behaviour and other customs involved with Phrygian worship of Cybele, was open to such charges as Numanus expresses (9.841–50), Hyparba earlier (4.314–17), and Turnus later (12.154–6): charges of indecorum and worse ('Lydia', the name of a nation of western Asia Minor which succeeded in dominating Phrygia, carries comparable meanings); (2) applied to 'Fire', 'Phrygian' produces a possible word-play on the term 'Greek fire', an incendiary compound employed in naval warfare (*OED*, *'fire'*, sb., 8.b); (3) applied to 'round', the ceremony of Cybele's tour through Phrygian cities (*A*)

pictures 1.169: *A*: *tabulae*, planks

piety (pious): reverential dutifulness, to the gods but very much to one's father or parents and other ancestors, and to other relatives and associates. Dryden's general note on Book 5 gives the opinion that the description of 'Sports' there excels Homer's, and adds that Virgil 'seems ... to have labour'd them the more, in Honour of *Octavius*, his Patron [i.e. Augustus]; who instituted the like Games for perpetuating the Memory of his Uncle *Julius* [Caesar]. Piety, as *Virgil* calls it, or dutifulness to Parents, being a most popular Vertue among the Romans'

Pilumnus: see *Goddess-born*

Pinarian House: the *gens* Pinarius, members of which served, with members of the *gens* Potitius, as priests for the rites of Hercules' 'Holy Shrine', the Altar to Hercules (*Ara Maxima*, 'Greatest Altar') in Rome

pin'd: exhausted

place 6.518: the cape now called Capo Palinuro, some miles south of the '*Velin* Coast'

plac'd 2.717: placed Priam (*A*)

Ploughman Consul: M. Atilius Regulus who, like the famous 5th-century Cincinnatus, was summoned from his farm to serve Rome. Regulus led a campaign in the First Punic War. Captured and paroled to advise Roman acceptance of Carthage's peace terms, he recommended otherwise, then kept his word by returning to his captors and to his death

plumes: plucks the feathers from

plump: flock

Pluto's Love: Proserpina (compare 6.213–14)

ply'd: plied, persistently rivalled

Podalyrian Heroe: Machaon (*A*), evidently as brother of Podalirius

Pollux: the immortal brother of mortal Castor; their father, Jove, when Castor was killed, permitted Pollux to take his place in Hades on alternate days

Pomptina: the Pomptine (or Pontine) Marshes, east of Circeii

Porsena: Lars Porsena, king of Clusium, an Etruscan who campaigned to restore the Tarquin monarchy only to find his advance across the Tiber blocked by Horatius Cocles' single-handed defence of the bridge. Porsena ultimately withdrew, expressing magnanimous appreciation of Roman heroism – particularly as exhibited by Clo-elia; she had led a group of hostages who escaped from the Etruscans by swimming the Tiber

Porter, barking [or] triple: Cerberus, the three-headed 'dog' of 6.540

Portunus: god of harbours

Potitius: see *Pinarian House*

Præneste, Preneste: ancient Latian city, now Palestrina. The other places referred to in lines 7.943–7 are the town of Anagnia, south-east of Praeneste, in the territory of the people named the Hernici, and the area about the town of Gabii, halfway between Praeneste and Rome in the valley of the river Anien (Anio)

Præneste's Founder: Caeculus (A)

præscious: conscious beforehand

preace: same as *press*

prefer: put forth; 'prefer' in the sense now conventional ordinarily required 'before'

prepossess: take defensive control of

press: as in the familiar phrase 'press of battle', throng

prevent: precede

Priam's eldest Daughter: see *Thrace*

Priam's Race, Maid of: Polyxena, daughter of Priam slain by Pyrrhus, Achilles' son

process: form of judicial procedure

Prochyta: island between Ischia and the Italian mainland

Procris: wife whose troubled marriage ended when she was slain by her husband in a hunting accident

produc'd 2.168: presented Calchas, possibly as if a performer or judicial witness

Progeny, doubtful: the Minotaur (see *Theseus*)

progress: a course or an itinerary

promiscuous: mixed

Proserpine: Proserpina, whose parents were Ceres and Jove, and who was carried off by Pluto to become his wife and 'Queen' of Hades and her 'nightly Reign' (6.177, in *A* the woods surrounding Avernus)

protend: extend forward

prove: experience

Punic, Punique [< Phoenician]: Carthaginian, and most notably referring to the three Punic Wars between Rome and Carthage

pye: pie (*pica* in Latin), a magpie or kind of crow; *picus* is Latin for 'woodpecker'

Pyrrhus: son of Achilles (and also known as Neoptolemus)

quaint: deft

queen: 7.445, 10.997, see *fire*; 8.921, see *Egyptian Wife*

Quirinus: Romulus, regarded as having become a god; Romulus and Remus became enemies, and Romulus slew Remus

race: (1) a people or nation (*A: gens, genus,* etc.); (2) offspring, individual or collective, of a particular progenitor or of a line of them, extending to multiple kindred and generations. This second, less modern set of senses conforms closely to usage in *A*. There, *genus* and related words indicate 'origin' and what Dryden calls 'Kind', as distinctly 'kin' not 'classification', and connote analogies between familial lineage and processes of nature basic to an agricultural way of life. Dryden's 'Stock' (e.g., 1.390) reflects *A*'s repeated *stirps* (which refers literally to a tree's lower trunk and roots and figuratively to a progenitor, also to a scion [*L*], as does Dryden's 'Brood', e.g., 9.819, translating *A*'s reference to a *genus* proceeding from a certain *stirps*). (3) a particular *gens*, e.g., 'the Sergian Race' (5.160), for those bearing the name 'Sergius' – comparably the 'Memmian Kind', 'the Julian Stock', etc.; (4) 'Progress, course' (*J*)

rack: 'The clouds as they are driven by the wind' (*J*)

rampire: rampart, a mound employed in fortification

ranch'd: torn

random: in *A*, the shepherd pursuing a deer wounds it without being aware that he has done so

reclaim: restrain

recreant: admitting defeat, typically with cowardly self-abasement

redeem'd: rescued

Refuge, Sacred: a sanctuary opened by Romulus to attract outsiders and increase Rome's population (Livy 1.8)

refuse: people who are rejected

reins: loins

remurmur: 'To answer with murmurs *to* a sound' (*OED* 1.b)

renown 1.637: possibly referring to the 'Fame' (1.640, 648), to which the art bears witness, of its Trojan War subject-matter

resort: betake oneself, themselves, etc. ('thick', 4.432: together)

rest: 'the butt-end of the lance' (*OED*, *sb.*³, 2, citing 12.641)

review: behold again

Rhœtean: Trojan (< Rhoeteum, a promontory and a city on it near Troy)

rob'd: robbed

rods: see *Brutus*

rotten: soft, loose

Roman King: Numa Pompilius, from the Sabine town of Cures (which *A* describes as small and poor)

Romulus: one of the twin sons – the other was Remus – of Mars and Ilia, daughter of Numitor, a king of Alba Longa. Numitor was 'injur'd' by his brother Amulius, who deposed him and sought to drown the twins in the Tiber. Surviving, the twins 'drain'd' – were suckled and preserved by – a wolf, and Romulus grew up to found Rome, become its king, and have it named after him

Rules of War: *belli commercia* (*A*), the conventions or commercial transactions of warfare

Rutuli: Rutulians

Saban, Sabæan: from Saba; referring to incense or warriors from the luxurious kingdom of Saba (biblical Sheba) in southern Arabia

Sabine: names a people of the area north-east of Rome, some of whom were brought under Roman rule as part of the political reconciliation following Roman abduction of the 'Sabine Dames' – that is, female Sabines and others seized at a festival entertainment staged by Romulus to make up for early Rome's scarcity of women. The Sabine towns referred to in 7.979–93 are Cures, Mutusca, Eretum, Amiterna, Casperia, Foruli, Orta, and Nursia; the landscape features are Lake Velinus, the mountains Severus and Tetrica, and several tributaries of the Tiber: Himella, Fabaris, and the 'fatal' river Allia, scene of a Roman defeat by the Gauls

Sacrana: the town of the Latian people called the Sacrani

sacred: 'accursed' (*OED* A.6)

Salian Priests, Salij (< *salio*, 'leap'): the Salii, an ancient Roman order of priests of Mars. They preserved a shield which had descended from heaven and which guaranteed Rome's prosperity, and carried that shield and others like it in spirited annual demonstrations (*L*)

sallows: willows (for the framework of shields [*A*])

salute: kiss

salvage: savage, wild

Samian: referring to the island of Samos in the Aegean Sea

Samothracia: Samothrace

sanguine: blood-red

Sarpedon: a king of Lycia who died fighting the Greeks at Troy; greatly esteemed and mourned not only for his valour and eloquence but also because he was the only son of Jove among the mortals in the Trojan War (*Iliad* 5, 12, 16). In 10.187–91, Clarus and Haemon are the two brothers of Sarpedon (*A*)

Saticulans: from Saticula, a town in Campania

Saturn, Saturnia (Saturnian): (1) see *Titan*; (2) Saturnia is also a fortress which Saturn built on the Capitoline Hill, across the Tiber from Janiculum

scarce: scarcely

Scipio's: both (1) P. Cornelius Scipio Africanus, 'Africanus' because he invaded Africa and defeated Hannibal in the Second Punic War, and (2) his adopted son of the same name, the general who destroyed Carthage

Scylla: see *Charibdis*

Scyrian: pertaining to the island where Achilles' son Pyrrhus was raised (*Iliad* 19), Scyros, near Euboea

Scythian: see *Thrace*

seam: animal fat

seat: site

Seats, fatal: destined homes

secret: (1) secluded; (2) unnoticeable

secure of: invulnerable to

self-conscious: see *conscious*

Semethis: Sebethis, nymph of a stream, Sebethos, in Campania

Seresthus: Serestus

Sergesthus: Sergestus; the reference to Sergesthus in 5.648 (where *A* refers to Serestus) suits what is said of Sergesthus and his 'shatter'd' ship in 5.355–6 (and in *A* there as well)

Sergian Race: the *gens* Sergius

Seven against Thebes: a military campaign preceding the Trojan War, against the Greek city of Thebes. At the death of Oedipus the Theban throne was to be shared by his two sons, but one of them, Eteocles, took it for himself. His brother Polynices sought restoration by force, aided by his father-in-law King Adrastus of Argos and five other heroes. Of the seven only Adrastus survived. The slain confederates included another son-in-law of Adrastus, Tydeus (see *Calydon*); also Amphiarius, whose participation resulted from a bribe accepted by his wife, Eryphile; and Capaneus, whose wife Evadne killed herself on his funeral pyre

shade 9.4: a grove within a sacred vale

shake 2.934: shake [the fire] from (*A: excutere*)

share: blade of a plough; 'shar'd' (9.1019) is 'cut, divided, cloven' (*OED v.*¹)

shock: as noun, a collision of opposing military forces; as verb, for them to collide

shoot: speedily traverse a place considered dangerous

Shrine, Holy: see *Pinarian House*

Sicanians: as indicated at 8.435, a people among the earliest to inhabit Latium

Sicheus: Sichæus

Sidonian: deriving from Sidon, the major Phoenician city

Sila: a forest in southernmost Italy

silvan, Silvanus [< *silva*, a wood]: respectively, (1) wooded or located in a wood (hence a woods–dweller) and (2) Silvanus, god of woods

Silvius: the impossibility of reconciling the prophecy concerning Silvius with prophecies concerning Ascanius/[I]ulus elsewhere in the poem (1.364–70, 5.777–9, 9.878–81) is evidence that Virgil did not finish revising it. Livy says Silvius was the son of Ascanius and father of Aeneas Silvius; but Livy also confesses uncertainty about whether Ascanius' mother was Creusa or Lavinia (1.3). The passage on Silvius in *A*, as well as Dryden's wording of it, is likewise indeterminate. That the same 'Silvius' suggests what Dryden takes to be a silvan birth (6.1036) may be related to the origins of the Latins as described in 8.417–19

Simois: a river near Troy, a tributary of the river Xanthus (as Virgil and Dryden call the river Scamander) – both rivers remembered especially as scenes of carnage by Achilles in *Iliad* 21

simples: healing herbs

Sirius: the main star in the constellation Canis Major ('Larger Dog'), prominent in the summer 'dog days'

Sirtes: same as *Syrtes*

Sister of the Day: Diana

sisters: 4.1000 and 7.452, see *fate* 2; 10.241, see *Muses*

Sister's Court: the court of Priam's sister Hesione, who became queen of the Greek city of Salamis after her rescue by Hercules

Sisters of the Woods: see *Driads*

slack: idle away

somewhat: something

Soracte[']s: belonging to Mount Soracte in Etruria, site of a temple of Apollo

sounding: resounding

sowse: souse, swoop

Spear, wreathy: the thyrsus, a staff woven round with ivy (see 7.549) and vines, an emblem of Bacchus and Bacchanalian celebrants

species: 'reflection[s]' (*OED* 3.c)

spires: spiral convolutions ('Curls', 5.115) of a serpent's body

spurn: strike, strike at

squander'd: dispersed

standard: a pole surmounted by some kind of sign (e.g., the Roman 'Eagles', 7.839) identifying a body of troops, their commander, or both

steerage: rowing apparatus (*OED* 3.c); see *Cyllenius*

stock: see *race* 2

stretcher: 'A foot-rest in a rowing-boat' (*OED*, *sb.*, 7)

stridour: stridor, a harsh sound

struck 2.318: *A* has *substitit* (came to a stop)

Stygian, Styx: referring to the infernal river Styx or more generally to Hades (see *Hell*). 'Stygian Jove' is, figuratively, Pluto as the Jove or supreme god of that region; Proserpina would be the Stygian Juno

sublime: 'set or raised aloft, high up' (*OED, a.,* A.1) – physically or
spiritually exalted, or both

suborn: tamper with or dishonestly procure

Subvertor, great: Achilles (*A*)

succeed: (1) follow; (2) take the place of; (3) accede to

successive: 'hereditary' (*OED, a.,* 3)

succor, succour: 'military assistance in men or supplies; *esp.* auxiliary
forces; reinforcements' (*OED,* 'succour', *sb.,* 3)

suffice: (1) 'To ... supply' (*J*); (2) to replenish

Sun, the: see *Day, the*

supply: provide a substitute for

suspect: mistrust

sute: suit, commitment to the pursuit of an objective

Sybilla: Sibylla (Latin for 'Sibyl')

sylvan, Sylvanus: see *silvan*

Syren's: the Sirens, monsters whose songs drew mariners towards lethal
rocks; Ulysses contrived to hear and sail past the Sirens in
Odyssey 12

Syren South: Auster, the south wind (named earlier in *A,* 5.764)

Syrius: Sirius

Syrtes, the: two perilous sea-passages off the North African coast (*A* refers
to them as Gaetulian)

Taburnus: a mountain in Campania

tagg'd: held together

tale, took the: counted

target: shield

Tarpeian Rock: a cliff of the Capitol

tempt: attempt

terms: obscure oracular phraseology

Teucer: (1) a founder of Troy, from Crete, his name is also spelled
'Teucrus' and 'Tucer' (see *Dardanus*); (2) from Salamis, son of
Hesione and Telamon who took part in the siege of Troy (see
Sister's Court)

Teucrus: same as *Teucer* 1

their Sacrifice, augments: the sense of the expression in *A* is, increases
the number of the gods being worshipped

Thermodon: river in north-eastern Asia Minor

Theseus: Athenian hero. Because Athens had had a part in the death of
Androgeos, a son of Minos and Pasiphaë, the monarchs of Crete,
Crete forced Athens to send, at regular intervals, several children
to be devoured by the Minotaur. The Minotaur was Pasiphaë's
'doubtful Progeny', 'doubtful' as a not readily classifiable or accept-

able hybrid, to whom Pasiphaë gave birth after amorous relations with a bull. (She was 'incestuous' in the obsolete sense 'adulterous' [*OED* 1.b].) To make that union practicable, Daedalus had contrived for Pasiphaë an artificial cow in which she could enclose herself. To confine the Minotaur, Daedalus devised the Cretan labyrinth or 'Maze', from which Theseus, after slaying the monster, managed to escape. Theseus retraced a thread or 'Clue' which he had laid down when making his way in. (This stratagem had been communicated by Daedalus to the Cretan princess Ariadne, and by her to Theseus, whom she loved.) Theseus also captured an Amazon, sometimes identified as Hippolyte (the Amazonian queen whose girdle Hercules acquired to complete one of his 'Labours'). She and Theseus became the parents of Hippolytus. Later Theseus repulsed an Amazon attack on Athens and withstood another Amazon reprisal for his marriage to Phaedra. (The consequences for Hippolytus of this marriage are set forth in 7.1049–68.) In yet another exploit, Theseus descended to Hades with Pirithous to rescue Proserpina, but the attempt failed and Theseus was himself rescued, by Hercules. Pirithous was not rescued, and Theseus after death rejoined him – both evidently suffering punishment for the impiety of their mission.

Thessalian: pertaining to Thessaly (see *Thrace*)

Thetis: (1) a sea-nymph, mother of Achilles; (2) figuratively, the sea

this 5.843: this person, i.e. the impersonator of Beroe

this, by: by this time

Thrace, Thracia (Thracian): a region at the south-eastern tip of Europe, opposite Asia Minor and ascending along the Black Sea towards the area of the Scythians, north of that sea. Like the Scythians and Thessalians, the Thracians had a reputation for military prowess in horse- and bowmanship, and for ferocity. To Romans these traits, particularly when combined – and combined extraordinarily in the Centaur horse-men of Thessaly (to some extent also in the Amazons, whom the text repeatedly locates in Thrace) – were evidently signs of barbarism or at least a lack of virtues maturely Greco-Roman; Scythia, Thrace, and Thessaly were all far from centres of Greek and Roman civilization. (In a note to 12.888–9 Dryden digresses to 'observe, not only in this [book], but in all the [six] last Books, that *Æneas* is never seen on Horse-back, and but once before as I remember, in the Fourth when he hunts with *Dido*. The Reason of this, if I guess aright, was a secret Compliment which the Poet made to his Countrey-men the *Romans*; the strength of whose Armies consisted most in Foot; which, I think, were all *Romans* and *Italians*. But their Wings or Squadrons, were made up of their *Allies*, who were Foreigners.') Thrace largely resisted Greek influence and became a Roman province only as late as 46 B.C. Hecuba, Priam's wife, was the daughter of a Thracian king, Cisseus, and the Thracian 'Tyrant' who slaughtered Polydore was Polymnestor, husband of 'Priam's eldest Daughter', Ilione

Thracian Bard: Orpheus; 'they' in 6.880 would seem to refer to the dancers who immediately 'fill' his notes up to the 'Measures' of 6.876 (*OED*, 'fill', *v.*, 17.e. A clearly connects Orpheus' music with the rhythm of the dancers)

Thuscan: Tuscan (see *Tyrrhene*)

Thymbræus: Apollo (< Thymbra, a city near Troy with a temple of this god)

Tibur, Tybur: Tibur (now Tivoli), a town in Latium

Tideus: Tydeus, father of Diomede (see *Adrastus* and *Calydon*)

Tisiphone: see *fury* 2 and *Atè*

tissue: 'A rich kind of cloth, often interwoven with gold or silver' (*OED* 1.a, adding that the word is obsolete except in historical use)

Titan, Titanian: referring to the Titans, divinities whose mother was Earth. (Earth is regardable as the goddess named Tellus or Gaea, but Virgil refers only to Tellus; he does not name the Titans' father, regardable as Uranus, the Sky.) The chief Titan was Saturn, father of, among others, Jove, Juno, and Neptune. Hence Juno and Neptune are called 'Saturnian' (and Juno is 'Saturnia'). Not Jove; Jove overthrew Saturn, consigning some of the Titans to Hades (Saturn took refuge in Crete and later in Italy). Earth's later offspring, the Giants (regardable as divinely sired by personified Tartarus [6.729]), renewed the campaign with like results. The Giant Typhœus (see *Hercules*) met a fate like that of the Giant Enceladus (3.755–60, 9.969–72)

Tithon: Tithonus, son of Laomedon beloved by Aurora

Tityus: Tityos, son of Jove who tried to rape Latona

toil: 'Any net or snare woven or meshed' (*J*)

Torquatus: same as *Manlius* 2

tortoise: massed soldiers with shields held overhead, a 'moving Shed' (9.672) or 'Penthouse' (9.681)

tow: oakum or other plant fibre used to caulk a ship's seams

train: 'a number of followers', 'a procession', or 'a stratagem of enticement' (*J*), i.e. in the last case, a trap

Tree, holy: see *Phœbeian Bays*

trenchers: platters or plates

Trinacrian: Sicilian

Tripod, Tripos: see *Delphian Oracle*

Triton, Tritons: respectively, a particular horn-blowing sea-god (as represented 10.298–304) or several such gods

Trivia: Diana (see *Diana's, three*); (Lake of) Lake Nemi, sacred to Diana

Troilus: son of Priam mentioned in *Iliad* 24 as slain in battle

Trojan Dames: see *Helenus*

trunchions: 'fragment[s] of a spear or lance' (*OED*, 'truncheon', *sb.*, 1.b)

truth: loyalty

Tucer's: see *Teucer* 1

turbants: turbans (see *mitre*)

turn'd: converted

Tuscan: see *Tyrrhene*

twin Gods: Apollo and Diana; regarding their Temple (6.106), see *Apollo's Porch*

Tyburs: in *A* Tiburtus (or Tiburnus [*L*])

Tydides: Diomede, as son of Tydeus

Typhœus: a Giant (see *Hercules* and *Titan*)

tyrant's 3.75: see *Thrace*

Tyre (Tyrian): a Phoenician city in what is now Lebanon; the adjective frequently refers to Carthage, founded by Dido after she fled from Tyre

Tyrian dye: a purple dye, originally from Tyre

Tyrrhene: adjective generally synonymous with 'Etrurian' and 'Tuscan', denoting not only the region of Etruria, mainly north of the Tiber, which was the centre of Etruscan power, but also its inhabitants; also the portion of the Mediterranean Sea west of Italy

Tyrrheus 7.708–12: the sense in *A* is only that he summoned his crew, was enraged, and employed an axe as a weapon because he happened to be splitting an oak at the time

Ucalegon: Ucalegon's house

unawares, at: 'without ... warning' (*OED*, 'unawares', 4)

undiscern'd: *pariter*, 'together' (*A*), as Dryden explains in 5.768

van: vanguard

vaulted: curved as if an arched ceiling

veer 3.527: in *A* the sense of the statement here is to stay clear of the shore and waves on the right

Velin Coast: by the ancient town of Velia on the south-west coast of Italy, about as far below Capri as Capri is below Caieta

Velinum (Veline): the area surrounding Lake Velinus, north-east of Rome and within the southern angle formed by the Tiber and the Nar

vent: to catch the scent of a prey

Venus 4.334: 'twice she' saved the life of Aeneas – not only at the fall of Troy but also, earlier, in his battle against Diomede (*Iliad* 5); 5.1046, regarding her 'birth', see *Dionæan Venus*

vest: 'A loose outer garment worn . . . in Eastern countries or in ancient times' (*OED, sb.*, 1.a)

Vesta (Vestal): see *gods* 2

victor 8.949: same as *Cæsar*

Virgin's Blood: that of Agamemnon's daughter Iphigenia, sacrificed by him to procure winds needed for the voyage to Troy

visionary: (1) having prophetic sight; (2) visible supernaturally

Volcians: Volscians, a people to the south of Rome who were notably resistant to its early expansion (see *Camillus*)

volumes: things 'rolled' (*J*) as scrolls are – here always applied figuratively to serpents (see *spires*)

Vulcan's Name: referring to the 'Isle' now named Vulcano, one of the Aeolian Islands (English 'volcano' < *Volcanus*, Vulcan's name in Latin); Mount Aetna is some fifty miles south of Vulcano

vulgar: 'Of or pertaining to the common people' (*OED, a.*, 8)

want: as verb, to lack or to be missing; as noun, neediness

wanted 10.906: though the word is used comparably at 9.346 and 10.182, this instance of it is conceivably a misprint or another inadvertence for 'wonted', i.e. 'usual' or 'characteristic'; *A* emphasizes imitation of Aeneas' stride, and Dryden employs 'wonted' similarly at 6.661, 8.516, and 10.1242. The fact that Dryden tends to deploy an unusual word more than once in a limited context – say, that of a given epic Book – does not decide the question

want to: exclude

ward, warder: guard

Warriors, winged: the sons of Boreas, who prepared a feast to attract the Harpies who had prevented the prophet-king Phineus from eating, and then drove them away (*Argonautica* 2)

wast, waste: (1) waist; (2) 'The middle deck, or floor of a ship' (*J*)

wat'ry 3.675: rainy (*A: pluvias*, applied to the Hyades)

Way, starry: see *Year, Solar*

weazon: 'trachea or windpipe' (*OED*, 'weasand,' 2)

weigh: lift anchor

wicker: pliant; applied to 'wings', possibly indicating those of 'various sinister creatures' (*OED*, 'wicker', *sb.*, 4.b)

without: outside

writh'd: hurled (for *A*'s *intorquens*, which suggests a twist or spin put on the hurled dart; compare 'whirling force' [11.435], where *A* has also *turbine*, a rotation, and Dryden's 'whirl'd along' applied to a lance in 9.956)

wrought: (1) wrought up; (2) manipulated

Xanthus (Xanthian): (1) same as *Simois*; (2) another of the rivers named
Xanthus, such as the one in Lycia

yellow Year: harvest (where Dryden has 'Year', *A* has *sata*, 'crops')
Year, Solar: the annual course of the sun as perceived from the part of
the earth controlled by the Romans before Augustus expanded that
part; 'starry Way' is the course of the stars perceptible from the
former vantage-point
yough: yew
Youth, Godlike: same as *Marcellus* 2

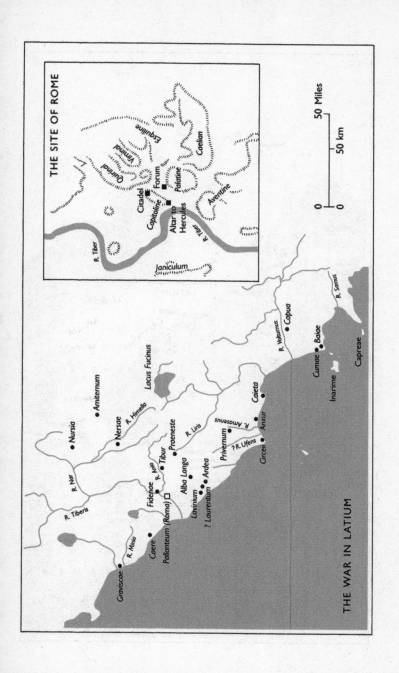

THE SITE OF ROME

R. Tiber

Citadel
Capitoline
Altar to
Hercules

Janiculum

R. Tiber

Quirinal
Viminal
Esquiline

Forum
Palatine
Coelian

Aventine

0   50 km
0   50 Miles

Nursia

Amiternum

Locus Fucinus

Nersae

R. Himello

R. Nar

R. Anio
Tibur
Praeneste

Fidenae
Pallanteum (Roma)

Caere

R. Liris

Alba Longa
Lavinium
Ardea

? Laurentum

R. Amasenus

Privernum
? R. Ufens

Circeii

Anxur

Caieta

R. Volturnus

Capua

Cumae Baiae

Inarime

Caprae

R. Savus

R. Minio

Graviscae

THE WAR IN LATIUM

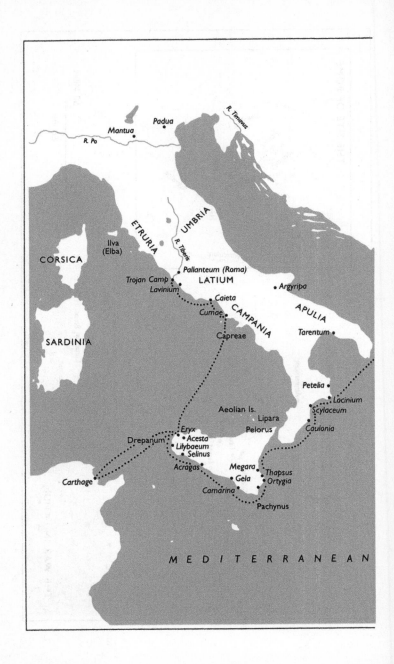

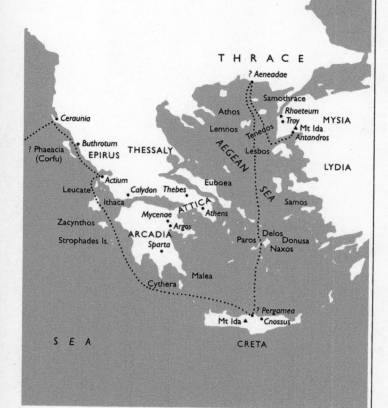

THE VOYAGES OF AENEAS

0   100   200 Miles

0   100   200 km

T H R A C E

? *Aeneadae*

Samothrace

Athos   *Rhoeteum*   MYSIA

Lemnos   Tenedos   *Troy*   ▲ Mt Ida

• *Ceraunia*   *Antandros*

                 AEGEAN   Lesbos

? Phaeacia   • *Buthrotum*   THESSALY   LYDIA
(Corfu)   EPIRUS

           • *Actium*   *Calydon*   *Thebes*   Euboea   SEA

Leucate•   ATTICA   Samos
     Ithaca   *Mycenae*   • *Athens*

Zacynthos   • *Argos*   *Delos*

Strophades Is.   ARCADIA   Paros   Donusa
              Sparta   Naxos

           Malea

       Cythera   ? *Pergamea*

                         Mt Ida ▲   • *Cnossus*

S E A   CRETA

READ MORE IN PENGUIN

In every corner of the world, on every subject under the sun, Penguin represents quality and variety – the very best in publishing today.

For complete information about books available from Penguin – including Puffins, Penguin Classics and Arkana – and how to order them, write to us at the appropriate address below. Please note that for copyright reasons the selection of books varies from country to country.

In the United Kingdom: Please write to *Dept. EP, Penguin Books Ltd, Bath Road, Harmondsworth, West Drayton, Middlesex UB7 0DA*

In the United States: Please write to *Consumer Services, Penguin Putnam Inc., 405 Murray Hill Parkway, East Rutherford, New Jersey 07073-2136.* VISA and MasterCard holders call 1-800-631-8571 to order Penguin titles

In Canada: Please write to *Penguin Books Canada Ltd, 10 Alcorn Avenue, Suite 300, Toronto, Ontario M4V 3B2*

In Australia: Please write to *Penguin Books Australia Ltd, 487 Maroondah Highway, Ringwood, Victoria 3134*

In New Zealand: Please write to *Penguin Books (NZ) Ltd, Private Bag 102902, North Shore Mail Centre, Auckland 10*

In India: Please write to *Penguin Books India Pvt Ltd, 11 Community Centre, Panchsheel Park, New Delhi 110017*

In the Netherlands: Please write to *Penguin Books Netherlands bv, Postbus 3507, NL-1001 AH Amsterdam*

In Germany: Please write to *Penguin Books Deutschland GmbH, Metzlerstrasse 26, 60594 Frankfurt am Main*

In Spain: Please write to *Penguin Books S. A., Bravo Murillo 19, 1°B, 28015 Madrid*

In Italy: Please write to *Penguin Italia s.r.l., Via Vittorio Emanuele 45/a, 20094 Corsico, Milano*

In France: Please write to *Penguin France, 12, Rue Prosper Ferradou, 31700 Blagnac*

In Japan: Please write to *Penguin Books Japan Ltd, Iidabashi KM-Bldg, 2-23-9 Koraku, Bunkyo-Ku, Tokyo 112-0004*

In South Africa: Please write to *Penguin Books South Africa (Pty) Ltd, P.O. Box 751093, Gardenview, 2047 Johannesburg*

READ MORE IN PENGUIN

A CHOICE OF CLASSICS

Francis Bacon	**The Essays**
Aphra Behn	**Love-Letters between a Nobleman and His Sister**
	Oroonoko, The Rover and Other Works
George Berkeley	**Principles of Human Knowledge/Three Dialogues between Hylas and Philonous**
James Boswell	**The Life of Samuel Johnson**
Sir Thomas Browne	**The Major Works**
John Bunyan	**Grace Abounding to The Chief of Sinners**
	The Pilgrim's Progress
Edmund Burke	**A Philosophical Enquiry into the Origin of our Ideas of the Sublime and Beautiful**
	Reflections on the Revolution in France
Frances Burney	**Evelina**
Margaret Cavendish	**The Blazing World and Other Writings**
William Cobbett	**Rural Rides**
William Congreve	**Comedies**
Cowley/Waller/Oldham	**Selected Poems**
Thomas de Quincey	**Confessions of an English Opium Eater**
	Recollections of the Lakes
Daniel Defoe	**A Journal of the Plague Year**
	Moll Flanders
	Robinson Crusoe
	Roxana
	A Tour Through the Whole Island of Great Britain
	The True-Born Englishman
John Donne	**Complete English Poems**
	Selected Prose
Henry Fielding	**Amelia**
	Jonathan Wild
	Joseph Andrews
	The Journal of a Voyage to Lisbon
	Tom Jones
George Fox	**The Journal**
John Gay	**The Beggar's Opera**

READ MORE IN PENGUIN

A CHOICE OF CLASSICS

READ MORE IN PENGUIN

A CHOICE OF CLASSICS

Aeschylus	**The Oresteian Trilogy**
	Prometheus Bound/The Suppliants/Seven against Thebes/The Persians
Aesop	**The Complete Fables**
Ammianus Marcellinus	**The Later Roman Empire (AD 354–378)**
Apollonius of Rhodes	**The Voyage of Argo**
Apuleius	**The Golden Ass**
Aristophanes	**The Knights/Peace/The Birds/The Assemblywomen/Wealth**
	Lysistrata/The Acharnians/The Clouds
	The Wasps/The Poet and the Women/ The Frogs
Aristotle	**The Art of Rhetoric**
	The Athenian Constitution
	Classic Literary Criticism
	De Anima
	The Metaphysics
	Ethics
	Poetics
	The Politics
Arrian	**The Campaigns of Alexander**
Marcus Aurelius	**Meditations**
Boethius	**The Consolation of Philosophy**
Caesar	**The Civil War**
	The Conquest of Gaul
Cicero	**Murder Trials**
	The Nature of the Gods
	On the Good Life
	On Government
	Selected Letters
	Selected Political Speeches
	Selected Works
Euripides	**Alcestis/Iphigenia in Tauris/Hippolytus**
	The Bacchae/Ion/The Women of Troy/ Helen
	Medea/Hecabe/Electra/Heracles
	Orestes and Other Plays

READ MORE IN PENGUIN

A CHOICE OF CLASSICS

Hesiod/Theognis	**Theogony/Works and Days/Elegies**
Hippocrates	**Hippocratic Writings**
Homer	**The Iliad**
	The Odyssey
Horace	**Complete Odes and Epodes**
Horace/Persius	**Satires and Epistles**
Juvenal	**The Sixteen Satires**
Livy	**The Early History of Rome**
	Rome and Italy
	Rome and the Mediterranean
	The War with Hannibal
Lucretius	**On the Nature of the Universe**
Martial	**Epigrams**
	Martial in English
Ovid	**The Erotic Poems**
	Heroides
	Metamorphoses
	The Poems of Exile
Pausanias	**Guide to Greece (in two volumes)**
Petronius/Seneca	**The Satyricon/The Apocolocyntosis**
Pindar	**The Odes**
Plato	**Early Socratic Dialogues**
	Gorgias
	The Last Days of Socrates (Euthyphro/
	The Apology/Crito/Phaedo)
	The Laws
	Phaedrus and Letters VII and VIII
	Philebus
	Protagoras/Meno
	The Republic
	The Symposium
	Theaetetus
	Timaeus/Critias
Plautus	**The Pot of Gold and Other Plays**
	The Rope and Other Plays

READ MORE IN PENGUIN

A CHOICE OF CLASSICS

Pliny	**The Letters of the Younger Pliny**
Pliny the Elder	**Natural History**
Plotinus	**The Enneads**
Plutarch	**The Age of Alexander (Nine Greek Lives)**
	Essays
	The Fall of the Roman Republic (Six Lives)
	The Makers of Rome (Nine Lives)
	Plutarch on Sparta
	The Rise and Fall of Athens (Nine Greek Lives)
Polybius	**The Rise of the Roman Empire**
Procopius	**The Secret History**
Propertius	**The Poems**
Quintus Curtius Rufus	**The History of Alexander**
Sallust	**The Jugurthine War/The Conspiracy of Cataline**
Seneca	**Dialogues and Letters**
	Four Tragedies/Octavia
	Letters from a Stoic
	Seneca in English
Sophocles	**Electra/Women of Trachis/Philoctetes/Ajax**
	The Theban Plays
Suetonius	**The Twelve Caesars**
Tacitus	**The Agricola/The Germania**
	The Annals of Imperial Rome
	The Histories
Terence	**The Comedies (The Girl from Andros/The Self-Tormentor/The Eunuch/Phormio/ The Mother-in-Law/The Brothers)**
Thucydides	**History of the Peloponnesian War**
Virgil	**The Aeneid**
	The Eclogues
	The Georgics
Xenophon	**Conversations of Socrates**
	Hiero the Tyrant
	A History of My Times
	The Persian Expedition